MORAL

DEVELOPMENT
& REALITY

PENGUIN ACADEMICS

MORAL DEVELOPMENT & REALITY

BEYOND THE THEORIES OF KOHLBERG AND HOFFMAN

SECOND EDITION

JOHN C. GIBBS
The Ohio State University

Allyn & Bacon

Boston   New York   San Francisco
Mexico City   Montreal   Toronto   London   Madrid   Munich   Paris
Hong Kong   Singapore   Tokyo   Cape Town   Sydney

Senior Editor: Stephen Frail
Editorial Assistant: Kerri Hart-Morris
Marketing Manager: Nicole Kunzmann
Production Supervisor: Patty Bergin
Editorial Production Service: Pine Tree Composition/ Patty Donovan
Manufacturing Buyer: JoAnne Sweeney
Electronic Composition: Pine Tree Composition
Photo Researcher: Martha Shethar
Cover Administrator: Joel Gendron

Library of Congress Cataloging-in-Publication Data

Gibbs, John C.
   Moral development and reality : beyond the theories of Kohlberg and
Hoffman / John C. Gibbs.
     p. cm.
   Includes bibliographical references and index.
   ISBN-13: 978-0-205-59524-2
   ISBN-10: 0-205-59524-3
  1.   Moral development.   I. Title.
   BF723.M54G5 2010
   155.2′5—dc22

                          2008052870

10 9 8 7 6 5 4 3 2 1   HAM   13 12 11 10 09

**Allyn & Bacon
is an imprint of**

www.pearsonhighered.com

ISBN-10: 0-205-59524-3
ISBN-13: 978-0-205-59524-2

*Dedicated to
the Memory of
J. Lowell Gibbs*

contents

Foreword ix
  by Daniel K. Lapsley
Figures and Tables xiii
Personal Preface and Acknowledgments xv

CHAPTER 1   Introduction 1

- Social Perspective Taking, Reversibility, and Morality 2
- Introducing Chapters 2 through 9   8

CHAPTER 2   "The Right" and Moral Development: Fundamental Themes of Kohlberg's Cognitive Developmental Approach 17

- Early Childhood Superficiality 19
- Beyond Early Childhood Superficiality 27
- Stages of Moral Judgment Development 36
- Summarizing Comment 54

CHAPTER 3   Kohlberg's Theory: A Critique and New View 57

- Background 58
- Adult Moral Development in Kohlberg's Theory 67
- A Critique and New View 70
- Conclusion 74

CHAPTER 4   "The Good" and Moral Development: Hoffman's Theory 76

- The Empathic Predisposition 77
- Empathy and Prosocial Behavior: Cognitive Complications and Empathy's Limitations 85
- Empathy, Its Cognitive Regulation, and Affective Primacy 92
- The Empathic Predisposition, Socialization, and Moral Internalization 94
- Conclusion and Critique 102

CHAPTER 5   Moral Development, Moral Self-Relevance, and Prosocial Behavior 106

- Prosocial Behavior: A Rescue 107
- Individual Differences in Prosocial Behavior 112
- Conclusion: Two Spurious "Moral Exemplars" 121

CHAPTER 6 Understanding Antisocial Behavior 128

- Limitations of Antisocial Youths 129
- A Case Study 144

CHAPTER 7 Treating Antisocial Behavior 151

- The Mutual Help Approach 152
- Remedying the Limitations: The Cognitive Behavioral Approach 162
- Social Perspective-Taking for Severe Offenders 181

CHAPTER 8 Beyond the Theories: A Deeper Reality? 185

- Two Case Studies 188
- A Deeper Reality? 194
- Moral Insight, Inspiration, and Transformation 207
- Conclusion 214

CHAPTER 9 Conclusion 218

- Revisiting the Issue of Moral Motivation and Knowledge 221
- Moral Perception and Reality 228

References 235
Appendix 266
Author Index 271
Subject Index 281

foreword

It can be confidently ventured that the present work by John C. Gibbs will be one of the most widely discussed contributions to moral psychology in quite some time. The achievement is not simply one of fine exegesis or cogent summary. Although the book is a comprehensive primer on foundational matters, it also provides insights of astonishing integrative power across a wide range of literatures and disciplines. Even those who are well versed in the theoretical subtleties of moral cognition, empathy, and development will find the present work rich with penetrating insights. For example, the critical distinction between constructivist and internalization processes in moral development is drawn with remarkable clarity. A social-cognitive framework is folded quite easily into the theoretical narrative, including the vast literatures on social-cognitive distortions (or sanitizing euphemisms) that corrupt our moral appraisal. The analysis of antisocial youth and how to treat them is the best that I have seen on this question. Relevant case studies—for example, of Osama bin Laden and Timothy McVeigh—will be read with keen interest. On top of this, the text is quite alive intellectually, a real page-turner for those who are animated by cutting-edge debates in the moral domain. This is a work of accomplished and assured scholarship. It offers the best analysis of the contribution of Kohlberg and Hoffman to moral development theory currently available. And the best part is this: *It has a surprise ending!*

For all the helpful insights and integrative work evident in this book, it would be a mistake to see it simply as an attempt to clear away the theoretical detritus that has grown up around these venerable theories. It does this, certainly, but the objective is more ambitious. It is, in addition, a sustained argument for a way of understanding the very nature of our existence. It asserts a reality that is deeper, Platonic, noumenal, but not entirely hidden from us. This deeper reality can, indeed, be glimpsed after careful excavation of moral development theory. A more fundamental reality is said to lie "beyond" our theoretical understanding of moral cognition and empathic arousal, but these theories can point us in the right direction if properly considered. Professor Gibbs takes on this task with admirable skill. The reader is gradually seduced into a project of moral archeology that progressively uncovers a remarkable find but only after sifting through the fine points of developmental theory, brushing away the incoherence of the empirical record, and reconstructing the linkage between cognition and empathy in moral functioning. Not everyone will be happy with the speculative conclusions. The book's ontological claims will be a source of enduring reflection, debate, and controversy. Yet the ambition is breathtaking and cannot be faulted. Indeed, if Piaget's genetic epistemology can dare to resolve epistemological problems with the empirical facts of cognitive development, and if Kohlberg's project can aim to defeat ethical relativism with the data of moral development, then it is just a short step to use developmental theory to face up to questions of existence and reality.

I want to give just one example of how careful theoretical excavation yields an insight that sustains the central claims of this book. Professor Gibbs argues that Kohlberg's theory fails largely because Kohlberg's best Piagetian insights were corrupted by his fascination with Dewey's writings on internalization and group conformity. Hence, Kohlberg's formulation of moral stages has a strong Piagetian source, but his formulation of the preconventional, conventional, and postconventional typology can be traced to Dewey. Grafting this typology to developmental stages was, according to Gibbs, a big mistake. Kohlberg's embrace of this typology led him to confuse construction with internalization and to underestimate the moral competence of children and adolescents. To put it differently, Kohlberg to some extent abandoned Piagetian constructivism for an internalization view of moral maturity. Hence, constructivist notions of the "active child" and schema building were assimilated to a modified version of moral internalization—and this to keep faith with Dewey's notions about group conformity. To call Kohlberg's Deweyan commitments the "Procrustean bed" that distorts his developmental theory is a startling claim.

The attack on exclusive internalization views of morality is sustained throughout the text. Professor Gibbs argues that the construction of moral structures, or of moral reciprocity, cannot be reduced to the internalization of moral norms, principally because reciprocity and justice are sui generis cognitions that have the necessity of logico-mathematical knowledge. Logical necessity is the operational property of Piagetian structures and, when applied to moral judgments, sustains the view that morality entails a sense of obligation related to the necessities of logic. In short, moral reciprocity is akin to logic. If this is true, then justice develops a motive power all its own independently of affect or empathy. The claims for logical necessity and the auto-motivating quality of moral judgments are a crucial thematic point. It allows Professor Gibbs to press the following analogy that underwrites the central claims of the book. Just as physicists use mathematics to describe reality that we cannot see, then, if decentered moral judgment or moral reciprocity is akin to mathematics, moral reciprocity also can point to an unseen deeper reality. Hence, the claim of logical necessity for moral judgments, derived from a Piagetian source and wielded against the rival internalization view, is pressed into the service of ontological claims about the nature of a deeper, Platonic reality. The possibility of a deeper reality is suggested not only by the logical foundations of such moral notions as ideal reciprocity, mutual respect, or the Golden Rule but also by empathic love and the meta-cognitive reflection of adults on the "limit questions" that Kohlberg once instantiated as a "Stage 7" concern.

This brief example is just an invitation to join Professor Gibbs in the most interesting exploration of moral development theory that one is likely to encounter. This book offers a compelling reason to believe in the ability of social-cognitive development to offer cogent, powerful explanations of cognitive-emotional development and a framework for understanding and treating troubled, antisocial youth. It will be of profound interest to developmental theorists and practitioners who draw inspiration from clinical-developmental theory. Each chapter will be read with profit, is rife with fresh insights, and will make a contribution to the literature. And be ready to confront the most interesting questions of our moral existence.

Daniel K. Lapsley, Ph.D.
University of Notre Dame

figures and tables

Figures
7.1 Alonzo's Problem Situation: Reasons for Proposed Group Decisions 171

8.1 Diagram of the Operating Room at the Barrow Neurological Institute 189

Tables
2.1 Cross-Cultural Samples in Rank Order by Mean Sociomoral Reflection Maturity Score (SRMS), Grouped by Age Period 49

3.1 Outline of the Life-Span Development of Moral Judgment and Reflection 72

4.1 Arousal Modes and Developmental Stages of Empathic Distress 79

6.1 Cross-Cultural Samples of Male Delinquents and Non-Delinquents in Rank Order by Mean Sociomoral Reflection Maturity Score (SRMS) 131

7.1 Problem Names and Thinking Errors 155

7.2 The Equipment Meeting Curriculum in a Nutshell 165

7.3 Alonzo's Problem Situation 170

7.4 Gary's Thinking Errors 175

7.5 Victims and Victimizers 177

personal preface and acknowledgment

First among my acknowledgments in this personal preface are the two names in the title: the late Lawrence Kohlberg and Martin L. Hoffman. Their theories have been central to moral psychology. Kohlberg's and Hoffman's works were already prominent in 1971, the year I asked each of these men to contribute to my doctoral study of social influences upon children's resistance to temptation (Gibbs, 1972). Hoffman mailed, from the University of Michigan, his measure of parental nurturance, and Kohlberg, on my campus (Harvard University), participated as a member of my reading committee.

After completing my dissertation in 1972, I continued collegial interaction with both theorists, especially with Kohlberg. In 1975, Larry, as everyone called him, invited me to join him at the Harvard Graduate School of Education. This I did gladly, collaborating as a research faculty member in the completion of his longitudinal moral judgment project (Colby, Kohlberg, Gibbs, & Lieberman, 1983; Gibbs, Kohlberg, Colby, & Speicher-Dubin, 1976) and assessment manual (Colby, Kohlberg, Speicher, Hewer, Candee, Gibbs, & Power, 1987). In the free atmosphere of Harvard, I also was encouraged to develop certain theoretical and empirical contributions. After reading the page proofs of my 1977 *Harvard Educational Review* revisionist critique of his stage typology, Larry told me that I "could be right."

I remain deeply appreciative that Larry continued to support and encourage my work in moral development even after I left Harvard (in 1979) for a faculty appointment at The Ohio State University. He wrote the foreword to an early group-administrable moral judgment assessment instrument that colleagues and I developed (Gibbs, Widaman, & Colby, 1982). He also continued to consider sympathetically my revisionist argument, even proposing (in part along the lines of that argument) a reconceptualization of adult moral development (Kohlberg, 1984). He appreciated our (Gibbs & Schnell, 1984) juxtaposition of his moral developmental approach vis-à-vis with moral socialization approaches such as Hoffman's. He was interested in our work on exemplary prosocial behavior (see Chapter 5). He even shared my interest in the near-death experience and the question of a deeper reality of human existence (see Chapters 8 and 9). Hence, although he died in 1987, years before the emergence of this book, Larry Kohlberg, in effect, nurtured its advance shoots. I know that Larry would have nurtured the book's progress as well, along with our (Gibbs, Basinger, Grime, & Snarey, 2007) "revisiting" with new data his universality claims for moral development (see Chapters 2 and 6 of this new edition of *Moral Development & Reality*).

I have also kept in touch with Martin Hoffman, for whose continued encouragement and help I am also grateful. Like Larry, Marty appreciated our (Gibbs & Schnell, 1984) overview of his and Kohlberg's approaches to moral development (indeed, he had provided helpful comments on a preliminary version). He also constructively commented on a subsequent chapter and article of mine (Gibbs, 1991a, 1991b) that proposed an integration of his and Kohlberg's theories. He (Hoffman, 1991) even wrote a commentary on that article. (Remarkably, Marty's commentary began, "The last time I saw Larry Kohlberg, about a year before he died, we decided to get together some day soon and try to integrate our theories. We never did" [p. 105].)

Marty's help has continued in recent years. He encouraged me to write this book, including this second edition. In 2008, he shared his most recent work, provided valuable feedback for two of this book's chapters, and even developed with me a summary table of his stages for Chapter 4. In his own book (Hoffman, 2000), Marty commented that he was "impressed with the variety of [social perspective-taking] methods" (p. 293) used in our intervention program for antisocial youth (see Chapter 7). Marty provided crucial consultation as my graduate students Julie Krevans and, subsequently, Renee Patrick fashioned their respective dissertations concerning the impact of inductive discipline (one of Hoffman's most important contributions to moral socialization; see Chapter 4).

Marty's first "encouragement" was actually a one-word challenge. At the 1987 American Educational Research Association meeting in Washington, D.C., Martin Hoffman and Nancy Eisenberg presented an Invited Dialogue. As the discussant for their presentations, I commented that Hoffman's theory presumed "affective primacy" (empathic affect as the exclusive source) in moral motivation. Marty replied, "So?" Unpacked, that meant, I think: So what's wrong with that? *A fair question*, I thought, *and one that I should answer*. This book contains my answer, and not only to Marty. This second edition of *Moral Development & Reality* includes my answer as well to other "exclusive affective primacy" moral theorists, such as Jonathan Haidt, Joshua Greene, and Dennis Krebs. I still answer mainly Hoffman, but the referent for my answer has broadened.

Writing this book has meant for me the thrilling opportunity to seek closure concerning questions that have consumed my interest over the decades since 1971: What is morality? Can we speak validly of moral *development*, as Kohlberg and Hoffman claim, or is morality totally relative to the particular values and virtues emphasized in particular cultures? Is the moral motivation of behavior primarily cognitive, a matter of justice (Kohlberg)? Or is it primarily affective, a matter of empathy (Hoffman) or other intuitive feelings? Are Kohlberg's and Hoffman's theories integrable? Can they adequately account for exemplary prosocial—and, for that matter, antisocial—behavior? What are their implications for treating antisocial behavior? Finally, going beyond the theories: Does moral development, including moments of moral insight, inspiration, and transformation, reflect a deeper reality?

This book seeks to answer these questions. I have been deeply gratified by the praise elicited by the book's first edition in 2003 from reviewers, colleagues, and students. In the years since the first edition, I have conducted extensive research, corresponded with national and international colleagues, and kept up with the remarkably diverse literature on moral psychology; hence, this second edition features over 150 new references. Every chapter has been thoroughly updated and refined. Several chapters have been expanded to address certain new trends in the field. My hope is that this new edition will find its place not only as a supplementary text in graduate and advanced undergraduate courses pertinent to one or more of these questions (facilitating this role are chapter questions listed in the appendix) but also as a contribution to the broader dialogues in the academic and intellectual community.

I will use "we"—as in, "we will explore moral development through the theories of Kohlberg and Hoffman"—frequently throughout this book. At some points, the pronoun may seem odd, but its use is quite intentional. In part, "we" is used for ordinary reasons: to convey in the writing "an impersonal character" (*Funk & Wagnalls New International Dictionary of the English Language*, 2000, p. 1425) and a presumed partnership with the reader. A special reason, however, is that at many points I do mean *we* not in some impersonal sense but, instead, quite literally and personally. I did write this book and do accept any credit or blame that may ensue. Fundamentally, however, not "I" but *we* accomplished this book. It exists only because of the collaboration, critiques, and encouragement of so many: not only mentors such as Larry Kohlberg and Marty Hoffman (and, even before 1972 at Harvard and once again in 2002, Herb Kelman) but so many other good and thoughtful people: coauthors, other colleagues, graduate students, advanced undergraduates, friends, and family.

Let me express first my appreciation to my coauthors over the years. In addition to my abiding appreciation of Larry Kohlberg (*qua* coauthor as well as mentor), I thank, most notably, Helen Ahlborn, Kevin Arnold, Alvaro Barriga, Karen Basinger, George Bear, Daan Brugman, Kate Brusten, Marvin Berkowitz, Larry Brendtro, Phil Clark, Anne Colby, Renee Devlin, Ann-Marie DiBiase, Dick Fuller, Lance Garmon, Barry Glick, Arnie Goldstein (now deceased), Ginny Gregg (Jelinek), Becca Grime, Mary Horn, Keith Kaufman, Julie Krevans, Jennifer Landau (Harrold), Leonard Leeman, Albert Liau, Marion Mason, Fara McCrady, Renee Patrick, Bud Potter, SaraJane Rowland, Steve Schnell, Randy Shively, Susan Simonian, John Snarey, Geert Jan Stams, Bobby Lee Stinson, Ann Swillinger, Mike Vasey, and Keith Widaman.

Among my current and recent colleagues (in addition to my coauthors) here at Ohio State and in the local intellectual community, I am so grateful for the helpful feedback or encouragement of Randy Anderson, Bob Batterman, Sally Boysen, Harold Cheyney, Jane Cottrell, Russ Crabtree, Don Dell, Sy Dinitz (now deceased), Dorothy Jackson, Norm Knapp, Herb Mirels, Ray Montemayor, Steven Robbins, Bob Rodgers, Linda Schoen, Ping Serafica, Vladimir Sloutsky, George Thompson, Mike Vasey, Charles Wenar (now deceased), and Jerry Winer. Among colleagues— again, in addition to my coauthors—at other institutions, I thank MaryLou Arnold, Diana Baumrind, Roger Bergman, Laura Berk, Gustavo Carlo, Bill Damon, Jim DuBois, Carolyn Edwards, Nancy Eisenberg, Ed Giventer (now deceased), Bruce Greyson, Patrick Grim, Sam Hardy, Marty Hoffman, Ray Hummel, Tobias Krettenauer, Dan

Lapsley, David Lorimer, Ron Mallett, Dave Moshman, Frank Murray, Elena Mustakovia-Possardt, Ulric Neisser, Larry Nucci, Fumi Ohnishi, Clark Power, Don Reed, Don Richardson, Mike Sabom, Stanton Samenow, Ping Serafica, Henry Stapp, Elly Vozzola, Cecilia Wainryb, Larry Walker, and Katsuyuki Yamasaki. For extending to me invitations to participate in special national and international conferences—and thereby indirectly contributing to the cutting-edge quality of this second edition—I thank Daan Brugman (Universiteit Utrecht, 2005), Roek de Bruijn (Teylingereind Center, 2005), Wayne Ramsey (The Fetzer Institute, 2007), and Dawn Schrader (Cornell University, 2008).

Special thanks go to Stephen Frail, Dede Saelens, Kate Motter, Patty Donovan, and Patty Bergin at Pearson Allyn & Bacon, who have wonderfully supported the accomplishment of this second edition; Dan Lapsley, for his insightful and gracious foreword; Jennifer Kuehn and Marty Jamison for their superb literature searches; Tom Sawyer (now deceased), for taking the time to critique Chapter 8 and to update for me his remarkable saga; and the graduate students of Psychology 832 (Life-Span Sociomoral Development). Among the graduate students, Renee Patrick, Kristin Rohrbeck, and Carisa Taylor merit special praise for their remarkably thoughtful and discerning feedback on the chapter drafts; they saved this book from numerous ambiguities and deficits. I also especially thank Charlie Campbell and Becca Grime (now on the faculty of Washington and Jefferson College) for their invaluable assistance as I prepared portions of this book and related work for PowerPoint presentations at conferences.

Other contributors and supporters include the members of my family. This book is dedicated to the memory of my father, John Lowell Gibbs, the first great love of my life, with whom I first discovered the joy and deep connection of true dialogue (as well as the fun of trading puns and other half-witticisms). I also thank Jonathan Lowell Gibbs, Louise B. Gibbs, Stephanie Gibbs Kamath, Sophia Gibbs Kim, Sung Clay Kim, Lea Queener, Llewelyn Queener (now deceased), Carol Gibbs Stover, JohnAlexis Viereck, and Peter Viereck (now deceased). Lastly, I thank Valerie V. Gibbs, my life's greatest love, my co-adventurer, my wife and partner in the most personal sense of "we" of all.

John C. Gibbs, Ph.D. (Harvard University, 1972) is Professor of Developmental Psychology at The Ohio State University. His work on moral judgment assessment and on interventions with antisocial youth has not only seen widespread use in the United States and Great Britain but has also been translated and adapted for use in Germany, Italy, Taiwan, The Netherlands, and other countries. Dr. Gibbs and coauthors' EQUIP intervention program won the 1998 Reclaiming Children and Youth Spotlight on Excellence Award. He has served as a member of the Ohio Governor's Council on Juvenile Justice, as well as the Social Cognitive Training Study Group of the Centers for Disease Control and Prevention (Division of Violence Prevention). He also serves on the editorial board of the *Journal of Near-Death Studies*. Some of his other books are *Moral Maturity: Measuring the Development of Sociomoral Reflection* (with coauthors Karen Basinger and Dick Fuller) and *The EQUIP Program: Teaching Youth to Think and Act Responsibly Through a Peer-Helping Approach* (with coauthors Granville Bud Potter and Arnold Goldstein). In addition to his books, Dr. Gibbs has published (alone or with coauthors) more than 70 book chapters and articles pertaining to the topics involved in *Moral Development & Reality*.

CHAPTER 1

Introduction

Cᴇʀᴛᴀɪɴ ᴄᴀᴍᴘᴇʀs ᴏɴᴇ sᴜᴍᴍᴇʀ ʀᴇᴘᴇᴀᴛᴇᴅʟʏ ᴘᴜʟʟᴇᴅ ᴀ ᴘʀᴀɴᴋ ᴏɴ Edward. Ed was a small, uneven-legged, mildly retarded adult who was the basic maintenance staffer for the camp. He was kind, conscientious in his duties, and proud that he was earning his way in life. There was just one thing: At a point of frustration or moment of embarrassment, Ed would invariably unleash a torrent of profanities that was surprising and, to some campers, entertaining. Several campers had devised a way to set off this "entertainment." Ed worked hard mowing and doing other chores on the camp grounds and would sometimes take a nap during the day. His bed was located in the boys' wing of the campers' open barracks-style sleeping quarters. Seeing Ed asleep, the plotters would move in. They would gently sink one of Ed's hands into a pail of water. Ed would wet his pants in bed and awaken, swearing madly and running frantically after the hysterically laughing campers.

Imaginatively putting oneself in the place of another, or social perspective taking, is central to moral development and behavior. Social perspective taking relates to the right and the good of morality, that is, to justice or mutual respect and to empathy or caring. What if the plotters that summer had truly taken Ed's perspective, including Ed's limited ability to take such a prank in stride? Might they have sensed a certain unfairness to their planned act, a certain violation of justice or respect? Might they have anticipated feeling a certain empathy-based guilt? Had the campers put themselves in Ed's place, they might have successfully resisted their temptation to tease and humiliate.

This book addresses the development of justice and caring, especially as seen through the works of their preeminent theorists, Lawrence Kohlberg and Martin Hoffman. Their works identify certain progressive trends: Human moral understanding as well as feeling grows beyond the superficial. A morality of mutual respect and caring becomes increasingly evident—if not always in behavior, at least in competence. A Kohlberg colleague, Elliot Turiel, posits an objective right and wrong definitive of the moral domain. Kohlberg even posited a deeper reality, a cosmic perspective that can affirm the moral life of love and respect for persons.

Fundamentally, Kohlberg's and Hoffman's theories imply that acts such as the campers' against Edward are morally wrong and harmful, period. Morality and its development have an objective basis; a more mature morality is a more adequate morality. But let us step back a bit. Aren't evaluations of moral right and wrong basically subjective? Aren't they relative to the values and virtues approved of and inculcated in this or that particular culture? And if there is no objectively "right" or more adequate morality, then isn't it of overriding importance not to impose our own subjective morality upon others?

William Damon (2006) noted that precisely such questions have led to challenges to the legitimacy of studying "broad concerns of development," indeed, to the very "notion of development itself" (p. xv). Challenges to broad concerns of human *moral* development—and even to objectivity or rationality—continue to abound in the social and behavioral sciences.[1] These relativistic challenges prompt us to ponder the basis for moral developmental theories such as Kohlberg's and Hoffman's, as well as the nature of the moral domain. In so stepping back, we will present an objective basis for morality as well as for moral development in a non-relative sense. This presentation will serve as a prelude to the chapters to follow. In these chapters, we will ponder Kohlberg's and Hoffman's theories and use them to explore moral development, behavior, and reality.

Social Perspective Taking, Reversibility, and Morality

At the least, social perspective taking means mentally adopting or considering another's "beliefs, desires, intentions, opportunities, preferences, and other psychological attitudes" (Kane, 1994, p. 20), along with what Hoffman calls the other's life condition. In Edward's case, social perspective taking in the mature sense would mean taking into account Edward's limited ability to take a prank in stride. This the campers did not do; instead, they indulged their self-centered desire for "entertainment." The campers could and should have asked themselves (implicitly or explicitly): "If I were Edward, would I want that done to me?" The right and mature answer would have been "No." Moral growth beyond the superficial has much to do with social perspective taking, evaluation, decision-making, and behavior in this mature sense.

The campers' act can be evaluated as objectively wrong because it was not reversible or impartial. In victimizing Edward, the campers' behavior failed to satisfy what Kurt Baier (1965) called "the condition of reversibility, that is, that the behavior in question must be acceptable to a [mentally and emotionally healthy, adequately informed, etc.] person whether he is at the 'giving' or 'receiving' end of it" (p. 108). Steven Pinker (2008, January 13) suggested that reversibility or "interchangeability" of perspectives may "point any rational [person away from] what privileges my interests over yours" (p. 56) and toward what is right and good. A reversible or interchangeable perspective is "independent, unbiased, impartial, objective, disinterested, ... [and] in the interest of everyone alike" (Baier, 1965, p. 107). Such a perspective is sometimes called the moral point of view; its opposite is a self-centered attitude or act such as the campers'. "Granted, I might be a bit better off if I acted selfishly at your expense" (Pinker, p. 56); but because the actor would not wish to be on the receiving end of such behavior (i.e., because it is not reversible), doing so would be morally wrong. As Immanuel Kant (1785/1993; cf. Kane, 1994; Singer 1981) might have put it: The moral point of view is the morality of mutual respect and justice, of reciprocity and equality—not of one person using (or abusing) others as a means to attain his or her selfish (even if "entertaining") ends. A self-centered social act is objectively and *intrinsically* wrong or "wrong in itself" (Baier, 1965, p. 108).

Let us relate our argument for an objective basis for moral evaluation and development to other views in the field of moral psychology. Similar to our objective view is that of social domain theorists such as Turiel (e.g., Smetana, 2006; Turiel, 2006a; Helwig, Turiel, & Nucci, 1996), although their referent for "objective" does not emphasize reversibility of perspectives.[2] Generally taking issue with the tenability of objective morality and leaving "little room for rational agency or developmental change" (Moshman, 2008, p. 280) are views such as post-modernism (e.g., Gergen, 2001), virtue or communitarian ethics (e.g., Campbell & Christopher, 1996; MacIntyre, 1981, 1988), "narrative" or Vygotskian psychology (e.g., Day & Tappan, 1996; Tappan, 2006), pragmatic accounts (Krebs, 2008; Krebs & Denton, 2005, 2006; critiqued by Gibbs, 2006b), aspects of neo-nativism (e.g., Hauser, 2006; Wilson, 1993), social intuitionist theory (e.g., Greene, 2008a, 2008b; Haidt & Bjorklund, 2008a, 2008b), and cultural psychology (e.g., Shweder, 1990, 2000; Shweder et al., 2006). Common across such views is the argument that morality is basically subjective or pre-rational, its formation largely relative to diverse personal and cultural values and contexts.

At the least, in the moral relativistic views noted above, universals in moral and cognitive development have been neglected in the focus on particular directions of moral socialization. For example, Jonathan Haidt and Frederick Bjorklund (Haidt & Bjorklund, 2008a, 2008b) claimed that a fully moral or virtuous individual is typically one who has been fully enculturated into the norms and values of his or her particular culture. What are we to make of such a claim? Is morality simply a matter of fully embracing and enacting this or that character virtue or value, such as benevolence or loyalty? Consider the case of "the physician who acts kindly and loyally by not reporting the incompetence of a fellow physician" (Beauchamp & Childress, 2001, p. 32). The physician is enacting the virtues of benevolence and loyalty, and in that context, might he not think himself (or herself) to be moral, his character good? How can others impose their views by judging him (or her) to be otherwise? Yet if the non-reporting physician were to put himself in the place of his incompetent colleague's patients—vulnerable, innocent, suffering, perhaps permanently harmed—he might have second thoughts about his "loyalty." Like that of the campers, the physician's perspective is wrong insofar as it is neither impartial nor reversible. As Tom Beauchamp and James Childress (2001) concluded, "The virtues need to be accompanied by an understanding of what is right and good" (p. 32;

cf. Blasi, 1995; Lapsley & Narvaez, 2006). In this case, benevolence and loyalty need to be "accompanied" or guided by an understanding of what is fair or just.

As noted, in such views, morality is often equated with the norms and customs of a particular culture. Can we legitimately evaluate another culture's established beliefs, values, traditions, and practices? Well taken are cultural psychologists' assertions that one's own culture is not always right, that diversity should be appreciated and even celebrated, and that one must make every effort to understand and respect the morality of a particular cultural context. Respecting and appreciating the other person or group, after all, is the start of social perspective taking. Nonetheless, we *can* justifiably engage in valid moral evaluation[3] even of a different cultural tradition or practice.

Consider, for example, the cultural custom of genital mutilation. It continues to be part of a girl's traditional upbringing in the village of Kisii, Kenya, although it is conducted secretly because of its having been declared illegal by Kenya's Parliament (Lacey, 2002). And it should be clear that the accurate term for this practice is *mutilating*, not merely "altering" (Haidt & Bjorklund, 2008a, p. 191): The custom involves removal of all or part of the girl's clitoris and labia minora (thereby diminishing or eliminating her capacity for sexual sensation) and, in some cases, severe constriction through suturing of the vaginal opening. The custom is intended to promote (by discouraging promiscuity) values of sexual purity and family honor. The practice can lead to infection, infertility, and even life-threatening complications. It is also excruciatingly painful as it is conducted without anesthesia; some girls cannot stand the pain and resist so much that they must be held down by men (Ali, 2007; Edgerton, 1992; Kopelman, 2001; Sinclair, 2008, January 20).

Given that the custom is still widely approved in the cultural context of the village of Kisii (although the practice is controversial in many villages), are these villagers right to persist in its practice? On what basis are the Kenyan lawmakers, representing the national culture, right to impose their views on this village subculture?[4] Yet there is a valid basis. Like virtues, cultural practices must be related to an understanding of the right and the good of morality. And like the acts of the campers and the physician, the acts of these practitioners fail the condition of reversibility. If the practitioners were adequately informed[5] and in the place of their vulnerable, innocent, suffering victims, the mutilators would likely not wish the act done to them. Although the practice follows a time-honored tradition, "an assertion of cultural tradition" to justify genital mutilation "is not enough to override...basic fairness" (Moshman, 2005, p. 52; see also Rest, Narvaez, Bebeau, & Thoma, 1999). Respecting cultural traditions and practices, in other words, should not require one to "condone the subjugation and brutalization of women" (Fowers & Richardson, 1996, p. 615). Is female genital mutilation functionally necessary to protect the village's cultural identity and preserve its traditional values?[6] Anthropologist Robert Edgerton (1992) noted dryly that "most societies in the world ... have managed to cherish female purity and family honor without practicing [clitorectomy and] infibulation" (pp. 9–10).

The Right and the Good: The Moral Domain

Once we have objectively justified an evaluation that the acts of the campers, the physician, or the mutilators are morally wrong, is our moral evaluation complete? Generally, does morality consist exclusively of fairness-based right or wrong? What are the foundations of ethics? There is clearly more to the moral domain than right and wrong based on impartiality or reversibility. What fundamentally completes the core of the moral domain? We have already alluded to some candidates. Note, for example, that moral sentiments pertaining to loyalty, group identity, purity, and honor figured into our evaluation of the acts of the complicit physician and the genital mutilator. Another moral value, respect for authority (even that of a mentally challenged adult), was violated by the campers' victimization of Edward. And then there is our disgust at the self-soiling inflicted on Edward. Might not that reaction have intensified our condemnation of the campers' act?

Values of in-group solidarity, loyalty, tradition, and conformity; respect for, honoring of, or obedience to authority; and purity (or disgust at impurity) are widely evident around the world and do impact moral evaluation. Jonathan Haidt (2003, Haidt & Bjorklund, 2008a, 2008b) has even claimed a primary or foundational status, comparable to that of fairness, for these values or "intuitions." This claim is dubious. As we have seen, simple appeals to loyalty, tradition, honor, and purity do not suffice to make a wrong act right. Although in-group solidarity and loyalty promote the sense of belonging or personal security of in-group members (Brewer, 2007), doesn't it matter how the culture treats *out*-group members, such as Edward (see Jacobson, 2008; Chapter 4)? And respect for authority is better framed as respect for and obedience to *legitimate* authority (see Damon, 1977), which again returns us to considerations of fairness. Pinker (2008, January 13) suggested that criteria of rationality or fairness (e.g., interchangeability of perspectives) may "provide a benchmark for determining" whether a moral evaluation or intuition is "aligned with morality itself" (p. 56). In-group loyalty, obedience to authority, and "purity" too often fail Pinker's benchmark to merit foundational status in ethics.

Feelings of impurity or disgust warrant further discussion as we seek to complete the basic core of the moral domain. Granted, disgust "can be a cruel and stupid emotion"; consider, for example, the "disgust" that ostensibly justifies the persecution of so-called "untouchables" in India (Bloom, 2004, p. 175). Indeed, given how often manipulations of disgust have led to "extreme in-group–out-group divisions followed by inhumane treatment," this feeling "wins the award as the single most irresponsible emotion" (Hauser, 2006, p. 199).

Nonetheless, the evolutionary function of this emotion points to an aspect of morality that may indeed assume a primary or foundational status alongside "the right" of impartiality or fairness. Consider that disgust prompts us to avoid contact with rotten meat, decaying flesh, vermin, vomit, feces, urine, or other "potential disease vectors" (Pinker, 2008, p. 37; see Bloom, 2004; Hauser, 2006). The core feeling of disgust or revulsion has served the function of protecting our bodies from harm.

What about considerations not specifically of infection to oneself or others, but of harm—or benefit—in general? Often complementary to the right or wrong of an act are its good or bad *effects* or *consequences* for oneself or others. Edward, for example, was not only wronged; he was harmed. He *suffered*, as did the village girls and the incompetent doctor's patients. And we *care* about their suffering. "Of the emotions that one could use as a moral guide," wrote Paul Bloom (2004), "I would prefer [over disgust] sympathy, compassion, and pity" (p. 175). Empathy or caring is indeed a worthy companion to fairness in the moral domain. Just as it is generally immoral to inflict harm, it is generally moral to promote the welfare, flourishing (*eudaimonia*) (Lourenco, 2000), or greater good of all participants in the moral sphere.

An adequate morality requires both the right and the good. Taken together, these basic considerations capture the core of the moral domain and define the primary strands of moral development. Largely consistent with our twofold representation is Beauchamp and Childress's (2001) conceptualization of morality in terms of two primary principles: first, justice and respect for the person[7] (autonomy) and, second, nonmaleficence or beneficence (along with its corresponding virtue, benevolence).[8] William Frankena argued that *justice* and *beneficence* collectively comprise the "substance of the moral point of view" (according to Beauchamp & Childress, 2001, p. 402). Beauchamp and Childress defined beneficence as "all forms of action intended to benefit other persons" (p. 166). Moral appeals for promotion of the good—not only for individuals but also for groups—are typically driven by empathy (see Chapter 4).

The right and the good strands of morality and moral development, although distinct, intimately interrelate and complement one another. The paradox is worth contemplating: The strands of morality are distinguishable yet inextricable. The "right" is the right of *something*. What is "the right" if not the right expression of love, the right balance of goods, the right sharing or reciprocating among *people*? Does not the right "presuppose" the good (Frankena, 1973, p. 44)? And the converse is also true: One can scarcely refer to the good in the absence of the right. Utilitarian and other consequentialist theories of the good prescribe not just the "greatest good" but the greatest good for *the greatest number*—an implicit appeal to equality. Baier (1965) referred to the moral point of view as "in the interest of *everyone alike*" (p. 107; emphasis added). Why should a utilitarian theory attend a whit to questions of distribution so long as the good is maximized (Frankena, 1973)? Does not equality or fairness seem almost inherent to promotion of the general good? No wonder Jean Piaget (1932/1965) concluded that "between the more refined forms of justice...and love properly so called, there is no longer any real conflict" (p. 324; cf. Barry, 1995).

Yet for all their intimacy (and perhaps ultimate compatibility), the right and the good do remain distinct and mutually irreducible: There simply is no way to assimilate justice into beneficence, nor beneficence into justice. We cannot say that the right *reduces* to the good any more than we can say that the good *reduces* to the right.[9]

The mutual irreducibility of the right and the good is not problematic for moral evaluations or decisions so long as these strands interweave compatibly. The campers' act was clearly immoral in that Edward was both wronged and harmed; much the same can be said for the medical patient and the child victims in Kisii, Kenya. In general, the case for objective morality is strongest where the strands are complementary. But what about cases where justice and caring would seem to be "unavoidably in conflict" and seem to "have equal weight in the circumstances" (Beauchamp & Childress, 2001, pp. 21, 390)? After all, "caring and justice are powerful, legitimate principles and both are valid" (Hoffman, 2000, p. 270; cf. pp. 267–270). Piaget's optimism notwithstanding, the good and the right do sometimes seem to conflict. In such cases, how does one decide whether caring or fairness takes precedence?

Hoffman (2000) provided a real-life case of conflict for us to consider. In Hoffman's psychology department, "an esteemed faculty member died and his wife, a part-time adjunct instructor with much-below-average teacher ratings, wanted to keep her job." The department faculty members were for a while at loggerheads: "The faculty who supported retaining the widowed part-time instructor were passionate about the matter and found it hard to believe that their colleagues could be so callous as to want to add to this woman's grief. [But] the other faculty were equally passionate [that] allowing a poor teacher to stay on" was unfair (and uncaring) to the students, who pay tuition and have a right to expect to learn from the best available teachers; to more competent and available prospective instructors who would be more deserving of the job; and to the meritocratic standards and legitimate expectations of the university (Hoffman, 2000, pp. 269–270). What to do?

Frankena (1980) suggested that, in cases of conflict between the right and the good, one might weigh the two sides. Although both are primary in principle, perhaps the right and the good are not after all comparably substantial in the given case. Then one could justifiably give precedence to whichever side is more substantial. "A considerable amount of good may outweigh a small inequality of treatment or a considerable gain in equality [or in what is fair] may outweigh a small amount of good" (p. 69). In terms of Hoffman's example: Is the good of letting the widow keep her job "considerable" and the attendant inequities of doing so "small"? Or does the right (fairness to the students, prospective teachers, university standards) outweigh the good (not adding to her grief)?

In the end, the faculty decided to replace the widow with a more competent instructor (Hoffman, personal communication, November 15, 2007), but perhaps not without some reluctance. Empathy for her plight was outweighed but not eliminated in the moral decision-making. Precisely because the lesser consideration remains, its subordination nonetheless often leaves in the judge a "trace" of sorrow, a residual regret that this other valid consideration had to be overridden (Beauchamp & Childress, 2001, p. 406; cf. Hill, 1996).

The right and the good not only capture much of the moral domain but also represent the main strands of moral development. We focus on moral development and its relation to reality in the remaining chapters of this book. To explore the development of the right and the good, we will use as vehicles the nonrelativistic and universalist theories of Lawrence Kohlberg and Martin Hoffman. Like the right and the good, these theories of moral development are distinct yet interrelated and generally complementary.

Introducing Chapters 2 through 9

Both Kohlberg's and Hoffman's theories posit that we develop morally in part as we truly take the perspectives of others and thereby go (or, perhaps better, grow) beyond the superficial. Young children might laugh at Ed because they would attend mainly to the salient or "surface" features of his colorful reaction: Ed's reddened face; the blaring and astonishing fluency of his blue streak; his odd, off-kilter way of running; and his ineffectual attempts to catch the culprits. More mature observers would have grown beyond this superficial laughter. They would truly and deeply take Ed's perspective: They would understand and object to the unfairness against him, discern and feel his suffering, and—one would hope—act on their moral motivation to help him. Their moral perception would be profound.

Moral perception can be profound in understanding (the right) as well as empathic feeling (the good). The development from superficial perception to a deeper understanding of right and wrong is addressed in Kohlberg's theoretical approach, discussed in Chapters 2 and 3. In Chapter 2, we discuss the fundamental themes of Kohlberg's theory or, more broadly, the cognitive developmental approach to morality. We revisit the works of Kohlberg's predecessor, Jean Piaget, as we consider the phenomenological world of the young child. Because preschoolers generally find it difficult to keep in mind and work with multiple sources of information, their moral understanding or moral judgment tends to be superficial. Broadly speaking, their attention is readily captured by or *centered* on that which is immediate and salient in their social and nonsocial worlds. Spontaneous altruistic thoughts do occur even in the young child's mind, and they may act on those thoughts and feelings for others. Nonetheless, highly salient is the chatter of one's own desires or impulses, and the immediate needs of one's own body, that is to say, one's egoistic perspective. Although Piaget's original concept of egocentrism as an *incapacity* did not prove to be valid, "egocentric bias," a *tendency* to center on one's own immediate perspective at the expense of others, lives on in the literature today.

Just as centration and superficiality characterize early childhood moral judgment, "decentration" and depth can be said to characterize moral understanding and perception in the school years and beyond. Taking into account others' perspectives (i.e., decentering from one's egoistic perspective) and growing beyond the superficial in a cognitive sense have to do with the construction of moral understanding and judgment, in particular, the right and wrong of ideal moral reciprocity. Again, mature persons would understand that the prank played upon Ed was unfair, that they—especially if they were Ed with his intellectual disability—would not wish to be treated that way. And out of that understanding, they might act, to refrain or intervene. In other words, the cognitive-developmental claim is that there is a primarily cognitive motive in morality. The motive is not insurmountable, to be sure; but it is there nonetheless.

In the course of our Chapter 2 discussion of this primarily cognitive strand of moral development, we do a number of things. We relate morality to logic; explain that the ideals of fairness or moral reciprocity are constructed, not merely socialized, internalized, or intuited; consider the role of peer interaction and perspective-taking opportunities in this moral constructive process; argue that reciprocity can be a moral motive in its own right; trace across diverse cultures the construction of moral judgment through social perspective taking during and beyond the years of childhood; and ponder issues in the concept and assessment of "stages" in the development of moral judgment. We interpret the stages as frameworks or "schemas," a construct that will evolve in the subsequent chapters of our exploration.

Given this Piagetian cognitive-developmental concern with superficiality-to-depth in moral judgment or understanding, Kohlberg was particularly concerned to discover and articulate an age trend and possible sequence of developmental advances or stages that may be universal. Although we argue in Chapter 3 that Kohlberg's specific stage typology was misguided and accordingly propose a new view, we stress Kohlberg's awesome achievements: This man almost single-handedly put cognitive moral development on the map of American psychology. He encouraged attention to the continued development of moral judgment beyond the childhood years. And he speculated from case studies of mature moral thinkers in existential crisis that there may be a deeper reality, one that underlies profound moral perception and that can support the moral life (see Chapters 3, 8, and 9).

Profound moral perception also entails caring or feeling. Accordingly, in Chapter 4, our focus shifts from the right to the good, from justice to empathy, from the primarily cognitive to the primarily affective strand of moral motivation and development. We examine the systematic, research-based theory of empathy and moral development articulated over the past three decades by Martin Hoffman and colleagues. As is Kohlberg's, Hoffman's work is described in virtually every current developmental psychology textbook. Although we will articulate our disagreements, we do agree with the evaluation of a prominent researcher, Carolyn Zahn-Waxler, that Hoffman's theory of empathy is "right on target" (Azar, 1997, November 11, p. 1) and that his research has "set the standard for the scientific study" of empathy (Zahn-Waxler, 2000). We draw heavily in Chapter 4 from Hoffman's (2000, 2008) integration of his impressive contributions to the field.

Hoffman has focused our attention on the key role of empathy in moral development. Thanks to cognitive development, language development, and moral socialization, empathy evolves from simple, biologically based responses to surface cues to a more complex and veridical emotional responsiveness to the joys, sufferings, and life situations of others. Because Ed's "funny" displays of agitation were so salient for them, young children might attend only to those cues and ignore cues of distress. Surface responding tends to be displaced in moral development by subtler and more authentic discernments: of the hurt behind Ed's anger, of his utter shame and humiliation at having wet himself, and of his distress at perhaps not quite knowing what to do or whom to tell about what was happening.

If empathy is to develop and motivate moral behavior, moral socialization (featuring the child's internalization of prosocial norms) is crucial. Within moral socialization, Hoffman focuses on parental practices of discipline. Through "inductions," or disciplinary teaching that makes salient the perspectives of others hurt by the child's transgression, the parent can elicit and cultivate a key psychological resource brought by the child to the disciplinary encounter: the empathic predisposition and its derivatives (chiefly, the potential for empathy-based guilt).

In the course of our Chapter 4 discussion of Hoffman's theory of empathy development and socialization, we address a number of topics: the complex nature of the empathic predisposition; the foundation of mature empathy in the development of the distinction between self and other; the use of both self-focused and other-focused perspective taking in mature empathy; the roles of causal attribution, inference, principles, and other cognitive processes in the formation of empathic anger, empathy-based guilt, and other empathic affects; the problems of empathic bias and empathic overarousal; the roles of nurturance and optimal arousal of attention in moral socialization; and the favorable impact, found for example in our research (Krevans & Gibbs, 1996; Patrick & Gibbs, 2007), of expressing one's disappointed expectations in the discipline encounter. The chapter concludes with our argument that the motivation to correct an injustice is, at least in part, cognitive. In other words, empathic affect stands not alone in moral motivation; the special structures constructed within the *cognitive* strand of moral development can also impel action. The most plausible position in moral motivation is neither "affective primacy" (Hoffman's position) nor "cognitive primacy" (Kohlberg's position) but *co*primacy (*both* empathy and justice as primary motives; in effect, a "dual process" model).

In Chapters 5 through 7, we apply Kohlberg's and Hoffman's theories to social behavior and, in the process, expand certain variables—most notably, moral self-relevance, self-serving cognitive distortion, and social skills—that neither Kohlberg nor Hoffman adequately developed. Chapter 5 focuses on some of the variables accounting for individual differences in the likelihood of prosocial behavior, where "prosocial behavior" can range from a particular intervention to a lifetime dedicated to just and good causes. Ed needed someone to intervene on his behalf against his tormentors. I know. As one of the campers, I witnessed Ed's torment on at least one occasion. Although I did not intervene (I feared sinking from anonymity into downright unpopularity, an excuse that even today fails to neutralize my guilt), I have learned since then (Gibbs et al., 1986) that there are those who would intervene. Our account of prosocial behavior in Chapter 5 includes the case of a White youth who surprised even himself as he intervened against his peers to save an African-American youth from imminent attack.

INTRODUCTION

10

Individuals who seem primed to discern and act against unfairness and harm amid the complexities of social conformity, ideology, and distorted thinking in the "field" of human social existence (discussed in Chapter 5) tend to be those for whom morality is central to their sense of self. Increasingly in moral development, moral self-relevance can join the main primary (affective and cognitive) sources of moral motivation. Individuals differ markedly in moral self-relevance: Some individuals, called moral exemplars by Anne Colby and William Damon (1992), achieve a life characterized by almost total integration of self and morality (at this high level of moral self-relevance, we refer to *moral identity*). Finally, to take effective sustained action, even those high in moral self-relevance need ego strength, which we define as affect-regulating follow-through skills. Distinguishing features of genuine versus spurious "moral exemplars" are considered at the end of Chapter 5.

Chapters 6 and 7 apply Kohlberg's and Hoffman's moral developmental theories to the understanding and treatment of antisocial behavior. Kohlberg's and Hoffman's theories primarily use the concept of developmental delay in perspective taking to account for antisocial behavior. One conjures the stereotype of children growing up in the conditions typical of inner cities, victims of abuse and neglect. The picture is of children managing to survive and cope as best they can, taking no one's perspective except their own, still superficial even as adolescents in their moral judgment and empathy, and accordingly acting in a manner unfair and unfeeling toward others. Abuse and neglect are in fact associated with developmental delays and other risk factors for antisocial behavior. Yet the adolescents who tormented Edward were not from a high-risk inner-city environment but instead were largely from the relatively affluent suburbs of northern New Jersey in the 1960s. Here we have an apparent anomaly: How do we account for antisocial behavior among those who, at least at the first blush of Kohlberg's and Hoffman's theories, should have gone beyond egocentric bias and other superficialities of centration to reach deeper, more mature levels of moral functioning? Why didn't they take Ed's perspective? Let us suggest three answers.

The first answer is that Ed was not among the campers' small circle of friends. The middle-class suburbs of New Jersey were rather exclusively White, mainstream neighborhoods. To the parochial members of that rather homogeneous culture, the relatively few individuals of other ethnic groups, and certainly disabled individuals, were, so to speak, invisible. Although Ed was similar in one salient respect (racially), he was different in other respects. The perpetrators were friendly enough with their peers but cared little about the feelings of those who were "different." To use Hoffman's term, their perspective taking was quite *empathically biased* (Chapter 4) in favor of their narrowly defined, familiar in-group at the expense of dissimilar others such as Edward. He was small, yet an adult; they were neither. He was mentally retarded; they were not. His legs were disparate; theirs were not. His occupational orientation was that of manual labor; theirs (or their parents') for the most part was not. It was as if Ed were too different to qualify for perspective taking, for decent (fair and caring) treatment, for inclusion within their "moral circle" (Singer, 1981). Haidt's emphasis on group loyalty as a moral foundation notwithstanding, robust in-group identity typically prompts far more *immoral* than moral behavior, indeed, "is a major cause of strife and suffering in the world today" (Tomasello, 2008, May 25; cf. Moshman, 2007).

Our second answer as to why the campers did not take Ed's perspective refers not to their in-group empathic bias but instead to their egoistic motives or desires. Ed was not simply different, but different and *vulnerable*. Although vulnerability can elicit empathy, it can also invite exploitation, and the latter motive can overpower empathy and preempt perspective taking. Hoffman and others (Chapter 4) are correct to assert that Kohlberg's cognitive-developmental approach suffers from an inadequate appreciation of the egoistic motives that morality must overcome through moral development and socialization:

> Humans ... have a desire for ... dominance *[power or control over others, supe-riority to them]* that has deep biological roots. Sociobiologists trace it to the drive to maximize reproduction of one's genes. But whatever the source, it plays important social roles and is deeply embedded in primate behavior generally. (Kane, 1994, p. 55)

Might the campers have been motivated in part to assert their power, their superiority over Ed, an ostensibly higher status but vulnerable adult? Ed may have been a tempting target among the adults in the campers' world. Ed was an adult, and hence occupied higher status and authority in the social hierarchy. The campers knew they should respect adults or others in authority (at least legitimate authority). But because Edward was mentally challenged, he could readily be outmaneuvered and dominated—in Kant's words, used as a means instead of respected as an end. To overcome such egoistic motives, moral socialization must cultivate children's fairness (Chapter 2), empathy (Chapter 4), and respect (Damon, 1995).

There is a third possible answer. Perhaps the campers were on the verge of perspective taking, with its attendant intimations of wrong and harm, of unfairness and empathy-based guilt. But perhaps they used cognitive distortions to sabotage that incipient perspective taking so that they could continue to tease and humiliate. After all, although their sphere of morality was small, they did not generally act like bullies or "proactive" aggressors (Chapter 6). Consider Hoffman's (and others') suggestion that empathy-based motives are just as much a part of human nature as egoistic ones, that the empathic predisposition is broadly evident and reliable (Chapter 4). Perhaps the campers were not so in-groupish and egoistically motivated as to preclude all empathy for Edward. Perhaps, indeed, precisely because of some degree of perspective taking and empathy, they needed to neutralize their incipient moral feelings by rationalizing their actions. I do remember how the campers who were engaged in tormenting Ed seemed motivated to talk about how much they needed "entertainment": This camp is so boring, you see, that it forces you to think up things to do for kicks. You just have to get some relief. Everybody pulls pranks, that's just what happens at any summer camp. And, you know, Ed's so funny when he's mad—you just can't help setting him off; it's sort of his own fault.

Blaming the victim and other rationalizing distortions neutralized the good and right of taking Ed's perspective. Accordingly, the campers failed to take into account that Ed was mentally challenged; that Ed had done nothing to them; that, in fact, he had shown them little kindnesses from time to time and tried to be their friend; and that their "entertainment" inflicted humiliation and distress on him.

We spend considerable space in Chapter 6 analyzing such self-serving cognitive distortions, especially as exemplified in the phenomenology of a notoriously antisocial individual, Timothy McVeigh. This case makes particularly clear how cognitive distortions can insulate a self-centered worldview (itself a primary distortion, linked to feeling superior), that is, can preempt or neutralize social perspective taking, moral understanding, and veridical empathy.

Again, we ask: What if the campers had veridically and profoundly taken Ed's perspective? What if they had seen Edward's common humanity with them and had thereby sensed the unfairness and felt the harm of their prospective act? Then they might have found the ego strength to refrain from "setting him off" for the purpose of their self-centered and egoistically motivated entertainment. Most offenders, from petty pranksters to ideological terrorists, fail (at least in any moral sense) to take the perspective of their victims. Hence, social perspective taking—in particular, perspective taking that is veridical, rationalization busting, reciprocally ideal, discerning, caring, socially skilled, and inclusive—should be a basic theme pervasive across the components of any effective treatment program. As we move from understanding to treating antisocial behavior (Chapter 7), we will focus on a multicomponent treatment program that incorporates a wide variety of social perspective-taking opportunities, namely, our EQUIP program (DiBiase, Gibbs, & Potter, 2005; Gibbs, Potter, & Goldstein, 1995; Gibbs, Potter, DiBiase, & Devlin, in press; Potter, Gibbs, & Goldstein, 2001). Chapter 7 concludes with illustrations of social perspective-taking treatments available for severe offenders.

Although most of this book concerns Kohlberg's and Hoffman's theories of moral development and behavior, we do go beyond those theories in Chapter 8 to consider the question of a deeper reality. As noted, Kohlberg argued that existential thinkers in their soul-searching sometimes discern such a reality, that is, come to see their earthly moral life from an inspiring "cosmic perspective." If there is such a deeper reality, perhaps it is sometimes glimpsed through physically life-threatening as well as existential crises. Accordingly, we study in this chapter cases of persons who have had a so-called "near-death experience," or a set of "profound psychological events with transcendental and mystical elements, typically occurring to individuals close to death or in situations of intense physical or emotional danger" (Greyson, 2000b, p. 316). Concerning the ontological significance of this phenomenon, a review of the literature—especially, recent medical research literature—leads us to the tentative conclusion that it is not entirely a matter of subjective projection, that the experience involves something real. To some extent, then, we corroborate Kohlberg's suggestion that there is a cosmic reality that underlies moral development and inspiration. In this light, "growing beyond the superficial" and "taking the perspectives of others" take on radical new meaning.

In our final chapter (Chapter 9), we conclude our use of Kohlberg's and Hoffman's theories to explore growth beyond the superficial in morality. We culminate our argument for a coprimacy in moral motivation by relating their theories to motivationally and qualitatively distinct categories of knowledge. We conclude the chapter with some final thoughts on moral development, perception, and behavior vis-à-vis a deeper reality of human interconnectedness. If we are deeply connected, then acts that wrong and harm one individual—Edward, a medical patient, a young girl in Kisii, Kenya—ultimately wrong and harm us all.

Notes

[1]In the physical sciences, however, post-modernist or subjectivist critiques of objectivity and rationality have lost considerable credibility (Gross & Leavitt, 1994; Sokol & Bricmont, 1999).

[2]Moral objectivity is linked instead to "intrinsic effects [of an act] for others' rights and welfare" (Smetana, 2006, p. 121). Social domain theorists may overstate the sophistication of young children's understanding of morality and the independence of social conventions from the moral domain (see critiques by Fowler, 2007; and Glassman & Zan, 1995). Turiel (2008) is correct, however, that unjust or oppressive social conventions and power structures must be clearly identified and resisted.

[3]Moral evaluation must be distinguished from moral reform. Although moral evaluation (by the consideration of the right and the good) can be valid, effective moral reform does not necessarily follow. Well-intentioned initiatives may only provoke hostility. For example, a doctor in Italy who served Somali immigrants was reluctant (having treated serious medical complications from the procedure) to cut the genitals of their daughters. He proposed to parents that he use a pin-prick procedure as a harmless symbolic alternative. The proposal outraged both culturally embedded immigrants as a travesty of their tradition, and reformist immigrants as an implicit approval of their culture's subjugation and brutalization of women (Bruni, 2004; cf. Ali, 2008). The latter outrage was justifiable, but the doctor's initiative seemed only to make things worse. (Interestingly, if we seek to specify "worse," we find ourselves back at the right and the good.)

[4]Haidt and Bjorklund (2008a) would presumably argue that the lawmakers were right in that their position represented the overall culture's majority "endorsement" (p. 216). An endorsement, however, does not necessarily constitute a valid moral justification (Jacobson, 2008), i.e., a belief "that everyone ought to follow the customs [or endorsements] of his own society" does not in itself provide "a rational basis for action" (Singer, 1981, p. 98).

[5]Practitioners may appeal to various demonstrably erroneous cultural beliefs concerning harm, such as that clitorises left intact grow hideously long or sprout branches that prevent conception, consigning an unexcised female to a childless future (Ali, 2008; Lacey, 2002; see also Kopelman, 2001; Nussbaum, 1999). Prospective victims who have been taught to accept such erroneous ideas are not in a position to give informed consent (James, 1994; Kopelman, 2001). Taking the perspective of "the victim" presupposes that the actual victim is adequately informed. As for victimizers, Cecilia Wainryb (2000) called for research on the conditions under which appeals to erroneous beliefs are seen as legitimate excuses. Generally, the condition of

reversibility presupposes that persons' perspectives are adequately informed, "healthy" in mental and emotional terms, and offered in good faith.

[6]Note the contradiction between the relativistic premise and the non-relative appeal:

> Relativists who say it is wrong to eliminate rituals that give meaning to other cultures [or] ... make [other] intercultural judgments about tolerance, group benefit, intersocietal respect, or cultural diversity ... are ... inconsistent in making a judgment that presumes to have genuine cross-cultural moral authority. (Kopelman, 2001, pp. 319–320)

Similarly inconsistent are "students who reject the language of morality [yet] have no qualms about expressing their disapproval of sexual harassment, child labor in sweatshops, and unfair treatment of graduate teaching assistants" (Bloom, 2004, p. 130). Colby (2008) also noted that college students' meta-ethical nihilism or relativism does not appear to deter their willingness to take "normative positions on specific ethical questions" (p. 399).

[7]Along with justice, "respect for the person" is often deemed to be integral to intrinsic, right-or-wrong-in-itself considerations in morality. Intrinsic moral considerations are typically termed "deontological" and contrasted with approaches that posit morality to reside not in the right or wrong of the action per se but instead in the human social utility or consequences of a given action. Joshua Greene (2008a) has argued against deontological (cognitive or rationalist) accounts of respect for the person. More broadly, Greene has rejected the intrinsic-versus-consequences distinction in ethics in favor of an affect-cognition (or emotion-reason) distinction. In Greene's argument, "respect for the person" is "up close and personal" (p. 70), a matter of primary "emotional moral intuitions" (Greene, 2008b, p. 105). Hence, "rational" or cognitive reconstructions of deontological evaluation are seen as largely post hoc rationalizations (p. 105). Whereas "deontological judgment is affective at its core" (Greene, 2008a, p. 65), utilitarian calculations of greatest-good consequences for the group are seen as fundamentally and qualitatively distinct insofar as calculations are "grounded in moral *reasoning*" (p. 36).

Greene's argument is questionable. Is the motive to consider consequences for others or identify the greatest good of the group primarily cognitive? Are its motivational origins fundamentally distinct from those of "up close and personal" care for the distressed individual? It is true that "our feelings of benevolence and sympathy are more easily aroused by specific human beings than by a large group in which no individuals stand out" (Singer, 1981, p. 157; see Chapter 4). Furthermore, implementing the best beneficence for the group may indeed entail some low-affect utilitarian calculations as evidenced in greater working-memory- than emotion-related brain-neuronal activation (e.g., Greene, Sommerville, Nystrom, Darley, & Cohen, 2001). But note that the difference favoring the individual is essentially quantitative ("*more easily* aroused"), as indicated in reaction time differences (e.g.,Greene, Morelli, Lowenberg, Nystrom, & Cohen, 2008). Despite these brain activation and reaction time differences, empathy (affective primacy) for others directly or indirectly drives *both* individual and group concern (see Chapter 4). As Vivek Viswanathan (2008) put the point: "It is not a lack of empathy that brings about utilitarianism. It is full empathy" (Viswanathan, 2008, February/March, p. 35).

Greene and colleagues' argument may be characterized as a "dual process" model (e.g., Valdesolo & DeSteno, 2008), but one that clearly differs from ours. We will argue in this book for a formulation of "dual process" (we prefer the term "coprimacy") that takes seriously the traditional deontological-consequentialist distinction in ethics. In these terms, we have posited a distinction between the right (fairness, impartiality, respect for the person in his or her own right) and the good (empathy, caring for the individual or group). Respect for the person does have a place along with justice under "the right" rubric. This placement is justified given that *dis*respect is logically inconsistent and unfair, i.e., fails the condition of reversibility: Treating another person (or even one's long-term self) as a means to one's own selfish ends contradicts how one expects to be treated by other persons. Hence, both justice and respect for the person may be considered to be deontological or rational (Beauchamp & Childress, 2001). Greene does not consider the referent for "deontological" used in this book and elsewhere, namely, the condition of reversibility (or interchangeability of perspectives).

[8]Actually, Beauchamp and Childress (2001) keep these concepts distinct on the grounds that

> conflating nonmaleficence and beneficence into a single principle obscures relevant distinctions. Obligations not to harm others (e.g., those prohibiting theft, disablement, and killing) are distinct from obligations to help others (e.g., those prescribing the provision of benefits, protection of interests, and promotion of welfare). (p. 114)

They do acknowledge, however, that "no sharp breaks exist on the continuum from not inflicting harm to providing benefit" (p. 165).

[9]Correspondingly, cognition and affect "always remain indissociable although distinct" (Piaget, 1973/1972, p. 47; cf. Cowan, 1978, pp. 49–53). It is sometimes argued that cognition and affect (and, for that matter, overt behavior) are so intimately interrelated in so many diverse ways that the very distinctions even for heuristic purposes are spurious, and therefore human functioning should be conceptualized anew using distinctions and constructs that may be more tenable (e.g., Damon, 1977; Rest, 1983). Others (e.g., Zajonc, 1984; Haidt, 2003; Metcalfe & Mischel, 1999) argue that affect is a separate system that can function prior to and independently of cognition (even *qua* appraisal). Coprimacy represents an intermediate or "dual process" position, positing that affect and cognition are distinct yet inextricably interrelated (cf. the relationship between the good and the right).

CHAPTER 2

"The Right" and Moral Development:

Fundamental Themes of Kohlberg's Cognitive Developmental Approach

IN THE LAST CHAPTER, WE NOTED THAT YOUNG CHILDREN MIGHT BE SO taken with a mentally disabled man's (Edward's) colorful reaction to a prank that they might not perceive his suffering and the pranksters' self-centered unfairness. Generally, young children often overattend to, or "center upon," one or another salient feature of a situation and accordingly fail to infer underlying realities. What does it mean, in a cognitive sense, to say that children grow beyond the superficial in morality? Does the construction (through social perspective-taking) of a deeper understanding of fairness or moral reciprocity contribute to one's moral motivation? Would an older person's grasp of an injustice, a violation of how people should treat one another, generate a desire to right the wrong?

Lawrence Kohlberg called his theoretical approach to morality and moral motivation "cognitive developmental" to describe his contextualization of moral development within social and nonsocial (or physical) cognitive development. One of Kohlberg's chief sources of inspiration, Jean Piaget, considered mature morality to be a logic or rationality inherent in social relations. Morality in the cognitive developmental approach refers mainly to the moral *judgment* (or reasoned evaluation) of the prescriptive values of right and wrong.[1]

In this chapter, we articulate the fundamental themes of the cognitive-developmental approach to morality. We have already hinted at them in the use of certain words in our opening paragraph, among them *superficial, center upon* or *self-centered, social perspective taking, construction*, and *moral reciprocity*. To be explicit, we will discuss these themes:

Superficiality, Self-Centration.   The young child's overattention in moral judgment to this or that eye- or ear-catching feature of a situation reflects a general cognitive tendency to center upon salient stimuli. Although one's own immediate perspective is salient throughout life, the young child tends to be especially egocentrically biased or centered on the self.

Growing beyond Superficiality/Self-Centration through Social Perspective Taking.   To "decenter" or grow beyond these centrations upon the self or upon some salient, here-and-now feature of a situation, the child needs not only to gain in working memory capacity but also to take and reflect upon the perspectives of others through social interaction.

Decentration, Mental Coordination, Social Construction.   To decenter from biasing centrations is to mentally coordinate multiple features (some salient, some not so salient) of a situation. Through this process, one eventually constructs a cognitive structure. As we will see, the "construction" of knowledge in Piagetian usage is irreducibly distinct from the internalization of a norm. *Social* construction (construction through social interaction, social perspective taking, and hypothetical reflection) is especially important in moral judgment development.

Moral Reciprocity.   The constructed structures most relevant to growth beyond the superficial in a cognitive sense are those of reciprocity. Advanced stages of moral reciprocity in human development surpass those attained by any other species.

Moral Necessity, Cognitive Primacy.   A constructed structure of moral reciprocity is "right" or necessary (e.g., moral equality must not be violated), much as logical reciprocity is right or necessary (e.g., mathematical equality cannot be violated). Real or apparent violations of reciprocity prompt a primarily *cognitive* motive to right the wrong.

Stages.   A network of structures such as those that pertain to moral reciprocity can be conceptualized as a basic framework, complex schema, or *stage* by which a child or older person perceives (meaningfully experiences), interacts with, and reflects upon events or situations. Because they are so mixed in one's overall functioning at any given time, stages in moral judgment development define only the qualitative levels of a rough age trend. As we will see, this age trend has been evidenced in over twenty countries or regions around the world.

The pervasiveness of these fundamental themes across social and nonsocial cognitive development reflects the broad sense of "cognitive" in Kohlberg's and Piaget's theoretical approach.[2] Indeed, Kohlberg (1964) began his work in part by identifying stable moral judgment trends that may "reflect cognitive development"

(p. 398). After all, it is the same child who meaningfully interacts with social and nonsocial (or physical) objects. We stress, however, the uniqueness of *social* interaction and perspective taking. Consider that social cognitive "objects" such as people are also conscious, intentional *subjects*. There is something quite unique about taking the perspective of an "object" that can also take *your* perspective! Pervasive cognitive-developmental themes notwithstanding, the story of socio*moral* development (to use Hugh Rosen's [1980] term) does not reduce entirely to the story of nonsocial cognitive development (Damon, 1977, 1981; Hoffman, 1981b).

Although Kohlberg's and Piaget's cognitive-developmental approach is clearly crucial to our exploration of the cognitive strand of moral development (a number of Piagetian constructs are quite helpful), we do not feel bound to the orthodoxy of either theorist's work. Indeed, although we do not systematically critique Piaget's version of the cognitive-developmental approach (see Beilin, 1992; Flavell, 1996; Gopnik, 1996; Lourenco & Macado, 1996; Siegler & Ellis, 1996), we will spend the entire next chapter critiquing (and offering a new view based on) Kohlberg's stage theory. This chapter goes "beneath" Kohlberg's theory. In other words, we explicate *basic* cognitive-developmental themes as a context for exploring the right and wrong of morality, in particular, the justice or reciprocity strand of moral development.

Early Childhood Superficiality

Because preschoolers generally have difficulty keeping in mind multiple sources of information, their moral judgment and, more generally, their social and nonsocial cognition tend to be superficial. Impressive appearances often capture their attention or imagination. In other words, young children evidence a "vulnerability to salient features of the here-and-now" (Flavell, Miller, & Miller, 2002, p. 181). This pronounced tendency to center upon the salient includes their own immediate viewpoint, especially their egoistic motives or desires. We will consider the superficial judgments of early childhood in terms of both social and nonsocial cognition.

Superficiality in Social Cognition

Young children overattend in their social (including moral) cognition to one or another salient appearance or consequence. Despite their evaluations of acts such as hitting as wrong even if adults were to approve (Turiel, 2006a), young children may legitimize the commands of authority figures such as parents or teachers by appeal to an imposing feature of size or power (e.g., "Dad's the boss because he's bigger"; Kohlberg, 1984, p. 624). Keeping a promise may be evaluated as important because "otherwise the other person will be mad or beat you up"—that is, may be justified by appeal to concrete consequences. Among children asked "What happens when lies are told?," 80% of 5-year-olds but only 28% of 11-year-olds mentioned punishment by an adult authority figure (Peterson, Peterson, & Seeto, 1983). Preschoolers, in contrast to older children, evaluate lies that lead to punishment more negatively than lies that do not (Bussey, 1992). Charles Helwig and Angela Prencipe (1999) found that 6-year-olds were more likely than 8- or 10-year-olds to suggest severe consequences ("a lot of trouble") for flag burning. The preschoolers also appealed to the material damage of the act and preferred the decisions of authorities among various approaches to changing a flag's design. Young children's orientation to salient authority and to visible or punitive consequences partly inspired Piaget's *heteronomy* (meaning "rules from others") term for their morality. It also inspired Kohlberg to characterize his moral judgment Stage 1 as "punishment and obedience" (see Chapter 3). The essential theme, however, is superficiality.

Perhaps the most famous example of superficiality in young children's moral judgments is found in one of Piaget's (1932/1965) early studies. Presenting pairs of stories of transgression, Piaget asked children which story entailed a "naughtier" act and why. One of the story pairs contrasted one child who accidentally breaks 15 cups as he comes to dinner with another child who breaks 1 cup as he tries to sneak a treat out of the cupboard. The younger (6- and 7-year-old) children, impressed by the "tangible" (p. 166) consequence of so many broken cups, often judged the coming-to-dinner child to be naughtier, even though that child was not the one with the mischievous intention.[3] Piaget's research design was criticized in subsequent literature (e.g., S. A. Miller, 2007) for confounding intention with consequence. The "confounding," however, was strategic: Piaget's aim was not to investigate whether young children understand intentions (his own research established that they do) but rather to study whether young children favor the salient over the subtle (e.g., an underlying intention) when the two conflict in a morally relevant task or situation.

Young children's tendency not to keep in mind intangible or subtle considerations means that their moral evaluations tend to be simplistic or inflexible (although their "inflexibility" may also reflect a recognition of the distinctly invariant character of the moral domain; Turiel, 2006a). For example, in the Peterson et al. (1983) study, 92% of the 5-year-olds (but only 28% of the 11-year-olds) stated that lying is "always wrong" (because, for example, the lie will always be found out and punished). Similarly, in the Helwig and Prencipe (1999) study, 96% of the 6-year-olds but only 46% of the 10-year-olds thought that flag burning could never be acceptable as a ritual showing respect for the country. Despite such "all or none" or inflexible evaluations (Harter, 2006, p. 522; Sigelman & Waitzman, 1991), young children's sociomoral judgments can also be quite capricious, as we will see.

Besides moral judgment, other areas of social cognition (understanding of self, others, social relations and situations, friendship, emotions, gender, death, and so on) also provide evidence of young children's vulnerability to the impressive or salient. Preschoolers' spontaneous descriptions of themselves or others tend to emphasize physical or directly observable attributes, abilities, and possessions ("I live in a big house," "I can run faster than anyone," "I have brown hair," etc.; Flavell & Miller, 1998; cf. Damon & Hart, 1988; Harter, 1999, 2006). Similarly, their social explanations, person description, and narrative comprehension tend to emphasize overt actions or expressive features (e.g., Livesley & Bromley, 1973; J. G. Miller, 1986; Paris & Upton, 1976).

Preschoolers' accounts of having been hurt or having hurt another person "lack depth" and tend to be "utterly behavioral," featuring simple one-way acts of physical harm (e.g., "Um, Jack hit me. And he also, he also kicked me"; Wainryb, Brehl, & Matwin, 2005, p. 54). Similarly, preschoolers' conceptions of friendship tend to focus on surface aspects such as playing together and sharing toys or other material goods (Selman, 1980). Gender is stereotyped by outer or situational features such as clothing, hairstyle, and occupational activity (Signorella, Bigler, & Liben, 1993). In the development of children's understanding of death, references to cessation of overt functions such as sight, hearing, or movement precede references to cessation of more subtle functioning in terms of feeling, thought, or consciousness (Lazar & Torney-Purta, 1991).

Young children's vulnerability to the pull of this or that particular overt feature does not preclude recognition of their own or others' wishes, preferences, or intentions. Indeed, broad characterizations of cognition in early childhood as "external" rather than psychological are untenable (Miller & Aloise, 1989). Various avenues of social cognitive research have found that early childhood judgment can be "internal," that is, can take into account psychological factors. As noted, despite young children's tendency to focus on external damage in naughtiness judgments, they are able—especially in the absence of conflicting, highly salient external features—to make judgments based on intentions (Flavell & Miller, 1998; cf. Piaget, 1932/1965). Self-descriptions, although generally concrete, often include psychological assertions ("I like pizza," "I love my dog Skipper," etc.). Indeed, young children even prefer to describe an emotional reaction in terms of psychological states (e.g., "he's scared of the dog") over behaviors (e.g., "he's holding his mommy's hand") when psychological and behavioral descriptions are both made salient as options (Lillard & Flavell, 1990).

Paucity of Ongoing Mental Coordination

Yet something is curiously amiss in the "internal" or psychological judgments of young children. Consider a 6-year-old's reply to Robert Selman's (1976) famous social cognitive task called Holly's Dilemma, pertaining to whether a girl named Holly would rescue a kitten stuck in a tree despite having promised her father that she wouldn't climb trees. Asked "What do you think Holly will do: save the kitten, or keep her promise?," the 6-year-old replied,

> She will save the kitten because she doesn't want the kitten to die. (How will her father feel when he finds out?) Happy, he likes kittens. (What would you do if you were Holly?) Save the kitten so it won't get hurt. (What if her father punishes her if she gets the kitten down?) Then she will leave it up there. (Why?) She doesn't want to get in trouble. (How will she feel?) Good, she listened to her father. (p. 303)

Although this 6-year-old's judgment is "internal" insofar as it appeals to psychological states such as wishes or preferences ("she doesn't want the kitten to die," "she doesn't want to get in trouble," etc.), the responses evidence a capricious quality. Attending to the kitten, she predicts Holly will climb the tree and suggests the father will be "happy" because "he likes kittens" (an attribution that ignores the father's likely upset over the broken promise). But then, prompted to consider the prospective salient consequence of punishment, the child abruptly switches focus from the kitten to the father: She would "leave it [the kitten] up there" and thereby avoid trouble with her father; she would even feel "good" having listened to and obeyed him (a judgment that neglects her feelings for the kitten). This 6-year-old seems blithely oblivious to the contradictions across her successive judgments. Is this not the whimsical charm of a young child?

Young children typically attend to one feature at a time, then, captured by that which is salient for him or her. Their focus is on the here-and-now. Robbie Case (1998), Robert Siegler (1996b), and other developmental psychologists called this attention to and consideration of one feature at a time "unidimensional thinking." What preschoolers tend *not* to do in their judgments is to keep in mind multiple sources of information (e.g., both the "kitten" and "father" facets of Holly's dilemma)—what Paul Bloom (2004) called "double bookkeeping" (p. 21)—and coordinate them to make a more adequate judgment (cf. Feffer, 1970). Ongoing mental coordination of the here-and-now with other facets of a situation—*multi*dimensional thinking—is precisely what is amiss in young children's "internal" yet still superficial judgments.

This paucity of ongoing mental coordination in social perspective taking is evident whether the social cognitive task is descriptive or prescriptive. In other words, one can discern the same unidimensional tendency whether the task questions ask what *will* or *would* happen and why (as in Selman's [1976] social cognitive dilemma) or what *should* happen and why (as in a moral dilemma). Consider young children's moral judgment responses to moral dilemmas such as William Damon's (1977) obedience-to-authority task. The protagonist of the dilemma story, Peter (Michelle for girl respondents), has been told that he can't go anywhere until he cleans up his messy room, but now he has an opportunity to go with his friends to a picnic. What should Peter do? A 4-year-old replied,

> *Go to the picnic. (Why should he do that?) Because he wants to and all his friends are going. (But what if his mother says, "No, Peter, you can't go until you clean up your room first"?) He would do what his mama says. (Why should he do that?) Because he likes to. (What if Peter really wants to go on the picnic and he doesn't want to clean up his room at all because if he does he'll miss the picnic?) His mama will let him go out with his friends. (But what if she won't let him?) He will stay home and play with his sister and clean up all his toys in his toy box. (Why will he do that?) Because he wants to. (p. 182)*

Once again, we find a capricious sequence of momentary preferences and wishful attributions, with no discernible regard for consistency. Young children do not seem to engage in much mental coordination in forming their judgments.

Paucity of mental coordination also seems to characterize young children's responses in studies that address development in the understanding of emotions. Young children tend not to take into account the influence of prior emotions upon current mood (e.g., that a person's upset from an earlier negative experience, or prior harm to another, could dampen or complicate his or her elation in a current pleasant situation; Arsenio, Gold, & Adams, 2006; Berk, 2009). Furthermore, young children have difficulty understanding mixed emotions, that is, that two emotions can occur at once (Harter, 1999, 2006).

Young children especially have difficulty inferring appropriate emotions in situations with conflicting features. In several studies (Fabes, Eisenberg, Nyman, & Michealieu, 1991; Gnepp, 1983; Hoffner & Badzinski, 1989; Hoffner, Cantor, & Thorson, 1989), questions regarding pictures depicting incongruous scenes such as a happy-faced boy with a broken bicycle elicited among the preschoolers explanations of emotion that centered on salient features such as facial expression (e.g., "He's happy because he likes to ride his bike"). Complex inferential judgments—for example, responses that coordinate or integrate the "happy face" and "broken bicycle" features of the scene (e.g., "He's happy because his father promised to help fix his broken bike")—did not become prevalent until somewhat older ages (7 years of age or so).

Egocentric Bias

This here-and-now immediacy or vulnerability to one or another salient feature of a present situation inclines the young child toward egocentric or self-centered judgments, perceptions, and behavior. After all, what is more immediate and salient than one's own mental chatter or "self-talk"? And the mental stream of young children's thought is especially self-oriented. Preschoolers are likely to describe the (less salient) perspectives of others in egocentric terms (e.g., "She gives me things"; Livesley & Bromley, 1973). They are also especially prone to attribute their own privileged-information perspective to others, not realizing that others, being uninformed, could not share their perspective (see Flavell et al., 2002). Alluding to the social problems that can ensue from such attributions, Paul Bloom (2004) labeled this presumptuous tendency "the curse of knowledge" (p. 22).

Other social cognitive research also points to the pronounced salience of self—that is, a paucity of taking and keeping in mind the perspectives of others—in early childhood. Although young children may infer that others are engaged in thought if others are depicted with a thoughtful expression or challenging task, they tend not to attribute *spontaneous* thoughts to others (Flavell & Miller, 1998). Nor do they attribute spontaneous thought to *themselves*: the "minds" encompassed within their superficial "theory of mind" include their own. Yet in many respects, young children are especially prone to attend to their own immediate thoughts, feelings, or knowledge, more than to the perspectives of others. Although it is easy for young children to keep in mind what *they* know to be true, they tend to forget what someone *else* would *not* know. In so-called "false belief" research (reviewed by Bloom, 2004; Chandler & Carpendale, 1998), young children attribute what they see (pertaining to, say, the new location of a chocolate treat) to an observer who (unlike themselves) did not see the relocation and hence would actually have a false belief (that the treat is still in the original location). Young children's typically inflated self-esteem and overestimation of their skills and abilities have been seen as following from the fact that children generally do not compare their competency with that of others until the elementary school years (Harter, 2006). The youngest children on distributive justice (how to share) tasks tend to confuse fairness with personal desire (e.g., "I should get it because I want to have it"; Damon, 1977, p. 75). In transgression-related tasks, young children typically judge that a child who gets to swing by pushing off the swing's current user would feel "happy" or "good" because he got what he wanted (Arsenio, Gold, & Adams, 2006). In a study of understanding the effects of lying (Peterson et al., 1983), none of the 5-year-olds (versus nearly a fourth of the 11-year-olds) made reference to a guilty conscience. Egocentric impulses of physical aggression are 3- to 6-year-olds' prevalent approach to resolving social conflict (Selman & Shultz, 1990).

The sense in which young children tend to be egocentric must be specified. Ample research has demonstrated the untenability of Piaget's classic definition of egocentrism as an *inability* or *lack of capacity* to differentiate others' perspectives from one's own (e.g., Flavell & Miller, 1998). Rather, egocentrism should be construed as a pronounced *bias* favoring one's own perspective over others' or a *distortive tendency* to assimilate others' perspectives to one's own, to forget that another person does not know or feel what we know or feel (Bloom's "curse of knowledge" noted earlier), or, occasionally, to assimilate one's own perspective into another's. This bias, cognitive distortion, or centration upon self may decline with gains in working memory and social perspective-taking experiences (discussed later) but does not disappear entirely:

> Our own points of view are usually more cognitively "available" to us than another person's views (Tversky & Kahneman, 1973). Furthermore, we are usually unable to turn our own [immediate] viewpoints off completely when trying to infer another's. Our own perspectives produce clear signals that are much louder to us than the other's, and they usually continue to ring in our ears while we try to decode the other's. For example, the fact that you thoroughly understand calculus constitutes an obstacle to your continuously keeping in mind a friend's ignorance of it while trying to explain it to him; you may momentarily realize how hard it is for him, but that realization may quietly slip away once you get immersed in your explanation. (Flavell et al., 2002, p. 182)

Interestingly, and in fairness, Piaget (1962) in later writings was amenable to this view of egocentrism as a tendency or bias rather than an inability or incapacity. He interpreted nondifferentiation of viewpoints as merely "an unconscious *preferential* focus" (emphasis added) on one's own perspective and depicted such a preferential tendency as evident even in adulthood:

> Every beginning instructor discovers sooner or later that his first lectures were incomprehensible because he was talking to himself, so to say, mindful only of his own point of view. He realizes only gradually and with difficulty that it is not easy to place oneself in the shoes of students who do not yet know what he

knows about the subject matter of his course. As a second example we can take the art of discussion, which consists principally in knowing how to place oneself at the point of view of one's partner in order to try to convince him on his own ground. (p. 5)

This preferential focus on self—especially, the "automatic positivity bias with respect to evaluations involving the self" (Valdesolo & DeSteno, 2008, p. 1335)—can undermine not only effective communication but also impartiality or objectivity. For example, egocentric bias can lead to hypocrisy and its maintenance by self-serving cognitive distortions (Valdesolo & DeSteno, in press; see Chapter 6). Although present throughout life, egocentric bias is especially evident during childhood. It is integral to the superficiality of early childhood moral judgment.

Superficiality in Nonsocial Cognition: The Conservation Task

Superficiality also characterizes young children's judgments in nonsocial cognition, for example, in responses to Piaget's famous "conservation tasks" (so called because an amount is conserved despite changes in its appearance). Immediate appearance-oriented (preconservation) judgments on a classic Piagetian task concerning conservation of quantity are described by Flavell et al. (2002) as follows:

(1) The child first agrees that two identical glasses contain identical amounts of water; (2) the experimenter pours the water from one glass into a third, taller and thinner glass, with the child watching; (3) she then asks the child whether the two amounts of water are still identical, or whether one glass now contains more water than the other. The typical preschool nonconserver is apt to conclude, after the liquid has been poured, that the taller and thinner glass now has more water in it than the other glass. Why? One reason is that it looks like it has more to her, and she is more given than the older child to make judgments about reality on the basis of the immediate, perceived appearances of things. (p. 140)

As on social cognition tasks, young children's judgments on nonsocial cognition tasks such as conservation center on whatever is immediately salient and accordingly may meander from moment to moment. In the conservation task (the example pertains to fluid or continuous quantity, one of many referents for conservation), most young children are more impressed with the height of a tall, thin glass and hence say there is now more water. Some children, however, are more impressed with the narrowness of the glass and say there is now *less* water. Either way, of course, the young child is thinking unidimensionally (whether the dimension is height or width). A given child's preconservation judgments can be made to shift from one (inaccurate) appearance-based judgment to another, from "more" to "less," as a function of which dimension is made salient in the task procedure. If water is poured from a tall glass to a washtub, such that the water scarcely even covers the bottom of the tub, the young child who had judged that there is now *more* water may blithely and abruptly switch to a judgment of *less* water (Brown, 1965)! The contradiction does not seem even to be noticed. And why would we expect young children to notice contradiction, given their paucity of ongoing mental coordination? We again encounter the curious caprice of the young child, this time in a *non*social cognitive context. But again, as we will see, children do grow.

Superficiality and Centrations

Whether in terms of social or nonsocial cognition, then, the young child's judgments tend to be superficial. Common to their performance on social and nonsocial cognition tasks is their unidimensional focus on a one or another (usually, highly salient) momentary feature to the exclusion of important other features, that is, their tendency not to keep in mind and coordinate aspects of a situation. We have repeatedly seen this paucity of mental coordination on social cognition tasks, but it is particularly clear on the conservation tasks.

A Piagetian construct helps us to analyze the young child's unidimensional thinking. With respect to conservation tasks, Flavell et al. (2002) invoked the Piagetian term *centration* in their analysis of young children's here-and-now immediacy in conservation task performance:

> The preschooler is more prone to concentrate or center (hence, centration) their attention exclusively on some single feature or limited portion of the stimulus array that is particularly salient and interesting to him, thereby neglecting other task-relevant features.... The difference in the heights of the two liquid columns is what captures most of the child's attention (and "capture" often does seem the apposite word), with little note given to the compensatory difference in column widths. (p. 141)

The capricious social and nonsocial judgments of the young child center not only on the "here" (a particular interesting feature or limited portion) but also the "now" (the present state of the problem): "When solving problems of all sorts they [young children] are less likely to call to mind or keep in mind relevant previous states of the problem, or to anticipate pertinent future or potential ones" (p. 142). Pertinent to what has been called temporal centration may be their (earlier noted) tendency to neglect the impact of an earlier emotion upon a subsequent one.

Incidentally, Flavell et al. (2002) speculated that—as with egocentric bias (self-centration)—temporal centration may never disappear altogether. Indeed, temporal centration may be thought of as an egocentric bias favoring one's *present* perspective:

> Interestingly, the "other" can be oneself in another time and condition, rather than a different person.... For example, it can be hard to imagine yourself feeling well and happy next week if you feel terribly ill or unhappy today. Taking the perspective of yourself when that perspective is different from your current one, can sometimes be as hard as taking the perspective of another person. (p. 182)

Again, egocentric bias or inadequate perspective taking (whether the perspective is that of another person or one's own in another time or condition) is a variant of the centrations or unidimensional thinking so intimately involved in young children's superficial moral judgment. We again emphasize that this cognitive superficiality, whether in its egocentric, social, moral, or nonsocial contexts, is a *tendency* of thought characteristic of preschoolers, *not* a fixed incapacity of all preschoolers in all circumstances. With age, young children's superficial and blithe caprice attenuates as ongoing mental coordination produces more considered judgment. As we will see in the next section, child cognitive development involves an overlapping shift from less to more mature modes of functioning and responding. Cognitive development does *not* mean "that young children never make inferences about unperceived states of affairs or that older children never base conclusions on superficial appearances" (Flavell et al., 2002, p. 141). Optimal circumstances (interesting and familiar stimuli, simplified task, absence of misleading salient features, nonintimidating questioner, simpler questions, etc.) reveal young children's nascent ability to coordinate features and make inferences (literature reviewed by Flavell et al., 2002). By the same token, *less than* optimal circumstances, as we all know too well, tend to induce, even among adults, less than mature cognitive performance (even though basic knowledge or competence generally is not lost). Indeed, Judy DeLoache, Kevin Miller, and Sophia Pierroutsakos (1998) concluded from a literature review that children are more—and adults less—"logical and rational than was previously believed" (p. 802). Nonetheless, one can discern a rough age trend characterizable as growth beyond the superficial, one that involves certain crucial qualitative changes.

Beyond Early Childhood Superficiality

Growth beyond the superficial in moral and other judgments means that those judgments are no longer so tied to this or that perceptual appearance or impressive feature. Although (in Piaget's earlier noted study of transgression judgments) the imagined consequence of 15 broken cups still looms large in the judgment of the older child, the older child *keeps in mind* more, considers more, coordinates more: Yes, to do so much damage is bad, but *keep in mind* the story protagonist's underlying good intentions, and *keep in mind* the naughty intentions of the other protagonist, the one who happened to break fewer cups. Underlying intentions—a *deeper* consideration—ascends against the superficial in the older child's moral judgment. Deeper still will be the appreciation of "good intentions" *guided by ideals of do-as-you-would-be-done-by morality,* an understanding that, as we will see, typically ascends in late childhood or early adolescence.

This growth beyond the superficial is evident not only in moral judgment but broadly in the growing child's social and nonsocial cognitive development. In the conservation task, for example, the child grows from judgments captured by misleading superficial appearances to a judgment of conservation, "an inference about *underlying* reality" (Flavell et al., 2002, p. 141, emphasis added). Growing *beyond* the superficial naturally follows early childhood superficiality in the broad cognitive-developmental approach.

If superficiality relates to centration, then, by the same token, growth beyond the superficial has much to do with *decentration*. As we will see, growth beyond the superficial and decentration in morality involve a constructive process fundamentally distinct from the internalization processes of moral socialization. Construction is as much a *social* as it is a nonsocial process, and *social* construction through perspective taking (in interaction with individual reflection) is particularly important for the emergence of "necessary" moral ideals that can motivate moral behavior (we will call the cognitive motivation of behavior "cognitive primacy"). Generally, the construction of more profound moral judgment constitutes an age trend involving a sequence of qualitative developmental advances or stages. Those stages may be universal in human development, entailing a level of potential maturity that would seem to surpass that of any other species. Just as our coverage of early childhood superficiality spanned the social and nonsocial, our depiction of growth beyond the superficial will be similarly broad. We will depict key growth-beyond-the-superficial themes—"decentration," "mental coordination," "social construction," "reciprocity," "necessity," "cognitive primacy"—in the context first of nonsocial cognition, especially conservation judgments. We then revisit the themes in the context of social cognition, especially moral judgment.

Beyond Superficiality in Nonsocial Cognition

Decentration and Construction

Decentration can be discerned most clearly in judgments of conservation. In contrast to the centrations of young children, older children are "apt to be distributing [their] attention in a more *flexible* [and] *balanced* way," that is, "to achieve a broader or '"decentered' (hence, *decentration*)" judgment (Flavell et al., 2002, p. 141). Decentration, then, means a more balanced perspective taking over time: a broader attention to multiple features of the situation, an ongoing and responsive mental coordination of those changing features, and hence a more consistent or profound judgment.

These Piagetian constructs merit delineation. Decentration refers to the process that Piagetians call construction. Decentration and construction both refer to the developmentally relevant qualities of ongoing mental coordination. *Decentration* highlights the liberation effected by mental coordination from narrow, imbalanced, and biased attentions (centrations), whereas *construction*, in the Piagetian sense, highlights mental coordination as a process that builds knowledge of a special sort (such as logical or moral reciprocity). Decentration, mental coordination, and construction contribute to the fundamental themes of the cognitive developmental approach.

Social Construction of Conservation Knowledge

The construction even of nonsocial cognition such as conservation knowledge involves social interaction. We shorten construction through social interaction to "social construction," although it has also been called co-construction[4], collaborative learning, dialogue, or collaborative argumentation. Basically, in social construction, participants who respect each other engage in "a balanced exploration of differences of perspective" (Rogoff, 1998, p. 711). Each participant in the dialogue is aware that his or her partner (a) may have a different perspective and (b) can actively take one's *own* perspective (Tomasello, Kruger, & Ratner, 1996). Social construction may be especially important if the learner is to achieve not just a quantitative increase in a skill or other proficiency but instead a qualitatively new, basic understanding (Damon, 1984).

Social construction in the Piagetian sense can build knowledge that is epistemologically distinct, even unique (a theme to which we return in our concluding chapter). Constructed knowledge (again, in the Piagetian sense) is not "internalized" (used loosely here to mean transmitted, acquired, picked up, copied, imitated, or learned) from some model in the environment; nor is it simply innate.

The fundamentally distinct character of constructed knowledge à la Piaget was demonstrated in a series of brilliant studies of collaborative argumentation in connection with conservation tasks or social issues (reviewed by M. Miller, 1987; Rogoff, 1998). The most fascinating (and epistemologically critical) condition[5] in these experiments involved pairing preconservational children whose pretest judgments involved opposing centrations. For example, a preconservational child who judged that the taller, narrower glass holds more water would be paired with a preconservational child who (centering instead upon the narrowness) judged the glass to hold *less* water. The dyads would be instructed to resolve their differences. The experimenter gave neither child the right answer. Nonetheless, even though there was no external source or "model" of conservation knowledge, many of the initially preconservational children made conservation judgments on the posttest. How could that be?

A typical study using such dyads, that of Gail Ames and Frank Murray (1982; cf. Doise & Mugny, 1984; Glachan & Light, 1982), was aptly titled "When Two Wrongs Make a Right." In each dyad, both children's judgments were wrong—but wrong in a mutually heuristic way. Each child, in attempting to resolve the difference, enhanced the salience of the feature of the task that the other child was neglecting. The children were typically 6 to 7 years old, old enough to have the working memory or "executive attention" (e.g., Case, 1998; Chapman & Lindenburger, 1989; Kane, Hambrick, & Conway, 2005) needed to experience as at least somewhat perplexing the other's challenges: "Look here, this glass is skinnier . . . there's *less* water"; "No, look there, the glass is taller . . . there's *more* water." Again, the "right" or more profound judgment (in this example, conservation of quantity; Ames and Murray actually used conservation of length) *could not* have resulted from any direct imitation or internalization from the environment; after all, neither experimenter nor partner provided conservation information. It seems most plausible that the conservation judgments reflected each child's decentration and mental coordination, or construction stimulated by the opposing child's challenge. Such studies have been cited to suggest that the child, at least in part, achieves knowledge such as that of conservation through a constructive process not reducible to internalization.

Although children do not usually argue with each other over questions such as that of conservation, social construction may in general play a role even in *non*social cognitive advances. These advances beyond the superficial entail important cognitive developmental properties—"reciprocity," "necessity," and "cognitive primacy"—noted at the beginning of this chapter.

Depth, Decentration, and Reciprocity

Constructed knowledge such as that of conservation represents a deeper understanding. Such judgments involve "an inference about underlying reality," for example, that two amounts of water, despite misleading appearances from a transformation, "*are really* still the same" (Flavell et al., 2002, p. 141). This inference as to underlying reality represents a qualitatively new, more adequate understanding and a kind of knowledge that, as we will see, has much to do with the right and wrong of morality. Although conservation "research has not so far yielded really clear answers" as to the significance of the phenomenon (Halford & Andrews, 2006, p. 577), decades ago Roger Brown (1965) made an insightful observation. Brown described a "crucial difference" between an older and a younger boy's (or girl's) responses to a conservation task:

> *After pouring, the experimenter asks [the older boy] the familiar question: "Is there the same amount or more or less?" The boy promptly says, "The same," and there is an implicit "naturally" in his intonation. If we continue with other containers of varying size he will become impatient and say, "It's the same, it's always the same."*
>
> *It is important to watch the older boy's performance carefully. There is a crucial difference between his reaction to each problem and the reaction of the younger boy. The younger boy when he is asked the critical question intently examines the materials before him. The older boy scarcely looks at them. For him it does not seem to be a problem in perceptual judgment. The correct answer appears to have a necessity in it that removes it from the sphere of matters requiring empirical verification.[6] (p. 201)*

As noted, the older child's inference of this underlying "necessity" is effected through mental coordination or decentration. Remedying the temporal and spatial centrations described earlier are temporal and spatial *decentrations*:

> *Conservers are likely to [temporally decenter, that is, to] say that the two quantities had, after all, been identical at the outset..., or that the experimenter had merely poured the water from one container to the other, and without spilling any or adding any.... They might even say that the continuing equality of amounts could be proved by pouring the liquid back into its original container. (Flavell et al., 2002, p. 142)*

The older child's analysis may also coordinate and balance the lesser width with the greater height of the liquid in the thinner but taller container.

That the temporally and spatially decentered response called conservation knowledge is balanced means that such knowledge derives from *reciprocity*. *Reciprocal* means "done or given by each of two to the other" (*Funk & Wagnalls New*

International Dictionary of the English Language, 2000, p. 1053), implying a counter-balancing of each feature with the other. *Temporal* decentration and reciprocity ("you can pour it back and see it's the same") involve a counterbalancing through an "equal reaction to an initial action" (Damon, 1977, p. 284), that is, a second action that completely undoes or inverts the first. *Spatial* decentration and reciprocity ("it's taller but also thinner"; "nothing is added or spilled") also involve a compensatory counter-balancing or equating of actual or potential changes (taller with thinner; additions of water could compensate for spills). Damon (1977) pointed out that "precise" (p. 284) reciprocities or compensations imply stable equalities.

Logical Necessity and Cognitive Primacy in the Motivation of Behavior

As in mathematics, the precise reciprocity and equality entailed in conservation judgments have a logical quality; they refer to what Piaget called logico-mathematical knowledge. For example, the precise reciprocity, "nothing added or taken away," means that $x + o - o = x$. It is logic that makes the "crucial difference" to which Brown (1965) referred, the qualitative change that removes conservation knowledge "from the sphere of matters requiring empirical verification." The older child's con-servation answer "appears to have a [logical] necessity to it," as Brown put the point. Granted, conservation judgments are not purely a matter of logic. As Thomas Shultz and colleagues (Shultz, Dover, & Amsel, 1979) noted, "Conservation judg-ments are neither wholly logical nor wholly empirical" but rather "derive from a combination of logical and empirical knowledge" (p. 117). Hence, conservation judgments do *partially* involve logic. For that reason, judgments such as those of conservation, transitive relations, and class inclusion are experienced as necessary rather than contingent, as that which "*must* be true" and not simply as "facts about the world that *are* true but might have been different" (Miller, Custer, & Nassau, 2000, p. 384; cf. Piaget, 1967/1971).

The sense of logical necessity means that this constructed, qualitatively new understanding of underlying reality (in the present case, of conservation) generates a compelling feeling that can motivate behavior. Consider the typical responses of children in so-called "countersuggestion" or "contrary feedback" research initiated in the 1960s by Jan Smedslund (1961) using a conservation of weight task. Those who make judgments of conservation (or other logic-related judgments) and give reciprocity explanations are upset upon being confronted (through the trick of sur-reptitiously removing some of the material) with an apparent violation of inferred or "necessary" reality. They seek some explanation, some logical way to account for or correct the imbalance. Mature conservers confronted with violations of weight conservation may make comments such as, "We must have lost some clay on the floor," or, "There must be something wrong with the scale." In general, although the mastery of necessity is "gradual and multifaceted" (Miller et al., 2000, p. 400), mature judges tend to act as if illogical imbalances or violations of precise reciprocity and equality "shouldn't be." The nonconservation that confronts them doesn't make sense logically, and that illogic prompts a feeling of distress or action tendency. The conservers are motivated to try to restore (through some logical explanation or action to find missing material) the "necessary" reciprocity or equality. The parallel with moral judgment and motivation is striking, as we will see.

Beyond Superficiality in Social Cognition

The fundamental themes of the cognitive-developmental approach to morality emerge as we revisit social decentration or construction and related concepts (reciprocity, necessity, cognitive primacy), this time in the context of *social* cognition. We start by examining a traditional treatment of reciprocity in the social sense, namely, as a norm that is internalized through moral socialization.

Reciprocity: Internalized Norm or Constructed Ideal?

Decades ago, Alvin Gouldner (1960) interpreted reciprocity as a societal norm. Essentially, the reciprocity norm prescribes that one should reciprocate if one receives help or that one should receive help in return if one has given help. Gouldner posited that the reciprocity norm somehow gains motivational power as it is internalized by members of society (particularly through parental socialization). He noted that the norm is cross-culturally pervasive and attributed such universality to reciprocity's functional value for promoting and stabilizing social relationships. He saw the norm as particularly helpful in preventing "system-disrupting exploitation" (p. 174) from interpersonal power inequalities in which the more powerful individual would—were it not for internalized inhibition from the reciprocity norm—simply take from the less powerful and (according to Gouldner) feel no compunction to return any benefit. Also helpful in preventing exploitation and reducing the tension of unequal exchanges or "reciprocity imbalances" are certain other norms, such as those prescribing one-sided generosity (e.g., Christian charity or "noblesse oblige") and magnanimity ("It's not the gift but the thought behind it that counts").

Given its functional importance for any society, the reciprocity norm is widely taught and should be part of moral socialization. We find Gouldner's (1960) functionalist argument generally compelling in this regard. Also compelling, however, is the cognitive-developmental view of moral reciprocity as a product of construction and decentration. The emergence in human development of nonsocial and sociomoral forms of reciprocity may relate to the "natural" human preference for balance or harmony (Heider, 1958), as well as consistency or logical noncontradiction, cognitive dissonance reduction, congruity, and symmetry (Abelson et al., 1968). Could the motive power of the reciprocity norm represent not only the power of an internalized norm but also the power of a constructed ideal? Reciprocity may not be *either* a "norm" or "ideal," but *both*! And is only one level of moral ideal constructed? As we will see, the cognitive-developmental approach provides a crucial clarification of the "moral reciprocity" co-existent with the reciprocity norm.

Social Construction (vs. Internalization) Revisited

It is time to revisit social construction in the context of *social* cognitive development. In this context, we find not only logical reciprocity and necessity, but *moral* reciprocity and necessity; correspondingly, we now find "cognitive primacy" generating *moral* feelings that in turn can motivate *moral* behavior. Piaget (1932/1965) regarded social construction (again, construction through social interaction) as "the main mover of [moral] judgmental change during the childhood years" (Youniss & Damon, 1992, p. 280). For Piaget, constructive social interaction chiefly meant peer exchanges that involve "comparison, ... opposition ... [and] discussion" (Piaget, 1932/1965, p. 393). The experimental condition described earlier, in which peer dyads exchanged viewpoints and thereby helped one another to decenter and construct conservation knowledge, parallels the social construction of the "necessary equilibrium" of moral reciprocity:

> For true equality and a genuine desire for reciprocity there must be [an ideal] that is the sui generis product of life lived in common. There must be born of the actions and reactions of individuals upon each other the consciousness of a necessary equilibrium binding upon and limiting both "alter" and "ego." And this ideal equilibrium, dimly felt on the occasion of every quarrel and every peacemaking, naturally presupposes a long reciprocal education of the children by each other. (Piaget, 1932/1965, p. 318, emphases added; cf. L. J. Walker, 1983)

For example,

> In the course of discussion [about how to distribute candy] the children may realize that ... an equal division of the candy, although not giving any child as much as she or he might like, avoids giving any child a valid basis for complaint. In the course of multiple such interactions, all the children may come to recognize the inherent fairness of no one getting more or less than anyone else—at least not without reason. (Moshman, 2005, p. 53)

Such a socially constructed moral understanding cannot, according to Piaget, be simply learned or internalized from parents or other socialization agents:

> But would it not be more efficient for an adult to simply tell the children to divide the candy equally? In the short run, an externally imposed rule to this effect might indeed avoid hostility and/or violence. Piaget believed, however, that such a rule would be perceived by a child as simply one of many rules that must be followed because they come from those with power and/or authority.... Genuine ... morality, then, is not a matter of culturally specific rules learned [or externally imposed] from parents or other agents of society. (Moshman, 2005, p. 53)

Piaget emphasized egalitarian peer interaction, then, as the crucial vehicle for the construction of genuine morality. Consistent with Piaget's claims, Ann Kruger and Michael Tomasello (1986) found that, relative to children paired with a parent, children in peer discussion generally evidenced more active reasoning followed by gains in moral judgment. Larry Walker, Karl Hennig, and Tobias Krettenauer (2000) found that parents, too, can contribute to children's moral judgment development if their interactive style is nonthreatening or Socratic and "inductive" (cf. Kruger, 1992; Taylor & Walker, 1991; see Chapter 4). Marvin Berkowitz and I (Berkowitz & Gibbs, 1983, 1985) found that college peers who reasoned from the hypothetical premises of one another's moral arguments (e.g., identifying a logical inconsistency or implication of the other's reasoning, questioning the other's premises, or suggesting a premise underlying both positions) were those who evidenced greater pre-post gains in mature moral judgment. Piaget (1972) considered such "just for the sake of argument" considerations of another's perspective in a discussion to exemplify the social expression of "formal operations." Socially applied formal operations (or hypothetically based deductive reasoning) change the nature of discussion: "A fruitful and constructive discussion means that by using hypotheses we can adopt the point of view of the adversary (although not necessarily believing it) and draw the logical consequences it implies" (pp. 3–4).

As in nonsocial cognition, social construction and decentration in *social* cognition mean the decline of egocentric bias or an increasing tendency to consider and keep in mind multiple perspectives. Later levels of sociomoral judgment are less egocentric: "The self's welfare is still important, but ... self-interest is increasingly seen in the context of the welfare of everyone in the relation" (Damon, 1977, p. 221). Older children no longer need salient cues to infer that the minds of others are active, and are more cognizant of what other persons would or would not know in a situation. The self-esteem level becomes less inflated or more realistic as children during the elementary school years begin to base their self-evaluations on social comparisons (Harter, 1999, 2006). They begin to grasp mixed emotions (Harter, 1999, 2006) and to include guilt among the emotions that may follow a transgression (Arsenio et al., 2006; Peterson et al., 1983). In their accounts of having been hurt or having hurt someone else, they are increasingly likely to coordinate social perspectives, refer to subtle mental states or emotions such as intentions, and describe violations of trust (Wainryb et al., 2005). Indeed, in all of the areas of social cognition surveyed earlier, one can discern in later childhood and beyond an increasing prevalence of decentered and deeper understanding.

Conditions Promoting Social Construction   That social construction differs irreducibly from internalization is a key theme of the cognitive-developmental approach, whether that which is constructed is social or nonsocial. Constructive benefits from peer interaction cannot be taken for granted, however. With reference to the earlier example of candy sharing among children, Moshman (2005) noted that "one child may grab all the candy and run off" (p. 53). Generally, Piaget's presumption that peer interaction will always be egalitarian and constructive seems a bit optimistic. Hoffman (2000) argued that Piaget and Kohlberg underplayed the problem of egocentrically biased expressions of egoistic motives. As Kenneth Rubin and colleagues (Rubin, Bukowski, & Parker, 2006) commented, "If the exchange of conflicting ideas is marked by hostility, dysregulated or disabling emotions are not likely to promote cognitive growth and development" (p. 583). Indeed, Damon and Killen (1982) found that children who simply contradicted or ridiculed their partners' ideas were *less* likely to show posttest moral judgment gain. The downward spiral of gratuitously violent peer interaction depicted in William Golding's classic *Lord of the Flies* (1954/1962) seems to be validated by numerous media reports of bullying and other violence perpetrated by children upon children.

Hoffman and others have collectively suggested four conditions that are probably important if peer interaction is to work as a constructive process. Hoffman (1988, 2000) suggested three conditions. First, to preempt tendencies to dominate or bully, the children involved should be comparable not only in age but also in social status or "pecking order" within the peer group context (but cf. Taylor & Walker, 1997). Indeed, Rogoff (1998) argued that perceived status equality was more important than equality in chronological age among factors conducive to cognitive-developmental change. Second, to further counteract tendencies to dominate, the interacting children's disciplinary background should be characterized primarily by inductions (inducing consideration for others) rather than power assertions (see Chapter 4). Third, conflicting children should be "coached" or encouraged by a supervising adult to consider one another's perspectives. Finally, Rubin and colleagues (Rubin et al., 2006) suggested that peer interaction is most likely to lead to moral judgment development if the peers are friends and hence can interact in a positive and nondefensive fashion. These four conditions enhance the likelihood that peer interaction will be constructive.

Morality and Logic: Necessity and Cognitive Primacy Revisited

In the cognitive-developmental approach, morality is a close kin to logic and rationality. The intertwining of morality with logic is expressed in Piaget's famous assertion: "Morality is the logic of action just as logic is the morality of thought" (Piaget, 1932/1965, p. 398). In other words, the two intimately interrelate: Moral reciprocity is rational just as rationality is prescriptive. Corresponding to the motive power of the logical necessity discussed earlier is the motive power of *moral* necessity. Violations of reciprocity or justice, like violations of logic, "shouldn't be." The inference of unfairness generates a motivation to restore the "necessary" reciprocity or equality (cf. Hammock, Rosen, Richardson, & Bernstein, 1989). As Kohlberg (1984) put the point, "Violation of logic and violation of justice may arouse strong affects" (p. 63).

In this connection, Laura Berk (personal communication, April 1, 2002) recounted an incident in which both logic and justice were violated (although logic was not actually violated, fairness or respect was). Several years ago, during her course on methodology, a student

> replicated Smedslund's [1961] research by surreptitiously removing a piece of the play dough while making the transformation in a conservation-of-weight tasks. In one instance, an 8-year-old girl was so secure in her grasp of the logic of conservation that she knew she had been tricked. Her emotional reaction was

strong: Why, she asked the college student, would an adult be so dishonest as to [try to] deceive [and upset] a child in that way? In this case, simultaneous violation of conservation and [justice] did, indeed, "arouse strong affect."

The motivation to account for or correct a "reciprocity imbalance" in the social context, then, may be no less cognitively based than is the corresponding motivation in the nonsocial or physical context. And note that in either context, the affect follows the cognition. Indeed, the affect of logical or moral necessity owes its very existence to the cognitive construction of logic or justice. Violations of logic or justice not only arouse, but in the first place *generate*, a desire to rectify the imbalance, to right the wrong.[7] Again we encounter cognitive primacy, this time in the context of *moral* motivation.

Stages of Moral Judgment Development

Growth beyond the superficial in moral judgment entails an overlapping sequence of basic frameworks or *stages*. Beyond the centrations of Stage 1 are two stages of moral judgment that have, at their core, structures of moral reciprocity (see Table 3.1 in Chapter 3). The second moral judgment stage—and the more primitive stage of moral reciprocity or justice—is that of a concrete and simple "you scratch my back so I should scratch yours," or "eye for an eye" morality. It is a morality of exact payback, of strict equality, of "getting even" in favors or blows. As C. S. Lewis (1962) recollected,

Once when my brother and I, as very small boys, were drawing pictures at the same table, I jerked his elbow and caused him to make an irrelevant line across the middle of his work; the matter was amicably settled by my allowing him to draw a line of equal length across mine. (p. 93)

Piaget (1932/1965) labeled this tit-for-tat morality of short-term exchanges "reciprocity as a fact" involving "crude equality" (p. 323) and sometimes even "vengeance ... in all its brutality" (p. 217). Kohlberg's label for this form of reciprocity was "Stage 2" or "pragmatic" and "instrumental exchange": "For example, it is seen as important to keep promises to insure that others will keep their promises to you and do nice things for you, or it is important in order to keep them from getting mad at you" (Kohlberg, 1984, pp. 626–628). Incidentally, Piaget's "reciprocity as a fact" depiction of Stage 2 moral reciprocity may be misleading. Although pragmatic or instrumental, crude (albeit literally exacting), short-term, and sometimes brutal, moral reciprocity is nonetheless *prescriptive* (e.g., "I *should* share with her because she shared with me"). Precursors in the preschool years are "purely descriptive ... as in, 'I share with her and then she shares with me' or 'If she hits me, I'll hit her'" (Damon, 1977, p. 291).

Prescriptive if still pragmatic perspective taking overlaps in time and increasingly displaces the centrations in moral judgment (Stage 1) characteristic of the preschool years. Stage 2 represents an advance beyond Stage 1 insofar as substantial mental coordination and moral logic (albeit pragmatic) are evident. Whereas the child with centered or unidimensional tendencies in thought may understand social influence in one direction at a time (self to others or others to self; Selman, 1980), the child whose thinking is designated Stage 2 is beginning to realize that each of two friends evaluates the other's actions, needs, and attitudes. In this sense, the social perspective-taking coordinations of Stage 2 pragmatic reciprocity produce a morality that, although still superficial, is less so than that produced by the centrations of Stage 1.

Pragmatic (Stage 2) Moral Reciprocity in Primate Societies

Moral reciprocity has a primate heritage, raising the question of what is and is not uniquely human in the development of moral maturity. Frans de Waal (1996) argued that judgments and norms of moral reciprocity evolved from practices of social exchange and cooperation evident throughout the primate world. Even Old World (macaque) monkey societies "may be veritable marketplaces in which sex, support, grooming, food tolerance [passive food sharing], warnings of danger, and all sorts of other services are being traded" (de Waal, 1996, p. 156). Primates may be biologically prepared to engage in reciprocal social activity (Levitt, Weber, Clark, & McDonnell, 1985; Tooby & Cosmides, 1996). Furthermore, the emotional and behavioral rudiments of reciprocity can be discerned in infants' interactions with caretakers, and young children can learn to take turns with toys during play activities (e.g., Damon, 1977; Mueller & Brenner, 1977). One can discern in human society rituals of exchange ranging from a tacit nod after a "pardon me" to formal treaties. Consistent with both Gouldner's functionalist and Piaget's constructivist analyses is de Waal's (1996) suggestion that exchanges can serve to restore social balance.

Sociomoral advances in exchange and reciprocity may have been linked to *cognitive* advances in the evolution of primates. The social and nonsocial cognitive abilities of Old World (macaque) monkeys are less advanced than those of their relatives, the chimpanzees. In contrast to monkeys, mature chimps can recognize themselves in a mirror, engage in intentional deception, and even, it would seem, infer concrete logic (Bjorklund & Pellegrini, 2002; Boysen, 1993; Boysen, Berntson, Shreyer, & Quigley, 1993; deWaal, 1996; Premack & Premack, 1983; but cf. Tomasello et al., 1996). Correspondingly, social reciprocity in chimp societies takes on more systemic and prescriptive (moral or normative) properties conducive to the restoration of balance or equilibrium. For example, not until one studies chimpanzee societies in the primate world does one find instances of punishment for nonreciprocation of favors. In the following incident, Puist became furious at her erstwhile ally Luit and even attacked him, apparently because he declined to support her after she had supported him against a rival:

> A high-ranking female, Puist, took the trouble and risk to help her male friend, Luit, chase off a rival, Nikkie. Nikkie, however, had a habit after major confrontations of singling out and cornering allies of his rivals, to punish them. This time Nikkie displayed at [threatened] Puist shortly after he had been [chased off]. Puist turned to Luit, stretching out her hand in search of support.

But Luit did not lift a finger to protect her. Immediately after Nikkie ... left the scene, Puist turned to Luit, barking furiously. She chased him across the enclosure and even pummeled him. (p. 97)

In another incident, the group shared food with those group members who had shared—but not with a selfish chimp named Gwinnie:

If [the female chimp] Gwinnie obtained one of the large bundles of browse [in the enclosure], she would take it to the top of a climbing frame, where it could easily be monopolized. Except for her offspring, few others managed to get anything. [Another female chimp] Mai, in contrast, shared readily and was typically surrounded by a cluster of beggars. Guess who met with more resistance if she herself was in need and tried to get food? ... It is as if the other apes are telling Gwinnie, "You never share with us, why should we share with you!" (p. 160)

From Stage 2 to Stage 3: Construction of Reciprocity as an Ideal

Although chimpanzees' prescriptive reciprocity norm in fighting, feeding, grooming, and so on is remarkable, its form is (literally!) no more than that of you-scratch-my-back-I'll-scratch-yours. Pragmatic moral reciprocity—Stage 2 in the Kohlberg stage typology (Chapter 3)—is also prominent in human societies. Indeed, as Thomas Lickona (1983) declared, "Stage 2 is alive and well in most of us adults" (p. 134). Stage 2 is not considered to be the optimal end state of moral development, however. As Piaget (1932/1965) suggested, "the best adult consciences ask for something more than" pragmatic morality (p. 323).

Children's—if not chimps'—quid pro quo social cognition typically develops into "a third perspective, that of ... mutuality of expectations" (Kohlberg, 1984, p. 34; cf. Selman, 1980, 2003). "My friend is thinking about what I am thinking" evolves into "true friends should understand each other" (Damon, 1977). This third-person, mutual perspective affords a more contextual and ideal justice in which "the circumstances of the individual are taken into account" (Piaget, 1932/1965, p. 272; cf. Damon, 1977). In one of Piaget's distributive justice stories, concerning whether a family's youngest child who had accidentally dropped his allotment of bread should be given another piece, 95% of 13- to 14-year-olds but only 17% of 6- to 9-year-olds made allowance for the young child's ineptness. Older children and adolescents, then, are much more likely to "attempt to understand the psychological context" in their moral judgments (Piaget, 1932/1965, p. 267; cf. Sigelman & Waitzman, 1991).

This third-person perspective affords a truly *ideal* normative reciprocity, recognizable as Golden Rule, do-as-you-would-be-done-by morality. Such ideal morality represents the quintessential expression of what philosophers have called the moral point of view (see Chapter 1). In Brian Barry's (1995) terms, it is the transition from "justice as mutual advantage" to "justice as impartiality" (p. 51). The hypothetical ideal of "*would be* done by" transcends the temporal sequences of exchanges entailed in concrete moral reciprocity.

The concrete origins of such hypothetical reflection in moral perspective taking are evident in its nascent expressions. Kohlberg (1971), following Selman, cited the "intellectual effort" made by a 10-year-old boy to justify the Golden Rule:

Well, the Golden Rule is the best rule, because like if you were rich, you might dream like that you were poor and how it felt, and then the dream would go back in your own head and you would remember and you would help make the laws that way. (p. 197)

The intellectual ability to reflect on the basis of a contrary-to-fact hypothesis (such as a rich person imagining and reasoning on the basis of how it would feel to be poor) represents the qualitative advance represented by formal operations: "To be formal, [logical inference or] deduction must detach itself from reality and take up its stand on the plane of the purely possible" or hypothetical (Piaget, 1928/1969, p. 71).

Although the shift from the concrete to the hypothetical represents only a rough age trend discernible during late childhood and early adolescence, it is nonetheless a distinct, qualitative change. David Moshman (1998) found "surprisingly strong support" for Piaget's thesis "that formal or hypothetico-deductive reasoning—deliberate deduction from propositions consciously recognized as hypothetical—plays an important role in the thinking of adolescents and adults but is rarely seen before the ages of 11 or 12" (p. 973). Such thinking is a prime example of metacognition or "thinking about thinking": The child reflects upon the processes and propositions of cognition.

Piaget suggested that the third-person perspective in social cognition emerges as children use their newfound hypothetical and deductive reasoning abilities to infer the limitations and "deeper trend" of tit-for-tat morality. Piaget's description of the child's reflection upon pragmatic reciprocity is suggestive of the process that he would later term *reflective abstraction* (Piaget, 1967/1971).

[The child's] concern with reciprocity leads [him or her] beyond ... short-sighted justice.... The child begins by simply practicing reciprocity, in itself not so easy a thing as one might think. Then, once one has grown accustomed to this form of equilibrium in his action, his behavior is altered from within, its form reacting, as it were, upon its content. What is regarded as just is no longer merely reciprocal action, but primarily behavior that admits of indefinitely sustained reciprocity. The motto "Do as you would be done by," thus comes to replace the conception of crude equality. The child sets forgiveness above revenge, not out of weakness, but because "there is no end" to revenge (a boy of 10). Just as in logic, we can see a sort of reaction of the form of the proposition upon its content when the principle of contradiction leads to a simplification and purification of its initial definitions, so in ethics, reciprocity implies a purification of the deeper trend of conduct, guiding it ... to ... the more refined forms of justice. (pp. 323–324)

Ironically, reflective abstraction from *temporal* justice (based on short-term, unstable sequences of "merely reciprocal action") yields a time*less* justice ("do as you *would be* done by") and the potential for "indefinitely sustained" relationships. As Peter Singer (1981) put it, the resulting

> *higher and wider standard of conduct.... is not a recommendation that we do to others as they have done to us, but that we do to them what we* would wish *them to do to us. Nor is anything said about doing this only if they are likely to respond in kind. (p. 137; emphasis added.)*

Reflective Abstraction and Social Construction

Although reflective abstraction and other metacognitive processes play an important role in sociomoral and nonsocial cognitive development, that role is embedded in social construction. So do individual reflection and reasoning derive from social construction, or is it individual reasoning that makes possible constructive social interaction? Going beyond the traditional Vygotskian emphasis on the sociocultural origins of individual thought, Jonathan Haidt and Fredrik Bjorklund (2008a) depicted reasoning as a process that remains mainly social: "reasoning happens between people quite often..., and within individuals occasionally" (p. 200). In contrast, Piaget is often depicted as emphasizing the primacy of individual reasoning. Deanna Kuhn (1997) suggested a "dual focus.... on the social process of development from the outside in (as forms originating in social interaction become interiorized) as well as from the inside out (as newly constructed forms are consolidated and applied in social interactions" (p. 257). Similarly, Moshman (1998) suggested a "reciprocal influence" between the social and the individual reasoning processes:

> *Reasoning is traditionally viewed as [simply] taking place within an individual. An alternative is to view reasoning as a fundamentally social process of group interchange, with individual reasoning a derivative phenomenon involving internalized aspects of the group process [cf. Vygotsky, 1930–1935/1978, 1934/1986]. A middle-ground possibility is that individual and collaborative reasoning are partially distinct and equally fundamental, developing via a complex process of reciprocal influence. (p. 962)*

Stage 3 Reciprocity and Cognitive Primacy

Unlike that of Stage 2, Stage 3 reciprocity is a reliable cognitive source of mature moral motivation. Granted, in the context of positive interpersonal relations, both forms or "structures" of reciprocity motivate moral behavior: Reciprocating someone's help may be prompted by the aim of gaining future favors from a valued other (Stage 2), as readily as it can be prompted by the aim of cultivating a mutually caring relationship (Stage 3). The importance of the distinction between the structures of reciprocity becomes clear, however, once tensions or frictions jeopardize those positive relations. The payback logic of Stage 2 motivates action to restore a balance of equality or "get even,"[8] whereas Stage 3 thinking prompts efforts to resolve any misunderstanding for the sake of the relationship. In this connection, we know of no data to suggest that chimpanzees can appreciate forgiveness or *non*reciprocation the way humans can (see Chapter 5).[9]

Robert Kegan (1982) discovered the importance of the distinction between Stage 2 and Stage 3 in the cognitive primacy of moral motivation during his work as a secondary school teacher. One day, he asked his seventh-grade English class of 12-year-old boys to explain the moral of a story called "The New Kid" (Heyert, 1976). Heyert's short story depicts the feelings and behavior of an unathletic boy named Marty. In the choosing of sides for baseball, Marty experiences the humiliation of always being chosen last. He must also endure verbal abuse as he plays poorly. When a new kid arrives who is found to be even more unathletic, the new arrival receives even worse treatment, especially from—guess who—Marty. Kegan noted the Stage 2 level at which many of the 12-year-olds understood the point of the story:

> The story is saying that people may be mean to you and push you down and make you feel crummy and stuff, but it's saying things aren't really all that bad because eventually you'll get your chance to push someone else down and then you'll be on top.... Fair is fair! (p. 47)

Dramatically different from these students' Stage 2 understanding of the story was the emergent Stage 3 understanding of some other 12-year-olds in the class who argued that "Marty should be able to think about how he felt when he was picked on and therefore not pick on the new kid" (p. 55). Marty, in other words, should treat another as he (or most anyone) would want to be treated. The ensuing discussion, Kegan (1982) surmised, gave the less advanced thinkers in the class some stimulus for development. The discussion was stimulating in part because the prescribed behavior differed so greatly: Whereas the "fairness" of pragmatic moral reciprocity prescribed abusive behavior (one was abused so it's fair to abuse others), that of ideal moral reciprocity (one was abused and should take into account how that would feel) prescribed *restraint*.

Along with sociobiologists and other theorists (e.g., Alexander, 1987; Burgess & Huston, 1979; Hauser, 2006; Jensen, 2008; Krebs & Denton, 2005; Trivers, 1971; Wright, 1994), Hoffman (2000) fails to make this crucial distinction between pragmatic (Stage 2) and ideal (Stage 3) moral reciprocity. Hoffman's general view of reciprocity is similar to ours, namely, as a "perception of balance . . . which in the moral domain translates into fairness or justice" (p. 241). Furthermore, he concurred that the perception of violations of reciprocity presupposes "the ability to focus on multiple aspects of a situation" (p. 243; cf. Gibbs, 1991a). Note, however, that he does not separate ideal reciprocity ("treat others as one would wish to be treated by them") as motivationally distinct among his examples of reciprocity in the moral domain: "earning what one deserves, being rewarded for good deeds and punished for bad; punishments fitting the crime ([an] eye for [an] eye); treating others as one would [wish to] be treated by them" (p. 241).

Interestingly, Hoffman (2000) did acknowledge that "a cognitive preference for reciprocity" may exist, although he cautioned that such a motive "has not been established" (p. 243). Perhaps a purely cognitive motivation to "rectify nonreciprocity," de-confounded from empathic motives, can in some contexts be activated, for example, if "one encounters someone who gets more than he or she deserves" (p. 243). In a similar vein, de Waal (1996) acknowledged that a motive to correct an unfairness or to see balance restored may account for the satisfaction one feels if a bad or undeservingly fortunate individual "gets his comeuppance, as when a pompous or dishonest man loses his fortune" (p. 85). The motive or satisfaction pertains to the primarily cognitive realm of unfairness or just consequences (although one might still feel a twinge of empathic distress for the victim, however richly deserved his loss).

Despite his acknowledgment of the possibility of a cognitive primacy in moral motivation, Hoffman (2000) argued that there is no *inherently* moral cognitive motivation. Reciprocity per se is morally "neutral" or "can serve many masters," including "non-prosocial 'eye-for-an-eye' thinking" (p. 243), Stage 2 in Kohlberg's typology. Insofar as reciprocity does play a role in prosocial behavior, its contribution (according to Hoffman) is not to motivate in its own right so much as to shape or transform motivating empathic affect. For example, "if one encounters a victim, one feels empathic distress, and if he or she is a victim of injustice, reciprocity may also be activated and transform the empathic affect into a feeling of injustice" (p. 243). In short, Hoffman champions *affective* primacy to the near exclusion of cognitive primacy in moral motivation. We will return to this limitation in Hoffman's theory in Chapters 4 and 5.

The distinction between Stage 2 and Stage 3 reciprocities is crucial for an adequate analysis of cognitive primacy and mature morality. We suspect that Hoffman did not distinguish "treating others as one would be treated by them" because doing so is inconsistent with his thesis that reciprocity is morally neutral. It is difficult to make the case that *ideal* (third-person, mutual, Golden Rule, Stage 3) reciprocity is morally neutral or can intrinsically motivate non-prosocial behavior. Again, however, even pragmatic reciprocity may in *some* contexts motivate (or comotivate along with empathy) moral behavior: For example, not only empathy but also the Stage 2 logic that hard work should be rewarded may prompt one to reward a hard worker.

Mature Morality, Socialization, and Culture

It is crucial that mature morality (especially, ideal reciprocity) be supported in the moral socialization practices, religious teaching, and social ecology of a society. For Kohlberg (1984), the essence of "socialization" was the provision of social role- or perspective-taking opportunities (a disciplinary practice that encourages perspective taking is discussed in Chapter 4). The child was seen as actively seeking these opportunities, which could derive not just from home experiences or peer interactions (as Piaget emphasized) but from various aspects of the child's social world:

If moral development is fundamentally a process of the restructuring of modes of role-taking, then the fundamental social inputs stimulating moral development may be termed "role-taking opportunities.".... Participation in various groups ... [stimulates] development.... The child lives in a total social world in which perceptions of the law, of the peer group, and of parental teaching all influence one another.... Various people and groups ... [stimulate] general moral development.... The more the social stimulation, the faster the rate of moral development. (pp. 74, 78)

Kohlberg's emphasis on the contribution to moral development of "various people and groups" in the child's social world is congruent with contemporary emphases in socialization research on "the interrelated effects of parenting, nonfamilial influences, and the role of the broader context in which families live" (Collins, Maccoby, Steinberg, Hetherington, & Bornstein, 2000, p. 228). A *communitarian* social context "where relationships between members are direct and multifaceted and where individuals can know and be known" may be crucial if perspective-taking experiences are to lead to interpersonally mature moral judgment and, in general, "a capacity for relatedness characterized by mutuality, reciprocity, and deepening intimacy" (Guisinger & Blatt, 1994, p. 109).

Cultures that fail to support and cultivate mature morality may place even their survival in jeopardy. Insofar as one can extrapolate from human development to cultural evolution, one can justify Napoleon Chagnon's (1988) characterization as "primitive" (p. 985) tribal or village cultures whose normative system prescribes revenge in blood (the culprit's or a relative's) for certain offenses. In any event, as de Waal (1996) suggested, despite the balance-restoring tendency of exchanges, their negative expression can get out of hand: "Revenge can be incredibly destructive if left untamed" (p. 161). Children and early adolescents living in an Arab village culture that prescribed practices of blood vengeance evidenced elevated levels of distress on scales measuring symptomatic behavior such as hostility, anxiety, phobias, paranoid ideation, depression, and somatic complaints (Al-Krenawi, Slonim-Nevo, Maymon, & Al-Krenawi, 2001). Chagnon (1988; cf. Anderson, 1999; Edgerton, 1992) found that practices of blood vengeance accounted for nearly one third of adult male deaths among the Yanomamo Indians of the Amazons. And apparently the Yanomamo are not atypical; homicide rates among hunter-gatherer tribes are generally so severe that modern per capita homicide rates—even factoring in massive wartime casualties—seem favorable by comparison (Bloom, 2004; Diamond, 2008, April 21). An adult Yanomamo man (who, we suspect, had constructed ideal reciprocity) visited

the territorial capital [of the Amazons].... There he discovered police and laws. He excitedly told [Chagnon] that he had visited the ... territorial governor and urged him to make law and police available to his people so that they would not have to engage any longer in their wars of revenge and have to live in constant fear. Many of his close kinsmen had died violently and had, in turn, exacted lethal revenge; he worried about being a potential target of retaliations and made it known to all that he would have nothing to do with raiding.[10] *(Chagnon, 1988, p. 990)*

In addition to their need for such judicial institutions, the Yanomamo were in desperate need of a mature culture whose moral climate, social institutions, and socialization practices facilitate the construction, internalization, and consolidation of ideal reciprocity, such that revenge can indeed be "tamed" (e.g., Damon, 1995; Fromm, 1955; Guisinger & Blatt, 1994). Social institutions that promote interethnic trust and connection, for example, are crucial in preventing or controlling cycles of violence and vengeance. Beyond simple social contact, interdependence in the context of integrated institutions such as business or professional organizations, trade unions, or political parties has been identified as particularly crucial (Varshney, 2002). Musafer Sherif and colleagues' (Sherif, Harvey, White, Hood, & Sherif, 1961) classic social psychological experiments established the effectiveness of joint activity toward shared superordinate goals in mitigating intergroup stereotypes and preventing cycles of violence. Such social perspective-taking opportunities should foster an expanded application of the impartial or moral point of view (see Chapter 1):

> Altruistic impulses once limited to one's kin and one's own group might be
> extended to a wider circle by reasoning creatures who can see that they and their
> kind are one group among others, and from an impartial point of view no more
> important than others. (Singer, 1981, p. 134)

Such an expansion may also entail development beyond the third stage of moral judgment.

Stage 3 to Stage 4: Beyond Peer Interaction in Moral Judgment Development

Although Kohlberg in effect reserved moral judgment maturity until his Stages 5 and 6 (see Chapter 3), our view is that moral judgment maturity (at least in the face-to-face interpersonal context) is already evident at Stage 3, the stage of third-person or ideal reciprocity. Stage 3 moral judgment, however, does not fully represent moral-cognitive adequacy for individuals living in a society more complex than that of a small community. For such individuals, moral judgment maturity must expand in scope from the dyadic or peer to the social system context.

As such adolescents or adults move beyond familiar peer interaction in small, local communities to societal institutions such as universities or complex work settings, they increasingly deal with anonymous individuals and relate to individuals with diverse or heterogeneous values. As a result of this broader role taking and the reflection it stimulates, their appreciation of the need for mutual trust and caring (Stage 3) expands into an appreciation of the need for commonly accepted, consistent standards and requirements (Stage 4) (see Edwards, 1975, 1978, 1982, 1985, 1986; Harkness, Edwards, & Super, 1981; Mason & Gibbs, 1993a, 1993b). James Rest and colleagues (1999) noted that "typically in adolescence there is the dawning awareness" of the need to establish "a system of cooperation at a societywide level (among strangers and competitors, not just among kin and friends) [that] calls for impartiality, generalizable norms, and 'a level playing field' among diverse ethnic, religious, and racial groups" (p. 15). In the words of one 18-year-old, the purpose of laws is "to set up a standard of behavior for people, for society living together so that they can live peacefully and in harmony with each other" (Adelson, Green, & O'Neil, 1969, p. 328). Commonly accepted standards, institutions, and requirements, then, "promote cooperation or social contribution and act as regulations designed to avoid disagreement and disorder" (Kohlberg, 1984, p. 632). As one of Kohlberg's longitudinal participants said, "You've got to have certain understandings in things that everyone is going to abide by or else you could never get anywhere in society, never do anything" (Colby et al., 1987, p. 375). In other words, individuals in a complex society must generally understand their interdependence and accept a balance between their rights or freedoms and their responsibility to respect the rights of others as well as to contribute to society. In the absence of such commonly accepted "understandings," not only will society "never get anywhere" but (in the words of another Kohlberg longitudinal participant) "chaos will ensue, since each person will be following his or her own set of laws" (p. 375).

Especially in relation to such advanced moral judgment, Kohlberg (1984), we note again, argued that peer interaction should be conceptualized as merely one mode of social perspective-taking (or role-taking) opportunity. He acknowledged that peer interaction "appears to stimulate development" (p. 77) and may be especially important during the childhood years. Nonetheless, Kohlberg argued that peer interaction "seems better conceptualized in terms of providing general role-taking opportunities than as having very specific and unique forms of influence" (p. 77).

Research Evaluation

Studies of social experiences in relation to moral judgment have generally been consistent with Piaget's and Kohlberg's claims that social perspective taking through peer interaction and group participation play an important role in moral judgment development. Kruger's (1992) findings concerning peer (as opposed to child-adult) discussions were noted earlier. Charles Keasy (1971; cf. Schonert-Reichl, 1999) found that the moral judgment stage in childhood is positively related to social participation, as evidenced by more social club memberships and leadership roles. Similarly, Anastasia Sedikides (1989), using a measure of childhood role-taking opportunities constructed by Steven Schnell and myself (Gibbs & Schnell, 1986; Schnell, 1986), found that for a sample of preadolescents, social role-taking opportunities were, in fact, related to movement through the first three stages of moral judgment. Consistent more with Piaget's than with Kohlberg's position, a peer interaction factor (relative to home and school factors also found in a factor analysis) accounted for the greatest percentage of moral judgment stage variance. Comprising the peer interaction factor were items such as "I have many friends and talk with them very often," and "My friend and I talk about our opinions when they differ."

In the context of moral judgment development beyond Stage 3, Kohlberg (1984) conceptualized the growing individual's new social interaction experiences in college or complex work settings as opportunities for "enlarged" (p. 428) or expanded role taking. Indeed, he claimed that such experiences were crucial for development beyond Stage 3. To investigate this claim, Marion Mason and I (Gibbs & Whiteford [Mason], 1989) devised a measure of postchildhood or expanded role-taking opportunities in which participants respond (on a 3-point scale from *not true or rarely true* to *somewhat true or sometimes true* to *very true or often true*) to items such as "I have encountered and become friends with other students or co-workers of different ethnic or cultural backgrounds (for example, a student from another country)," "I have been involved in a group or organization where it was necessary for me to deal with various points of view," and "I have learned just how culturally varied the world is since coming to college." We (Mason & Gibbs, 1993a, 1993b) administered both the Gibbs and Schnell childhood role-taking opportunities measure and the Gibbs and Mason postchildhood measure focusing on work and college role-taking experiences to a college sample evidencing mixtures of Stage 3 and Stage 4 moral judgment. The postchildhood measure, but not the childhood measure, was highly correlated with moral judgment level in this advanced sample. Using the postchildhood measure, Comunian and Gielen (1995, 2000) found significant gains (relative to a comparison group) in expanded social perspective taking and toward Stage 4 moral judgment among young adults who engaged in communitarian activities. Hence, Kohlberg was right to stress the distinct importance of *socially expanded* perspective-taking experiences for moral judgment development beyond childhood.

Assessing Stages of Immature and Mature Moral Judgment

Although we have not emphasized the stage construct in our depiction of cognitive-developmental themes, it should be clear by now that many of our conclusions regarding the products of moral judgment development can be summarized in terms of immature and mature stages. Immature moral judgment stages are superficial insofar as they confuse morality either with salient appearances, consequences, or other objects of centration (Stage 1) or with "you scratch my back I'll scratch yours" deals, that is, pragmatic reciprocity (Stage 2). The concrete decentration of Stage 2 moral judgment provides a certain rationality, especially in contrast to the capricious and blithe inconsistencies of Stage 1 thinking. Accordingly, Stage 2 is somewhat less superficial. Nonetheless, the light of subsequent stages exposes the superficiality even of Stage 2 judgment: Its rationality is interpersonally shallow, narrow, and unabashedly self-serving.

Perhaps through reflection upon pragmatic reciprocity, and especially with socialization support, a more ideal and profound morality typically emerges in child development. Mature moral judgment penetrates through superficial considerations to infer the bases of interpersonal relationships (Stage 3) or society (Stage 4). The Stage 3 ideal-reciprocity maturity constructed in the face-to-face interpersonal sphere extends across complex or diverse social settings (Stage 4).

To assess an individual's moral judgment maturity in terms of these stages and thereby to study moral judgment development across cultures, we start by defining a moral judgment stage as a structure of moral justifications, that is, of reasons supporting a decision or evaluation in the context of the right and the good (see Chapter 1). Accordingly, the decision or evaluation pertains to values such as keeping a promise, telling the truth, helping a friend, saving a life, and not stealing.

Our assessment measures (even multiple-choice measures; see Gibbs, Arnold, Morgan, et al., 1984; Basinger & Gibbs, 1987; cf. Rest, Narvaez, Bebeau, & Thoma, 1999) of moral judgment development are based on such a definition. In particular, the Sociomoral Reflection Measure–Short Form (SRM-SF) (Gibbs, Basinger, & Fuller, 1992; Gibbs, Basinger, & Grime, 2003; Gibbs, Basinger, Grime, & Snarey 2007; for reliability and validity, see Basinger, Gibbs, & Fuller, 1995) asks individuals to evaluate and justify the importance of specified moral values. The values are specified through certain lead-in statements (e.g., "Think about when you've made a promise ...").[11] Respondents' justifications are then matched to inductively and deductively derived "criterion" justifications found in the scoring manual (Gibbs, Basinger, & Fuller, 1992). At each stage, the justifications are depicted in terms of five to seven aspects that cohere into a gestalt or "montage" that serves to guide the matching. The immature Stages (1 and 2) can be illustrated in terms of their montages for the collective value of keeping a promise and telling the truth:

Stage 1. "You should always keep a promise, and never be a tattletale. If you made a promise to a friend, it wouldn't be nice to break it because then he wouldn't play with you and wouldn't be your friend any more. Or he'd cry and beat you up. Not only that, but your parents will punish you if you lie or break a promise."

Stage 2. "Your friend has probably done things for you and may return the favor if you help him by keeping your promise. Besides, you may like your friend, and this could be your only friend. Lies catch up with you sooner or later, and once they do you'll be in worse trouble because the other person may get even. If it's parents and children, then parents should keep their promises to the children if the children have kept their promises to the parents. But if the promise is to someone you hardly know, then why bother? They'll probably never know whether you kept it or not."

Illustrating mature-stage (Stages 3 and 4) moral judgment are these montages:

Stage 3. "Your friend has faith in you, and you shouldn't betray that trust or hurt his feelings. After all, you'd expect him to keep his promises to you, and having a friend to share feelings with means a lot. Even if it's not a friend, honesty is still the best policy and it's just common courtesy. It's selfish to break promises, and once you make a bad impression, people won't think much of you. If it's a child and the parents don't keep promises, the children will stop believing in their parents and will start thinking that lying is all right. Even if it's someone you hardly know, you may start a good relationship by showing that you care and can be trusted."

Stage 4. "Society is based on trust and reliability, and keeping promises is necessary for the sake of social order. Honesty is a standard everyone can accept, and you wouldn't want to live in a society where you couldn't trust anyone. After all, promises have intrinsic value, and a relationship is meaningless if there is no trust. In the case of a child, parents have an obligation to keep their word and to provide an example of character so that the child develops a sense of responsibility. Keeping a promise is a commitment and a matter of honor—failing to keep it, even if it's to someone you hardly know, reflects on your integrity. People must be consistent and not break promises whenever they feel like it, so that they can earn others' respect, to say nothing of their own" (adapted from Gibbs, Basinger, & Fuller, 1992).

These montages convey our sense of "stage" as a reasonably coherent, qualitatively distinct framework, complex schema, or cognitive structure. Do growing children in fact evidence such immature and mature stages in their moral judgment? Can an age trend in these terms be observed around the world, consistent with Kohlberg's claim of universality in moral judgment development?

Moral Judgment Stage Development across Cultures

These questions can, in fact, be addressed on the basis of findings from the measure just described. The SRM-SF has been used to measure moral judgment development in at least 75 research studies spanning 23 countries (see Gibbs, Basinger, Grime, & Snarey, 2007; cf. Snarey, 1985). These countries collectively represented cultural diversity: Although many of the samples were urban and Westernized, some were nonurban (rural communities in Armenia, Kenya, Nigeria), and others were outside Western Europe and North America (namely, Armenia, Bosnia, Bulgaria, and Russia in Eastern Europe; Sweden in Northwest Europe; China, Japan, Malaysia, and Taiwan in Asia; Kenya and Nigeria in Africa; and Bahrain and Saudi Arabia in the Middle East). In this connection, the SRM-SF was translated into sixteen non-English languages. SRM-SF protocol attrition (from unscorable justifications, etc.) was generally low (less than 10%), suggesting that the questionnaire's questions and moral values "made sense" to the respondents, and that a common core captures their reasons in support of those values, despite the diversity of the respondents' cultural contexts.

Table 2.1 presents an overall picture of moral judgment development across cultures aggregated across the studies (not included are juvenile delinquents' moral judgment levels; see Chapter 6). The moral judgment levels are presented in terms of both Global Stage range and Sociomoral Reflection Maturity Score (SRMS), a continuous variable ranging from 100 (pure Stage 1) to 400 (pure Stage 4). The Global Stage designations in the table are derived from SRMS values as follows: 100–124 = Stage 1; 126–174 = Transition 1/2; 175–225 = Stage 2; 226–274 = Transition 2/3; etc. The mean SRMSs for the samples reviewed are then ordered and grouped by Childhood (Late), Adolescence (Early/Middle, Late), and Adulthood (Young, Middle).

A full analysis of moral judgment development across these cultures is provided in our review, published elsewhere (see Gibbs et al., 2007). From even a brief inspection of the adapted table presented here, however, support can be seen for Kohlberg's universality claim: Growth beyond the superficial in moral judgment does indeed

Table 2.1 Cross-cultural samples in rank order by mean Sociomoral Reflection Maturity Score (SRMS), grouped by age period

Country, sample/age range (mean) in years	n	Global stage range	M
Late childhood (approx. 9–11 years old)			
Bosnia, primary school students/7–9 (8.1)	18	1/2	164
Kenya, primary school students/8–10 (NR)	69	1/2-2	179
Nigeria, primary school students/10–11 (NR)	37	1/2-2	181
USA, 5th grade students/NR	61	2-2/3	209
Canada, 5th grade students/10–12 (11.0)	45	NR	209
Ireland, primary school students/10–11 (NR)	96	2-2/3	221
Italy, 6th graders/NR (11.2)	52	NR	223
Taiwan, primary school students/9–12 (NR)	450	2-2/3	225
Japan, 4th graders/NR (10.3)	37	2-3	239
Early/middle adolescence (approx. 12–15 years old)			
Kenya, middle school students/11–13 (NR)	83	1/2-2	185
Belgium, primary school students/12–14 (NR)	48	NR	223
Bosnia, primary school students/11–12 (11.8)	23	2-2/3	230
Netherlands, secondary school students/ 12–17 (14.3)	216	2-2/3	237
USA, 6th graders/11–14 (11.8)	276	2-3	240
Englands, middle school students/12–15 (13.0)	789	2-3	242
China, non-delinquents/13–15 (NR)	10	NR	251
Scotland, middle school students/14–15 (NR)	157	2/3-3	255
Japan, 8th grade students/NR (14.3)	62	2-3	264
Canada, 6th and 7th grade students/10–13 (11.7)	47	NR	268
Taiwan, 5th and 6th grade students/11–12 (NR)	45	NR	272
Ireland, secondary school students/14–15 (NR)	325	2/3-3	278
Italy, 9th grade students/NR (14.4)	52	NR	291
Late adolescence (approx. 16–19 years old)			
Kenya, high school students/17-19 (NR)	94	2–3	250
Netherlands, high school students/14-17 (15.0)	120	2/3–3	260

(Continued)

Table 2.1   (Continued)

Country, sample/age range (mean) in years	n	Global stage range	M
Germany, non-delinquents/14–16 (15.6)	309	2/3-3	261
England, male high school students/14–16 (15.5)	149	2-3	264
Sweden, non-delinquents/13–18 (15.6)	29	2/3-3	266
Ireland, secondary school students/16–19 (17.3)	61	2/3-3	281
USA, high school students/13–19 (15.9)	163	2/3-3	286
Japan, 11th graders/NR (16.8)	95	2/3-3	289
Belgium, secondary school students/18–20 (NR)	37	NR	292
Russia, high school students/NR (15.6)	419	NR	311
Bahrain, non-delinquents/17–18 (17.7)	30	3-3/4	313
Japan, high school students/16–18 (17.1)	22	NR	320
Italy, community volunteers/NR (16.0)	70	NR	329
Young adulthood (approx. 20–35 years old)			
Japan, university students/NR (19.8)	80	2/3-3/4	300
Belgium, university and vocational students/ 21–24 (NR)	57	NR	311
Bulgaria, adults in romantic relationships/ 19–73 (29.8)	163	3-3/4	325
England, university students/18–25 (19.5)	64	3-3/4	327
Saudi Arabia, upper-division university students/ 20–26 (22.5)	60	NR	333
USA, university students/17–39 (20.8)	153	3-3/4	335
Australia, university students/NR (26.9)	94	3-3/4	340
Italy, adult community volunteers/NR (33.9)	154	NR	359
Middle adulthood (approx. 40–50 years old)			
USA, university parents/NR (50.1)	58	3/4	350

Notes: NR indicates information not reported. Students include both genders unless otherwise indicated. Non-delinquents are generally male high school students selected (sometimes matched) for use in comparison studies of delinquent moral judgment (see Table 6.1). Global stage range is estimated on the basis of plus or minus one standard deviation of SRMS. Pertinent studies are referenced in the source article.

Source: Adapted from J. C. Gibbs, K. S. Basinger, R. L. Grime, & J. R. Snarey (2007). Moral judgment development across cultures: Revisiting Kohlberg's universality claims, *Developmental Review, 27,* 443–500. Used with the permission of Elsevier ScienceDirect.

appear to take place across diverse cultural contexts. Apparently, moral development is not entirely relative to particular cultures and socialization practices.

Of particular relevance to this chapter is the crucial qualitative advance that takes place in the years from late childhood into early adolescence. In our terms, the advance is from Stage 2 pragmatic exchanges to Stage 3 mutualities. As the table indicates, Stage 3 already makes an appearance in the stage ranges of some late childhood samples, but generally gains prominence (sometimes even full-stage prominence) during early adolescence. By late adolescence, Stage 3 normally (at least for non-delinquents among the cultures studied) becomes the mean global moral judgment stage. Older adolescents (at least in national states) may also begin to extend their Stage 3 mutualistic understanding to grasp the importance of agreed-up standards and institutions for the common good (Stage 4).

Stage Mixture

The traditional cognitive-developmental approach claims that (a) a stage is a structure not only conceptually but also empirically, that is, that at any given time an individual is "in" mainly one stage or another (evidencing only minimal mixture with an adjacent stage) and (b) stage development occurs step-by-step in an invariant sequence, that is, with no reversals or skipping (see Chapter 3). Kohlberg's longitudinal research team (of which I was a member) reported results largely consistent with these claims (Kohlberg, Colby, Gibbs, & Lieberman, 1983; cf. L. J. Walker, 1988). The longitudinal results are arguably open to criticism, however, in that the low levels of stage mixture were to some extent an artifact of the scoring methods (see Krebs, Vermuelen, Carpendale, & Denton, 1991). Scoring methods less vulnerable to these criticisms, such as those used with the SRM-SF (see Basinger et al., 1995), do yield higher levels of stage mixture. We agree with Flavell et al.'s (2002) suggestion, then, that the qualitative changes in social and nonsocial cognitive development should be regarded "as rough age trends" (p. 140). Indeed, Kohlberg's longitudinal team (Colby et al., 1983) noted the overlapping "curves" of stage development, "with earlier stages dropping out as later stages enter, such that *the subject seems to be always in transition from one stage to the next*" (p. 49, emphasis added).

Piaget (1932/1965) himself noted the presence of considerable overlap in the age trend from superficial to more mature moral judgment. Even within a single child's interview, variability in the level of moral judgment can be discerned:

> [Const., age 7] (Let's pretend that you are the mummy. You have two little girls. One of them breaks fifteen cups as she is coming into the dining room, the other breaks one cup as she is trying to get some jam while you are not there. Which of them would you punish more severely?) The one who broke the fifteen cups. . . . (Have you ever broken anything?) A cup. (How?) I wanted to wipe it, and I let it drop. (What else have you broken?) Another time, a plate. (How?) I took it to play with. (Which was the naughtier thing to do?) The plate, because I oughtn't to have taken it. (And how about the cup?) That was less naughty because I wanted

to wipe it. (Which were you punished most for, the cup or the plate?) For the plate. (Listen, I am going to tell you two more stories. A little girl was wiping the cups. She was putting them away, wiping them with the cloth, and she broke five cups. Another little girl is playing with some plates. She breaks a plate. Which of them is the naughtiest?) The girl who broke the five cups. (pp. 125–126)

The 7-year-old's responses vary in maturity according to whether the questions address her direct personal experience (a condition of "high support" conducive to optimal or more mature functioning) (Fischer & Bidell, 2006) or hypothetical situations ("low support"). Because of such variability, Piaget refrained from referring to his modes of moral judgment as "stages," recommending instead the concept of overlapping "phases" (p. 317). Damon (1980) found in a 2-year longitudinal study that distributive justice stage development was "gradual, mixed, and uneven" (p. 1017). Siegler (1996a; cf. Colby et al., 1983; Flavell et al., 2002; Rest, 1979) suggested that the stage construct can be salvaged if each new stage were conceptualized not as a new step but rather as a beginning new "wave" that overlaps previous waves in the waxings and wanings of developmental advance.

Stages as Schemas

James Rest and colleagues (Rest et al., 1999) were sufficiently impressed with stage mixture and other problems to suggest replacing *stage* with the more generic and less theory-laden term *schema* in developmental theory. Schemas are frameworks for meaningful experience that can be activated in imagination, self-talk, or encounters with reality. Most schemas are dynamic, growing through cycles of interplay with the environment that take place over time (cf. Neisser, 1976). Through schemas, the self perceives or experiences (anticipates, attends to, interacts with) an environmental event. Surprises from that event elicit refinements or even reorganizations of the schemas. The newly refined schemas then contribute to more competent or adaptive interaction in the next environmental encounter. It is through such progressive cyclical interplay that growth beyond the superficial in morality takes place.

Various uses of the schema construct are evident in the literature of developmental psychology. The various operationalizations are, of course, not precisely equivalent; "boundary conditions" of each usage should be specified (Meichenbaum, 1990, p. 99). Roughly speaking, however, we can state that schemas motivate, guide, and structure. Fairly typical is Keenan and Ward's (2003) description of schemas as "structure[s] containing beliefs or attitudes that follow a similar theme or pattern" or as "organizing frameworks for processing new information" (p. 145). That schemas are dynamic is reflected in phrases such as "action-oriented representations" (Trzebinski, 1985) and "interlocking *cognitive-affective* representations" (Cason, Resick, & Weaver, 2002, emphasis added). Piaget claimed that schemas have "an intrinsic need ... to exercise themselves" (Feffer, 1970, p. 198). Seymour Epstein and colleagues (e.g., Epstein, 1991; Epstein & Morling, 1995; cf. Narvaez, 2008) suggested that schemas actively serve basic needs for pleasure or avoidance of pain, self-enhancement, consistency or predictability, and social relatedness. In social cognition, we build "relational schemas" (e.g., Baldwin, 1992) that guide and shape our expectations concerning others vis-à-vis the self. Whereas relational schemas pertain to particular contexts of social interaction, *internal working models* (Bowlby, 1980; Shaver, Collins, & Clark, 1996) are thought to influence our basic approach to social relationships. "Implicit theories" structure our perception and explanation of the empirical world (Gopnik & Wellman, 1994). In subsequent chapters, we will pay particular attention to *self* schemas (e.g., Harter, 2006) for which morality is highly relevant (Chapter 5), schemas of cognitive distortion and constructive social interaction (Chapters 6 and 7), schemas by which people attempt to describe the near-death experience (Chapter 8), and the epistemological distinction between *scripts* for event sequences in the environment (Hoffman, 2000; Nelson, 1981) and *logico-mathematical structures* of knowledge (Chapter 9).

In both Kohlberg's and Hoffman's theories, *stage* can refer to a relatively broad and complex schema that is qualitatively distinct from—yet related to—other such schemas in a developmental sequence. Anne Colby (2000) defined moral judgment stages as "cognitive-moral frameworks" representing "different sets of assumptions that help to inform and shape people's reactions to the micro-decisions they face" in everyday life (p. 162). As fundamental frameworks or sets of assumptions, moral judgment stages make only indirect contributions to everyday reactions, decisions, and perceptions. Nonetheless, a crucial point is that, once a stage has been constructed, its activation can be quick (as we will see in Chapter 5).

We continue to use the term *stage*, then, but with the caveat that its conceptual coherence typically does not mean concurrence in the emergence of its facets during childhood. In the broadest terms, *stages* in cognitive development refer to an individual's ways of knowing and interacting with the social and nonsocial world. Each stage paves the way for construction of the next, qualitatively new and more adequate or mature stage. During any ongoing interaction with reality, however, a given individual is likely to activate multiple stages and other schemas (cf. Fischer & Bidell, 2006; Siegler, 1996a).

If adaptive learning and development are to take place, schemas must be open to consolidation, refinement, transformation, and even radical reorganization as novelties and contradictions are encountered. In Piagetian terms, experience is assimilated to a preexisting cognitive structure, which itself undergoes (or should undergo) accommodation.[12] For example, a child who encounters a camel for the first time may distortingly assimilate it to horse schema but notice the hump and reflect, "That surely is a funny-looking horse!" Similarly, the preconservational children in the Ames and Murray (1982) study were perplexed (the Piagetian term is *disequilibrated*) by anomalous facts pressed upon them by peers who saw in terms of the opposing centration (e.g., a child judging "more" liquid after it is poured into the tall glass is pressed to attend to how *thin* the tall glass is).

Eventually, accommodation to the novel features (such as the camel's hump or the glass's other dimension) will induce a differentiation and the construction of a new structure or schema ("camel," or conservation knowledge). Once the accommodation and new equilibration are accomplished, these more differentiated and integrated schemas are available to inform future encounters. Accordingly, the next camel encountered is accurately construed, or the next conservation question understood to be a matter of logical inference rather than empirical perception.

We might describe a child as mainly "in" a certain social or nonsocial cognitive stage, so long as we specify the context or content domain and emphasize that stage mixture would characterize the child's cross-situational performance. Although disequilibration may not be necessary for developmental advance (Siegler, 1996a), high stage mixture in moral judgment development may generate disequilibration that in turn tends to facilitate longitudinal gain (Walker, Gustafson, & Hennig, 2001).

Summarizing Comment

Growth beyond the superficial in morality entails, then, a qualitative sequence of immature and mature stages (see Table 3.1 in Chapter 3). The mature stages are constructed through social perspective taking and hypothetical reflection. At the core of the mature stages is ideal moral reciprocity, which entails a sense of necessity and provides a primarily cognitive motivation. Mature morality penetrates through superficial considerations of immature morality (Stages 1 and 2) to infer the intangible bases of interpersonal relationships or society (Stages 3 and 4). An age trend from immature to mature stages was evident in a review of studies conducted in over 20 countries (Gibbs et al., 2007). Because the stages overlap so greatly, this stage sequence constitutes only a rough age trend in the use of increasingly mature ways of understanding and interacting with the social world. Bolder claims for extended stages of moral judgment development were made by Kohlberg, to whose theory we now turn.

Notes

[1]Kohlberg and colleagues' Moral Judgment Interview (MJI) (Colby et al., 1987) and related measures (e.g., the Sociomoral Reflection Measure–Short Form; Gibbs, Basinger, & Fuller, 1992) emphasize moral values (e.g., contract, truth, and property) that tend to "pull" for justifications of right and wrong. Beneficent moral values (e.g., helping others and saving another's life) are also addressed, however, in these measures (cf. Eisenberg, 1982). These moral values of the right and the good have generally been rated as important or very important in diverse cultures (see Gibbs et al., 2007). In these measures and the cognitive developmental approach, "moral judgment" refers to the justification of prescriptive social evaluations or decisions. It should be noted that "moral judgment" is used interchangeably with "moral evaluation" in the social intuitionist approach (e.g., Haidt & Bjorklund, 2008a, 2008b).

[2]Piaget generally took a strong domain-general view, depicting cognitive development as one and the same phenomenon whether viewed socially or nonsocially. In technical terms,

interindividual mental operations of a certain stage were seen as isomorphic to intraindividual operations of that stage (Piaget, 1967/1971). Kohlberg was initially sympathetic to Piaget's broad or domain-general view. In fact, he (Kohlberg, 1964) initially examined moral judgment trends that seemed to reflect cognitive development. Subsequently, however, Kohlberg (1984) came to stress temporal orders of parallel construction across subdomains (with each latter construction emerging contemporaneously or later in time, if at all): A given nonsocial cognitive stage is seen as necessary but not sufficient for the attainment of a parallel social perspective-taking stage, which in turn is necessary but not sufficient for the attainment of a parallel moral judgment stage. William Damon (1977) proposed an intermediate position: Although a certain logical operational construction may be necessary but not sufficient for a certain social cognitive construction, the logical construction may emerge in the social subdomain *before* it does in the nonsocial subdomain (which could happen if a child has, for example, "some kind of block against mathematical problems," p. 322). Damon's may be the most defensible position, given the problem of stage mixture discussed later in the chapter.

[3]Although mature moral judgment is primarily governed by intentions rather than consequences, consequences of course remain relevant to some extent—especially insofar as they may reflect negligence (in effect, an inadequate intentionality). Roger Brown (1965) observed that moral judgments acknowledge

> something that might be called the seriousness or importance of what happens. . . . If a pedestrian is killed by a motorist, that is more serious than if a pedestrian is only knocked down.
>   The law . . . often punishes in terms of the objective event rather than the intention. . . . It gives people a reason [or incentive] to acquire knowledge and control their intentions [or negligent behavior]. (pp. 239–240)

[4]"Social construction," in the Piagetian sense, differs almost diametrically from some other usages. For example, in the 1960s, Foucault, Derrida, and other post-modernists used social construction or "social constructivism" to characterize the scientific process as having more to do with social convention, contingency, and political power than with rationality, logical necessity, or objective knowledge of nature. Some non-Piagetian moral psychologists have similarly critiqued moral development, equating "social construction" with relativistic enculturation processes and expressing skepticism regarding rationality, objectivity, and moral knowledge (e.g., Haidt & Bjorklund, 2008a, 2008b).

[5]Although this condition is fascinating for its elucidation of construction as deconfounded from internalization, experimental conditions in which one disputant in the dyad is at a slightly more advanced level often stimulate greater gains in both logical and moral judgment (e.g., Kuhn, 1972; Murray, 1982; L. J. Walker, 1983). In Vygotsky's (1930–1935/1978) terms, optimal growth typically takes place within the child's "zone of proximal development."

[6]Although qualitative, the difference depicted by Brown (1965) does not reflect abrupt change. Through the child and adolescent years, understanding and appreciation of the logical-empirical distinction gradually becomes "more stable, more generalizable, and more imbued with feelings of necessity" (Flavell et al., 2002, p. 146; cf. Miller et al., 2000; Morris & Sloutsky, 2001; Winer & McGlone, 1993; Winer, Craig, & Weinbaum, 1992). The epistemological and ontological significance of the logical-empirical distinction is explored in Chapter 9.

[7]Although one can violate logical or moral necessity in thought or speech, the ideal remains: "Thinking or saying that one plus one equals three or that it is right to gratuitously harm

someone does not make it so." The logical-moral parallel stops there, however: "Although a moral rule violation may be wrong, it is nonetheless possible to commit it (to gratuitously harm someone); but in some sense [despite tricks] it is not actually possible to violate logic (to add one plus one and actually produce three)" (Laupa, 2000, p. 30).

[8]Retributive justice can have a more mature aim than that of mere retaliation or "getting even." If mixed with ideal reciprocity, revenge seeks to educate the offender, or shatter his or her self-centeredness and other self-serving cognitive distortions, as when the prospective avenger wonders "how he'd [the offender would] like it if the same thing were done to him" (Lewis, 1962, p. 94). Moral education and the correcting of self-serving cognitive distortions are discussed in Chapter 7.

[9]Appeals to the futility of cycles of vengeance and to forgiveness do not necessarily imply unqualified tolerance or pacifism. Some situations are accurately perceived as requiring defense of self or others.

[10]In contrast to this tribesman's enthusiasm for social institutions of law and conflict mediation, a New Guinea Highlands tribesman who worked for a multinational corporation was more ambivalent (Diamond, 2008, April 21). The New Guinea tribesman acknowledged that "Letting the government settle disputes by means of the legal system [is] better [than being] trapped in our endless cycles of revenge killings" (p. 84). Yet the New Guinea tribesman also expressed euphoria, pride, relief, and a sense of satisfaction in having accomplished a revenge killing, and regretted that he would not be allowed to continue such activity. Particularly thoughtful was a former boy soldier's conclusion that

> revenge is not good. We are all brothers and sisters. I joined the army to avenge the deaths of my family and to survive, but I've come to learn that if I am going to take revenge, in that process I will kill another person whose family will want revenge, then revenge and revenge and revenge will never come to an end. (Beah, 2007, p. 199)

[11]Such lead-in statements were as effective as moral dilemmas, a finding (see Basinger, Gibbs, & Fuller, 1995; Gibbs et al., 2007) that obviated various criticisms of Kohlberg's theory that were based on his use of dilemmas in stage assessment.

[12]Despite criticism (e.g., Klahr, 1982), Piaget's concept of adaptation as encompassing assimilatory and accommodative aspects—and in particular, of maladaptation in terms of overassimilation and overaccommodation—has continued to find valuable application in identity development (e.g., Whitbourne & Connolly, 1999), ego development (Rathunde & Csikszentmihalyi, 2006), parenting interventions with disturbed children (Cowan, Powell, & Cowan, 1998), and other areas of developmental psychology.

CHAPTER 3

Kohlberg's Theory:

A Critique and New View

LAWRENCE KOHLBERG'S CONTRIBUTION TO THE FIELD OF MORAL development was enormous. Indeed, Kohlberg almost single-handedly innovated the field of cognitive moral development in American psychology. Such work scarcely existed in the early 1960s when Kohlberg began to publish his research: "His choice of topics [namely, 'morality'] made him something of an 'odd duck' within American psychology.... No up-to-date social scientist, acquainted with [the relativism of] psychoanalysis, behaviorism, and cultural anthropology, used such words [as moral judgment development] at all" (Brown & Herrnstein, 1975, pp. 307–308). Yet these scientists could not ignore Kohlberg's claim—and supporting evidence—that morality is not basically relative to culture, that is, that across diverse cultures one can discern a qualitative sequence of progressively more adequate modes of moral judgment. Kohlberg became one of the most frequently cited psychologists in the social and behavioral sciences (Haggbloom et al., 2000). His work is described and discussed in virtually every major developmental psychology textbook on the current market.

This chapter provides a critique of Kohlberg's theory and concludes with a new view of "the right" in moral development. The basics of this view were introduced in our Chapter 2 depiction of the fundamental themes of the cognitive-developmental approach: themes such as growing beyond the superficial, construction, social perspective taking, and invariant stage sequence. Whereas Chapter 2 went "beneath" Kohlberg's theory, this chapter addresses Kohlberg's theory per se. Kohlberg's driving insight was that moral development is not complete by the end of childhood, but instead continues throughout the human life span. For background, we narrate how Kohlberg used the stage-developmental writings of philosopher John Dewey to fashion a six-stage sequence that would be (Kohlberg hoped) clearly invariant and life-span in scope. As we will see, that attempt was costly: It resulted in misrepresentations of developmental processes and the nature of moral judgment maturity. Kohlberg did succeed, however, in establishing the increasing importance of contemplative (or hypothetical-deductive) reflection in moral judgment development. Such reflection plays a key role in our proposed new view (outlined at the end of the chapter in Table 3.1).

Background

In 1985 (just 2 years before he died), Kohlberg referred to both Dewey and Piaget as he recollected how his moral judgment stages started and evolved in the course of his "search for universal morality":

> My views ... were based on John Dewey's philosophy of development and his writings concerning the impulsive, group-conforming, and reflective stages of moral development. The first empirical work to pursue this direction was taken by the great Swiss child psychologist, Jean Piaget, in 1932. ... Using [in my dissertation; Kohlberg, 1958] dilemmas created by philosophers or novelists, I was struck by the fact that adolescents had distinctive patterns of thinking which were coherent and were their own, just as Piaget had seen distinctive patterns of thinking in younger children. In my dissertation I tentatively characterized these patterns as qualitative stages and added three stages to those formulated by Piaget.
>
> When I completed my dissertation I was well aware that by describing ninety-eight American boys, aged ten to sixteen, I had not created a universal theory. The stages I had postulated had to meet criteria....The first step in determining this was to follow up my original subjects. ... The longitudinal study has led to refinement and revision in the description and scoring of the stages....Coordinate with [this] follow-up study was checking my doubts about whether the stages were really universal in non-Western cultures....The final stages have been found to be rare. (Kohlberg, 1991, pp. 14–15, emphasis added)

Kohlberg's empirical starting point as he began his 1955 dissertation work, then, was the work of Jean Piaget. Kohlberg saw in Piaget's (1932/1965) classic *Moral Judgment of the Child* the potential for establishing a stable cognitive developmental underpinning for morality, and, in particular, a universal sequence of moral judgment. Piaget had identified certain basic age trends, comprising successive schemas of moral thought that might be "invariant" across factors of social class, culture, sex, ethnic status, and cohort. The more advanced schemas were "constructed" through peer interaction (as well as, in Kohlberg's revision, other experiences of social perspective taking; see Chapter 2). Although social class, culture, and other factors might affect social perspective taking and hence the rate of a child's moral development, they would not alter the developmental *sequence*. Cognitive moral development involved a cross-culturally invariant and cross-culturally universal sequence with a "definite direction," an age trend of naturally upward, sustained change from "the more primitive" to "the more evolved" organizations or structures. Furthermore, the "more evolved" or mature schemas of judgment were expected to be fairly common or "universal" across diverse cultures (p. 335). Indeed, each structure is thought to transform into a qualitatively new and more adequate organization of thought. No schema could be skipped because each schema was needed to pave the way for the next. *Invariant sequence* meant for Piaget, then, a standard (cross-culturally evident) age trend of sustained progressive, qualitative change entailing a consecutive sequence of qualitatively distinct and basic schemas of action and reflection. Once constructed, the more advanced competencies could not ordinarily be lost. Hence, any regression in cognitive competence (beyond ordinary variations in performance) or skipping of one of the schemas would violate the expectations of invariant sequence.

Interestingly, Piaget (1932/1965) generally refrained from labeling these basic moral judgment schemas *stages* and from making strong invariant sequence claims for them. Instead, because of variability and mixture in usage (see Chapter 2), "invariant sequence" in this context referred merely to "phases" (p. 317) of moral judgment that "partially synchronize" (p. 124); development merely meant that the later phases gradually gain ascendancy. This ascending phases view of moral judgment development resembles contemporary models of cognitive development (Fischer & Bidell, 2006; Rest, 1979; Siegler, 1996a).

Piaget (1970, 1971, 1972) reserved for *non*social cognitive development the bolder claim that invariant sequence refers not just to overlapping phases but to *stages*. A basic schema or stage was a *structure d'ensemble*, an overall organization that would "hang together" in development and hence give rise to a distinct period or era of cognitive development. He saw his famous preoperational, concrete operational, and to some extent formal operational stages, then—but not his moral judgment phases—as characterizing such a clear sequence in cognitive development. Although he did allow for considerable variability or stage mixture (see Chapter 2), especially during transition, Piaget characterized the developing child as generally "in" one or another stage or period of development.

In moral judgment, Kohlberg had the courage of Piaget's bolder convictions. Kohlberg hypothesized, in effect, that Piaget was unduly conservative in his relegation of moral judgment development to overlapping phases in a rough age trend. To put the point positively, Kohlberg anticipated that moral judgment development data (if investigated from a more adequate conceptual, empirical, and methodological framework) could support a claim of *clearly* invariant *stage* sequence. Kohlberg (1964) scrutinized, in light of subsequent research, the various aspects of moral judgment studied by Piaget. Kohlberg found that: (a) certain aspects "reflect cognitive development" (p. 398), whereas others seemed more "socioemotional"; and (b) the age trends in the former (cognitive) but not latter (socioemotional) aspects held up across variations in children's nationality (at least in Western cultures), social class, or religion. Hence, the constituents of these cognitive age trends held promise for satisfying Piaget's bolder sense of invariant *stage* sequence. Indeed, beyond merely reflecting cognitive development, moral development would become "its own sequential process," a distinct domain in its own right (Kohlberg, 1971, p. 187).

The promise of these age trends could be actualized, Kohlberg surmised, if the structure of participants' moral judgments were more effectively probed for patterns of reasoning. Rather than Piaget's story pairs (see Chapter 2), Kohlberg in his dissertation used moral dilemmas ("created by philosophers or novelists"). The most famous dilemma is that of the husband Heinz, who must decide whether to steal a prohibitively overpriced drug to save his dying wife. Kohlberg also included adolescents in his dissertation (Piaget's sample was restricted to ages 6–13), which led to the identification of stages beyond Piaget's. As noted in his recollection, Kohlberg was "struck by the fact" that the adolescents in his sample "had distinctive patterns of thinking which were coherent and were their own."

As Kohlberg recollected, he based his work not only on Piaget's empirical work but also on Dewey's philosophy and writings concerning moral stages,[1] Indeed, Kohlberg saw Piaget's empirical work on moral judgment as pursuing the direction of Dewey's (Dewey & Tufts, 1908) philosophy of moral developmental stages as progressing through impulsive, group conforming, and, finally, reflective levels. It is possible that Piaget was pursuing such a direction in his moral judgment research. Yet Piaget (1932/1965), in his *Moral Judgment of the Child*, made no reference to Dewey's stage conceptions; nor do Piaget's phases bear much resemblance to those conceptions. Kohlberg's (1971) thesis that psychology and philosophy can respectively inform and guide each other is well taken. Nonetheless, as we will see, Kohlberg's Dewey-inspired three-level conception *mis*guided the formulation, extension, and refinement of the stages.

Kohlberg's Overhaul of Piaget's Phases

In effect, Kohlberg overhauled and added to Piaget's phases using an adaptation of Deweyan views. Dewey's "impulsive" (egoistic desires, needs), "group-conforming" (customs, rules), and "reflective" (conscience, principles) stages were at first labeled premoral, conventional, and "self-accepted moral principles" levels (Kohlberg, 1963, 1964, p. 400) and later as preconventional, conventional, and postconventional levels (Kohlberg, 1976; cf. Rest et al., 1999). To this trichotomy of levels were assimilated a total of six stages, two per level. Our critique asks, essentially: How well did this overhaul work? Did it result in a more valid model of universal moral judgment stages? Did it clarify our understanding of developmental processes or of moral judgment maturity? Did the six-stage scheme evidence an invariant sequence in Kohlberg's longitudinal research?

Dewey's trichotomy works adequately for the first two stages; that is, the term *preconventional* is not inaccurate. Generally lacking from these stages, after all, is an understanding of the intangible and ideal *bases* for interpersonal and societal norms or conventions. Piaget's and Kohlberg's descriptions of these stages roughly agree. Piaget's first phase, "heteronomous" morality—purged of what Kohlberg called its "socioemotional" aspects—constitutes a superficial childhood morality that relates fairly well to Kohlberg's "punishment and obedience" Stage 1 (even though "punishment and obedience" is a misnomer; see Chapter 2). Nor is there great harm in relating Piaget's Stage 2 "reciprocity as a fact" version of moral autonomy to Kohlberg's "individualism, instrumental purpose, and exchange" Stage 2 (Kohlberg, 1976). "Pragmatic exchanges" does depict this morality of concrete decentration.

After Stage 2, however, the Deweyan trichotomy seriously distorts the nature of moral judgment development. Although Kohlberg was right to point out the need to extend Piagetian stages[2] of moral judgment beyond childhood, his use of the Deweyan trichotomy meant that those later stages were misrepresented. As noted in Chapter 2, Piaget (1932/1965) hypothesized that "reciprocity as an ideal" (our referent for Stage 3) is achieved as the socially interacting child reflectively grasps the mutuality—the deeper ideal social logic, as it were—underlying reciprocal exchanges. Hence, Piaget's Stage 3 marks the construction of mature or profound moral understanding (albeit only within the sphere of the dyad or the homogeneous community). Unfortunately, Kohlberg lost Piaget's recognition of this stage's maturity. Ideal reciprocity was largely obscured and even distorted in Kohlberg's Deweyan characterization of interpersonal morality as essentially group conforming or conventional. Ideal reciprocity or Stage 3 became the stage of "interpersonal conformity" or even "'good boy–nice girl'" (Kohlberg, 1971, p. 164). Even later in Kohlberg's theoretical work, Stage 3 became part of the "member of society" sociomoral perspective in which "the self is identified with or has internalized the rules and expectations of others, especially those of authorities" (Colby & Kohlberg, 1987, p. 16).

Use of the Deweyan typology also distorted Stage 4. The growing person's grasp of the intangible bases for social cooperation may expand from the Stage 3 interpersonal to broader social spheres such as that of social systems, as indicated in Stage 4 (see Chapter 2); in other words, profound or mature moral judgment blossoms, and Kohlberg was right to explore its blossom beyond the childhood years. The expansion to a fourth stage through Kohlberg's Deweyan lens, however, was misrepresented as entailing an identification with the authorities and internalization of the legal and other norms of one's society, resulting in a "law and order orientation" (Kohlberg, 1971, p. 164), scarcely what one could characterize as basic moral judgment maturity.

Note Kohlberg's reference to "identified with" or "*internalized.*" Such appeals to moral internalization contradicted Kohlberg's appeals elsewhere (Kohlberg, 1984) for understanding stage transition processes in terms of social construction or "natural" development and maturity rather than "simpler conformity or internalization concepts" (p. 93). One may legitimately ask: Were Stages 3 and 4 in Kohlberg's hands to be understood as products of internalization or of construction?

Kohlberg's handling of the question of developmental process is subtle but in the end disappointing. Note that Kohlberg objected specifically to "*simpler* conformity concepts" or "*direct* internalization" (Kohlberg, 1971, p. 155, emphases added), imply-ing that some more complex or indirect version of internalization might be tanta-mount to construction. That implication undermined Kohlberg's original inspiration from Piaget: Piaget had challenged Durkheimian and other sociological views of morality, arguing that truly mature morality is socially *constructed*, not merely internalized. Yet, perhaps to retain continuity with the Deweyan group con-formity view, Kohlberg (1971) suggested a modified version of internalization that he called optimal match: "Some moderate or optimal degree of discrepancy" or "match" between the child's developmental level and "the [more advanced] structure of a specific experience of the child" accounts for "specific transitions from stage to stage" (p. 18) and constitutes "the most effective experience for structural change in the organism" (p. 356). Although Kohlberg used "optimal match" as if it were synony-mous with "cognitive conflict" (p. 18) in a Piagetian sense, it is not. Albeit complex and indirect, such an optimal-match process (cf. the Vygotskian notion of a zone of proximal development) still entails "an implicit moral internalization concept" because a match—unlike a genuinely constructive mental coordination—still refers to a preexisting model in the environment (Hoffman, 1988, p. 523). In short, optimal match reduced construction to internalization. As a result, we lose one of the truly revolutionary insights of Piagetian developmental psychology, as emphasized in Chapter 2: the understanding of ideal moral reciprocity as a social *constructive* product, of *construction* as a process fundamentally distinct from internalization.

Kohlberg hypothesized the existence not only of a fourth stage but also of a fifth and sixth stage, beyond the childhood moral judgment studied by Piaget. These final two stages comprised his Dewey-inspired postconventional level, rep-resenting a "prior-to-society" social perspective that "differentiates the self from the rules and expectations of others and defines moral values in terms of self-chosen principles" (Colby & Kohlberg, 1987, p. 16). The principles pertained to "social contract or utility and individual rights" (Stage 5) or "universal ethical principles" (Stage 6). In his original cross-sectional dissertation sample, Kohlberg (1963) interpreted 20% of the 16-year-olds' moral judgment protocols as evidencing Stage 5 thinking and a much smaller percentage (5%) as using Stage 6. Neither stage was used with more than negligible frequency among the other participants in the sample (the 10- and 13-year-olds). The irony is evident. In Kohlberg's search for a universal morality, the highest stages—even among the oldest participants in his dissertation sample, the adolescents—were far less than prevalent. As Kohlberg subsequently discovered and dealt with violations of the invariant sequence claim in his longitudinal research, the non-universality problem worsened. Indeed, as we will see, the high-est stages were to become (to use Kohlberg's word) rare.

Discoveries of Longitudinal Research

As Kohlberg noted in his recollection, his dissertation stages and levels did not nec-essarily constitute a "universal theory" of moral judgment development. Evaluation of the stage typology would require empirical research, especially longitudinal and cross-cultural studies. Kohlberg embarked on an ambitious longitudinal research project, following up his dissertation sample by conducting moral judgment interviews every 3 years, from the late 1950s until the early 1980s. The longitudinal results yielded problems that, as per Kohlberg's recollection, quoted earlier, "led to refinement and revision in the description and scoring of the stages."

Violations and Restoration of Invariant Sequence   The most substantial revisions were prompted by the discovery of major violations of invariant sequence in longitudinal interview data collected during the 1960s. The regressions were evidenced by participants whose high school moral judgment had been "principled-sounding," for example, who had conceptualized "the moral value of life as taking precedence over obedience to laws or authority" (Kohlberg, 1984, p. 447). During their college-years interviews, however, their moral judgments were scored as largely at Stage 2. The regressions back to Stage 2 during the college years were major not only in magnitude (much of it from the highest to the lowest stages) but also in frequency, involving approximately 20% of his sample. What a challenge to invariant sequence!

Kohlberg's strategy for dealing with this challenge evolved. His initial response (Kohlberg & Kramer, 1969) was to accept the apparently downward movement at face value as an ego development-related regression: the respondents had apparently "kicked ... their Stage 5 morality and replaced it with good old Stage 2 hedonistic relativism" (Kohlberg & Kramer, 1969, p. 109). Elliot Turiel (1974, 1977) argued, however, that the Stage 2 label for the college relativism belied its actual sophistication. Kohlberg came to agree; he (1973b, 1984) then reinterpreted the stage significance of selected longitudinal data, eliminating the "regression" through certain refinements in stage description and scoring. As Anne Colby (1978) and Kohlbergian colleagues (myself among them: see Colby et al., 1983; cf. Colby et al., 1987) explained, seven longitudinal cases were selected for the refinement work. The refined scoring system, constructed through scrutiny of these cases, was "used to score the remaining interviews in the longitudinal study" (p. 9), thereby providing a test of whether the refined stage constructs evidenced invariant stage sequence.

The refined system rested on Kohlberg's reinterpretation of the apparent regression from the highest stages to Stage 2 as in fact a transition ("$4^{1}/_{2}$"). Kohlberg (following Turiel) argued that, although the moral judgment of the "regressed" college students resembled in content the naive hedonism and instrumental pragmatism of the young Stage 2 participants, the college-level thinking was actually far more abstract and philosophical. For example, although a 20-year-old college student's initial moral judgment response to Heinz's dilemma ("If he values her life over the consequences of theft, he should do it.") resembled "good old Stage 2 relativism," further questioning revealed greater sophistication. Instead of offering instrumental reasoning, the student explained that people "have varying values and interest frameworks [that] produce subjective decisions which are neither permanent nor absolute" (Kohlberg & Kramer, 1969, p. 110). Kohlberg identified two distinct "levels of discourse" or "social perspectives": Whereas naive Stage 2 moral judgment aimed at "justifying moral judgment to an individual selfish actor," the discourse evident in the college students' moral judgment protocols was beyond Stage 4, aimed at "defining a *moral theory* and justifying basic moral terms or principles from a standpoint outside [or prior to] that of a member of a constituted society" (Kohlberg, 1973b, p. 192). The "theory," emphatically "defined" by the "4$^1/_2$," thinkers, was a meta-ethical skeptical relativism (Turiel, 1977) that Michael Boyes and Michael Chandler (1992) called extreme or "unbridled." Boyes and Chandler attributed this epistemological and moral relativism to the impact of "newfound" formal operations:

> The achievement of formal operational models of reasoning, while a decided advantage to those living in a culture as riddled with abstractions as our own, is not accomplished without certain short-run costs. One of these is that the new-found capacity for reflection characteristic of formal operational thinkers serves to transform the isolated or case-specific uncertainties of childhood into an altogether more ominous set of generic doubts... [leading for a time to] unbridled relativism. (pp. 284–285, emphasis added)

To establish the "4$^1/_2$" transition as part of an invariant sequence, the refined analysis scrutinized not only the college but also the high school data, specifically, the "principled-sounding" moral judgments. *Truly* principled moral judgment must be more sophisticated than that. After all, if the new 4$^1/_2$ thinking was at a meta-ethical, theoretical, even philosophical level of discourse, then should not the moral judgment beyond 4$^1/_2$ also evidence at least this level? Furthermore, should not 4$^1/_2$ skepticism naturally lead to more adequate levels of moral judgment? Unbridled relativism seemed to Kohlberg to be inherently unstable from internal contradictions: if all morality is subjective, arbitrary, and relative, then why wouldn't those characteristics apply to the attendant claim that one should not impose one's morality on others? Accordingly, relativism undermines itself. Hence, sooner or later (at least for reflective adults, postmodernists notwithstanding), 4$^1/_2$ should destabilize.[3] The internal contradictions of meta-ethical relativism should eventually "disequilibrate" or perplex the thinker and prompt a "reequilibration" leading to movement beyond unbridled relativism to the achievement of post-skeptical rationalism:

> What comes to be understood by this class of especially mature young persons is that, despite the inescapably subjective character of the knowing process, it is still possible to settle upon methods and standards for deciding that certain beliefs and courses of action have better legs to stand on than do others.
> (Boyes & Chandler, 1992, p. 285)

Postskeptical rationalism in turn provides the nonrelative epistemological "legs" for principled, philosophical moral judgment stages. "From reflection upon the limits of customary morality in very varied cultural and educational circumstances"—and upon the internal contradictions of unbridled relativism—emerges the "natural" (as opposed to professional) philosophical (Stage 5) structure comprising "notions of natural rights, social contract, and utility" (Kohlberg, 1973a, p. 634). Whereas the level of discourse of the philosophical post-college adult data was seen as *genuinely* principled and scored accordingly, the discourse of the ostensibly principled high school adolescent moral judgment was judged in the refined analysis to be merely social conformist or member-of-society.

Dealing with Two New Problems

Although they restored invariant sequence, these refinements of the stages created two major new problems: (a) a strain upon the logical coherence of the so-called conventional level and (b) a worsening of nonuniversality at the so-called postconventional level.

Straining "Conventional" The first problem was that the revised "conventional level" (now also called "member-of-society" perspective) was internally contradictory. The two supposedly "conventional" stages, 3 and 4, now included profound expressions of "principled-sounding" moral ideality. How could a participant whose moral judgment represents an internalization of "the rules and expectations of others, especially those of authorities," produce moral judgment conceptualizing "the moral value of life as taking precedence over obedience to laws or authority"?

Innovation of Moral Types A/B. Perhaps in an effort to deal with this problem and save the "conventional level" designation for Stages 3 and 4, Kohlberg (1984) introduced Moral Type A or B (see Chapter 5). Roughly speaking, in Kohlberg's 1960s revision, the dissertation-version Stage 3 (good boy–nice girl) and Stage 4 (law and order) moral judgment became designated respectively as Stage 3 Type A and Stage 4 Type A, whereas the previously postconventional, "principled-sounding" moral judgment became designated as either Stage 3 Type B (basic and universalized interpersonal ideals) or Stage 4 Type B (basic and universalized societal ideals). Alongside caring for friends and living up to interpersonal expectations (Stage 3A) were placed concerns for *mutual* good faith or understanding and for *universalized* caring (Stage 3B). Alongside concerns with fixed responsibilities or authority and the givens of the law (Stage 4A) were placed concerns with *ideal* responsibility to contribute to a *better* society and with *moral* law (Stage 4B).

Although Stages 3B and 4B embody moral ideality, Kohlberg argued that they are still at the conventional level because, like Stages 3A and 4A, their expression is only "intuitive," not theoretical in any clear or precisely articulated way. Intuitive appeals to the priority of life in the Heinz dilemma, for example, might be (see Colby et al., 1987) that "a person's life is more important than money" (Stage 3B) or that "the value of human life is more important than society's need for law in this case" (Stage 4B). For a postconventional score, the expression would have to make the point in a more explicitly principled way, such as "a human life was at stake ...

that transcends any right the druggist had to the drug" (Stage 5) or, best of all, a Stage 6 formulation from a philosopher:

> Since all property [such as the drug] has only relative value and only persons can have unconditional value, it would be irrational to act in such a manner as to make human life—or the loss of it—a means to the preservation of property rights. (Kohlberg, 1971, p. 209)

This insistence upon explicit theoretical or philosophical formulation struck an odd note in the cognitive developmental endeavor to identify *implicitly* evident patterns or structures in social and nonsocial cognitive development.

The Rarification of Postconventional Moral Judgment The elevation of theoretically over intuitively expressed justifications led to a second problem: rarification or elitism of the highest stages (Gibbs, 1979). Although this refinement did restore invariant sequence, it also generated "a fairly radical change in age norms" (Colby et al., 1983, p. 67). In addition to straining the meaning of "conventional," the relocating of "principled-sounding" but merely intuitive justifications to the conventional level and the criteria of sophistication for the postconventional stages left for those stages precious little material. This problem was evident despite an effort, in the final scoring system, "to put the focus of the scoring back on operative moral judgments rather than in ultimate justification and metaethical assumptions" (Colby, 1978, p. 93). Given this problem, it is no wonder that, as Kohlberg recollected, the "final stages" were "found"—or, more accurately, *refined*—to be "rare." As we noted, Kohlberg's Stages 5 and 6 were already uncommon in his original 1950s formulation, but now the problem became severe. By the new scoring stringency, *none* of Kohlberg's longitudinal participants reached postconventional moral judgment before adulthood. Even in the adult years, only 13% fully or partially reached Stage 5, and *all* of those "had some *graduate* education" (Kohlberg, 1984, p. 458, emphasis added). Stage 6 became so rare that Kohlberg was led to "suspend" (p. 273) his empirical claims for it and eliminate it from the scoring manual.[4] He acknowledged that his revised description and scoring of Stage 6 "came from the writings of a small elite sample, elite in the sense of its *formal philosophical training* and in the sense of its ability for and commitment to moral leadership" (p. 270, emphasis added).

The rarity problem with the philosophically trained "discourse" of the final stages was also evident in cross-cultural research. As Kohlberg (1984) noted in his recollection, he was especially concerned with "whether the stages were really universal in non-Western cultures." In a cross-cultural review, John Snarey (1985) noted that Stage 5's "frequency within any particular sample is seldom high" and that *none* of Kohlberg's longitudinal participants unambiguously reached Stage 6. Snarey concluded that even Stage 5 is based on the individualistic philosophies of "Kant, Rawls, and other Western philosophers" and hence is "incomplete" (p. 228). Snarey suggested that the characterization of Stage 5 be supplemented with more "collective"

(p. 226) postconventional principles from non-Western societies (cf. Vasudev & Hummel, 1987). Yet even Stage 5 is inappropriate as a description of moral judgment maturity, not because it is cross-culturally incomplete but more basically because *any* theory-defining level, even in broadened form, misrepresents moral judgment maturity as the exclusive province of the philosophically or theoretically articulate.

Why Not Discard Dewey's Trichotomy?

The two problems created by Kohlberg's stage revisions—contradiction within the conventional-level construct and rarification at the postconventional level—both derive from a generic problem: Kohlberg's persistence through his three decades of work in assimilating his longitudinal moral judgment data to a Procrustean bed, namely, his Deweyan conceptual trichotomy (preconventional, conventional, post-conventional). Kohlberg was correct that there is more to moral development than the basics of childhood and adolescence. Aspects of Kohlberg's stage refinement were quite valid; for example, his innovations of the Moral Types A and B. Indeed, the moral clarity or ideality of Type B judgment represented a newer and more appropriate sense of "postconventional thinking"—not as an elite level but rather as an insightful mode of moral perception (see Chapter 5). Precisely because of these valid contributions, however, it is time finally to discard Dewey's preconventional-conventional-postconventional trichotomy so that a more accurate depiction of basic moral judgment development and maturity can emerge.

Adult Moral Development in Kohlberg's Theory

Dewey's influence on Kohlberg's theory was not entirely adverse. Although the imposition of Dewey's tri-level sequence (impulsive, group conforming, reflective) led to serious problems of misrepresentation and elitism in Kohlberg's work, the Deweyan association of metacognitive *reflection* upon morality with the achievement of moral *maturity* is in principle valid. As Michael Tomasello and colleagues (Tomasello et al., 1996) observed, "Human beings have the seemingly unique capacity to treat their own behavior and cognition as 'objects of contemplation' in their own right" (p. 509). To treat as objects of contemplation one's thought and behavior—and, indeed, the phenomena and contexts of one's life—is to disembed oneself from those contexts, to become aware of the constellation in which one finds oneself (Fromm, 1955; cf. Kegan, 1982; Mustakova-Possardt, 2000). Accordingly, "the mature thinker may think about all manner of abstract ideas and ideals in such areas as morality, religion, and politics" (Flavell et al., 2002, p. 182). Although Kohlberg's conceptualization of reflective moral principles in terms of adult moral judgment stages ($4^1/_2$, 5, 6) can be questioned, his association of hypothetical reflection or contemplative disembedding with growth in moral judgment maturity is valid.

Beyond Invariant Sequence

Besides relating metacognitive reflection to the achievement of higher moral judgment stages, Kohlberg also discussed two ways in which such reflection contributes to adult moral development *beyond* an invariant sequence of stages. First, a contemplative adult may propose a systematic or formal philosophy of ethics. Second, a contemplative adult *in existential crisis* may derive a deeper and broader perspective on the moral life.

Formal Philosophy

Adults who become professional philosophers may reflect on basic "natural" ethics and go on to develop and publish formal theories. A formal theory may systematize or build from a "'natural' moral-stage structure" such as the Stage 5 judgment of laws "by the light of a social contract, by rule-utilitarianism, and by some notion of universal or natural rights" (Kohlberg, 1973a); or from the Stage 6 ethics of universalizable claims. Indeed, Kohlberg saw "natural" Stages 5 and 6 as the generative sources, respectively, for these "two major families of formal moral theory," namely, contractarian and Kantian ethics (p. 634). But after attaining the maturity of the natural and even the professional moral philosopher, then what?

Metaphorical "Stage 7"

Metacognitive, contemplative reflection can lead not only to formulations of professional philosophy but also to existential concerns:

> Even after attainment of Stage 6's clear awareness of universal principles, a fundamental ethical question still remains, namely, "Why be moral? Why be just in a universe that appears unjust?" This question asks whether there is any support in reality or nature for acting according to universal moral principles.... This question entails the further question, "Why live?"; thus, ultimate moral maturity requires a mature solution to the question of the meaning of life. This in turn, is hardly a moral question per se. (Kohlberg & Ryncarz, 1990, p. 192, emphasis added; cf. Kohlberg & Power, 1981)

Mature metacognitive thinkers encountering ultimate questions—meta-ethical, existential, even spiritual and ontological—often first experience "despair," which "can arise when we first begin to see ... the finitude of our individual self" (p. 192). There is hope, however, for movement beyond despair. After all, individual finitude cannot be seen except from some (at least dimly intuited) perspective of holistic infinity. Emerging from the despair of finitude, then, is a

> cosmic perspective [in which] what is ordinarily ground [i.e., nature or the universe] becomes foreground, and the self is no longer figure to the ground. We sense the unity of the whole and ourselves as part of that unity. In the state of mind I metaphorically term Stage 7, we identify ourselves with the cosmic or infinite

perspective and value life from its standpoint. . . . If we are aware of the relationship of all people and things to the whole of Nature, then we continue to love the whole in spite of the disappointments or losses [of life]. (Kohlberg & Ryncarz, 1990, pp. 192, 196)

This initially dim but increasingly clear transcendent intuition, characterizable as a gestalt-like shift in figure-ground perception, parallels the earlier movement through the

adolescent crisis of relativism, [transition] $4^1/_2$, [which] can occur only because there is a dim apprehension of some more universal ethical standard in terms of which the cultural code is relative and arbitrary. To explore the crisis of relativism thoroughly and consistently is to decenter from the self, reverse figure and ground, and see as figure the vague standpoint of principle that is the background of the sense of relativity. (Kohlberg & Ryncarz, 1990, p. 195)

Unlike the rational, theory-defining resolution of $4^1/_2$, however, the resolution of existential despair cannot be resolved "solely on the basis of formal operational thought." Rather, the existential resolution seems also to require a "mystical experience" (p. 206) or "experience of a nonegoistic or nondualistic variety. . . . Even persons who are not religious may temporarily achieve this state of mind in certain situations, as when on a mountaintop or before the ocean" (Kohlberg & Ryncarz, 1990, p. 192).

Despair is overcome and the moral life is again valued as existential thinkers and meditators shift to this cosmic perspective. Such a perspective brings some resolution of ultimate questions: "Well-developed moral intuitions [are seen to] parallel intuitions about nature or ultimate reality" (p. 197). For example, we see that "our consciousness of justice . . . is parallel to, or in harmony with, our consciousness of . . . the larger cosmic order" (Kohlberg & Ryncarz, 1990, p. 196). Concurrently, an eternal love displaces temporal desires:

If pleasure and power are not intrinsic ends, only the love of something eternal and infinite . . . can be an intrinsic end. . . . The knowledge and love of Nature is a form of union. Our mind is part of a whole, Spinoza claims, and if we know and love the eternal, we ourselves are in some sense eternal. (Kohlberg & Ryncarz, 1990, pp. 200–201)

The resonance between mind or morality (justice, love) and a larger, supportive reality will be explored further in Chapter 8. Pertinent to our present concerns is Kohlberg's speculation regarding his metaphorical Stage 7 as "essential for understanding the potential for human development in adulthood" (Kohlberg & Ryncarz, 1990, p. 207). Adult moral development goes beyond invariant stage sequence: grasping a sense of a deeper reality "relies in part upon the self's particular and somewhat unique life experiences" and hence is not a universal "developmental stage in the Piagetian sense" (p. 207).

A Critique and New View

In our view, moral development beyond "natural" moral stages need not await the formal enterprises or meta-ethical struggles of the adult years. For that matter, the so-called postconventional stages (5, 6) of "natural" moral philosophy already represent a kind of human development beyond basic moral judgment stages of maturity, one in which even the bright, well-read, contemplative adolescent can and sometimes does participate.

It is not that professional philosophical theorists draw inspiration from the discourse of postconventional-stage thinkers (as Kohlberg would have it), but rather that moral theorists (whether professional ethical philosophers or "postconventional" thinkers) draw inspiration from the *basic* stages of human moral understanding or social perspective taking found in childhood and adolescence. Analogously, the intuitive starting points for mathematical philosophers' theories of number can be found in children's constructions of the number concept. Philosophers and developmental psychologists interested in the scientific enterprise ponder analogs to scientific problem solving in the hypothetical and deductive reasoning of adolescents (e.g., Kuhn & Franklin, 2006).

Particularly interesting are the contributions to moral philosophy made by the basic moral judgment stages. The more promising philosophies tend to be those that start from more mature basic assumptions. The emphasis on authoritarian, unilateral power in Hobbesian (Leviathan) and might-makes-right philosophies would seem to reflect the centration- and appearance-oriented perspective taking of Stage 1. Social contract or libertarian theories that emphasize "maximum liberty consistent with the like liberty of others" (Locke, Mill) require and expect no more than Stage 2–level "pragmatic reciprocity" perspective taking. Finally, Kantian ethics, with its emphasis on respect, reversibility, and consistency, would seem to draw upon and gain richness from the moral point of view or Stage 3–level "ideal reciprocity" perspective taking. In this sense, Rawls's (1971) version of the social contract, in which initially egoistic participants do not know which position in the society will be theirs (the "veil of ignorance"), induces participants to adopt something tantamount to the moral point of view and agree to principles for a just society (Hoffman, 2000).

It must be stressed that these philosophies, whether of number, science, or ethics, are just that: philosophies. They may derive their starting assumptions from one or another basic stage, but they are not *themselves* basic stages.

Adult moral development in Kohlberg's theory includes not only the development of philosophies of ethics but also existential development. Again, whereas Kohlberg attributed prior-to-society, existential, and ontological reflection to the sophisticated adult, such reflection can also be found among contemplative Stage 3 and 4 (perhaps especially Type B) adolescents. That even adolescents can think from a prior-to-society vantage point about social contractarian and communitarian issues is suggested by their hypothetically reflective responses to Joseph Adelson and colleagues' classic "desert island" problem (How might the marooned individuals go about building a society?). One 18-year-old suggested that people would agree to laws "to set up a standard of behavior for people, for society living together so that they can live peacefully and in harmony with each other" (Adelson et al., 1969, p. 328). The adolescent was appealing, in effect, to the need for a social contract.

There is no reason that the objects of hypothetical contemplation must be restricted to the phenomena of dyadic exchanges, conventions, or even normative ethics. Sooner or later, the mature metacognitive thinker (whether chronologically adolescent or adult) may come to reflect on ultimate questions. Not only the theory-discoursing adult but even the Stage 3 but theory-discoursing *adolescent* can ponder meta-ethical, existential, spiritual, and ontological questions such as: Isn't all morality relative? Why be moral? Does our being alive matter? What is the meaning of life? What is reality? As did Carl Jung and Erich Fromm, Harold Kushner (1986) stressed that, at some point in our lives, "these are not abstract questions suitable for cocktail party conversations. They [can become] desperately urgent questions. We will find ourselves sick, lonely, and afraid if we cannot answer them" (p. 19).

A New View of Life-Span Moral Judgment Development

Hypothetical reflection and contemplation, then, play a pivotal role in our broad reconceptualization[5] of moral development. We see the life span development of "the right" (i.e., moral judgment and reflection concerned mainly with right and wrong) as entailing two major phases: standard and existential (see Table 3.1). Terming these modes of development *phases* is appropriate in that they overlap in time. Like other animal species, humans undergo certain standard sequences of cognitive and social-cognitive development, although we (through reflective contemplation) *surpass* other species in the method and flower of our intellectual achievement. The aim of Piaget's and Kohlberg's work was mainly to describe this standard intellectual development, which, as John Flavell and colleagues (Flavell et al., 2002) argue, can continue to grow in sophistication, scope, and consistency even in the adult years. Intriguingly, the hypothetical metacognitive ability that emerges in the course of standard development—the ability to disembed from the context of a thought or phenomenon and hold it as an object of contemplation—makes possible not only basic cognitive maturity but also existential awareness and the need for development in a poststandard sense. Particularly relevant to moral judgment and behavior is the emergence in existential development of an ethic of interconnectedness (Lorimer, 1990). The potential contribution of a "near-death experience" to existential or spiritual awareness and a moral life of connection is discussed in Chapter 8.

Table 3.1   Outline of the Life-Span Development of Moral Judgment and Reflection

Moral judgment involves ways of understanding the bases for moral decisions or values of right and wrong (but also of caring) in morality. The life span development of moral judgment and reflection consists of two overlapping phases (standard and existential).

I.   *Standard Development* (invariant albeit high-mixture stage sequence; USA age norms provided in Gibbs et al., 1992; and Basinger et al., 1995; cross-cultural age norms reviewed in Gibbs et al., 2007)

A.   *The Immature or Superficial Stages.*   Constructed in early childhood; typically, by adolescence, Stage 1 usage is negligible and Stage 2 usage has appreciably declined. The level is superficial in that the moral is confused with the physical or momentary (Stage 1) or with the pragmatic (Stage 2). Morality is also confused with egocentric bias and motives (blatantly at Stage 1, more subtly at Stage 2).

1.   *Stage 1: Centrations.*   Morality tends to be confused with physical size or power ("Daddy's the boss because he's big and strong") or with the momentary egocentric desires of one's mental life ("It's fair because I want it"). The overattention to a particular salient here-and-now feature of others or of one's egoistic perspective is called *centration* in Piagetian theory. The young child's vulnerability to the immediately salient is evident not only in moral but more broadly in social and nonsocial cognitive. Adult might-makes-right philosophies find inspiration from this stage.

2.   *Stage 2: Pragmatic Exchanges.*   Gains in mental coordination, perspective taking, and logic-related inference bring about a more psychological if pragmatic and still self-centered morality (e.g., the Golden Rule is misinterpreted as "do for others if they did or will do for you"). This concrete moral reciprocity underlies norms of "blood vengeance" found in some cultures and seems to be evident in the social behavior of chimpanzees. The emphasis on pragmatic deals provides foundational inspiration for social contractarian philosophies such as those of John Locke.

B.   *The Mature or Profound Stages.*   (Typically constructed and socialized during late childhood and adolescence, with elaboration in later years; but developmental delay sometimes seen among adolescents and even adults.) Moral judgment is mature insofar as it appeals to the intangible, ideal bases (mutual trust, caring, respect) and moral point of view (ideal reciprocity, How would you or anyone wish to be treated?) of social life. Mature morality applies mainly to interpersonal relationships (Stage 3) but may expand in scope to social systems (Stage 4). Care-related aspects of these stages are more prevalent among highly empathic individuals (Eisenberg et al., 2006). These stages presuppose attainment of the hypothetical and deductive abilities Piaget referred to as formal operations (these abilities also make possible poststandard development; see below). Although "Type A" versions of these stages tend to confuse this ideal morality with the maintenance of given interpersonal (Stage 3) or societal (Stage 4) expectations, "Type B" versions entail particularly clear perceptions of ideal reciprocity and render problematic Kohlberg's designation of these stages as necessarily "conventional level" and "member of society."

1.   *Stage 3: Mutualities.*   Do-as-one-would-be-done by or Golden Rule morality, based on third-person perspective. The core appeal is to ideal

reciprocity, mutual trust, or intimate sharing as the basis for interpersonal relationships. Kohlberg's early "good boy-nice girl" label applies to the Type A version; Type B may inspire moral-point-of-view (Baier, 1965) and other Kantian philosophies. A relativized version of Stage 3 (a truly sincere person's morals are right for him or her) is termed Transition 3/4 R (Gibbs et al., 1992) or $3^1/_2$ (Colby, 1978).

2. *Stage 4: Systems.* The social contexts for mutualities expand beyond the dyadic to address the need for commonly accepted values, institutions, and standards in a complex social system. Kohlberg's "law and order" label applies to a version termed Type A; Type B appeals to the values of an ideal society.

II. *Existential Development* (qualitative changes but no longer characterizable as an invariant stage sequence. Although associated with adulthood, this phase of life can begin as early as adolescent for some individuals; throughout the lives of others, however, this phase may remain absent). Existential development transcends the standard moral judgment stages. The existential phase involves hypothetical contemplation, meta-ethical reflection, the formulation of moral principles or philosophies, and spiritual awakening or ontological inspiration. In epistemological terms, meta-ethical reflection tends to evolve from relativism (cf. Kohlberg's "$4^1/_2$") to postskeptical rational perspectives. The theoretical products of contemplation can include those of "natural" (cf. Kohlberg's "Stage 5" and "Stage 6") or professional philosophies. The most profound expressions of existential development involve transcendent ethical insights (such as an ethic of interconnectedness; Lorimer, 1990) emergent from meditation, existential crises (cf. Kohlberg's metaphorical "Stage 7"), or near-death crisis events. Such deep inspiration can diminish cognitive distortions and revitalize dedication to the moral life.

Source: Adapted from J. C. Gibbs (2003). *Moral development and reality: Beyond the theories of Kohlberg and Hoffman (1st ed.).* Thousand Oaks, CA: Sage Publications. Used with permission.

Our two-phase view of life-span moral judgment development, then, involves the following points, articulated in this and the preceding chapter:

- Life-span moral judgment development consists of two overlapping phases: standard (involving an invariant sequence of stages comprising a rough age trend) and existential (involving meta-ethical, philosophical moral judgment as well as ontological and spiritual concerns and intuitions).
- Standard development consists of two overlapping levels, each of which nests two stages: immature (Stage 1, Centrations and Stage 2, Exchanges) and mature (Stage 3, Mutualities and Stage 4, Systems). The crucial event is the emergence of ideal moral reciprocity (Stage 3).
- The standard stages are at least in part "constructed," particularly through certain facilitative conditions of peer interaction and, beyond childhood, broader contexts of social perspective taking. The constructive process also entails reflection and presupposes gains in working memory. An advanced metacognitive ability—namely, hypothetical and deductive reflection (in

particular, reflective abstraction)—may play a key role in the emergence of ideal moral reciprocity.

■ Although at least Stage 3 of the mature level is reached in most human societies, such maturity must be supported by societal norms, institutions of social interdependence toward common goals, and moral internalization if it is to displace immature morality in the social life of the culture.

■ Hypothetical reflection or contemplation (e.g., upon the meaning of life or the universe) also plays a key role in the emergence (during adolescence or adulthood) of the existential phase of human development. Persons may develop existentially from sustained contemplation but also from sudden insights or inspirations (as may occur during meditation, "soul-searching" crises, life-threatening circumstances, or other existentially profound events).

Conclusion

The late Lawrence Kohlberg deserved considerable credit for championing and elaborating the themes of the cognitive-developmental approach, putting cognitive moral development on the map of American psychology, relating moral psychology to philosophy and vice versa, encouraging attention to moral judgment development beyond the childhood years, and recognizing the role of reflection or contemplation in the achievement of moral judgment maturity. Nonetheless, as his stage theory evolved, it increasingly distorted basic moral judgment development and maturity. In Kohlberg's theory of stages and Deweyan levels, construction is confused with internalization and basic understanding with reasoning that reflects philosophical training. Contractarian and Kantian philosophies should be seen not as postconventional, final stages in an invariant sequence but rather as products of hypothetical reflection on normative ethics, stemming from the morality of one or another of the basic moral judgment stages. Adults who contemplate their morality and formulate ethical principles have *not* thereby constructed a new Piagetian stage. They *have*, however, engaged in a developmental process of existential inquiry with personal relevance for ethical living:

> Merely the explicit formulation of principles about obligations should make us more sensitive to those obligations. It should make us less liable to be deceived by selfish ethical reasoning in ourselves or others. It should make us more perceptive in our moral assessment of ourselves and our motivation. (Brandt, 1959, p. 14)

In other words, formulating principles of ethics should render us less vulnerable to self-serving cognitive distortions (see Chapter 6). Generally, disembedding from and reflecting on moral right and wrong should promote moral development and the cognitively based motivation of behavior. "The right" plays a key role in morality and moral development. Also figuring into any *comprehensive* discussion of moral development and the motivation of moral behavior, however, is "the good." At the core of promoting the good is empathy—the primarily *affective* motive—to which we now turn.

Notes

[1]Roger Bergman (2006) correctly pointed out that the three-level typology represented a minor element in Dewey's overall constructivist philosophy of development, and that Kohlberg was also inspired by Dewey's constructivism. The fact remains, however, that Kohlberg (1991) did explicitly attribute his preconventional-conventional-postconventional scheme to Dewey (Gibbs, 2006a).

[2]Despite his own caveat regarding variability in usage, Piaget (1932/1965) did at numerous points refer to his overlapping phases as "stages."

[3]Colby (2008) urged college educators to move beyond a laissez faire attitude:

> College students' moral relativism ought to be cause for concern among educators, because beliefs such as "everyone is entitled to his own opinion and there is no way to evaluate the validity of those opinions," prevents students from engaging fully in discussions of ethical issues, learning to articulate and effectively justify their views, and adopting new perspectives when presented with high quality evidence and arguments. (p. 399)

[4]Stage 6's suspension was only temporary. Despite its empirical rarity, Stage 6 was subsequently revised further and reintroduced as the philosophical end state of moral judgment development (Reed, 1997; see Kohlberg, Boyd, & Levine, 1990).

[5]Although our reconceptualization offers a new view of life-span moral judgment and reflection, the view derives from an initial formulation in the late 1970s (see Gibbs, 1977, 1979).

"The Good" and Moral Development: Hoffman's Theory

OUR EXPLORATION OF MORAL DEVELOPMENT SHIFTS IN THIS CHAPTER from the right to the good. In particular, we shift from a concern with how we grow beyond superficial moral *judgment* to a concern with how we grow beyond superficial moral *feeling* and from *cognitive* sources of moral motivation such as justice or reciprocity to *affective* sources such as benevolence or empathy.[1] Accordingly, our conception of moral motivation will expand. Moral motivation derives not only from cognitively constructed ideals of reciprocity but as well from what Nel Noddings (1984) called an "attitude ... for goodness" (p. 2) and what Carol Gilligan (1982) claimed[2] was a distinctly feminine "voice" that urges responsible caring. Nancy Eisenberg (1996) called empathy "the good heart" and made impressive contributions to its measurement. Frans de Waal (2008) saw empathy's underpinning in a socially and emotionally sensitive "perception-action mechanism" common among mammals. Particularly impressive has been a theory that empathy researcher Carolyn Zahn-Waxler (Azar, 1997) concluded was "right on target" (p. 1): namely, the systematic, integrative work of Martin Hoffman (2000, 2008). As is Kohlberg's, Hoffman's work is described in virtually every developmental psychology textbook currently on the market.

Hoffman's theory of empathy-based moral development involves a socialization approach that starts with functional and biological considerations. Empathy in Hoffman's view is a multifaceted predisposition that eventuates in mature prosocial behavior through three key factors: biological bases, cognitive development, and socialization (especially, a parental discipline that fosters the child's empathy and internalization of prosocial moral norms).

The Empathic Predisposition

What is empathy? Metaphorically, it is the "spark of human concern for others, the glue that makes social life possible" (Hoffman, 2000, p. 3) and "the bedrock of prosocial morality" (Hoffman, 2008, p. 449). Literally, it is "feeling in," or with, another's emotion, that is, "feeling what another is feeling" (Hauser, 2006, p. 347). Phenomenologically, it can mean enduring another's suffering by imaginatively "enter[ing], as it were, into [the sufferer's] body," becoming "in some measure the same person with him" (Smith, 1759/1965, p. 261). Strictly speaking, mature empathy is "a vicarious response to others: that is, an affective response appropriate to someone else's situation rather than one's own" (Hoffman, 1981a, p. 128). Broadly speaking, it is a biologically and affectively based, cognitively mediated, and socialized predisposition to connect emotionally with others.

Background: Prosocial Behavior and Empathy

Ethologists, sociobiologists, and evolutionary moral psychologists have posited genetic programming as well as more complex bases (such as the empathic predisposition) for the cooperative, prosocial,[3] and even sacrificial behaviors that have been observed in many animal species. An intrusion into the hives of ants, bees, or termites will trigger genetically programmed suicidal attacks against the intruder by certain members of that insect group. Such behaviors are adaptive for the insect group because only some are programmed for sacrificial defense; others are programmed to carry out the group's reproductive activity (Campbell, 1972). Genetically programmed separation of survival and reproduction functions is not seen within groups of phylogenetically higher animal species.

Cooperative or prosocial behavior is also observed among social groups of mammalian species. Chimpanzee groups practice adoption of a motherless infant; they also engage in cooperative hunting and in sharing meat after a kill (Goodall, 1990). Baboons "may suddenly increase their vigilance if one among them is injured or incapacitated. When a juvenile in a captive baboon colony had an epileptic seizure, other baboons immediately turned highly protective" (de Waal, 1996, p. 52). Humans of all ages are likely to help others in distress, especially when other potential helpers are not around (e.g., Latane & Darley, 1970; Staub, 1974).

Groups whose members engage in such cooperative and prosocial behavior have obvious adaptive advantages. Such behavior can also be adaptive for the helper insofar as the individual helped is genetically related (even if the helper does not survive, some percentage of the helper's genes are passed on through the surviving recipient) (Hamilton, 1971). Prosocial behavior is also adaptive where the recipient may eventually reciprocate the help (Trivers, 1971). Robert Trivers described this reciprocal altruism in terms of "the folk expression ... 'you scratch my back—I scratch yours'" (de Waal, 1996, p. 25).

A certain minimum of cooperative and prosocial or altruistic behaviors is essential for the survival of human societies. It is unfeasible for any society to have "a cop on every corner" to deter egoistic motives or to have a moral exemplar on every corner to encourage prosocial ones. Requisite to the essential minimum of cooperative and prosocial behavior, then, is in turn some minimum degree of moral self-regulation. More than a century ago, the sociologist George Simmel (1902) depicted the indispensable role of moral self-reward in the regulatory functioning of society:

The tendency of a society to satisfy itself as cheaply as possible results in appeals to "good conscience," through which the individual pays to himself the wages for his righteousness, which would otherwise have to be assured to him through law or custom. (p. 19; quoted by Hoffman, 2000, p. 123)

Such moral self-reward derives partly from moral socialization and the internalization of a society's moral norms. A society needs help to accomplish moral socialization, however. Given the cross-cultural diversity of societal norms and of approaches to moral socialization, it is unlikely that requisite levels of prosocial behavior could be commonly achieved without some universal starting place in the child, as it were, for such socialization. Put positively, moral socialization and internalization must have help from a biological readiness or receptivity to altruistic appeals in socialization, that is, a predisposition to accept such norms.

Hoffman's word for such a biologically based predisposition is *empathy*. Empathic responsiveness emerges at "an early age in virtually every member of our species" and hence may be "as natural an achievement as the first step" (de Waal, 1996, p. 45). The biological substratum for empathy may inhere in neurophysiological pathways between the limbic system (specifically, the amygdala) and the prefrontal cortex (Blair, 2005; Brothers, 1989; Decety & Chaminade, 2003; Greene, Sommerville, Nystrom, Darley, & Cohen, 2001; Maclean, 1985).[4] Heritable individual differences in neural sensitivity may account for the higher correlation between identical, compared to fraternal, twins in their degree of empathic responsiveness (Zahn-Waxler, Robinson, Emde, & Plomin, 1992). Although biology imparts to empathy its earliest modes of arousal, more advanced cognitive modes subsequently enrich the empathic predisposition. These multiple modes promote the reliability and subtlety of the empathic response. That the complex human tendency to connect with the sufferings or joys of others is overdetermined and hence reliable suggests its functional importance for the life of the group.

Modes of Empathic Arousal

The empathic predisposition is complex at least partially because its modes of arousal in the human adult are both immature and mature. Hoffman argues that empathy has biological roots and can be activated by multiple modes or mechanisms. These modes are classifiable as basic (involuntary mechanisms of mimicry, conditioning, direct association) or as mature (representational or symbolic; mediated association, perspective taking). Although the basic modes are broadly shared across mammalian species (de Waal, 2008), the higher-order cognitive or mature modes flower most fully in humans. Depending on whether one's referent for empathy is basic or full-fledged, then, empathy is or is not common among mammals. We now review the immature and mature modes (see Table 4.1).

The Basic Modes

The three basic or primitive modes—mimicry, conditioning, direct association—constitute empathy in the preverbal years of childhood. These modes continue throughout life and give face-to-face empathic distress or joy an involuntary or compelling quality.

1. Mimicry   Mimicry involves motoric imitations that rapidly trigger feelings:

> The observer first automatically imitates and synchronizes changes in his facial expression, voice, and posture with the slight changes in another person's facial, vocal, or postural expressions of feeling....The resulting changes in the observer's facial, vocal, and postural musculature then trigger afferent feedback which produces feelings in the observer that match the feelings of the victim. (Hoffman, 2000, p. 37)

Table 4.1   Arousal Modes and Developmental Stages of Empathic Distress

I. Modes of Empathic Affect Arousal (operate singly or in combination)

Three (A, B, C) basic or non-voluntary mechanisms
A. Motor mimicry (automatic facial/postural imitation plus feedback)
B. Conditioning (self's actual distress paired with other's expression of distress)
C. Direct association (self's past distress resembles other's current distress)

Two (D, E) higher-order cognitive or mature modes (presuppose self-other differentiation, other milestones of cognitive development)
D. Verbally mediated association (other's distress communicated through language)
E. Social perspective taking (imagining self or anyone in other's place; self-focused and/or other-focused)

II. Developmental Stages of Empathic Distress (formed as arousal modes coalesce with cognitive development)

Three (1–3) immature stages
1. Global (newborn reactive cry)
2. Egocentric (can't tell other's distress from own empathic distress, seeks to comfort self)
3. Quasi-Egocentric (can tell the difference but seeks to comfort other with what comforts self)

Three (4–6) mature stages
4. Veridical (feels what other feels or would normally feel in the situation)
5. Beyond the situation (feeling for other's distressing life condition)
6. Distressed groups (feeling for group's life condition)

Hoffman (2000) suggested that mimicry "may not only be a prosocial motive but also a prosocial act" (p. 45) insofar as instant, ongoing nonverbal imitation communicates emotional connection: "By immediately displaying a reaction appropriate to the other's situation (e.g., a wince for the other's pain), the observer conveys precisely and eloquently both awareness of and involvement with the other's situation" (Bavelas, Black, Chovil, Lemery, & Mullett, 1988, p. 278).

2. Conditioning   Like mimicry, conditioning can induce quick and involuntary empathic responses. In terms of classical conditioning, basic empathy is an acquired or learned response to a stimulus that is temporally associated with one's previous affect (distress, joy, etc.). Hoffman (2000) suggested that empathic learning in this sense may be inevitable as mothers hold their infants and communicate through bodily contact, at one or another time, anxiety or tension: "The mother's accompanying facial and verbal expressions then become conditioned stimuli, which can subsequently evoke distress in the child even in the absence of physical contact" (pp. 45–46).

By the same token, the mother can condition positive empathic affect:

> When a mother holds the baby closely, securely, affectionately, and has a smile on her face, the baby feels good and the mother's smile is associated with that feeling. Later, the mother's smile alone may function as a conditioned stimulus that makes the baby feel good. (p. 46)

3. Direct Association   Empathy by association can take place even in the absence of conditioning. A child may, for example, become distressed upon seeing another child fall down on ice and cry simply because the scene evokes one's painful memory of a similar accident one experienced.

The Mature Modes

As Hoffman (2000, 2008) notes, empathy aroused by the basic modes (mimicry, conditioning, direct association) is relatively superficial: simple, passive, and here-and-now, "based on the pull of surface cues and requiring the shallowest level of cognitive processing" (p. 48). Superficiality persists even with the advent of language and rudimentary self-other differentiation (enabling awareness of others as independent selves with inner states). A young child, for example, may simply laugh along with a momentarily laughing but terminally ill peer.[5] As we have seen, a lack of mental coordination or decentration means superficial moral judgment. It also means superficial empathy. Although there are precocious exceptions, children's attention tends

> to be fixed or "centered" on the more salient personal and situational cues of another's distress in the situation. Owing to the powerful impact of conditioning, association, and mimicry, the "pull" of these cues may be powerful enough to capture a child's attention, with the result that his empathic response is based [exclusively] on these cues. (Hoffman, 2000, pp. 84–85)

With continued language and cognitive development (especially the metacognitive "awareness that one's feeling of distress is a response to another's distressing situation," Hoffman, 2000, p. 49), two more advanced modes of empathy arousal take root and make possible more subtle and expanded empathic responding. These two higher-order cognitive modes are verbally mediated association and social perspective or role taking.[6] The mature empathy made possible through these advanced modes is a deeper emotional connection with others. Although the mature modes are more "subject to voluntary control" and effort, "they too can be fast-acting, involuntary, and triggered immediately on witnessing the victim's situation" (Hoffman, 2000, p. 61).

4. Verbally Mediated Association   Empathy by association can also take place through the cognitive medium of language. For example, one may read a letter describing another's situation and affective state. Empathic responding through language-mediated association entails the mental effort of semantic processing and decoding. In the process, some "psychological distance" is introduced between observer and victim (Hoffman, 2000, p. 50). Accordingly, mediated association is a relatively low-intensity mode of empathic arousal.

5. Social Perspective Taking   Empathy is also aroused when one takes the role or situational perspective of the other person, especially, imagines oneself or anyone in the other person's place. Hoffman (2000) suggested that perspective taking can be either self-focused (imagining how one would feel in the other's situation) or other focused (imagining how the other person feels or how most people would feel in that situation). Although other-focused perspective taking is more readily *sustained*, self-focused perspective taking tends to be more *intense*, probably because it "activates one's own personal need system" (p. 56). This activation, however, renders self-focused perspective taking vulnerable to what Hoffman calls "egoistic drift," in which the observer "becomes lost in egoistic concerns and the image of the victim that initiated the role-taking process skips out of focus and fades away" (p. 56). One of Hoffman's students, after hearing that a pregnant friend's unborn child had Down syndrome, "became so engrossed in [her] own thoughts" and fears that she "forgot all about" her friend's specific circumstances (Hoffman, 2000, pp. 57–58). "Fully mature" (p. 58) social perspective taking achieves the best of both worlds—that is, sustained intensity—by "co-occurring, parallel processing" of both self and other (Hoffman, 2008, p. 442). Furthermore, it specifies the optimal sense of the social perspective taking entailed in ideal moral reciprocity.

The Complex Empathic Predisposition

The coalescence of the basic and mature modes of development renders the full-fledged empathic predisposition flexibly responsive to a diverse array of distress cues. Accordingly, the complex empathic predisposition is rich with contrasting qualities: shallow but also penetrating; fleeting or immediate and intense but also stable and sustained; narrow or here-and-now but also broad in scope (encompassing victims who are absent); automatic or involuntary but also voluntary; passive and unconscious but also effortful and conscious.

Given our thesis that moral development is growth beyond the superficial, we find most intriguing the developmental progression in the arousal modes from shallow processing (attention to surface or physically salient cues) to more subtle discernment and expanded caring. This superficial-to-profound theme becomes particularly evident in Hoffman's stages of empathy development.

Empathy and Cognitive Development: Stages of Empathic Distress

"Growing beyond the superficial," then, applies not only to moral judgment (Chapter 2) but also to the development of empathy. As the modes of the empathic predisposition interact with cognitive advances, we again see a cognitive developmental age trend toward more mature stages of moral perception, motivation, and behavior. When the trend beyond the superficial in morality refers not to moral judgment but to empathy or caring, however, cognition—although still crucial—loses the limelight. As we will see, it is depth of *feeling* in morality that is highlighted in Hoffman's theory.

In Hoffman's latest rendition of his model (Hoffman, 2008), "empathy develops along with the development of cognitive self-other concepts, in six stages" (p. 444; see Table 4.1), from immature (Stages 1–3) to mature (Stages 4–6). Hoffman does not emphasize the stage construct. Although he would presumably expect his sequence to be fairly standard across cultures, he does not explicitly claim that the stage sequence is invariant. Much as Piaget might have said for moral judgment phases, Hoffman points out that "the age levels assigned to the stages and transitions between stages are approximate and individual differences can be enormous" (Hoffman, 2000, p. 64). The developing arousal modes interact with the child's growing understanding of the self and other to produce overlapping stages of increasing discernment and subtle empathic emotion. One can say generally that the empathy stages emerge for the most part in infancy and early childhood (in contrast to the stages of moral judgment). However, the emergence of Hoffman's most mature stage may await adolescence (in any event, Hoffman's examples of this stage are drawn exclusively from adolescents and adults). Like Kohlberg's later moral judgment stages, Hoffman's later stages of empathy entail expansions in social scope, e.g., "an awareness that others (and oneself) have 'personal histories, identities, and lives beyond the immediate situation'" (p. 64). We now describe Hoffman's immature and mature stages of empathy development.

The Immature Stages

The immature stages of (reactive, egocentric, quasi-egocentric) empathic distress are seen during the first year or so of life, when nonexistent, dim, or superficial self-other distinctions mediate the impact of the preverbal arousal modes upon social behavior. Hoffman discusses three immature stages of empathy.

Stage 1. Global Empathic Distress: Newborn Reactive Cry   When the newborn cries in reaction to hearing another's cry, that reactive cry is more than a weak imitation or simple reaction to a noxious stimulus. Rather, the newborn reactive cry is just as intense and vigorous as if the newborn itself were in distress. Hoffman (2008) regards the newborn's reactive cry as "the first instance of empathy without awareness" (p. 444) of self and other as at all distinct: "The 'other' to which the newborn is responding is probably sensed by the newborn as connected to the 'self,' that is, as part of the same global psychological entity as the self" (pp. 65–66). Yet the newborn's reactive cry is more likely to be triggered by the unfamiliar cry of another human newborn than by control stimuli that have included a computer-simulated cry, the cry of a chimpanzee, and even the newborn's own previous cry (Dondi, Simion, & Caltran, 1999; Martin & Clark, 1982; Sagi & Hoffman, 1976; Simner, 1971). Marco Dondi and colleagues (Dondi, Simian, & Caltran, 1999) noted that a newborn's familiar-unfamiliar distinction among the auditory stimuli is further evidence that even infants process new experience in relation to established prototypes or rudimentary schemas (Walton & Bower, 1993). Hoffman (2000, 2008) argued that the newborn's innate reactive cry response is triggered by mimicry, conditioning, or both.

Stage 2. Egocentric Empathic Distress   After several months of life, the reactive cry typically attenuates (less automatic, instant, or intense crying). Six-month-olds typically look sad and pucker their lips before crying, perhaps a beginning emotional regulation. By the end of the first year, infants engage in rather curious behavior upon witnessing a peer's distress: whimpering and watching the peer followed by behavior that relieves their *own* distress (thumb-sucking, head in mother's lap, seeking to be picked up and comforted, etc.). Although they can identify the unfamiliar and differentiate the other child as physically separate, they may still be "unclear about the difference between something happening to the other and something happening to the self" (Hoffman, 2000, p. 68)—hence their egocentric seeking of self-comfort as if that would remediate the observed distress. Empathically driven behavior in the egocentric or cognitively immature sense—and its uselessness for the distressed other—has been observed among infant rhesus monkeys:

> Once, when an infant had been bitten because it had accidentally landed on a dominant female, it screamed so incessantly that it was soon surrounded by many other infants. I counted eight climbing on top of the poor victim—pushing, pulling, and shoving each other as well as the infant. Obviously the infant's fright was scarcely alleviated; the response seemed blind and automatic, as if the other infants were as distraught as the victim and sought to comfort themselves rather than the other. (de Waal, 1996, p. 46)

Although "blind" or egocentric, such reactions can still marginally be considered prosocial insofar as their trigger is *another's* distress.

Stage 3. Quasi-egocentric Empathic Distress During the second year, children try to help the distressed peer, suggesting a clear sense of the peer as a separate other. Nonetheless, their "help" is still more appropriate to relieving their own discomfort (e.g., bringing a distressed peer to one's own mother even though the friend's mother is present or offering one's own rather than the peer's favorite toys)—suggesting a somewhat egocentric projection of one's own onto others' inner states and needs. This egocentric projection is a bias that, as we have learned from cognitive-developmental work (Chapter 2), dissipates but does not disappear entirely even among adults. Hoffman (2000) argued that egocentric projections are especially evident in the empathic responses of infants.

The Mature Stages

Mature empathic distress is profound in that it connects with the authentic inner experience and life situation of another individual or group. This deep level of empathic experience can be intense and even life-changing (see examples in Hoffman, 2008; and Chapter 9).

Contributing to the decline of egocentric bias and foundational to deep, veridical empathy is a key developmental milestone in the self-other distinction, namely, the recognition of one's bodily self.[7] Some time around the middle of the second year, children begin to realize that their mirror image is a reflection of their physical selves (Lewis & Brooks-Gunn, 1979). Physical self-recognition may signify an awareness of self (and, by extension, others) as an active self with inner experiences. Self-recognizing children

> sense their body as containing, and being guided by, an inner mental self, an "I,"
> which thinks, feels, plans, remembers . . . [and understand] that one is somebody
> separated from others not just physically but also in terms of inner experience;
> and that one's external image is an aspect of one's inner experience. This makes
> it possible for one to realize that the same holds true for others: Their external
> image is the other side of their inner experience. (Hoffman, 2000, pp. 72–73)

Such a metacognitive awareness of others *qua others* may enable the child to decenter from self, experience veridical empathic distress, and appropriately perspective take (e.g., to recognize and appreciate that one's upset, crying friend would be better comforted by his or her *own* teddy bear, parent, etc.).

Accordingly, although children upon seeing others in distress continue to experience some ego-oriented discomfort, they also come to experience compassion or sympathetic distress. This partial "transformation" of egocentric empathy into sympathetic empathy means that, from childhood on, people "want to help because they feel sorry for the victim, not just to relieve their own empathic distress" (Hoffman, 2000, p. 88). Again, however, egocentric bias and "a purely [egocentric] empathy may remain . . . even in adulthood" (p. 89).

Mature empathic distress is accurate or veridical and evident both in the context of the immediate situation and beyond that situation. Hoffman (2008) delineates three stages of mature empathic distress.

Stage 4. Veridical Empathy   Less egocentric or more aware of the other as distinct from self, the young child begins to experience socially accurate or veridical empathy. "Veridical empathy has the basic features of mature empathy, but becomes more complex" or profoundly discerning with cognitive development (Hoffman, 2008, p. 445). For example, preschoolers begin to understand that an event can evoke different emotions in different people and that people can control the expression of their feelings. Older children begin to grasp mixed or subtle emotions and to take into account social context in judging another's feelings (see Chapter 2). A child may be judged to be sadder if distress over a broken toy occurs despite friends' entreaties not to be a "crybaby" (Rotenberg & Eisenberg, 1997).

Stage 5. Empathic Distress Beyond the Situation   As temporal decentration (or extension of time perspective; Chapter 2) develops, self and others are increasingly understood to have not only present inner states and situations but also experiential histories and prospective futures, that is, to have coherent, continuous, and stable identities. The preadolescent responds, then, not only to immediate expressive or behavioral cues but as well to information concerning the other's life condition, knowing that momentary expressions can belie deeper emotions or mood states. In contrast to the child's simple empathic connection with the laughter of a terminally ill peer, for example, mature individuals may experience a more complex emotion that encompasses joy and sadness (but see Note 5).

Stage 6. Empathy for Distressed Groups   With broader social experience, beyond-the-situation veridical empathic distress can lead to a sixth stage, as empathy for an entire group's life condition emerges:

> It seems likely that with further cognitive development, especially the ability to form social concepts and classify people into groups, children will eventually be able to comprehend the plight not only of an individual but also of an entire group or class of people such as those who are economically impoverished, politically oppressed, social outcasts, victims of wars, or mentally retarded. This combination of empathic distress and the mental representation of the plight of an unfortunate group would seem to be the most advanced form of empathic distress. (Hoffman, 2000, p. 85)

Empathy and Prosocial Behavior: Cognitive Complications and Empathy's Limitations

Although empathy may be the "bedrock of prosocial morality" (Hoffman, 2008, p. 449), activated empathy even at the mature stages does not necessarily eventuate in prosocial behavior. Empathy's relationship to prosocial behavior is complicated by the intervening role of certain cognitive processes, as well as by certain biases or limitations that may be natural to empathy itself.

How Is the Situation Interpreted? Cognitive Complications of Attribution and Inference

Although individuals with mature empathy tend to help distressed others, whether and how that tendency actualizes depends to a great extent on how the situation is perceived or interpreted. In other words, cognitive processes complicate the relationship between empathy and prosocial behavior. Cognition has thus far played a constructive role in the morality of the good: understanding or awareness of self and other facilitates a progressive maturity of caring for others. It is a matter of common observation, however, that mature empathy does not necessarily eventuate in prosocial behavior. Causal attributions and other interpretive cognitive processes can critically shape empathic emotion and hence the character of its contribution to social behavior.

People are mentally active, especially as mental coordination increases during childhood (Chapter 2). As persons perceive another's distress, they bring to that perception not only their empathic predisposition but as well their tendencies to make causal attributions and inferential judgments (Hickling & Wellman, 2001; Weiner, 1985). These cognitive tendencies can play a crucial mediating role. For an observer who is aware that it is another person who is in distress, empathy for the distressed other generally takes the form of, in Hoffman's terminology, *sympathy* (Hoffman, 2000, 2008). The formation of this empathy-based sentiment (empathy is sometimes used loosely to mean sympathy) requires a certain causal attribution, namely, that the distressing circumstances were beyond the sufferer's control (perhaps a natural disaster, unavoidable accident or illness, or death of a loved one). Empathy may not form sympathy, however, if the observer attributes responsibility to the victim for his or her plight. Especially in ambiguous circumstances, observers may be motivated to make precisely that causal attribution to reduce empathic overarousal (discussed later) or to support their belief in moral reciprocity (studied in social psychology as the motivated "just world hypothesis" or need to believe that the world is just; Lerner, 1980; see Hafer & Begue, 2005). Accordingly, it is often tempting to blame the victim even when such a causal attribution is unwarranted (cf. Chapter 6). When that happens, instead of being shaped into sympathy and thereby prompting prosocial behavior, empathy is reduced or neutralized as the victim is derogated.[8]

Attributing blame to the victim illustrates one transformation of the empathic predisposition into a specific empathy-based sentiment. There are others. Attributing the cause of another's distress to an aggressor (whether an individual or group or even a corrupt system) can shape one's empathic distress into *empathic anger*, even if the distressed victim is not angry at the time. *Empathy-based transgression guilt* derives from attributing the victim's plight to one's own actions. *Bystander guilt* derives from attributing that plight to one's *in*actions (for example, more than 40 years after having witnessed a continuing victimization, the author has still experienced bystander guilt over his passivity; see Chapter 1).

Closely related to blame attribution are justice inferences. Hoffman (2000) discussed not only causal attributions but also "inferences about whether victims deserve their plight" (p. 107) as cognitions that can fundamentally shape the nature of empathy's impact on behavior. "If the victim is viewed as bad, immoral, or lazy, observers may conclude that his or her fate was deserved and their empathic/sympathetic distress may decrease." As noted, there is a temptation to view the victim in precisely this way. If, however, the victim can only be "viewed as basically good, observers may conclude that his or her fate was undeserved or unfair and their empathic/sympathetic distress, empathic anger, or guilt may *increase*" (p. 107, emphasis added).

Such a perceived unfairness entails the violation of one's sense of justice or reciprocity and belief in a just world: Bad things should happen to bad—not good—people. As noted in Chapter 2, Hoffman (2000) acknowledges a common "preference for reciprocity" (p. 242) or fairness and even a motive to correct reciprocity imbalances or violations, to right a wrong. An inference of injustice (or activated moral principles, discussed later) can even "increase" the intensity of empathic emotions. Generally speaking, however, Hoffman grants reciprocity only a mediating or shaping role: The reciprocity-based perception of an undeserved or unfair fate "may transform [the viewer's] empathic distress into an empathic feeling of injustice" (p. 107). Hoffman's characterization of injustice as fundamentally a *feeling* is critiqued in Chapter 5.

Empathy's Limitations: Overarousal and Bias

In addition to transformative cognitive complications, certain limitations of empathy itself can compromise its contribution to rational moral evaluation or prosocial behavior. Hoffman identifies two such limitations: overarousal and empathic bias. As we will see, cognitive strategies, beliefs, principles, and other factors or processes can remedy these limitations and even promote prosocial moral development.

Empathic Overarousal

Overly intense and salient signs of distress can create an experience in the observer that is so aversive that the observer's empathic distress transforms into a feeling of personal distress; the personally distressed observer may then shift into egoistic drift (described earlier) and avoid the sufferer. The intensity level of empathic distress, in other words, can be postoptimal. Empathic overarousal is the downside of empathy's multiple arousal modes: combined arousals (especially if they include self-focused perspective taking, generating vivid mental images) often account for the postoptimal level of distress, a level that, ironically, can exceed the victim's actual level of distress. Chronic empathic overarousal, or compassion fatigue, is a problem well known to critical care nurses and other helping professionals.

There are exceptions to empathic overarousal or compassion fatigue. Consider dedicated clinicians, nurses, rescue workers, and other helping professionals, as well as other individuals highly committed to helping (perhaps as a loved one) or to caring principles. For these persons, "empathic overarousal may *intensify* rather than destroy one's focus on helping the victim" (Hoffman, 2000, p. 201). Beyond commitment to the role demands of a helping profession or to a principle of care, Hoffman refers to an important additional motivating factor—"the kind of person one is or wishes to be"— that we term *moral self-relevance* (see Chapter 5):

> *An observer may feel empathically motivated to help someone in distress, but he may in addition feel obligated to help because he is a caring person who upholds the principle of caring. This activation of a caring principle and the addition of one's "self" (the kind of person one is or wishes to be) should add power to one's situationally induced empathic distress and strengthen one's obligation to act on principle. (Hoffman, 2000, p. 225, emphasis added)*

In general, however, states of empathic overarousal do tend to induce egoistic drift and hence undermine the contribution of empathy to prosocial behavior.

Empathic Bias

Empathic bias is the second limitation of empathy. Within empathic bias, Hoffman distinguishes between familiarity-similarity bias and here-and-now bias. A prototype of the familiarity bias is the preference that develops for a stimulus to which one is repeatedly exposed (e.g., Zajonc, 1968). Roger Brown (1965) once wondered whether the Mona Lisa owes its popularity at least partly to its recognition value among museum tourists. The familiarity bias may be adaptive in an evolutionary context where survival and security of the group against external threat is of paramount importance. In this context, the functional value of prosocial behavior pertains to the survival of the prosocial actor's familiar "in-group" of family, friends, and others similar to oneself. Accordingly, arousal modes such as self-focused perspective taking are more readily activated by the distress cues of someone perceived as similar to oneself. By the same token, others perceived as dissimilar (such as Edward in the camp incident; see Chapter 1) are less likely to elicit empathy.

These considerations also apply to what Hoffman refers to as a "here-and-now" version of empathic bias, pertaining to distressed persons who are immediately present. Again, these are likely to be the members of one's in-group; such persons are especially likely to stimulate the primitive empathic arousal modes (physical salience-driven modes such as mimicry or conditioning). Although children with their pronounced centrations (see Chapter 2) are especially vulnerable, even mature observers capable of representing others' life conditions beyond the immediate situation are vulnerable to here-and-now bias. In experiments (e.g., Batson et al., 1995) and in real life, individuals often act to relieve the distress of an immediately present other, even when that prosocial act is unfair to comparably distressed but absent others. Indeed, distressed victims who are no longer salient may lose out in sympathy even to "*culprits* who are now the focus of attention and, for one reason or another, appear to be victims themselves" (Hoffman, 2000, p. 212). Moral perception may become further distorted as attributions of blame shift from the culprit to the victim.

Remedying Empathy's Limitations

The limitations of empathy might not be all bad; indeed, modest levels of empathic overarousal and bias might have some adaptive value. Might not some limitation or regulation of empathic distress promote more effective and sustainable prosocial behavior? After all, "if people empathized with everyone in distress and tried to help them all equally, society might quickly come to a halt" (Hoffman, 2000, p. 14). Beauchamp and Childress (2001) put the point in philosophical terms: "The more widely we generalize obligations of beneficence, the less likely we will be to meet our primary responsibilities [to those to whom we are close or indebted, and to whom our responsibilities are clear], which many of us already find difficult to meet" (p. 169). This issue relates to what has been called the "multiple claimants dilemma": How can one legitimately help some needy claimants but not others equally in need? Yet total equality of all claimants near and far, with no bias or gradient of care whatever, would place an impossible strain on the prospective helper. Of course, this practical point should not be stretched to excuse doing nothing to help alleviate distant suffering. Although their total elimination might be counterproductive, empathy's limitations of overarousal and bias should nonetheless be *reduced*.

Reducing Empathic Overarousal   As noted, states of empathic overarousal typically undermine the contribution of empathy to prosocial morality and hence should be reduced. Fortunately, empathic arousal levels are modifiable, especially through cognitive strategies and beliefs. Helpful in reducing empathic intensity to a more manageable level are (a) temporary "defensive" strategies such as thinking or looking at something distracting or looking ahead to a planned interlude (e.g., the "rest and relaxation" breaks of emergency care workers); (b) a self-efficacy belief (Bandura, 1977) that one has the requisite skills and other competencies to substantially alleviate the victim's suffering; (c) the activation of moral principles; and (d) habituation. As noted, principles of caring can sustain the prosocial work of highly committed individuals. Also, the broad scope or abstract quality of moral principles can help the empathizer "to 'decenter' from the salient features of the victim's plight, and thus respond with more appropriate ... empathic distress" (Hoffman, 2000, p. 238). As we will see, moral principles are particularly helpful in the regulation of empathic distress. Less conscious and voluntary than strategies, beliefs, or principles is habituation through repeated and excessive exposure to distress cues. If unchecked, however, habituation can reduce empathic arousal to suboptimal levels and even eliminate it.

Reducing Empathic Bias   Hoffman (2000) suggested that empathic bias reflects our evolutionary tendency to help those with whom we share the most genes, i.e., our primary group. He also suggested, however, that we can "transcend" our empathic bias if we make a "conscious deliberate effort to use our knowledge to reduce empathic bias through moral education" (p. 267). Similarly, Singer (1981) suggested that we "can master our genes" (p. 131) to expand our "moral circle" through the use of reason (cf. "moral insight," Bloom, 2004, p. 146).

Interestingly, our here-and-now and similarity-familiarity biases can be used against themselves. Hoffman suggested that moral educational or cognitive behavioral programs (see Chapter 7) make prominent use of a technique that, ironically, recruits our empathic bias to the service of its own reduction. The technique is called reframing or relabeling, as when we reframe an otherwise abstract outgroup with a suffering individual. Empathic distress for a vividly presented victim can generalize, as when a well-publicized, highly salient victim of a widespread disaster or severely crippling illness (say, a poster child for muscular dystrophy) elicits empathic distress and help that extends to the entire group of victims. Those who might not help a distressed group of anonymous individuals may help a needy child who becomes in effect a "foster child" in a long-distance relationship (photos received, letters exchanged, etc.; Singer, 1981). Similarly, a stranger in need can be assimilated into one's sphere of familiarity if the stranger is imagined as a friend or family member. Parents and moral or religious educators often attempt to broaden the scope of social perspective taking by encouraging contact and interdependence with other groups and appealing to "the universal qualities that make strangers similar to the self—for example, 'all men are brothers'" (Maccoby, 1980, p. 349).

Reframing, Aggression Inhibition, and Moral Development   Empathy for the "human face" of a group can not only broaden the referent for prosocial behavior but also inhibit aggression and promote moral development. And reframing may refer not to a "technique" but to an epiphany of social experience. Mark Mathabane (2002), a Black South African, remembered "learning to hate" white people as he grew up during the years of apartheid and oppression of Black people.

> *Learning to hate was...simple.... All it took was a gradual twisting of my humanity while I was growing up in the impoverished ghetto of Alexandria.... White policemen ... would invade our neighborhood in the middle of the night, break down our door and march my parents half naked out of bed, interrogate and humiliate my father and then arrest him for the crimes of being unemployed and harboring his family as illegal aliens in "white" South Africa ... White people could not be human. If they were, why did they not feel my pain? (p. A21)*

Yet Mathabane also remembered that, when he was 7 years old, a White person, a nun, did feel the pain of his family's oppression and predicament. When he saw the nun cry while listening to his mother's plight, he was

> *stunned by her tears, for they were the first I'd seen streak a white face. I remember saying to myself: "She feels my mother's pain. She's human after all, not a monster." (p. A21)*

Perhaps, then, "not all white people were unfeeling like the police." He wondered whether

by killing whites I would also kill people like the nun whose empathy had given my mother hope and whose help had saved me, by making it possible for me to get an education, from the dead-end life of the street and gangs. As long as there was that chance, I couldn't bring myself to kill in the name of hate. (p. A21)

He reflected that

guns, bombs, and tanks cannot defeat hatred. It can be vanquished only by humanity.... One is not fully human until one acknowledges and affirms the humanity of others—including one's enemies. Ultimately, the enemy is within the human family and not without. And once we acknowledge that, we will all have the courage ... [to] move beyond the darkness of mutually destructive hatred and revenge into the light of reconciliation and forgiveness. (p. A21)

It is worth noting that Mathabane's growth beyond the superficial in morality is captured in Kohlbergian as well as Hoffmanian theories. Mathabane's moral development was in part an *empathy-based* story of how empathy, reflection, and reframing humanized an enemy and thereby inhibited aggression. Mathabane's moral development was also in part a *cognitive-developmental* story, one of an appreciation and reflection that grew his moral judgment from Stage 2 retaliation to Stage 3 reconciliation and forgiveness. Although distinguishable, the Hoffmanian and Kohlbergian aspects of the story are intimately interrelated and complementary. Finally, Mathabane's growth into a deeper perception of common humanity was perhaps ultimately a *spiritual* story with ontological implications. We will save for later consideration (in Chapters 8 and 9) the question of moral development and reality.

Role of Moral Principles

Besides reframing and other cognitive processes, the activation of moral principles or "philosophical ideals" (Hoffman, 2000, p. 223) can also serve to remedy the limitations of empathy. Although moral principles per se are seen to "lack motive force" (p. 239) and are originally "learned in 'cool' didactic contexts [such as those of lectures, sermons]" (p. 239), they do have an affective motive power through bonding with empathy (we would add that moral principles can also gain *cognitive* motive power from moral reciprocity). Hoffman argues (and we would agree, Chapter 1) that there are basically two families of moral principle: caring and justice. Hoffman's additional claim that empathy bonds with and motivates moral principles is straightforward with respect to the principle of caring: "The link between empathic distress and [principles of] caring is direct and obvious. Indeed, caring seems like a natural extension of empathic distress in specific situations to the general idea that one should always help people in need" (p. 225). Empathy transforms caring ideals *into prosocial hot cognitions—cognitive representations charged with empathic affect, thus giving them motive force. How is this accomplished? I suggest that people in a moral conflict may weigh the impact of alternative courses of action on others. This evokes images of others' being harmed by one's actions; these images and empathic affects activate one's moral principles. The concurrence of empathy and principle creates a bond between them, which gives the principle an affective charge. (p. 239)*

Hoffman posits the same bonding process for principles of justice, that is, ideals of equality and reciprocity. Distributive justice emphasizes equality, but includes consideration (and images) of particular individuals' special neediness or effort in the determination of how much of a given set of goods should be distributed to whom.

Affectively charged moral principles can reduce empathic overarousal and biases insofar as they give "structure and stability to empathic affects" (p. 216). They embed empathic affects in cognitive representations, thereby imparting longevity: the empathic affects should survive in long-term memory. Structure, stability, and longevity mean that the mature individual is less vulnerable not only to overarousal but to underarousal as well. In other words, moral principles can serve to regulate and optimize the level of empathic distress. Moral principles "charged with empathic affect" can help to "stabilize" empathic responses or render them "less dependent on variations in intensity and salience of distress cues from victims, and over-arousal (or under-arousal) is less likely" (Hoffman, 2000, pp. 238–239). Moral principles and other cognitive regulators of empathy level, along with low impulsivity, permit effective and sustained prosocial behavior (Eisenberg et al., 2006; Chapter 5).

Empathy, Its Cognitive Regulation, and Affective Primacy

Beyond its "complicating" or transformative role, then, cognition can also regulate empathy. The optimal regulation of empathic affect is seen not only in terms of the stabilizing role of moral principles but also broadly in moral or rational decision-making. Although empathic feelings affectively charge an airplane pilot's knowledge and goals of safe landing, for example, those feelings must not be allowed to become disruptive. An optimal level is called for:

The airplane pilot in charge of landing his aircraft in bad weather at a busy airport must not allow feelings to perturb attention to the details on which his decisions depend. And yet he must have feelings to hold in place the larger goals of his behavior in that particular situation, feelings connected with the sense of responsibility for the life of his passengers and crew, and for his own life and that of his family. Too much feeling at the smaller frames and too little at the larger frame can have disastrous consequences. (Damasio, 1994, p. 195)

Although cognition can be quite active as it stabilizes, optimizes, or otherwise regulates affect, it is nonetheless affect that in the final analysis "comes first" in the motivation of much situational behavior. Cognition then mediates or moderates (regulates, transforms, directs, etc.) the impact of that initial affect on behavior. De Waal (1996) suggested that social perspective taking and other cognitive processes permit humans to direct more appropriately and effectively ("fine-tune") the empathic and helping tendencies shared with other cooperative animals:

> The cognitive dimension [has] to do with the precise channeling of [empathy].... Thus, in aiding a friend, I combine the helping tendency of cooperative animals with a typically human appreciation of my friend's feelings and needs. The forces that propel me into action are the same, but I carry out the mission like a smart missile instead of a blind rocket. Cognitive empathy [the ability to put oneself in the "shoes" of this other entity without losing the distinction between self and other] is goal directed; it allows me to fine-tune my help to my friend's specific requirements. (pp. 69, 80)

Like de Waal, Hoffman (1986, 2000) argues that affective forces (arousal modes of the empathic predisposition; cf. "action tendencies," e.g., Saarni, Campos, & Witherington, 2006) propel action (affective primacy) but gain more or less "smart" direction from cognition. Hoffman's (1986) emphasis, however, is on the interaction between affective and cognitive processes, rather than on affect as a prior force that can operate independently of cognition (e.g., Haidt & Bjorklund, 2008a, 2008b; Zajonc, 1984).

Is Empathy "the" Moral Motive?

That Hoffman views empathy as the exclusive motivator of moral behavior is suggested by his reference to empathy as providing "the" motive to rectify injustice or nonreciprocity—even though he also refers to motivation generated by a probable "preference" for reciprocity:

> If humans prefer reciprocity over nonreciprocity (most do, I think), *then a person who works hard and produces as much as someone else but gets paid less will feel angry, unjustly treated, and motivated to rectify the injustice. He will also,* to the extent that he is empathic, *feel empathic anger, have empathic feelings of injustice, and be motivated to rectify the injustice when someone else is treated unjustly [cf. cognitive primacy].* Thus, while empathy may not make a structural contribution to justice, it may provide the *motive to rectify violations of justice to others.* (Hoffman, 2000, pp. 228–229, first and third emphases added)

Our theoretical position can be reconciled with Hoffman's in this passage with the change of one word in the last sentence: Given our view of moral motivation, the *the* should be an *a*! Empathy provides *one* motive to rectify injustice, but the other motive—cited by Hoffman himself—is the reciprocity preference (especially, the ideal moral reciprocity motive).

Whether it is *a* or *the* moral motive, empathic or affective primacy also empowers the mental representations and causal schemas entailed in moral internalization. A mental representation of an event has been termed a "generic event memory," or "script" (cf. schema, Chapter 2):

> Scripts are derived from experience and sketch the general outline of a familiar event. . . . 3- and 4-year-olds are quite good at telling what happens in general in a familiar event such as having lunch at the preschool or going to the beach, the zoo, or MacDonald's (Hudson & Nelson, 1983; Nelson, 1981). . . . Discipline-encounter scripts . . . can be charged with the affects [e.g., empathy, empathy-based guilt] that accompany the event. (Hoffman, 2000, pp. 156–157)

Like moral principles, then, mental representations such as scripts owe their moral motive power to empathic affect. The development of scripts (or, more broadly, schemas) into morally "hot" cognitions is discussed further in the context of moral internalization.

The Empathic Predisposition, Socialization, and Moral Internalization

As noted at the outset of this chapter, the empathic predisposition is fairly reliable insofar as it is composed of multiple arousal mechanisms. Under optimal circumstances, one who sees another in distress is likely to help. More specifically: Biologically normal, cognitively and linguistically mature humans are likely to experience in bystander situations where no one else is around to help (or other situations where egoistic motives and biasing cognitive complications are not strong) a multidetermined empathic distress that generates sufficient motive power to elicit prosocial behavior.

Nonetheless, in addition to biological bases and cognitive development, socialization is crucial for an empathic predisposition to eventuate into mature and effective prosocial behavior. Most situations in life, after all, are less than optimal. In the broadest terms, the development of functionally adequate levels of cooperative and prosocial behavior in a human society requires not only appropriate biological and cognitive/linguistic development but also appropriate socialization and moral internalization. Socialization is needed especially because many situations are more conflictual than is the simple bystander situation and, accordingly, elicit basic egoistic motives or desires (hunger, thirst, sex, safety, dominance, etc.), egocentrically biased self-chatter, and associated emotions (impulses or immediate desires or pleasure, pain, fear, anger, etc.). These motives and biases—especially pronounced during the childhood years—can override empathy (see Chapter 5; cf. Zahn-Waxler & Robinson, 1995). Consider a situation in which a child in the first place *caused* another's distress:

> Child A says it is his turn and grabs a toy from child B, who grabs it back. They argue until A pushes B away, grabs the toy and runs. B starts to cry. A ignores B's crying and plays with the toy. (Hoffman, 2000, p. 138)

Such ambiguous conflict situations beg for adult intervention because they allow "each child to blame the other"; the neutralizing effect of other-blaming causal attributions on empathy was noted earlier. Furthermore, although cognitively developing children are increasingly able to decenter ("that is, to transcend the egoistic pull, free themselves from the grip of their own perspective, and take another's perspective as well"; Hoffman, 2000, p. 160), the ability to coordinate one's own with other viewpoints "is not enough to keep children's own viewpoint from capturing most of their attention in a conflict situation" (p. 160) that has elicited powerful egoistic and angry emotions. Such emotions can "blind" (p. 135) children to the harm they have done. Socialization support for decentration is necessary if each child is to understand the other's perspective and realize it is like his own ("He expects to be given a reason, not a flat refusal, just as I do"). It is also necessary if each child is to empathize with the other and anticipate his disappointment at not getting what he wants and for each child to accept his share of blame and be ready to make amends or compromise (p. 138).

Adult intervention, then, is often needed in child conflict situations. After all, "even highly empathic children can get emotionally involved when pursuing their goals or when their desires conflict with [those of] others" (Hoffman, 2000, p. 169). Adults may also react after a child has already done harm or damage, especially if the harm was serious and intentional (reflecting awareness and deliberation) or negligent (the child could have been aware and more considerate) and did not evidence spontaneous guilt or reparative behavior. Such interventions in the midst of or following transgression are discipline encounters. Although parent-child interactions during discipline encounters constitute but one dynamic in the family system (Parke & Buriel, 2006), they are, according to Hoffman, at the heart of moral socialization.

Socialization through Discipline Encounters

Not surprisingly, Hoffman (2000) advocates interventions in the discipline situation that encourage decentration or perspective taking through the elicitation and cultivation of empathy and transgression guilt—natural "allies" (p. 151; cf. Damon, 1988[9]) of the parent's prosocial cause. Specifically, Hoffman advocates the use of "inductions" or parental messages that "highlight the other's perspective, point up the other's distress, and make it clear that the child's action caused it" (p. 143).

To be effective, inductions must be delivered appropriately and with optimal power or influence. Parents who make effective inductions cast the message in a form appropriate to the maturity level of the child's available empathic arousal modes and cognitive development. Inductions with a preverbal toddler can point up an act's physical harm and thereby activate classically conditioned and direct associations. An intervening induction may point to the still-present crying victim:

> For inductive information to be understood well enough to arouse empathic distress
> and guilt at that age, it must simply and clearly point up the victim's distress and make
> the child's role in it salient ("You pushed him and he fell down and started to cry").

In processing their very earliest inductions, children probably integrate the cause-effect relation between their act and the victim's distress into the simple, non-moral physical cause-effect scripts. [These] scripts are [thereby] enriched and given a moral dimension (my actions can harm others). Furthermore, the scripts can be infused with empathic distress and a (rudimentary) guilt feeling, which gives them the properties, including the motivational properties, of affectively charged representations, or hot cognitions. (Hoffman, 2000, pp. 159–160)

With cognitive and linguistic advances, the child develops role or perspective taking and mediated association modes of empathic arousal. Accordingly, parents can now communicate more complex and subtle information concerning *emotional* harm.

Through this process [of progressively integrating the information in literally thousands of inductions over the childhood years], children's early, physical, non-moral causal scripts are gradually transformed into complex, generalized, affectively charged scripts pertaining to the effects of one's actions on others. (Hoffman, 2000, p. 161)

Of particular theoretical interest is Hoffman's construal of this moral internalization as a "constructive" process: Children "build up" or "*construct* an *internalized* norm of considering others" (p. 144, emphases added). At first blush, the juxtaposition of "constructing" with "internalizing" is odd; we saw in Chapter 2 (cf. Chapter 9) that construction has a special referent in Piagetian usage to logic and, in that sense, is not reducible to internalization. In a broader context, however, construction in Piagetian theory refers to an interplay in which the person actively assimilates, transforms, and adapts to environmental information. Insofar as Hoffman conceptualizes internalization not as simple transmission but instead in terms of constructive transformation, his usage is not inconsistent with a broad Piagetian (or, for that matter, Vygotskian) conceptualization (cf. Lawrence & Valsiner, 1993). Some knowledge, however adapted or transformed, *does* originate in the environment or culture (Piaget called it empirical knowledge; see Chapter 9). In this sense, *social* construction can be expanded beyond peer interaction to encompass inductive influences and moral internalization. The constructive value of inductive discipline suggests that Piaget (1932/1965) underplayed the role that parents can play in the moral development of the child (see Chapter 2; see also Walker et al., 2000).

Effective inductions are not only developmentally appropriate but are also conveyed in the context of an optimal level of parental power or influence. Children experience a certain degree of pressure to comply in a discipline encounter once they become aware of the relative power of parents. Furthermore, they care about parental approval and are vulnerable to anxiety in response to indications of parental disapproval. Induction and power (which generate in the child anxiety about the parent's approval) are the dimensions of any discipline initiative. Parental power is expressed either in physical terms (demands, threats, actual punitive or restraining force, or deprivation of a privilege or possession, i.e., "power assertion";

Hoffman, 1960) or psychological terms (love withdrawal). Even the most nurturing, inductively disciplining parents bring an implicit power dimension to the discipline encounter. Hoffman argued that parents' judicious use of power can promote moral socialization. Parents should bring to bear an optimal level of "pressure":

> *Too little pressure obviously gives children no reason to stop, attend, and process inductive messages.... Too much power assertion or love withdrawal directs children's attention to the consequences of their action for themselves.... Induction's explanatory feature reduces the arbitrary quality of the parent's demand, and by focusing on the parent's disapproval of the act and its harmful effects rather than on the child,... makes a high-anxiety, cognitively disruptive response less likely. (Hoffman, 2000, p. 153)*

The optimal level of pressure to attend to an inductive discipline is congruent with the broader balance between parent-centered (authoritarian) and child-centered (permissive) orientations achieved in authoritative parenting (Baumrind, 1989; Damon, 1995). Considerations relevant to the question of what constitutes "optimal" pressure for an induction include the type of situation (an intense conflict requires more pressure than, say, a negligent act to reach the "optimal" attention level[10]), a particular child's temperament (a higher level of pressure defines "optimal" for a willful than for a shy or inhibited child; cf. Kochanska, 1995), and cultural context (physical discipline is less likely to be viewed as rejecting where such discipline is more normative; Dodge, McLoyd, & Lansford, 2005).

Inductive Discipline and Moral Internalization

Children's transition from compliance with parental discipline to acceptance of parental induction constitutes, then, moral socialization or the internalization of a society's prosocial norms. It should be emphasized that an internalized moral norm is one that has been *appropriated* or adopted as one's own. In other words, the child (a) experiences the normative information "as deriving autonomously from within oneself" (Hoffman, 2000, p. 135), (b) feels compelled by an inner obligation to live up to it even in the absence of witnesses or external reward and punishment, and (c) feels empathy-based transgression guilt and/or engages in reparative or other prosocial behavior toward the victim in the event of a failure to live up to the norm.

Hence, given moral socialization and internalization—along with the biological and cognitive-developmental factors already discussed—an older child will at least experience an inner moral conflict in a moral encounter. When a moral requirement and motive (for example, one promised to visit and feels sympathy for a sick friend) conflict with an egoistic desire (one is tempted instead to accept an invitation to join a party), the morally internalized person seeks a responsible balance or priority (even if it means forgoing the party). Moral socialization or internalization can be construed as the transition from a child's compliance to a constraining adult in a *discipline* encounter to an inner conflict and resources for autonomous *self*-regulation (Bugental & Grusec, 2006) in a subsequent *moral* encounter. The common features of conflict (outer, inner) and influence (compliance, self-regulation) in discipline and moral encounters form the basis of Hoffman's (1983) argument for the importance of discipline practices to the outcome of moral socialization. Although nurturance and warmth or prosocial role modeling foster a more receptive child, neither does what inductions in the discipline encounter can do: teach the impact of the child's selfish act on another and empower that teaching with empathy, the crucial connection for moral internalization.

Evidence for Hoffman's Theory of Moral Socialization

The socialization component of Hoffman's moral developmental theory, then, features empathy. Specifically, the empathic predisposition is seen as playing a key role in the contribution made by inductive discipline to children's subsequent prosocial behavior. Discipline that emphasizes power does not cultivate empathy; indeed, unqualified power assertion fosters in the child self-focused concerns with external consequences, which can in turn *reduce* prosocial behavior. Severe levels of power assertion, or physical child abuse, can inculcate in the child a schema or internal working model of the world as dangerous and threatening, of others as necessarily having hostile intentions; such biased or distorted social information processing has been linked to subsequent antisocial behavior (Dodge, Coie, & Lynam, 2006). In contrast, inductive discipline elicits empathic distress and empathy-based transgression guilt by directing the child to consider how his or her behavior has affected others. The elicited empathic affect charges or renders "hot" the other-oriented induction, empowering it to prevail over egoistic motives in subsequent moral situations.

The key claim of Hoffman's moral socialization theory is that empathy mediates the relation between parents' use of inductive discipline and children's prosocial behavior. Two contemporaneous[11] studies that have examined this claim both found results consistent with it. Using LISREL analyses, Jan Janssens and Jan Gerris (1992) found that postulating children's empathy as a mediator between authoritative parenting (including inductive discipline; Baumrind, 1971) and prosocial development (including prosocial behavior) yielded a more adequate causal model than did alternative models of empathy. Julia Krevans and I (Krevans & Gibbs, 1996) found that inductive discipline no longer predicted children's prosocial behavior when variance attributable to children's empathy was removed from regression analyses. Put positively, empathy provided the crucial variance in the link between inductive discipline and prosocial behavior. In other results, both studies found that parental use of harsh power assertions related *negatively* to both children's empathy and children's prosocial behavior.[12]

The findings of these studies established a precondition for further research using Hoffman's theory. If the researchers had found, for example, that the relation between inductive discipline and children's prosocial behavior remained significant after the variance attributable to empathy was removed, then the validity of

Hoffman's inductive discipline theory would have been seriously undermined. Such a finding would have meant that, whatever the reasons for the induction-prosocial behavior relation, it could not be attributed to parents' promotion of children's empathy.

Krevans and I (Krevans & Gibbs, 1996) also evaluated the mediating role of empathy-based guilt, for which the results were less consistent. The mediational status of empathy-based guilt could not be adequately tested because the component correlations using guilt were significant only for some of the measures of the variables. Notably, however, guilt did strongly relate to empathy and to prosocial behavior for *high*-empathy children, the portion of the sample for which the guilt variance was most likely to be attributable to empathy-based guilt as opposed to other kinds of guilt. This result pointed to the importance of Hoffman's empathy-based guilt construct and to the need to develop more valid measures that target specifically this type of guilt.

Because the design of these studies was cross-sectional and correlational, the results are amenable to alternative causal interpretations. For example, it can be argued that high empathy in children leads not only to prosocial behavior but also to inductive discipline in the first place: After all, the responsiveness of such children to inductions (they might already be noticing their act's consequences for their victim) would presumably encourage parents to use this discipline technique. Hoffman and we argued, however, that the relations between parental and child variables were most likely bidirectional—in particular, that induction and empathy "feed each other ... in complex, interlocking ways" (Hoffman, 2000, p. 169). Much the same can be said of the interaction between socialization contexts in general and other child variables such as temperament (Collins et al., 2000). Hoffman suggested that a longitudinal research design and structured equation modeling would yield more definitive data and conclusions regarding the causality question.

Expressing Disappointment

An unexpected finding in the Krevans and Gibbs (1996) study pointed to the importance of a construct not currently included in Hoffman's discipline typology: parental expression of disappointment and higher expectations. "Disappointment" is an elusive construct. Insofar as the message highlights harm to another (namely, the parent, who may comment, "What you said made me unhappy"), it is classifiable as an induction. Other versions clearly communicate love withdrawal (e.g., "I can't trust you any more"). A number of the items in the original Hoffman and Saltzstein (1967) measure of inductive discipline were statements of disappointed *expectations*, for example, "I never would have expected you to do that"; such expressions may connote induction or love withdrawal but may also go beyond both in their meanings. They seem to say in effect to the child, "You know better, you can do better, and I think much more highly of *you* than I do of what you did" (Berk, personal communication, April 1, 2002; cf. Damon, 1995). Given such a message, children may be induced to reflect on the kind of persons they are or wish to be, appropriate the parental values for themselves, feel a disappointment in themselves, and determine to be more honest or considerate toward others in the future.

An adaptation of the Hoffman and Saltzstein (1967) measure was used in our (Krevans & Gibbs, 1996) replication of the relationship between inductive discipline and children's prosocial behavior. According to Hoffman's theory, other-oriented inductions specifically account for this relationship. To evaluate this claim empirically and improve the construct validity of the Hoffman and Saltzstein measure, we retained some disappointed-expectations items but added items (e.g., "point out how his friend must feel") that were clearly other-oriented induction appeals. We then created disappointment and other-oriented induction subscales and correlated each with prosocial behavior. We expected to find that other-oriented induction mainly accounted for the inductive-discipline–prosocial behavior relation. Instead, the results indicated the opposite: The disappointment subscale was the stronger component factor. Hence, parental expression of disappointed expectations may be even more important than other-oriented induction for the socialization of cooperative and prosocial behavior, at least for older children (our participants were early adolescents).[13]

Disappointment is related to other-oriented induction in positive discipline. In our study, disappointment statistically "behaved" like other-oriented induction (cf. Patrick & Gibbs, 2007): Both correlated positively with maternal nurturance, negatively with parental power assertion, and positively with child empathy. A similar pattern of correlations was found in the Janssens and Gerris (1992) study for a disappointment-like variable, demandingness (in which parents "appeal to their child's responsibility, make demands about mature behavior, and control whether their child behaves according to their expectations," p. 72). These findings that disappointment generally "behaves" like other-oriented induction led Hoffman (2000) to conclude that disappointment messages are often interpreted by the child as other-oriented inductions specifying the parent as the hurt "other" (but that rejecting or ego-attacking expressions of disappointment might be interpreted as love withdrawal). Accordingly, Hoffman suggested that disappointment items be assimilated either to induction or love withdrawal, "depending on how the parent usually responds in similar situations" (p. 155).

Yet parental disappointment might also foster in the child a sense of the relevance of morality to self-concept (Patrick & Gibbs, 2007; see Chapter 5). Hoffman (1963) suggested that parental expressions of disappointment (as distinct from parental "ego attacks") could promote positive behavior by communicating that the child was "capable of living up to an ideal" (p. 311). In other words, such expressions "may connect [the] parent's expectations and hopes for the child with the child's own self-image and developing expectations and hopes for himself" (Hoffman, personal communication, February 24, 2007). Indeed, parent's more frequent expression of disappointment in discipline encounters is related to higher levels of moral self-relevance among adolescents (Patrick, 2008), in some cases even among older children. Consider the following childhood recollection from a young woman (she did not recollect her age at the time of the incident):

> *I once stole some candy from a food store and was caught by the manager. He demanded to know my name, and, terrified, I told him. He phoned my parents, told them what I had done, and sent me home.*
>
> *As I rode my bicycle home in the dark, I thought about the reception and probable spanking I would receive. Looking scared, I entered the house and was met by a rather calm father and mother. They stressed that they were* very *disappointed in me that I hadn't lived up to their expectations. They said they hoped I would never do it again, because it was wrong to take what didn't belong to me.*
>
> *My initial feeling when I was back in my room was that I had escaped with my life. But as I thought about it, I, too, was disappointed in myself. I resolved never to do it again, and didn't. (Lickona, 1983, p. 155)*

Although the child initially reacted to the parents' calm eschewing of power assertion with relief at having avoided external consequences, she then contemplated her parents' disappointment in her. From this reflection emerged a sense of *self*-disappointment ("I, too, was disappointed in myself"). She (the "she" emergent through her reflection) then found immoral acts such as theft to violate who "she" is, her identity. To protect her newfound (or newly constructed and appropriated) moral identity against subsequent violations, she summoned her ego strength ("I resolved never to do it again, and didn't"). The contributions of moral self-relevance and ego strength to moral motivation are discussed further in Chapter 5.

Role of Nurturance

The studies also examined the relation of maternal nurturance or warmth to parental discipline styles as well as to children's empathy and prosocial behavior. In Hoffman's theory, nurturance or warmth is a "background or contextual variable" (Hoffman, 1970, p. 303) or an example of parenting *style* (Darling & Steinberg, 1993): Children of generally warm or affectionate parents should care more about the child-parent relationship and hence more readily experience attentional arousal during a disciplinary encounter. Eleanor Maccoby (1983) suggested that parental nurturance promotes cooperativeness in the child and hence reduces the necessity for parents "to resort to heavy-handed, power-assertive modes of control" (p. 363). Accordingly, parental nurturance should be negatively correlated with power assertion, a finding obtained in both studies. Both studies also found that maternal nurturance related positively to parental induction, parental disappointment, and child empathy—variables that in turn correlate with prosocial behavior (cf. Zhou et al., 2002). Little or no support was found, however, for a *direct* correlation between nurturance and child prosocial behavior, suggesting that Hoffman is correct to view nurturance as an interactional more than main-effect variable in moral social-ization. Nurturance combined with *low* levels of induction or demandingness (often called permissive or indulgent parenting), for example, does not predict child prosocial behavior.

Conclusion and Critique

Thanks to Hoffman's theory, we gain in our exploration of moral development a greater appreciation of the fact that morality must contend with the egoistic motives of the individual. We find relief in Hoffman's theory from a decades-old complaint against Kohlberg's theory as "cold" in that its cognitive-developmental approach "gives relatively little attention to the strong emotions" of the ego (Mac-coby, 1980, p. 325). In contrast, Hoffman consistently respects "the hot" in morality: the naturally hot desires of the ego; the countervailing, naturally hot basic arousal modes of the empathic predisposition; and the role of empathy and evoked images in rendering "hot" various aspects of cognition (we have encountered, for example, self-recognition, cognitive development, scripts, attributions, inferences, moral principles, internalized moral norms, and inductions).

Hoffman's attention to egoistic motives and "hot" empathic processes in moral socialization accounts for the major caveats he invokes as he uses cognitive-developmental themes. Doesn't the child actively construct moral schemas? Well, yes—but only if "constructing moral schemas" can be taken beyond its classic Piagetian context of necessary knowledge (see Chapters 2, 9) to mean "building up moral scripts" of social sequences and gaining motivation from empathic affect in the course of moral internalization. Doesn't peer interaction promote social decentration and moral development? Well, yes—but only if those interacting peers do not vie for dominance, and only if they have been socialized in inductive homes or are supervised in their conflict by inductive "coaches." Doesn't perspective taking promote moral behavior? Well, yes—but thanks exclusively to the primacy of empathy; otherwise, "why should perspec-tive taking serve prosocial rather than egoistic [e.g., manipulative] ends?" (Hoffman, 2000, p. 131).

Hoffman's caveats lead to a more balanced and comprehensive understanding of moral development. Our main *counter*-caveat is that "the right" is in a sense just as primary as "the good" in morality. The construction of ideal and "necessary" moral reciprocity through perspective-taking, for example, has a place in moral motivation that affective primacy fails to capture. If reciprocity is akin to logic—"the morality of thought" in Piaget's famous dictum—then reciprocity (or its viola-tion), equality, and impartiality generate a motive power in their own right, one that can join the motive power of empathy. Although Kohlberg's theory may underplay egoistic motives and empathy, it does recognize the moral motivation engendered by violations of fairness or justice. And we seek to represent not just prosocial morality, but the entire moral domain.

We will need the resources of both theories as we now turn our attention more fully to social behavior and its motivation. Do Kohlberg's and Hoffman's theories of moral development enable an adequate understanding of prosocial and antisocial behavior? This question will be explored in the next two chapters.

Notes

[1]Besides empathy or caring, other candidates for affective primacy include in-group loyalty, respect for authority, and purity (see Chapter 1).

[2]The more widely noted of Gilligan's (1982) claims, that female respondents are artifactually downscored in Kohlberg's stage system, is generally disconfirmed (Walker, 1995). In fact, females are often found to be more advanced than males in moral judgment during early adolescence (e.g., Garmon, Basinger, Gregg, & Gibbs, 1996; Gibbs et al., 2007; Silberman & Snarey, 1993). Gilligan also claimed that males favor justice and rights in their moral judgment, whereas females favor care-related concerns. There is some support especially for the latter part of this claim: Care-related concerns are more prevalent in the moral judgments of females than males, especially when open-ended assessment methods are used (Garmon et al., 1996; Gibbs, Arnold, & Burkhart, 1984; Gielen, Comunian, & Antoni, 1994; Jaffee & Hyde, 2000). This gender difference disappears when participants are asked to recollect "personal" (care-related) moral dilemmas and make moral judgments in that context (Walker, 1995), indicating that males *can* but tend not to use prominent levels of care-related concerns in their moral judgment. The reference to moral *judgment* more than moral *feeling* renders Gilligan's work a less suitable vehicle than Hoffman's for exploring the affective-primacy strand of moral development.

[3]Prosocial behavior refers to beneficence, or acts intended to benefit another. In our usage of *prosocial behavior*, we imply further that the acts are *altruistic*, that is, motivated by an intrinsic concern for others more than by external rewards or punishments. This further implication is often difficult to establish in practice, however (Eisenberg, Fabes, & Spinrad, 2006). *Exemplary* prosocial behavior appears, at least from the outside, to entail some substantial personal cost (see Chapter 5).

[4]Particularly suggestive of such a biological substratum are case studies of the behavior of patients with brain damage in these areas (cf. psychopathy). Patients who had sustained damage to the ventromedial prefrontal region of their brains no longer showed empathy or other feelings, rendering their emotions shallow and their "decision-making landscape hopelessly flat" (Damasio, 1999, p. 51). They could formulate plans but not implement them and could not maintain gainful employment (in our Chapter 5 terminology, they had lost all "ego strength"). They were sometimes actively cruel to others and tended to boast—with little or no foundation—of professional, physical, or sexual prowess. One patient's lack of moral enactment was evident despite his mature level of moral judgment, as measured by Kohlberg et al.'s Moral Judgment Interview (Colby et al., 1987). One should beware of any direct attribution of morality or immorality to a specific structure of the brain (Sarter, Berntson, & Cacioppo, 1996), or equate the lack of ego strength with a lack of motivation "to do the right thing" (Hauser, 2006, p. 416). Nonetheless, the case studies do suggest that certain structures and pathways of the brain are prerequisites for moral behavior.

[5]Although their underlying emotions are more complex, even "decentered" adults can be captured for a while by the salience of familiar cues. One of Hoffman's close friends, who had cancer,

> *just wanted to talk as usual about sports and the stock market, and with the usual gusto—about anything but his condition. Had I been openly empathic it could have disrupted his denial, so I went along, got lost in conversation and enjoyed myself; empathic distress was kept under control in the back of my mind, but it returned afterward. (Hoffman, 2000, p. 81, emphasis added)*

[6]*Perspective taking* is the more general term ("children may be able to understand another's perspective without knowing anything about the person's role [in a social structure]"; Maccoby, 1980, p. 317). Hence, Hoffman (personal communication, September 19, 2002) since the publication of his book (Hoffman, 2000) has dropped the role-taking term and uses *perspective taking* exclusively (e.g., Hoffman, 2008).

[7]Bodily self-recognition is a necessary but not sufficient condition for veridical empathy. Self-aware children still make egocentric or quasi-egocentric mistakes, but "are cognitively ready to learn from corrective feedback after making 'egocentric' mistakes. Eventually, feedback becomes unnecessary (although even adults need it at times)" (Hoffman, 2000, p. 72; cf. Flavell et al., 2002).

[8]An interesting question pertains to the degree of effectiveness of blaming the victim and other cognitive distortions in preempting or neutralizing empathic distortion. Maintaining self-serving cognitive distortions may require the expenditure of cognitive resources (see Chapter 6). That the success of such rationalizations is less than complete for many antisocial individuals offers some hope for intervention (see Chapter 7).

[9]Haidt and Bjorklund (2008a) even asserted that moral development is a matter of "assisted externalization," whereby cultural guidance and examples enable a child's innate morality to emerge and "configure itself properly" (p. 206). Hoffman's (2000) and Damon's (1988) position is more cautious and defensible, namely, that the child's innate empathic predisposition can and should be cultivated to foster the child's internalization of prosocial norms (but *not* that prosocial morality is already within the child and ready to emerge or "externalize").

[10]Intense conflicts involving a recalcitrant child are sometimes handled with the consistent, sustained application of a time-out technique whereby the child is sequestered (e.g., placed in a "naughty corner," or, for older children, "reflection chair") for a period of time. As a popular television show "Supernanny" (Powell, 2008) demonstrated, the time-out consequence works best when it is framed in moral or social perspective-taking terms (the sequestered child is reminded in clear, simple terms of why their act was wrong or harmful, and a "sorry" is elicited and accepted; older children may progress from the "reflection chair" to the "communication couch" eventuating in [one hopes] apology and parent-child reconciliation).

[11]Krevans and I first presented our work as a conference paper in 1991 (Krevans & Gibbs, 1991) and subsequently published it in 1996. We were unaware of Janssens's and Gerris's (1992) research report, nor were they aware of ours (Janssens, personal communication, December 5, 2002). That two independent studies using different methods found such similar results bolsters confidence in the validity of the support for Hoffman's inductive discipline theory.

[12]Where power assertion is less harsh, corporal punishment is culturally normative, and the physical punishment is not interpreted as rejection by the child, the negative relationship

between power assertion and children's empathy or prosocial behavior may not hold (Dodge, McLoyd, & Lansford, 2005).

[13]It is even possible that other-oriented inductions can be counterproductive by preadolescence. Some mothers commented to researcher Julia Krevans that their early adolescent children were often already aware of how a transgression of theirs had harmed another and would have felt hurt, scolded, or "talked down to" by an explicit description (Krevans, personal communication, December 30, 2002). Perhaps expressing disappointment and hope for better future conduct is more effective once children reach adolescence, as some recent data (Patrick, 2008) would suggest.

Moral Development, Moral Self-Relevance, and Prosocial Behavior

TO KNOW THE RIGHT OR FEEL THE GOOD IS NOT NECESSARILY TO *DO* the right or good. One who has grasped ideal moral reciprocity or who, on multiple levels, empathizes with others may—or may not—actively seek to correct an injustice or come to the aid of someone in distress. Consistency across ideals of understanding, empathic feeling, and prosocial action in morality does occur in many instances. Those dedicated to humanitarian causes, who persevere through adverse circumstances, stand out as particularly admirable. One thinks of those who courageously campaign for equal human rights, engage in nonviolent protest, feed and nurture needy children of the world, care for the abandoned or neglected, heal the desperately ill, or comfort the dying (Ackerman & Duvall, 2000; Colby & Damon, 1992). Smaller scale prosocial or altruistic behavior—a parent's encouraging hug for a child, a teacher's tutoring for a struggling student—is also important and, fortunately, common.

In this chapter and the next two, we will apply what we have learned of Kohlberg's and Hoffman's theories to social behavior. The present chapter will focus on prosocial behavior and individual differences in its occurrence, the next two (Chapters 6 and 7) on antisocial behavior and its treatment. In our attempt to account for the complexity of sociomoral behavior, we will revisit in this chapter the question of moral motivation. We will also highlight the need to elaborate certain underdeveloped concepts in Kohlberg's and Hoffman's theories: chiefly, moral self-relevance in this chapter and cognitive distortion as well as social skills in the next two. Case studies to be introduced at the end of this chapter will serve to sharpen our understanding of the requirements for prosocial behavior. An initial case study, from Robert Coles's (1986) *The Moral Life of Children*, introduces our considerations.

Prosocial Behavior: A Rescue

In our usage, *prosocial behavior* is social action intended to benefit others (remedying injustice, promoting others' welfare) without anticipation of personal reward, indeed, perhaps at some cost or risk to oneself. Our case study of prosocial behavior in effect fits this definition: At some personal cost and risk, one youth rescued another from an imminent attack. The rescuer was White, the rescued African-American; both youths were students at a previously segregated high school in Atlanta, Georgia, in the 1970s. In the weeks prior to the near assault, the White youth, an "ordinary" 14-year-old from a so-called "redneck" family, had "meant it" as he had joined in shouting at the Black youth taunts and epithets such as "Go nigger, go!" Yet he had also noticed that the Black youth "knew how to smile when it was rough going [from the taunts], and who walked straight and tall, and was polite." The White youth remarked to his parents, "It's a real shame that someone like him has to pay for the trouble caused by all those federal judges" (Coles, 1986, p. 27). Concurrently, he "began to see a kid, not a nigger" (p. 27). "Then," as the youth recalled, "it happened":

> I saw a few people cuss at him. "The dirty nigger," they kept on calling him, and soon they were pushing him in a corner, and it looked like trouble, bad trouble. I went over and broke it up. I said, "Hey, cut it out." They all looked at me as if I was crazy. . . . But my buddies stopped. . . . Before [he] left, I spoke to him. I didn't mean to, actually! It just came out of my mouth. I was surprised to hear the words myself: "I'm sorry."
>
> As soon as he was gone, my friends gave it to me: "What do you mean, 'I'm sorry'!" I didn't know what to say.

The White youth characterized his sudden act of intervention and apology as "the strangest moment of my life." The incident marked a dramatic turning point in the moral life of this 14-year-old. Despite the continued scorn of his White "buddies" at school, the White youth subsequently became a friend of the African-American youth. Initially, the White youth still decried integration. As the friendship grew, however, he eventually began to "advocate 'an end to the whole lousy business of segregation'" (Coles, 1986, p. 28).

The Issue of Moral Motivation

What motivated this youth's act of intervention and apology, in the face of scorn from his peers—indeed, in the face of his own prior scorn against the victim? Can we find any motive for a moment so sudden, so without advance indication or apparent conscious forethought? The words of apology in that moment just sprang from the rescuer's lips, unintended, as surprising and inexplicable to the rescuer as they were to his shocked and perplexed White buddies. Perhaps morality, then, is in the main arational or irrational, a primarily affective phenomenon. Perhaps indeed, as the emotivists (e.g., Ayer, 1952) argue, moral prescriptions are merely intense expressions of feeling, such as a "hurrah!" or a shudder. Although they are not simple emotivists, many exclusive affective primacy theorists of morality (e.g., Greene, 2008a,b; Haidt & Bjorklund, 2008a,b; Hauser, 2006; Krebs, 2008) see little role for cognitive structuring or conscious reflection in prosocial behavior, especially in sudden prosocial acts such as the rescue. (Hoffman is the exception, as we will see.)

What makes this case particularly intriguing, of course, is the youth's surprise and bewilderment at his sudden "strange" act and words. Are we total "strangers to ourselves" (Wilson, 2002)? Why didn't the youth recall his prior lament at the unfair treatment accorded the African-American youth? Piaget (1972/1973) wrote that a person's thought and action are "directed by structures whose existence he ignores and which determine ... what he 'must' do." Especially ignored—even suppressed from awareness—are cognitive structures that contradict the person's conscious beliefs, self-concept, or ideology: An "incompatible scheme cannot, of course, be integrated into the system of conscious concepts" (pp. 33, 39).[1] Did the White youth not immediately recall his cognitive "structure" or "scheme" of unfairness to the Black youth because that unfairness concern was "incompatible" with his still-in-place "system of conscious concepts," i.e., his segregationist beliefs?

The White youth's own pondering of the incident leads us to suspect a dynamic of conscious and unconscious moral motivation. Although the prosocial moment seemed at first strange and inexplicable, he did, upon reflection, recognize its preparation in those crucial prior weeks:

> I'd be as I was, I guess, except for being there in school that year and seeing that kid—seeing him behave himself, no matter what we called him, and seeing him being insulted so bad, so real bad. Something in me just drew the line, and something in me began to change, I think. (Coles, 1986, p. 28)

Even before the scene of "trouble, bad trouble," the White youth had indeed already begun to change—to respect the erstwhile "nigger" as a person, a good person being insulted and made unfairly to "pay" (for the trouble caused by those federal judges). One might say that he had been "primed" for the moment, even though he did not know it at the time. His cognitive history counts as evidence that, at least in some cases, "fast and automatic moral intuitions are actually shaped and informed by moral reasoning" (Pizzaro & Bloom, 2003, p. 193). At the scene, the line drawn in the White youth's mind was activated as he witnessed, now not just insults, but their escalation to aggressive pushing and cornering the African-American youth, heading obviously toward physical assault. That moral line was crossed; it was just too much. Despite implicit pressure to conform to the behavior of his White peers, he could take it no longer. In that sudden but perhaps not-so-strange-after-all moment, he intervened and apologized.

Affective Primacy in Moral Motivation

Hoffman (2000) offered an empathy-based analysis of this incident that is brilliant, yet limited insofar as it reserves exclusively for empathy the role of moral motivation. But let us go with Hoffman's affective primacy analysis as far as it will take us. Consider the sudden, at-first inexplicable quality of the rescue and apology. We think first of Hoffman's involuntary mechanisms of the empathic predisposition, and then of the cognitive structuring of that empathic distress as the interpretive processes kick in (see Chapter 4).[2] The youth himself referred, in effect, to empathy and its cognitive alloys: sympathetic distress ("seeing him being insulted so bad, so real bad . . . soon they were pushing him in a corner"), the anticipation of worse sympathetic distress ("it looked like trouble, bad trouble"), and empathy-based guilt ("I'm sorry"). Also note the affective precedent in the youth's dramatic moral turnabouts. Specifically, the emotional shift from anger to empathy and friendship preceded the cognitive shift from his segregationist ideology to the emergence of his philosophy of integration.

In Hoffman's view, then, even the White youth's unfairness concern was primarily an empathic feeling, albeit one shaped by cognition. Consider what the White youth himself regarded as a crucial experience: seeing the African-American youth smile, be polite, and remain above trading insults "no matter what we called him." This "contrast between the Black youth's admirable conduct and the way he was treated" generated the inference that he was "a fine person who deserved better." Discerned during those weeks, then, was an "obvious lack of reciprocity between character and outcome" (p. 108). The inference of nonreciprocity, in Hoffman's analysis, "transformed . . . the boy's empathic/sympathetic distress . . . into an empathic feeling of injustice" (p. 108).

Hoffman's analysis of this case illustrates his claim that the motivation to correct a violation of justice or an imbalance of reciprocity derives ultimately and exclusively from empathy. Justice is treated as just another empathy alloy. In the beginning is empathy. Then comes the cognition, the formation of empathy into, say, sympathy or empathy-based guilt (see Chapter 4). In this case, empathic distress suffuses and affectively charges the inference of nonreciprocity to form an *empathic feeling* of injustice. Note that, in Hoffman's theory, the injustice cognition would have no motive power were it not for empathy. Furthermore, *moral principles* represent an empathy alloy once removed: In Hoffman's analysis, the empathic feeling of injustice itself then activated and primed (or charged with empathic affect) the youth's moral principle of "equal rights" (p. 244) or philosophy of integration.

For an exclusive affective-primacy moral theory, Hoffman's is remarkably cognitive developmental. His depiction of the cognitive development of empathy and the crucial role of cognition in structuring empathic intuitions renders his theory more nuanced and less extreme than, say, Haidt's affective-primacy claims that "the action in morality is in the intuitions, *not* in reasoning" and that reasoning's role in morality is mainly that of self-serving, post-intuition rationalization or "confabulation" (Haidt & Bjorklund, 2008a, pp. 190, 196, emphasis added). Although Hoffman is less extreme than other affective primacy theorists, he, like they, argues for *exclusive* affective primacy. Transformed and directed though it may have been by an inference of unfairness (and empathy-based guilt), empathy alone in Hoffman's theory provided the motive power that prevailed over the youth's egocentric biases and ethnocentric prejudices and impelled him to action, apology, and the advocacy of integration.

Coprimacy in Moral Motivation

In our view, Hoffman's *exclusive* affective primacy claim exceeds the proper bounds of primary affect in moral motivation. The evocative moral power of the African-American youth's moral dignity in the face of those bad-and-getting-worse insults and pushes, or, more generally, of the nonviolent protester against oppression or injustice (Ackerman & Duvall, 2000), is affective *and* cognitive. There is room among automatic unconscious and preconscious processes not only for the reactions of the empathic predisposition but as well for reactions stemming from the logically and morally necessary ideals of justice or reciprocity. As we argue throughout this book, justice is a moral motive in its own right, just as primary as empathy.

We have seen in previous chapters that, although Hoffman (2000) acknowledged the possibility of a "preference for reciprocity" (p. 242) or equality, he did not relate reciprocity to logical necessity or distinguish levels of moral reciprocity. Specifically, he did not distinguish *ideal* from pragmatic reciprocity, an important omission especially in this case. The nonreciprocity discerned by the White youth represented the violation of an *ideal*; he seemed to have been impressed with the African-American youth's dignity "no matter what we called him." Less mature youths (such as the rescuer's peers?) might not have been moved, indeed, might have thought the Black youth a fool not to pay back, not to reciprocate tit-for-tat every insult with a counterinsult (Kohlberg's moral judgment Stage 2). But the White youth may have constructed a more mature or ideal understanding of reciprocity: Again, he was moved as he appreciated a fine person, an authentic and dignified character morally *above* the level of trading insults. The sense of justice or reciprocity generates its own motivating affect, known as the feeling of logical or moral necessity. In this case, the White youth's inference of nonreciprocity, his perception of *in*justice generated a distress akin to that of "conservational" children confronted with (spurious) nonreciprocity outcomes in the conservation task (Smedslund, 1961; see Chapter 2). Unfortunately, in the sociomoral realm, nonreciprocity is not spurious but all too real and in need of correction.

If exclusive affective primacy is untenable, so is exclusive cognitive primacy as a sufficient account of moral motivation. Certainly, any attempt to argue for cognitive (justice) primacy *instead* of affective (empathy) primacy is an intellectual nonstarter. And empathy, insofar as it contributes to love, may be linked to the "ultimate" moral motive (see Chapter 9). We argue not for cognitive primacy as *the* motive, just for cognitive primacy as *a* motive. Given that we see justice as contributing moral motive power along with that of empathy, *coprimacy* (or dual process) aptly labels our view. Primary in the rescuer's social perception and impetus to act were both sympathetic distress ("seeing him insulted so bad, so real bad") *and* the violation of ideal reciprocity ("seeing him behave himself, no matter what we called him"). The rescuer's case illustrated coprimacy in the strong sense, given the apparent simultaneity of their activation. In other cases, either the affective or the cognitive is temporally primary and then the two coalesce. As Paul Bloom (2004) pointed out, "empathy and rationality [injustice inference] can be mutually reinforcing." A rational conclusion that slavery is unjust (entailing a primary motive in our view) can lead one to empathize with the plight of a slave (i.e., cognitive primacy leads to and coalesces with the affective motive into coprimacy); just as "someone who, for whatever reason, ... feels empathy [for a slave] might be driven to explore the notion that slavery in general is immoral [i.e., affective primacy leads to, coalesces with the cognitive motive into coprimacy]" (p. 144).

Like its affective counterpart, the cognitive aspect of coprimacy can motivate throughout life. As Anne Colby and William Damon (1992) observed in their brilliant study of 23 morally committed men and women, such individuals' expression of moral obligation

> evokes a quality similar to numerical necessity, as when one realizes that two plus two must equal four and therefore simply cannot be convinced to say that it equals something else.[3] Virginia Durr expresses this certainty when she says that all people must be treated equally and that this must apply to blacks as well as whites. Cabell Brand ... expresses it when he says that it is wrong for poor children to have less opportunity than rich children. ... The great certainty that we observed in our moral exemplars was the certainty established by logical necessity once the truth is found. (pp. 75–76)

Consistent with our coprimacy analysis of the basic motivation of prosocial behavior is the finding of a dichotomy among altruists: "helper" altruists and "reformer" altruists. The aims of the helper and the reformer respectively correspond to the good and the right: Whereas the helper empathically identifies with and seeks to alleviate the distress of the people they are helping, the reformer aims to correct social injustice (Carlson, 1982). Of course, many helpers are also reformers to some extent, and vice versa. Indeed, we interpret these aims as matters of emphasis and their motivational sources as distinguishable yet inextricable and complementary: Although the prosocial behavior of helpers concerns mainly the alleviation of suffering, helpers may also seek to alleviate a cause of that suffering pertaining to social injustice. Correspondingly, the reformer's cognitive motive to correct injustice or inequality as a logical or moral necessity coalesces with the motivating power from empathizing with the victims of that injustice. The interrelated helper and reformer categories of prosocial behavior are both primary—as are the basic sources of moral motivation to which those categories correspond.

Individual Differences in Prosocial Behavior

The prosocial behavior of rescue and apology in our case study is remarkable not only because of its suddenness but also because the rescuer-to-be, an ordinary youth (Coles, 1986, described him as "a tough athlete, a poor student, not a well-read boy of fourteen," p. 27) who had yelled "Go nigger, go!" at the very African-American youth he was subsequently to rescue, was a most unlikely candidate. We have argued that the White youth was impelled to act by a primarily cognitive motive to stop an injustice and a primarily affective motive to relieve or prevent another's pain and suffering. But then why were not his White buddies also moved by injustice and empathic distress? Why were they "not as swift as he to show a change in racial attitudes" (Coles, 1986, p. 28)? How was the White youth able to resist their social influence? More broadly, what factors might account for individual differences in the likelihood of prosocial behavior?

In a study of this question (Gibbs et al., 1986), we explored the extent to which individual-difference and moral judgment stage variables could account for the variance in prosocial behavior among high school students. Teachers characterized students they knew well in terms of one or another of five nutshell descriptions of "how the subject tends to act in social situations." The rating instrument was developed by Robert Havighurst and Hilda Taba (1949) and adapted by us to measure moral courage, which can be characterized as prosocial behavior in the face of major adverse circumstances. Representing the bottom of our adapted four-point scale was a description of a person who "would only consider joining a just or rightful cause if it is popular with his/her friends and supported by adult authorities. He/she would prefer to remain in the background even if a friend is being taunted or talked about unfairly." At the highest level was a person who

> consistently stands by his/her principles. He/she would stand up for a just or rightful cause, even if the cause is unpopular and will mean criticizing adult authorities. He/she will defend someone who is being taunted or talked about unfairly, even if the victim is only an acquaintance. (Gibbs et al., 1986, p. 188)

This description of moral courage is pertinent to our case study from Coles (1986), insofar as the White youth did indeed defend an acquaintance who was being taunted (and worse), and to many of the exemplars studied by Colby and Damon (1992). Of course, neither Coles's nor Colby and Damon's participants were among the high school students studied in our research. We can speculatively apply to these cases, however, our and other findings concerning individual differences in prosocial behavior.

Moral Types A and B

The main individual difference variable we studied was Moral Types A and B, introduced in Chapter 2. The Type A/Type B distinction pertains to the extent to which the prescriptive ideals of the mature stages are evidenced. Even the Type A versions of Stage 3 and Stage 4 judgments indicate a profound understanding of the bases for viable interpersonal relationships and societal systems. However, 3A and 4A thinking is more embedded in existing social arrangements and hence is less clearly ideal than that of 3B and 4B. High school students evidencing Stage 3 Type A judgment, for example, may "care so much about what others think of them that they can turn into moral marshmallows, willing to do something because 'everybody's doing it '" (Lickona, 1983, p. 161). In contrast to the asymmetrical social conformist tendencies of Type A, Moral Type B is

> more balanced in perspective. A 3A decides in terms of, What does a good husband do? What does a wife expect? A 3B decides in terms of, What does a good husband who is a partner in a good mutual relationship do? What does each spouse expect of the other? Both sides of the equation are balanced; this is fairness. At 4A, the subject decides in terms of the question, What does the system demand? At 4B the subject asks, What does the individual in the system demand as well as the system, and what is a solution that strikes a balance?
>
> Because of this balance, B's are more prescriptive or internal, centering more on their judgments of what ought to be. They are also more universalistic, that is, willing to carry the boundary of value categories, like the value of life, to their logical conclusion. (Kohlberg, 1984, p. 185)

Accordingly, we operationalized Moral Type B as composed of three components: *balancing* or reciprocal perspective taking, *fundamental* or universal *valuing*, and *conscience* or internality (cf. moral self-relevance, discussed below). Whereas "parents should not expect to be respected if they don't treat their children fairly" illustrates the balancing component, "parents will lose their self-respect if they treat their children unfairly" illustrates the conscience component. One component may support another in a moral justification. For example, a participant may evaluate saving even a stranger's life as important because "all life is precious" and "people shouldn't just care about those in given relationships but about all humanity" (fundamental valuing) and then support that universal appeal by asking, "How would you feel, if you were the stranger and no one cared enough to save your life?" (balancing).

A central finding of our study was that Moral Type B is related to prosocial behavior. Adolescents who make appeals in their moral judgment to balanced perspectives, fundamental values such as the basic humanity of people, and personal conscience are rated by their teachers as individuals likely to engage consistently in acts of moral courage and other exemplary prosocial behavior. AnnaLaura Comunian and Uwe Gielen (1995, 2000) found that Italian adolescents and adults evidencing Moral Type B (as well as those evidencing mature moral judgment in societal [Stage 4] as well as inter-personal [Stage 3] spheres) were more likely to engage in volunteer services assisting disabled, elderly, and refugee individuals. Relevant to fundamental valuing and proso-cial behavior is Sam and Pearl Oliner's (1988) finding that European rescuers of Jews during the Holocaust tended to perceive superficially dissimilar others as essentially similar to themselves.

Moral Type B, Field Independence, and Veridical Moral Perception

A clue to the significance of Moral Type B lies in its correlation with a cognitive style variable called field dependence-independence, also known as psychological differentiation (Ferrari & Sternberg, 1998). Traditionally, this variable pertains to perceptual or kinesthetic ability: Individuals high in field independence are able to orient vertically despite biasing influences, such as a tilted chair or window frame, or (as in the measure we used) discern and differentiate geometric figures that are embedded or concealed in more complex designs or "fields." The social relevance of the variable is indicated by the relative autonomy or independence from confor-mity influences of field-independent individuals in social judgment tasks (Witkin & Goodenough, 1977).

The relation we found between field independence and Moral Type B suggests that Moral Type B individuals are more likely to engage in prosocial activity because they are more able to discern a core injustice in a situation despite dis-tortive, obscuring, or distracting influences from the social context or "field" of a social group. The distorting field in which the White youth was embedded included the immediate social-conformity pressures from his peers and, more broadly, an ecological context (Bronfenbrenner & Morris, 2006) in which ideological norms of segregation and out-group rejection were prevalent. Nor were the field influences merely external pressures: In Kelman's (1958) classic terms of social influence, the White youth had not only complied with his buddies' expectations but had also identified with their anti–African American norms (although he may not have fully internalized those norms).

The field-independence interpretation of Moral Type B fits with the "moral clarity" (p. 173) and "resistance to illusory interpretations of events" (p. 289) shown by moral exemplars (Colby & Damon, 1992, p. 173), including whistle-blowers (Anderson & Morgan, 2007; Andrews, 2006, December 3; Glazer, 2002; Lacayo & Ripley, 2002; Walsh, 2007, November 18). Again, Moral Type B (vs. Type A) individ-uals clearly see moral wrong (even amid obfuscating norms, rationalizations, and ideologies). Accordingly, they experience a stronger sense of the violation of moral necessity and, at least in part because of this cognitive motive, feel impelled to act. For example, in light of the prominent concern with the ideal perspective-taking balance in Type B, would not a Type B-oriented individual be more primed to discern an essential moral *im*balance (nonreciprocity of treat-ment, unfairness) even in a complex and confusing social situation? Might not a

Type B-oriented be especially "able to discriminate between the demands of convention and the requirements of justice"—and, accordingly, "attempt to transform societal arrangements embedding inequalities and injustices" (Turiel, 2008, p. 4)? Moreover, in light of the prominent concern with fundamental values that go beyond superficial role boundaries, would not a Type B individual be more primed to discern the essential humanness of a member of an out-group? Significantly, a "human ability to treasure the spark of humanity in everyone" (p. 279) was common among Colby and Damon's (1992) exemplars.[4]

Given the perceptual emphasis in the field independence construct, it is interesting that the White youth in our case study repeatedly used a visual figure of speech in explaining his intervention: He kept "*seeing* him [the African-American youth] behave himself, no matter what we called him, and *seeing* him being insulted so bad, so real bad" (Coles, 1986, p. 28, emphasis added); "after a few weeks, I began to *see* a kid, not a nigger" (p. 27, emphasis added). It is as if the youth had a "good eye" for the ethical dimension of life. Much as a child penetrates through misleading appearances despite superficial impressions to infer an underlying reality of conservation, our White youth inferred injustice and penetrated through stereotypes and superficial differences to see a human being. Indeed, his maturity and growing clarity, accuracy, or veridicality of moral perception may have fed his empathic distress and his upset at the violation of morally necessary ideals. These factors may have related to the "something in him" that "began to change." Given that internal change, the remaining field pressures were restricted to the extrinsic (such as compliance) and were insufficient to suppress his mounting motivation to do something as the unjust victimization escalated.

Morality and the Self-Schema: Moral Self-Relevance

Individuals who seem primed to discern and respond to the ethical core in the complexities of human social existence tend to be those for whom morality is relevant to their sense of self or even, as David Moshman (2005) put it, "central to your deepest sense of who you are" (p. 75; cf. Blasi, 1995). In other words, mature and accurate or discerning moral perception should be related to moral self-relevance (Kohlberg & Candee, 1984). Colby and Damon (1992) concluded that their exemplars' "hopes for themselves and their own destinies are largely defined by their moral goals" (p. 300); that is, there is "a moral center" to their self-understanding or an exceptional degree of "unity between self and morality" (p. 300). Given this moral center, moral schemas in moral exemplars are "chronically accessible for appraising the social landscape" (Lapsley & Narvaez, 2006, p. 268). And the scope of their concerns is "exceptionally broad": "They drop everything not just to see their own children across the street but to feed the poor children of the world, to comfort the dying, to heal the ailing, or to campaign for human rights" (p. 303). Daniel Hart and colleagues (Hart, Atkins, & Donnelly, 2006; cf. Aquino & Reed, 2002) found that adolescents who engaged in extensive volunteer community work were more likely to describe themselves in terms of moral personality traits and goals. By the same token, those who use *fewer* moral terms in their self-description are more likely to engage in *anti*social behavior (Barriga, Morrison, Liau, & Gibbs, 2001; Aquino, Reed, Thau, & Freeman, 2007).

Individual differences in the relevance of morality to one's sense of self are greater than, say, individual differences in the relevance of gender to self-concept. As the toddler becomes aware of the distinction between self and other, the sense of self (or "self-schema") grows through interplay with the environment. Gender is perceived from the start as relevant to self. The toddler picks up the self-label "boy" or "girl" and accordingly differentially attends to, prefers, and remembers social information in the environment. Within a few years, gender becomes consolidated into the self-schema; the child has a gender identity (Martin, 2000).

Not necessarily so for morality. Whereas a sense of self as male or female develops relatively early as a stable and central feature of one's emergent identity, a sense of self as moral takes place more gradually (Blasi, 1995; Damon & Hart, 1988). "Early in life, morality and self are separate conceptual systems with little integration between them" (Colby & Damon, 1992, p. 305). By the end of the preadult years, some degree of integration of self with morality is typically achieved by various means (Giesbrecht & Walker, 2000). The rescuer had to bring his sense of self and even his worldview in line with his strange moment of intervention to reduce the cognitive inconsistency between his act of rescue and apology and his erstwhile beliefs in segregation (Abelson et al., 1968). As we noted in the last chapter, parental expression of disappointment after a transgression can stimulate the child (at least the adolescent) to reflect on self and gain in moral self-relevance. Individual differences in the degree of integration or of moral self-relevance, however, are still considerable even among adults (Colby & Damon, 1992, pp. 305–306). In George Kelly's (1963; cf. Markus & Wurf, 1987) terms, morality for some is a "core construct" in the maintenance of one's identity and in one's self-evaluation, whereas for others it is more peripheral. Along a continuum of the prominence of moral schemas in identity, those for whom schemas of morality are highly relevant to their self-schema and interpretation of social events define one pole (highly schematic; moral identity); defining the other pole are those for whom morality is entirely irrelevant (aschematic; cf. clinical sociopathy or psychopathy; Lykken, 1995). Most individuals are of course in the middle range of moral self-relevance (Baldwin, 1992).

The high moral schematicity or almost total integration of self and morality evidenced by Colby and Damon's (1992) moral exemplars was what "makes them exceptional" (p. 301). This integration, as well as the evolution of their goals, was achieved as the exemplar connected with others in a transformative process of social construction in the broad sense of the term, called "co-construction" by Colby and Damon:

> Both the exemplar and his or her colleagues are active agents in determining the shape of the transformation. All new ideas must owe their shape to some interaction between external guidance and internal belief: the transformation is, in one precise word, a "co-construction." Over an extended period of time, the new

or expanded moral goals are co-constructed in the course of many negotiations between the exemplar and other persons. (p. 184)

At one or another point during co-construction, there may occur a critical event or experience triggering an "abrupt change" (Colby & Damon, 1992, p. 185). "We never quite know ... how an event will connect with ourselves" (Coles, 1986, p. 29). The White youth of our case study certainly did not know that the encountered scene of worsening "bad trouble" would personally connect the way it did, that it would evoke his empathy and guilt and sense of injustice and stimulate a "strange" moment of moral intervention and apology. Nor could he have anticipated his subsequent transformation and expansion of friendships and attitudes—in effect, substantial changes in his identity, perhaps the "something in him" that "began to change." (Coles tells us nothing of the White youth's subsequent life. It is intriguing to fancy that he subsequently co-constructed such a life of moral commitment that in the 1980s, he was among those recruited for study as moral exemplars by Colby and Damon!)

For moral exemplars, moral self-relevance can be said to have consolidated into a *moral identity* that is a major contributor in its own right to moral motivation. Besides ideal reciprocity and empathy, then, a moral identity may motivate one to live up to (act consistently with, express, fulfill in life) profoundly self-attributed moral principles or goals (cf. Bergman, 2004; Blasi, 1995). Similarly, Hoffman (2000) suggested that a person with internalized moral principles will act morally not only because of empathy (and, we would add, ideal moral reciprocity) but also as "an affirmation of one's *self*" (p. 18). To do otherwise would be a *betrayal* of self. Although attention to self can become detrimental (Baumeister, 1991), moral self-relevance plays an important role in moral behavior. A person with a moral identity may refrain from padding his expense account not only because doing so would betray his employer's trust and because he would feel guilty, but also because "it would violate his sense of integrity" (Colby, 2002, p. 133). Kohlberg and Candee (1984) even posited that persons make "responsibility judgments" of the extent to which "that which is morally good or right is also strictly necessary for the self" (p. 57; cf. Blasi, 1995). The central place of moral self-relevance in our chapter title mirrors its mediating role (especially *qua* moral identity) in the dynamic relation between moral development and exemplary prosocial behavior; and within that dynamic, exemplary prosocial behavior may foster moral identity, as it may have for the Atlanta youth. For moral exemplars, moral identity even becomes, as it were, a *meta*-primary source of moral motivation, a dynamic framework of personally invested moral goals that encompasses the primacies of justice and care.[5]

Moral Judgment Stage, Empathy, and Locus of Control

Although Moral Type B and field dependence-independence were the main foci of our (Gibbs et al., 1986) study of prosocial behavior, we also explored the possible role of certain other variables: moral judgment stage, empathy, and locus of control.

Moral type correlated with moral judgment stage (cf. Comunian & Gielen, 1995, 2000, 2006; Krettenauer & Edelstein, 1999). Even controlling for moral type, moral judgment stage correlated with prosocial behavior (cf. Brabeck, 1984; Comunian & Gielen, 1995, 2000), indicating that the moral perception involved in prosocial behavior (at least in the sense of moral courage) is not only veridical but also mature. Empathy also related to prosocial behavior (the correlation only approached significance, perhaps because of the limitations of the self-report measure of empathy we used). Anecdotally, the rescuer in our case study did appeal to empathic distress ("seeing him insulted so bad, so real bad"). Other studies have found a fairly consistent relationship between empathic distress and altruistic or prosocial behavior (see Eisenberg, Fabes, & Spinrad, 2006; Krevans & Gibbs, 1996; Oliner & Oliner, 1988).

Finally, among the male participants, exemplary or courageous prosocial behavior related to internal locus of control. Internal locus of control is a belief that one's own actions are the main determinants of one's outcomes in life (cf. self-efficacy theory, Bandura, 1977). Within our adolescent sample, males who were rated high in moral courage were *less* likely to evidence *external* locus of control, in particular, to attribute events in their lives to the effects of chance or actions of powerful others. Perhaps the rescuer's overcoming of inhibitory peer expectations was attributable not only to accurate moral perception but as well to an implicit belief that his actions are not necessarily controlled by external forces. Accordingly, one would tend to hold oneself rather than others accountable for the consequences of one's actions. Colby and Damon (1992) observed that, among their moral exemplars, "blaming others, even impersonal forces" was rare, and personal accountability ("the importance of taking full responsibility for their actions") was common (p. 290). As bystanders among others in an emergency situation, moral exemplars would probably intervene rather than diffuse responsibility (Latane & Darley, 1970). In the long run, their lives of moral commitment had remarkable staying power, in part because failures were attributed to temporary, specific, and changeable factors and hence did not discourage new effort.

Moral Perception and Information-Processing Models

In our study of prosocial behavior thus far, we have mainly addressed the question of how such individuals see others and interpret their social world, that is, the variables entailed in their *moral perception*. Our and other studies suggest that the moral perception of prosocial actors is veridical, mature, and empathic and that they see or define *themselves* in moral terms. Perception in the broadest sense— that is, meaningful experiencing—is dissected in information-processing models of behavior. In Kohlberg and Daniel Candee's (1984) model of moral action, perception is composed of the "functions" of interpretation (based on one's stage, type, and other factors), choice or decision, and self-attribution (or nonattribution) of personal responsibility. Similar to these functions are the "components" of moral sensitivity (e.g., empathy), moral judgment, and prioritizing of moral values in James Rest's model (e.g., Narvaez & Rest, 1995). The broader model of Kenneth

Dodge and colleagues (e.g., Dodge & Schwartz, 1998; Dodge, Coie, & Lynam, 2006) specifies not functions or components but *steps*. The "steps" include encoding and interpreting situational cues, clarifying a goal (or orientation toward a desired outcome) in the situation, and evaluating and deciding among prospective responses pertinent to that goal.

Such analyses of perception in terms of components or steps have strengths and weaknesses. On one hand, these models do identify factors and processes that are typically involved in one way or another as individuals encounter events, that is, as we anticipate, experience, and react to the environment. On the other hand, they can give the misleading impression that the meaningful experience of events typically involves extensive calculations or sequential steps of decision making. Colby and Damon (1992; cf. Haidt, 2003) criticized such models insofar as their depiction of the individual as "constantly in the throes of decision" was not seen in the "simplicity of moral response" evident among their moral exemplars (pp. 69–70).

Colby and Damon (1992) might agree, however, that seemingly simple or sudden responses can stem from a complexity of cognitive factors and processes. In a reformulation of the social information-processing model, Nicki Crick and Kenneth Dodge (1994) suggested that a situational response is a function not only of the event per se but also of the schemas (proximal mental representations or attributions as well as "latent knowledge structures") that are brought to and activated by the event. The schemas may be complex and might have been slow to develop. Their development may even have entailed conscious reflection. Once the schemas have developed and become well practiced and dominant, however, their implicit activation can be very quick indeed (cf. post-conscious automaticity as described by Bargh, 1996). "That a concept is used rapidly does not mean that it does not involve [in its history] complex processes of reasoning" (Turiel, 2006b, p. 19).

The point can be made in terms of nonsocial cognition (e.g., conservation knowledge) as well as moral principles. Consider the older child who promptly justifies a conservation response with a complex appeal. The child's schemas and resultant sense of necessary reciprocity took a while to develop, but once they have become dominant, they can be readily activated—much like the schemas and sense of moral necessity of the moral exemplars. Gordon Moskowitz and colleagues (Moskowitz, Gollwitzer, Wasel, & Schaal, 1999; cf. Pizarro & Bloom, 2003) found that male undergraduates who had become highly committed to moral principles of gender equality were (in contrast to low-commitment controls) uninfluenced in a verbal task (concerning the pronunciation of female attributes) by prejudicial stimuli (negative female stereotypes). The equality principles to which they were highly committed can be regarded as complex and dominant schemas. The prejudicial stimuli—and their control by the activated equality schemas—happened quickly, even preconsciously: The stimulus was quite brief (presented for less than 200 milliseconds) and immediate (presented less than 200 milliseconds prior to the task judgment). The prejudicial stimuli (e.g., "irrational") facilitated the low-commitment participants' but *not* the high-commitment participants' response times, presumably because the stimuli were in the latter case controlled or inhibited by the activated equality schema. Again, it all happened very quickly. The schema had already been activated and done its implicit inhibition of the prejudicial stimulus before the respondent could even know what happened.

Similarly, sudden moments or simple responses of prosocial behavior can have a complex cognitive background. The rescuer's sudden intervention stemmed not just from the scene of imminent assault per se but also from the dominant, complex schemas that he had developed and brought to his perception of that scene. These were schemas of wrong (violation of ideal moral reciprocity) and harm (empathic alloys such as sympathy, guilt) that had been developed and, recently, applied to the African-American youth (perceived as "a kid, not a nigger"). The White youth was, in a way, primed to act, even though he didn't know it at the time. Only later did he realize that a (schema-based) line had been formed in his mind. That moral line divided levels of both wrong and harm. In both respects, the line was crossed as he saw his peers escalate from verbal abuse to imminent assault. In general, sudden and ostensibly simple responses can derive from complex processes and schemas that operate implicitly in various ways and degrees (Bargh, 1996; Bushman & Anderson, 2001; Pizarro & Bloom, 2003; Wegner & Bargh, 1998).

Ego Strength or Self-Control as the Regulation of Affect

Beyond moral perception, a final component or step included within processing models of social behavior links perception to action. This component has been characterized as "follow-through" skills (nondistractibility, intelligence, etc.) enabling goal attainment (Kohlberg & Candee, 1984), character or implementation (Narvaez & Rest, 1995; Rest et al., 1999), and enactment (Dodge & Schwartz, 1998). In traditional terms, this factor pertains to ego strength, self-control, perseverance, bravery, willpower, volition, conation. The moral exemplars evidenced ego strength in that they were extraordinarily persistent in pursuing their moral goals, partly because of their (earlier noted) positive attributional style in the face of failure. Similarly, the courageously prosocial male high school students we studied were less likely to attribute their actions to external influences (i.e., were higher in internal locus of control). Yet the moral exemplars did not need to struggle using all their ego strength to attain and maintain their resolve. Moral necessity, deep empathy, and moral self-relevance meant that they saw no morally acceptable alternative course of action and hence did not need to will themselves to overcome fear or doubt (Colby & Damon, 1992). The White youth regarded his rescue intervention as "the strangest moment of [his] life" partly because of its abrupt spontaneity, that is, the absence of any conscious reasoning and resolve to do the right thing despite the costs.

Nonetheless, ego strength is often needed for the attainment of behavioral goals. Ego strength links perception to action and goal attainment irrespective of the *content* of the goal. Ego strength is admirable when it promotes the attainment of moral goals, ranging from prosocial behavior to completing a task honestly (which may involve resisting a temptation to cheat). Honesty has been linked to nondistractibility or the stable maintenance of attention. Paul Grim, Sheldon White, and Kohlberg (1968) found that elementary school children's degree of attentional stability (operationalized as a low standard deviation in the reaction time of their response to a visual stimulus) was related to the extent to which they avoided cheating. "Stable attention seems to promote honesty primarily by leading to a higher threshold for distracting thoughts of the opportunity to cheat" (p. 250).

Processes contributing to the strength to resist a tempting distraction have been identified as strategies for achieving self-control or delaying gratification. The research question has been whether individuals of various ages can eschew a smaller immediate reward (such as a treat) in order to obtain a larger but later reward (perhaps two treats). Delay of gratification means regulating one's appetitive affect. Strategies or skills for regulating affect may include reducing the salience of the "hot" stimulus (e.g., covering the treat or avoiding attending to it), enhancing the salience of alternative stimuli or thoughts (e.g., singing a song or thinking of engaging in some alternative activity), and reinterpreting the meaning of the hot stimulus (e.g., minimizing a marshmallow treat's chewy, sweet, tasty qualities by reframing the marshmallow as "just a picture" or as a nonappetitive object such as a cloud or cotton ball) (Metcalfe & Mischel, 1999). Also functioning as an affect-regulatory strategy are the positive attributions (e.g., "learning opportunity") by which the moral exemplars interpreted the significance of failure.

Ego strength *qua* affect regulation tends to gain during child development. As we know from earlier chapters, the young child's behavior tends to be impulsive, egocentrically biased, and uncoordinated or centered on momentary here-and-now stimuli (in Metcalfe and Mischel's [1999] terms, "responsive primarily to the urgencies of internally activated hot spots and the pushes and pulls of hot stimuli in the external world," p. 8). The child gains ego strength through learning, socialization, language acquisition, cognitive development (primarily, decentration, mental coordination, and inferential ability), frontal lobe maturation, and increasing attentional stability. Accordingly, appetitive affect can be increasingly regulated and gratification delayed.

In later childhood, cognitive gains helpful for affect regulation come to include metacognitive awareness or understanding (e.g., understanding the value of "cool" ideation in sustaining gratificatory delay). A metacognitively savvy 11-year-old explained that, in the delay of gratification situation, he would tell himself, "I hate marshmallows, I can't stand them. But when the grown-up gets back, I'll tell myself 'I love marshmallows' and eat it" (Mischel & Mischel, 1983, p. 609).

Conclusion: Two Spurious "Moral Exemplars"

In addition to Coles's (1986) adolescent rescuer and Colby and Damon's (1992) 23 moral exemplars, two final cases (both men) warrant consideration. With charity, we might characterize these men as caring and imbued with a strong sense of justice; they apparently cared intensely for relatively defenseless people perceived to be suffering injustices at the hands of cruel bullies or arrogant governments. Each became totally dedicated to a campaign against those perceived cruelties and injustices; in Colby and Damon's terms, each merged his sense of self and his personal goals into his campaign. In the process, each evidenced impressive qualities of perseverance or ego strength, as well as self-efficacy or internal locus of control. Each sought to do something big or spectacular for his cause, and each succeeded. The names of these two exemplars? Timothy McVeigh and Osama bin Laden, ideological terrorists, willful prisoners of hate (Beck, 1999) whose big, spectacular events for their causes succeeded in killing hundreds or thousands of innocent men, women, and children. Despite the presence in their stories of factors we have seen to be associated with prosocial behavior, both men are exemplars not of love, mature and accurate perception, and compassion, but instead of distorted anger, vengeance, and hate (Damon, personal communication, October 14, 2001). Their ostensibly "moral" identities are more accurately identified as, to use David Moshman's (2004) term, *false* moral identities. McVeigh was found guilty of bombing a federal building in Oklahoma City, Oklahoma; he was executed on May 19, 2001. Bin Laden was believed to be still alive as of the autumn of 2008, although in hiding.

Taken together, these spurious "moral" exemplars prompt us to refine the thrust of the present chapter and move us toward our next topic, antisocial behavior. The acts of McVeigh and bin Laden reflect a nature-nurture interplay and are amenable to analysis on many scales of context or level (for a historical, political, and cultural analysis of the life of bin Laden, see Bodansky, 1999; Coll, 2008). Much as it would be fascinating to explore the gradual twisting of their humanity (to borrow a phrase from the South African Mark Mathabane, 2002; see Chapter 4), that is not our goal. Rather, we seek to use McVeigh and bin Laden as counterfoils in a discriminant analysis of the meaning of prosocial behavior. Hence, we will probe as best we can the minds of these men, their worldviews, their schemas for meaningful social experiencing. As Dodge (1993) suggested, it is the level of cognitive phenomenology that is the most "proximally responsible" (p. 560) for a person's overt behavior in a given situation. We will mainly use McVeigh (of whom more is known than of bin Laden) to make three points regarding full-fledged prosocial behavior.

First, *the moral basis for prosocial behavior must be mature.* Although even preschoolers can act prosocially (see Chapter 4), prosocial behavior in the full sense requires mature morality. The adolescent rescuer appreciated that the prospective victim (an African-American student and peer) was responding in a forgiving way to taunts and threats, and forgiveness was a common quality among the 23 exemplars (Colby & Damon, 1992, pp. 278–279). As Piaget emphasized, forgiveness and reconciliation (where feasible) are key indicators of ideal reciprocity or, more broadly, mature moral judgment (see Chapter 2). In contrast, forgiveness was absent in the pronouncements of McVeigh or bin Laden. Either might have seen the African-American youth's nonreciprocation as foolish or cowardly and perhaps deserving contempt.

Prominent instead in the pronouncements of both men was that of eye-for-an-eye reciprocity: vengeance, retribution, or retaliation. One fatwa or decree thought to be the work primarily of bin Laden used variants of the word *retaliate* nine times (Bodansky, 1999, pp. 224–225). He declared his aim to "show them [Americans and other infidels] the fist!" (p. 387) and to "pay back the Americans in their same coin" (p. 405). After the September 11, 2001, bombing attacks with their thousands of casualties, bin Laden declared, "What America is tasting now is only a copy of what we have tasted"[6] (Bradley, 2001). Similarly, McVeigh embraced a "philosophy" of "dirty for dirty" (Michel & Herbeck, 2001, p. 17). Particularly chilling threats of vengeance were reserved for McVeigh's former compatriots. Having reached a "philosophical impasse" with a former Army friend named Steve, McVeigh wrote Steve a 23-page letter that concluded with a transparent threat: "Blood will flow in the streets, Steve. . . . Pray it is not your blood, my friend" (pp. 153–155).

The case of Timothy McVeigh drives home just how crucial for social behavior is the difference between the initial, developmentally primitive version of "moral reciprocity" and its more advanced form—that is, between pragmatic reciprocity (moral judgment Stage 2) and reciprocity as an ideal (moral judgment Stage 3, especially Stage 3 Type B). Hoffman's (2000) claim that reciprocity "can serve many masters" (p. 243)—including hate—is tenable specifically with reference to pragmatic reciprocity. As we will discuss in the next chapter, moral judgment developmental delay is a risk factor for antisocial behavior.

Empathic distress as an empowerment of violence through immature moral judgment is illustrated with particular clarity in the case of McVeigh. As a child, McVeigh loved animals. He "cried . . . for days" after seeing kittens drown; he "let out a scream of shock and terror and ran for his parents in tears" (Michel & Herbeck, 2001, p. 17) to obtain help for an attacked and fatally injured rabbit. A decade or so later in McVeigh's life, a more complex empathic distress (specifically, self-focused perspective taking and empathic anger; see Chapter 4) partly motivated his primitive reciprocity, activated as he watched on television the violence at Waco:

> There it was. . . . Mount Carmel, the wooden complex where the Branch Davidians worshiped and lived under the rule of David Koresh, was engulfed in flames. Armored vehicles were ramming the walls. . . . The Davidians' Star of David flag . . . drifted into the fire. . . . tears were streaming down [McVeigh's] cheeks.
>
> When federal agents raised their own flag over the smoldering ruins, McVeigh's anger neared the point of exploding. People died in that house, he thought. How crude and ruthless and coldblooded can these guys be? . . . The government's use of CS gas, the tear gas McVeigh had been doused with as a soldier, enraged him. The memory of his own experience with the gas made the thought of using it on women and children unbearable to him. . . . In his mind, it was the ultimate bully attack. . . . Something . . . would have to be done. (pp. 135–136, 160)

Years later, after doing his "something," McVeigh invoked his Stage 2 vengeance philosophy to defend the murders of those in and around the federal building: "Women and kids were killed at Waco and Ruby Ridge. You put back in [the government's] faces exactly what they're giving out. . . . *Dirty for dirty,* he thought. *You reap what you sow. This is payback time*" (pp. 2, 225). The moral immaturity of McVeigh's social perception could scarcely be more explicit.

Second, *the social cognitive basis for prosocial behavior must be veridical.* The moral exemplars studied by Colby and Damon (1992) achieved not only mature moral understanding but also "ever greater moral clarity" (p. 173), which, again, we interpret as a kind of field independence in moral perception. As noted, they were rigorously truthful or veridical, resisting illusory interpretations of events: "Distortion . . . was not a mental process to which they would readily bring themselves" (p. 290). The vision or optimism that sustained them was, in Sandra Schneider's (2001) terms, "realistic" rather than biased.[7] In contrast, McVeigh's and bin Laden's visions and pronouncements, despite elements of truth, were rife with grandiose biases, cognitive distortions, and contradictions. Bin Laden's pronouncement favored "rhetorical effect over consistency of argument" (Coll, 2008, p. 570). McVeigh's cognitive distortions are examined more systematically in Chapter 6.

The distorted character of the terrorists' "moral" perception was especially evident as they attempted to cope with the problem that their acts of ostensible morality meant the murder of innocent human beings. After all, Stage 2 "dirty-for-dirty" reciprocity still meant that the act was, well, dirty (i.e., morally reprehensible), and these men were not devoid of empathy. Indeed, perhaps precisely because they *were* vulnerable to empathic distress, they needed to rationalize, distort, and thereby preempt any adverse feelings of self-blame or guilt for their actions. Bin Laden minimized the scale of the innocent victim problem and attributed it to the actions of the demonized enemy: "The few civilians caught up in the power games of the infidel Americans" were in effect "human shields held hostage" by the infidels (Bodansky, 1999, p. 368).[8] We term such cognitive distortions Minimizing/Mislabeling and Blaming Others, respectively (see Chapter 6).

McVeigh, too, found a way to blame the victims. He

> summoned an image that had remained with him since his childhood: the destruction of the Death Star in the 1977 motion picture Star Wars.
>
> McVeigh saw himself as a counterpart to Luke Skywalker, the heroic Jedi knight whose successful attack on the Death Star closes the film. As a kid, McVeigh had noticed that the Star Wars movies show people sitting at consoles—Space-Age clerical workers—inside the Death Star. Those people weren't storm troopers. They weren't killing anyone. But they were vital to the operations of the Evil Empire. . . . As an adult, McVeigh found himself able to dismiss the killings of secretaries, receptionists, and other personnel in the Murrah Building with equally cold-blooded calculation. They were all part of the evil empire. (Michel & Herbeck, 2001, pp. 224–225)

To elaborate on this rationalization, McVeigh used the military phrases he had learned as a soldier in the U.S. Army. As he prepared to bomb, he was "in a combat mode" (Michel & Herbeck, 2001, p. 156). "If he seemed devoid of feelings and sensitivity," then, "that was because he was a soldier" (p. xix) preparing for an "act of war" (p. 3), with a "duty to carry out … a mission" (p. 288). His "positive offensive action" (p. 332) against the government would need to generate a large "body count" (p. 169) if it was to make its point.

The military metaphor, then, enabled him to minimize the enormity of the crime with euphemisms. The dead among the "body count" who were peripheral to the evil empire were "collateral damage": "'In any kind of military action,'" he explained, "'you try to keep collateral damage to a minimum. But a certain amount of collateral damage is inevitable'" (p. 331). McVeigh's apparent need to use this minimizing distortion suggests that his assimilation of his killing innocent people to his Stage 2 dirty-for-dirty philosophy was not entirely successful. We do know from experimental research that maintaining distortions can require the expenditure of cognitive resources (Valdesolo & De Steno, 2008).

In other words, McVeigh's "field" of rationalizations and minimizing strategies could not entirely obscure the heinousness of his crime. Even the murderous bomber Theodore Kaszynski, a fellow inmate for several months, criticized McVeigh's allegedly moral perception as seriously flawed in its crudity; after all, "most of the people who died at Oklahoma City were … not even remotely responsible for objectionable government policies or for the events at Waco" (Michel & Herbeck, 2001, p. 364). A similarly global nondifferentiation in the conception of "the enemy" (Beck, 1999) was evident in the pronouncements and attacks associated with bin Laden.

Third, and in summary, *ego strength serves morality insofar as it links mature and veridical moral perception to action.* As noted, ego strength or persistence toward goal attainment depends partly on the use of strategies or skills for regulating affect and thereby maintaining attentional stability or avoiding distractions. Ego strength per se is neutral with respect to morality; hence, in Lawrence Walker's and Karl Hennig's (2004) study of moral exemplarity, the character attribute of "brave" is a moral quality only insofar as it is contextualized by "just" and/or "caring" qualities. Indeed, ego strength in the service of attaining *moral* goals (e.g., prosocial behavior or honest task completion) rests ultimately on processes of mature and accurate moral perception. A money-hungry and egocentrically biased man walking past a blind beggar is distracted by the sight of the beggar's many coins in a nearby cup and thinks how easy it would be to take them. This man will have little motivation to resist acting on this thought unless he processes the situation in moral terms. For example, the man might automatically activate a Stage 3 schema pertaining to how he or anyone would wish to be treated in that situation (ideal reciprocity à la Kohlberg or Piaget), or, relatedly, he might attend to that person's plight and imagine how he would feel or how that person must feel (empathic perspective taking à la Hoffman).

The terrorists' ego strength served an ideology of hatred. Against such perversely guided regulations of affect, empathic affect *for the prospective victims* scarcely had a chance. According to investigative interviewers Lou Michel and Dan Herbeck (2001), McVeigh did have at least one moment of moral clarity. As McVeigh drove his bomb-laden truck toward the federal building and "his eyes fell upon it," he was "hit … by the enormity of what he was about to do." But "just as quickly, he pushed the thought aside" (p. 230). Our speculative translation: As he saw all the unsuspecting, innocent people in and around the building, he anticipated with some beginning moral maturity and accuracy what his bomb would do to them. He experienced incipient moral inhibition from empathic distress, empathy-based guilt, and justice violation. Before the affective and cognitive moral motives could effectively inhibit, however, he mustered his resolve; that is, he empathized again with the Waco victims, generating empathic anger and reactivating his developmentally delayed morality (crude "payback" reciprocity) and distorted schemas of interpretation (e.g., "positive military action"). He thereby neutralized his moment of moral clarity. Such perverse use of ego strength, that is, such regulation of affect through cognitive distortion in the service of antisocial goals, is discussed further in the next chapter.

Notes

[1]Piaget's (1972/1973) explicit discussion of the influential role of "the cognitive unconscious," as well as his discussion of implicit moral cognitive structures evident in game playing behavior (Piaget, 1932/1965), challenges claims (e.g., Hauser, 2006) that Piaget "failed to consider the possibility that the knowledge driving … behavior is unconscious" (p. 170).

[2]Interestingly, Hoffman (2000) suggested that not only the basic but even the advanced arousal modes (verbally mediated association, perspective taking) can contribute to sudden responding: "If one is paying attention to the victim, they too can be fast-acting, involuntary, and triggered immediately on witnessing the victim's situation" (p. 61). This point challenges relegations of complex cognitive processes to "slow" and "cool" mental systems (e.g., Haidt & Bjorklund, 2008a, b; Metcalfe & Mischel, 1999).

[3]Marta Laupa (2000) suggested that "2 plus 2 equals 4" involves symbolic notation and hence does not illustrate numeric or logical necessity as well as propositions such as "the combination of two actual quantities is greater than either of the original quantities" (p. 22).

[4]Anthropologist Robert Edgerton (1992) provided a poignant example of profound moral perception of common humanity (and moral courage):

> Some time in the early nineteenth century, Knife Chief, the political leader of the Skidi Pawnee and a greatly respected man, decided that human sacrifice was cruel and unnecessary. … He began to speak against the practice, and in 1817 he attempted to halt the sacrifice of a captive girl. Just before the torture of the young victim was about to begin, Knife Chief's son, by all accounts the most honored warrior among the Skidi Pawnee, stepped in front of the girl and declared that it was his father's wish that she be set free. As the Pawnee audience looked on in

amazement he freed the girl, threw her on his horse, and delivered her safely to her own people. A year later, father and son again prevented a sacrifice—this time of a ten-year-old Spanish boy— by ransoming the captive from a warrior who was determined to offer the child for sacrifice.

As courageous, determined, and influential as Knife Chief and his son were, their efforts to put an end to the practice of human sacrifice failed. Led by their priests, the Skidi Pawnee continued to propitiate the Morning Star by sacrificing human captives at least until 1834 and perhaps much longer. Knife Chief and his son had failed, but they stand as striking examples of individuals who did everything in their power to change a custom that they found abhorrent even though that custom was held sacred by the rest of the society. (p. 143)

[5]We posit moral self-relevance as a major motivational primacy mainly in individuals for whom personal and moral goals are highly integrated (although salient wrong and harm to others can pose a problem of inconsistency and guilt for those with even modest moral self-relevance; see Chapter 6). In contrast, Damon (1996) saw a more widespread impact on motivation: "Toward the end of childhood, ... children ... begin thinking about themselves in terms of how kind, just, and responsible they are. ... This [closer link between their moral interests and their self-concept or identity] leads to a bit more predictability between children's moral judgment and their conduct" (p. 221).

[6]Although this statement would appear to indicate a Stage 2 moral developmental level, it could also be prompted to some degree by a Stage 3 moral educational concern (see Chapter 2, Note 8).

[7]Perhaps not totally realistic or veridical. Some studies suggest that seeing one's self and capabilities or prospects for success as "*slightly* better than they are" may be adaptive and mentally healthy (Baumeister, 1989, p. 182, emphasis added; cf. Haaga & Beck, 1994; Taylor & Brown, 1994).

[8]By the summer of 2008, bin Laden's minimizations of his movement's massacres of innocent lives—many of them Muslim—seemed to be wearing thin even among some of his erstwhile associates (Bergen & Cruickshank, 2008, June 11; Wright, 2008, June 2).

6 CHAPTER

Understanding Antisocial Behavior

THIS CHAPTER AND THE NEXT CONTINUE THE APPLICATION OF MORAL knowing and feeling—especially, what we have learned of moral knowing and feeling through study of Kohlberg's and Hoffman's developmental theories—to social behavior. From the last chapter's focus on variables of prosocial behavior, we shift at this point in our exploration to the understanding and treatment of *anti*social behavior. According to Kohlberg's and Hoffman's theories, the key principle of treatment for antisocial behavior is at least in part the same as that for facilitating children's social decentration and moral judgment development or for socializing prosocial norms and empathic motivation. Whether the aim is to cognitively facilitate or empathically socialize, the key is to give egocentrically biased or self-centered individuals—children, adolescents, adults—opportunities and encouragement to take the perspectives of others. Perspective-taking treatment programs will be discussed in Chapter 7.

This chapter will focus on self-centration and other limitations characteristic of youths with antisocial behavior problems. Two caveats to the term *limitation* should be noted. First, pronounced egocentric bias and other "limitations" are best construed as tendencies, not incapacities evident in all circumstances. Second, these tendencies result from "a complex interplay of nature and nurture" (Rutter, 1997, p. 390). "Nature" encompasses partially neurophysiological variables such as difficult temperament and hyperactivity, and "nurture" encompasses not only relatively direct effects such as those of abuse and neglect but also the indirect effects of macrocontexts such as social class, negative youth culture, and economic disadvantage (Collins et al., 2000; Kazdin, 1995; cf. Bronfenbrenner & Morris, 2006). Although they are not the focus of this chapter, the background factors of nature and nurture should be kept in mind as we discuss the limitations that tend to characterize antisocial youths.

Limitations of Antisocial Youths

After extensive work with antisocial and aggressive youths, Cleveland, Ohio, high school teacher Dewey Carducci (1980) reached three main conclusions regarding the limitations (problematic tendencies might be a better term) of such adolescents. First, according to Carducci's impressions, the antisocial juvenile is "frequently at a stage of arrested moral/ethical/social/emotional development in which he is fixated at a level of concern about getting his own throbbing needs [i.e., impulses and desires] met, regardless of effects on others." Second, such juveniles were seen to "blame others for their misbehavior." Third, they "do not know what specific steps [in a social conflict]... will result in [the conflict's] being solved [constructively]" (pp. 157–158). The research literature concerning conduct disorder, opposition-defiance disorder, and other patterns of adolescent antisocial behavior (e.g., Kazdin, 1995) strikingly corroborates Carducci's impressions.

We (Gibbs, Potter, Barriga, & Liau, 1996) have termed these limitations, respectively, (a) developmental *delay* in moral judgment, (b) self-serving cognitive *distortions*, and (c) social skill *deficiencies*—the "three Ds," so to speak, common among antisocial youths. Although distinguishable, the limitations are interrelated (Barriga, Morrison, Liau, & Gibbs, 2001; Larden, Melin, Holst, & Langstrom, 2006; Leeman, Gibbs, & Fuller, 1993). Following our review of the literature pertinent to these three main interrelated limitations of antisocial youths, we will revisit for illustrative purposes the case of Timothy McVeigh (who was still in his 20s when he committed his atrocity) that was introduced in the last chapter.

Moral Judgment Developmental Delay

Moral developmental delay refers chiefly to the persistence of immature morality into adolescence and adulthood. Just as prosocial behavior stems in part from the mature moral perception (or meaningful experience) of events (Chapter 5), *anti*social behavior stems in part from moral perception based on developmentally delayed morality. As discussed in Chapter 2, immature morality is composed of pronounced egocentric bias or, more broadly, superficial moral judgment.

Superficial Moral Judgment

Superficial moral judgment confuses the moral with the salient surface features of people, things, or actions: either with impressive physical appearances or physical consequences (Stage 1) or with concrete, tit-for-tat exchanges of favors or blows, that is, pragmatic reciprocity (Stage 2). Relative to controls, delinquent or conduct-disordered adolescents evidence a delay in moral judgment stage level (even after controlling for SES, intelligence, and other correlates), attributable mainly to a more extensive use of moral judgment Stage 2 (see meta-analyses by Nelson, Smith, & Dodd, 1990; and by Stams, Brugman, Dekovic, Rosmalen, van der Laan, & Gibbs, 2006; for an overview, see Blasi, 1980; Palmer, 2003). Our

(Gibbs, Basinger, Grime, & Snarey, 2007) cross-cultural review found that delinquents were delayed in moral judgment (relative to matched or group-selected comparison controls) in all seven countries where the question was studied (the delinquents' delay in the Netherlands became non-significant when participants from "a high-risk urban area" were added to the comparison group; Brugman & Aleva, 2004, p. 325). Inspection of Table 6.1 reveals an almost total absence of overlap between delinquents' and non-delinquents' moral judgment means across the seven countries.

We also studied moral judgment delay by area of moral value (keeping promises, helping others, respecting life, etc.). Although we found delay in *every* area (Gregg, Gibbs, & Basinger, 1994; Palmer & Hollin, 1998), the area of greatest delay concerned the reasons offered for obeying the law. Nondelinquents generally gave Stage 3 and Transition 3/4 reasons, for example, the typical selfishness of law-breaking such as stealing, and its ramifications in society for chaos, insecurity, or loss of trust. In contrast, the delinquents' reasoning mainly concerned the risk of getting caught and going to jail.

It should be emphasized that the superficiality of delayed moral judgment pertains to the *reasons* or *justifications* for moral decisions or values. I remember discussing moral values in the late 1980s with Joey, a 15-year-old at a specialized middle school in Columbus, Ohio, for juveniles with behavior problems. Joey seemed earnest and sincere as he emphatically affirmed the importance of moral values such as keeping promises, telling the truth, helping others, saving lives, not stealing, and obeying the law. "And why is it so important to obey the law?" I asked Joey. "Because, [pause], like in a store, you may think no one sees you, but they could have cameras!," he replied. His other explanations were generally similar: Keeping promises to others is important because if you don't, they might find out and get even; helping others is important in case you need a favor from them later; and so forth. The more Joey justified his moral evaluations, the less impressed I became. Could Joey be trusted to live up to his moral values in situations where his fear of observers and surveillance cameras would be less salient than his egocentric motives? Despite their evaluation of moral values as important (Gregg et al., 1994; Palmer & Hollin, 1998), many antisocial juveniles are developmentally delayed in that they do not evidence much grasp of the deeper *reasons* or bases for the importance of those values.

Pronounced and Prolonged Egocentric Bias

The high salience of egocentric biases and egoistic motives in superficial moral judgment means that the antisocial youth tends to be concerned with "getting his own throbbing needs [or desires] met, regardless of effects on others" (Carducci, 1980, p. 157). Accordingly, relative to non-delinquent adolescents, antisocial youths respond empathically to others less frequently and less intensely, and more frequently make self-references (Robinson, Roberts, Strayer, & Koopman, 2007). Like

Table 6.1 Cross-Cultural Samples of Male Delinquents and Non-Delinquents in Rank Order by Mean Sociomoral Reflection Maturity Score (SRMS)

Country, sample/age range (mean) in years	n	Global stage range	M
China, delinquents/13–15 (NR)	10	NR	182
Australia, delinquents (1 female)/14–18 (16.5)	38	1/2–2/3	211[a]
England, delinquents/14–17 (15.9)	147	2–2/3	223
Sweden, delinquents/13–18 (15.5)	29	2–2/3	228
Netherlands, delinquents/NR (16.5)	64	2–2/3	241
USA, delinquents/13–18 (15.9)	89	2–2/3	243
Germany, delinquents/14–17 (15.6)	39	2–3	243
Netherlands, non-delinquents/NR (15.1)	81	2–3	249
China, non-delinquents/13–15 (NR)	10	NR	251
Bahrain, delinquents/14–19 (16.8)	30	2/3–3	254
Germany, non-delinquents/14–16 (15.6)	309	2/3–3	261
England, non-delinquents/14–16 (15.5)	149	2–3	264
Sweden, non-delinquents/13–18 (15.6)	29	2/3–3	266
USA, non-delinquents/13–19 (15.7)	86	2/3–3	272
Bahrain, non-delinquents/17–18 (17.7)	30	3–3/4	313

Notes: NR indicates information not reported. Global stage range is estimated on the basis of plus or minus one standard deviation of Sociomoral Reflection Maturity Score. Non-delinquents are generally male high school students selected (sometimes matched) for a comparison study of delinquents. The studies are referenced in the source article.
Source: Adapted from J. C. Gibbs, K. S. Basinger, R. L. Grime, & J. R. Snarey (2007). Moral judgment development across cultures: Revisiting Kohlberg's universality claims. *Developmental Review, 27,* 443–500. Used with the permission of Elsevier ScienceDirect.
[a]Mean pretest score in an intervention study.

children, they tend to "complain of mistreatment if their wishes are not given priority over those of other[s]" (Beck, 1999, p. 236). Their

> *energy tends to go into asserting their needs and desires and making the world accommodate to them. They have a supersensitive Unfairness Detector when it comes to finding all the ways that people are unfair to them. But they have a big blind spot when it comes to seeing all the ways they aren't fair to others and all the ways parents and others do things for them. (Lickona, 1983, p. 149; cf. Redl & Wineman, 1957, pp. 153–154)*

As we have seen, it is normal for egocentric bias to be pronounced in early child-hood; young children have not yet decentered from their own very salient needs, desires, or impulses. With perspective-taking opportunities such as those afforded by peer interaction and inductive discipline, egocentric bias normally declines. In a study of the development of children's reasons for obedience, Damon (1977) found later rea-sons to be less egocentric: "The self's welfare is still important, but at ... later levels self-interest is increasingly seen in the context of the welfare of everyone in the rela-tion" (p. 221). The often highly power-assertive and harsh parenting homes of children at risk for conduct disorder (Kazdin, 1995), however, preclude opportunities to take the perspectives of others. Accordingly, bias of self over the welfare of others and superfi-cial moral judgment generally remain pronounced into the adolescent years.

Self-Serving Cognitive Distortions

Moral judgment stages are not the only schemas relevant to social perception and behav-ior. Just as prosocial behavior can stem from schemas of mature and veridical moral per-ception (Chapter 5), antisocial behavior can stem from perception structured by schemas of self-serving cognitive distortion. Cognitive distortions (cf. "thinking errors," Yochelson & Samenow, 1976, 1977, 1986; "faulty beliefs," Ellis, 1977) are inaccurate or nonveridical schemas for perceiving events. Reviewed below are self-serving cognitive distortions that, at elevated prevalence levels, facilitate aggression and other antisocial behavior.

Self-Centered: The Primary Self-Serving Cognitive Distortion

The longer that pronounced egocentric bias persists through childhood, the more it tends to consolidate into a primary self-serving cognitive distortion that we have called Self-Centered. In the absence of moral judgment perspective-taking opportunities, the self-centration (including "I want it *now*" temporal centration) characteristic of early childhood can evolve in later years into a network of self-skewed schemas that guides one's perception and explanation of events and indeed one's basic approach to life, one's worldview. We (Gibbs et al., 1996) have defined the Self-Centered schema network as "according status to one's own views, expectations, needs, rights, immediate feelings, and desires to such an extent that the legitimate views, etc., of others (or even one's own long-term best interest) are scarcely considered or are disregarded altogether"[1] (p. 108). The combination of a radically Self-Centered worldview with even the normal array and intensity of egoistic motives constitutes a risk factor for antisocial behavior.

Numerous clinicians working with antisocial youths have discerned a link between the youths' antisocial behavior and a self-centered attitude or approach to social relations. Stanton Samenow (1984) quoted a 14-year-old delinquent: "I was born with the idea that I'd do what I wanted. I always felt that rules and regulations were not for me" (p. 160). Redl and Wineman (1957) gave as an example the responses of a youth who had stolen a cigarette lighter and was confronted:

> His only defense seemed to be, "Well, I wanted a lighter." When further challenged, "Yes, you wanted a lighter but how about going to such lengths as to steal it

from someone?," he grew quite irritated. "How the hell do you expect me to get one if I don't swipe it? Do I have enough money to buy one?"... The act... was quite justifiable to him ..."I want it, there is no other way, so I swipe it—just because I want it." (pp. 154–155)

Similarly, in our group work with antisocial youth (see Chapter 7), one group member seemed to think that he had sufficiently justified his having stolen a car with this explanation: "I needed to get to Cleveland." Other group members, reflecting on their shoplifting and other offenses, have recollected that their thoughts at the time concerned whether they could do what they wanted and get away successfully. The only perspective these juveniles took was their own; spontaneous references to the victims' perspectives were almost totally absent. Indeed, a recent study (Wainryb, Komolova, & Florsheim, in press; cf. Carr & Lutjemeier, 2005) found that only 10% of violent youths (versus 89% of comparison youths) made reference to their victims' emotions in narrating a time of having harmed someone.

This primary cognitive distortion is especially clear in groups of aggressive male juveniles, for example, in their responses to the following vignette (used in connection with the anger management component of our EQUIP group program, discussed in Chapter 7):

Gary is in the kitchen of his apartment. Gary's girlfriend, Cecilia, is angry at him for something he did to hurt her. She yells at him. She pushes his shoulder. Thoughts run through Gary's head. Gary does nothing to correct the errors in his thoughts. Gary becomes furious. He swears at Cecilia. A sharp kitchen knife is nearby. Gary picks up the knife and stabs Cecilia, seriously wounding her. (Potter et al., 2001, p. 56; cf. Gibbs et al., 1995)

Our impression is that aggressive youths seem to identify with Gary. In response to the probe question, "What thoughts do you think ran through Gary's head?" the juveniles readily and with some genuine feeling offer thoughts such as, "Who does she think she is? She has no right to treat me that way. Nobody hits *me*. I wear the pants around here. I do what I want. How dare she *touch* me!" Self-centered and other self-serving cognitive distortions correlate highly with self-reports, parent or peer ratings, and records of violent or aggressive behavior (e.g., Barriga & Gibbs, 1996; Barriga, Landau, Stinson, Liau, & Gibbs, 2000; Liau, Barriga, & Gibbs, 1998; McCrady, Kaufman, Vasey, Barriga, Devlin, & Gibbs, 2008; Paciello, Fida, Tramontano, Lupinette, & Caprara, 2008).

Aggressive youths "generally believe that their entitlements and rights override those of others" (Beck, 1999, p. 27). Accordingly, their egoistic motives gain full sway in their social behavior. Although offenders victimize others, they generally misperceive their victims as the offenders and themselves as victims. After all, they have been thwarted or disrespected and thereby wronged, their (egocentrically elevated) entitlements or rights violated:

Consider the following scenarios. The driver of a truck curses a slow driver ... [or] a large nation attacks a smaller, resistant neighbor for its abundant

supply of oil. Interestingly, although there is clearly a difference between vic-
timizer and victim in these examples, the aggressor in each case is likely to
lay claim to being the victim: ... The object of their wrath, the true victim (to
disinterested observers), is seen as the offender by the victimizers. (p. 26,
emphasis added)

Proactive and Reactive Aggression   This inflated sense of one's self-esteem
and prerogatives and readiness to see oneself as wronged reflect a Self-Centered
ego that is either (a) grandiose from a sense of superiority or (b) vulnerable from
a sense of potential inadequacy. In the grandiose version of the Self-Centered
ego, the individual perceives and treats others as weaker beings who should not
dare to interfere and who can be manipulated or controlled through violence.
Aggression, then, is part of his basic approach to life. In the vulnerable version of
the Self-Centered ego, the individual views the world mainly as a place where
people do not adequately respect (and may actively seek to humiliate) him; he
becomes violence prone when he perceives (or misperceives) a threat or insult
(Beck, 1999). In the terms we will use, the aggression is either (a) *proactive* (at
clinically severe levels, psychopathic) or (b) *reactive* (Dodge & Coie, 1987). In either
case, the Self-Centered worldview is a risk factor for aggressive or other antisocial
behavior.

Both proactive and reactive offenders evidence inflated self-esteem (Baumeister,
1997) and "assert their prerogatives—for example, 'You have no right to treat me
that way'" (Beck, 1999, p. 138). The reasons behind such assertions differ, however.
The proactive offender "takes for granted that his rights are supreme and confidently imposes them on other people" (pp. 138–139). Following aggression, he feels
"triumphant" (after all, he has righted the wrong of interference or resistance). In
contrast, "the reactive offender feels that nobody recognizes his rights and reacts
with anger and sometimes violence when others reject him or do not show him
respect." His inflated self-esteem is more volatile, more vulnerable to bouts of
despair. After harming someone, the reactive offender on some occasions may feel
vindicated (he, too, has righted a wrong, the wrong of undeserved disrespect) but
on other occasions "may feel shame or guilt," suggesting a capacity for empathic
distress and self-attribution of blame (Beck, 1999, pp. 138–139).

Men who are wife batterers—the Garys of our vignette—may be either reactive or proactive (Chase, O'Leary, & Heyman, 2001). The majority are reactive; that
is, they hit "impulsively, out of rage after feeling rejected or jealous, or out of fear of
abandonment" (Goleman, 1995). In contrast, the proactive aggressive men hit

in a cold, calculating state.... As their anger mounts ... their heart rate drops,
instead of climbing higher, as is ordinarily the case.... This means they are growing
physiologically calmer, even as they get more belligerent and abusive. Their violence
appears to be a calculated act of terrorism, a method of controlling their wives by
instilling fear. (Goleman, 1995, pp. 108–109; see also Gottman et al., 1995)

Secondary Cognitive Distortions

To continue his Self-Centered attitude and antisocial behavior, the offender (at least the reactive offender) typically develops protective rationalizations, or what we term *secondary* cognitive distortions. These secondary cognitive distortions protect the offender against certain types of psychological stress that tend to be generated by his (or her) harm to others. One type of stress, primarily affective, refers to empathic distress and empathy-based guilt that may begin to be aroused by salient victim distress cues (Eisenberg, Fabes, & Spinrad, 2006; Redl & Wineman, 1957). If Hoffman's depiction of the common and multiple modes of empathy is accurate, then endogenous or primary psychopathy (marked by the total absence of empathic predisposition; Lykken, 1995) should be relatively rare. In positive terms, most of those who characteristically do salient harm to others must cope with incipient empathic distress and even guilt.

The second type of stress, primarily cognitive (but relating to guilt and moral self-relevance), results from the potential inconsistency with self represented by salient and unfair harm to others. Morality is less relevant to self for those with a pre-eminent sense of entitlement and who engage in antisocial behavior (Aquino et al., 2007; Barriga et al., 2001). Even so, the impression of many clinicians is that, like most individuals (Epstein & Morling, 1995), antisocial persons (even proactive offenders to some extent) seek to retain and maintain a "good" image (Beck, 1999; Samenow, 1984) in some sense (others are harmed only for good reason). Accordingly, highly salient, obviously unfair harm to others may contradict the good-person presentation to self and others and thereby generate psychological stress from cognitive inconsistency or dissonance (Blasi, 1995; Kelman & Baron, 1968; Swann et al., 1999).

Maintaining self-serving cognitive distortions to cope with these stresses often requires cognitive effort (cognitive resources in information processing terms; mental energy in psychodynamic terms). In many cases, one's distortions (the nobility of one's actions, the inhumanity or blameworthiness of one's victims, etc.) must be repeated if the stresses (empathic distress, threat to moral self-image) generated by one's antisocial behavior are again to be quelled. Experimental work has shown that self-protective (and self-deceiving) distortions attenuate once some of one's cognitive resources are diverted (Valdesolo & DeSteno, 2008), or once one is "primed" with salient moral terms (caring, compassionate, fair, friendly, kind, etc.; Aquino, Reed, Thau, & Freeman, 2007).

Nonetheless, secondary distortions can function as a perversely effective coping mechanism. Through their use, the antisocial individual can reduce the stresses of empathy and inconsistency (as well as other stresses, such as humiliation; see below) and preserve his primary Self-Centered orientation[2] as well as self-esteem. Higher self-esteem children with antisocial tendencies were more likely to use self-serving cognitive distortions (minimizing the harm of their aggression or blaming their victims; Menon, Tobin, Corby, Menon, Hodges, & Perry, 2007). Also, self-serving distortions relate inversely to empathy for victims (e.g., Larden, Melin, Holst, & Langstrom, 2006; McCrady et al., 2008; Paciello et al., 2008). Adolescents with high levels of self-serving distortion are more aggressive and subsequently less likely to express feelings of guilt (Paciello et al., 2008). In psychodynamic terms, Fritz Redl and David Wineman (1957) described the "special machinery [that the antisocial child] has developed in order to secure their [ego and impulse-gratifying] behavior against... guilt" (p. 146). In the language of Albert Bandura's (1999) cognitive social learning theory, rationalizations permit one to "disengage" one's unfair, harmful conduct from one's evaluation of self. In our typology (Barriga, Gibbs, et al., 2001; Gibbs, Barriga, & Potter, 2001), these empathy reducers and protectors of Self-Centered attitudes and self-esteem are termed *Blaming Others, Assuming the Worst,* and *Minimizing/Mislabeling.*

Blaming Others   As Carducci (1980) noted, antisocial or aggressive individuals tend to blame others for their own misbehavior. Blaming Others naturally follows from the Self-Centered sense of entitlement; in the example noted earlier, the aggressive truck driver blamed his verbal attack on the slow driving of his victim. In the Gary vignette (above), several of the group members suggested that Cecilia "was asking for it." "If she bothered to clean up around the kitchen," one group member opined, "she wouldn't have gotten hurt with that knife." Indeed, a man who expected others to accommodate to his every whim flew into a rage and fatally stabbed his wife upon discovering that she and their children had finally started eating dinner without him. He told her as she died, "You pushed me to the limits. You did this to yourself" (Aloniz, 1997, p. 5A). Harry Vorrath and Larry Brendtro (1985) noted the "elaborate systems" developed by antisocial youths

> *for displacing responsibility for their problems onto some other person or circumstance. When we ask a youth why he got into trouble he will say his parents were messed up, or he had the wrong friends, or the police were out to get him, or the teachers hated him, or his luck turned bad. Projecting, denying, rationalizing, and avoiding, he becomes an expert at escaping responsibility. (p. 37)*

Generally, Blaming Others can be defined as "misattributing blame for one's harmful actions to outside sources, especially to another person, a group, or a momentary aberration (one was drunk,[3] high, in a bad mood, etc.), or misattributing blame for one's victimization or other misfortune to innocent others" (Gibbs et al., 1995, p. 111). The misattribution of illegitimate aggression to military authorities ("I was just following orders") has been called "authorization" (Kelman, 1973; Kelman & Hamilton, 1989).

The ego-protective role of secondary cognitive distortions such as Blaming Others means that they serve as strategies for regulating or neutralizing interfering affects in the service of antisocial behavioral goals. Ordinarily, an individual may use cognitive strategies to regulate appetitive affect and thereby achieve prosocial goals (see Chapter 5). In contrast, an antisocial individual may use a cognitive distortion such as Blaming Others to preempt, neutralize, or at least attenuate inhibitory threats such as empathy-based guilt (or the aversive affect generated by inconsistency with self-concept) to achieve or resume the pursuit of *antisocial* behavioral goals. And the neutralization of guilt with self-serving cognitive distortions can require conscious effort (Valdesolo & DeSteno, 2008). Looking back on his burglaries and victims, one delinquent reflected, "If I started feeling bad, I'd say to myself, 'tough rocks for him. He should have had his house locked better and the alarm on'" (Samenow, 1984, p. 115). This delinquent would seem to be saying in effect, "Upon experiencing empathy-based guilt and bad self-concept for causing innocent people to suffer, I would neutralize my aversive affect by blaming the suffering on the victims; they were negligent in protecting their homes and so deserved whatever happened to them." Hoffman (2000) concurred with this view of externalizing blame as serving to neutralize, displace, or otherwise regulate affect, noting that it

> fits my [Hoffman's 1970] own finding that seventh graders with an external
> moral orientation (stealing is bad if you get caught) often respond with guilt
> feeling to story-completion items in which the central figure harms another, but
> it is only a momentary guilt feeling that is followed quickly by externalizing
> blame and other forms of guilt reduction. (p. 291, emphases added)

Besides neutralizing empathy-based guilt, externalizing blame can momentarily spare the ego the aversive affect of hurt or humiliation from an offense. This benefit may be especially important in the case of the reactive offender. One of Aaron Beck's (1999) patients was a mother who "became angry with her children for very minor infractions." In therapy, she recognized her belief that

> "If kids do not behave themselves, it means they are bad kids." The hurt came
> from a deeper meaning yielded by the belief, "If my kids misbehave, it shows I'm
> a bad mother." The overgeneralized belief led to an overgeneralized interpreta-
> tion. The mother diverted her attention away from the pain of the negative
> images of herself by blaming her children. (p. xii, emphasis added)

Although this woman's blame did not lead to physical child abuse, Blaming Others—especially when the pain experienced includes humiliation or negative self-image—does often eventuate in aggression. Blaming Others can support self-centered perceptions and anger. For example, an interpretation that the deliverer of a perceived insult or slight "is asking for it" or "deserves to be punished" can precipitate or rationalize an assault. If—as in the case of the reactive ego—the insult activates a negative self-image and attendant thoughts generating distress ("everybody thinks they can put me down, that I am weak, powerless, inferior"), that distress can be temporarily neutralized by an externalization of blame and punitive act of aggression. Although momentarily obscured, the underlying sense of inadequacy and vulnerability persists.

For some reactive offenders, "only a violent act would be sufficient to neutralize their deep sense of humiliation. Hitting and killing are strong forms of empowerment and powerful antidotes to a debased self-image" (Beck, 1999, p. 266). So is sexual violence. A sadistic rapist who believed that women deprecated him attributed his criminal "excitement" to "the prospect of having a young, pure, upperclass girl and bring[ing] her down to my level—a feeling like 'Well there's one fine, fancy bitch who [has been humiliated]. ... Bet she don't feel so uppity now'" (Groth & Birnsbaum, 1979, pp. 45–46). Timothy Kahn and Heather Chambers (1991) found higher sexual recidivism rates among juvenile sex offenders who blamed their victims for the offenses than for those who did not.

It is worth noting that the victim in the above example had not even known the offender, let alone deprecated him in any way; in the offender's mind, however, her mere membership in the offending class of humanity (women) was sufficient to justify the assault. Many offenders overgeneralize their grievances and targets of vengeance (Wilson & Herrnstein, 1985). One of Redl and Wineman's (1957) Pioneer House children "really tried to prove that his stealing [from other House children] was all right because 'somebody swiped my own wallet two weeks ago'" (p. 150). A 16-year-old who had just fatally shot several classmates explained the violence to the school's assistant principal (who was holding him until the police arrived): "Mr. Myrick, the world has wronged me" (Lacayo, 1998).

The sense that one has been *wronged* adds motive power to one's antisocial behavior. As Beck (1999) noted, an individual who has perceived himself to have been diminished in some way typically perceives that putdown to be unfair, prompting a mobilization of "his behavioral system ... in preparation for counterattack" (p. 31). One must rape, steal, or kill not only to neutralize one's hurt or restore one's self-esteem but more nobly to reestablish one's rights, to correct an injustice that has been committed against one, to "get even" or "settle the score." Hoffman (2000) characterized offenders' rationalization "that because they have been victimized in the past it is legitimate for them to victimize others" as representing "an inverted form of [eye-for-an-eye] reciprocity which ... illustrates my claim ... that reciprocity ... can serve antisocial as well as prosocial purposes" (pp. 292–293). The youth who killed to get even with the world that had wronged him was evidencing both Stage 2 moral judgment and a Blaming Others distortion to cover his highly salient, otherwise obviously unjustifiable harm to innocent others. Moral judgment delay and a tendency to externalize blame can be a deadly combination.

Assuming the Worst   The sadistic rapist who imagined that a young woman "felt uppity" and deprecated him not only evidenced a Blaming Others cognitive distortion ("it was her fault she was raped") but also an "Assuming the Worst" distortion that she specifically and deliberately meant to offend him (cf. Gannon, Polaschek, & Ward, 2005). We define Assuming the Worst as "gratuitously attributing hostile intentions to others, considering a worst-case scenario for a social situation as if it were inevitable, or assuming that improvement is impossible in one's own or others' behavior" (Gibbs et al., 1996, p. 290). Our EQUIP group members' responses to our "What thoughts went through Gary's head?" question (see above) included Assuming the Worst distortions such as "she hates me," "she thinks I'm no good," "she's trying to kill me, I have to defend myself!" and "she's going to leave me!" Much like Blaming Others, such exaggerated attributions can then function as facilitative and protective rationalizations for violence against the victim.

Attributing to another, on insufficient grounds, hostile attitudes or negative intentions toward oneself has been linked to antisocial behavior. Kenneth Dodge and colleagues (see Coie, Lynan, & Dodge, 2006; cf. Orobia de Castro, Veerman, Koops, Bosch, & Monshouwer, 2002) found evidence consistent with the thesis that such misattributions precede aggression: Although the other boys' intentions were actually ambiguous, highly aggressive (relative to low-aggressive) boys gratuitously attributed hostile intentions to the other's acts. Dodge and colleagues (Dodge, Price, Bachorowski, & Newman, 1990) found higher levels of hostile attribution among severely reactive-aggressive juvenile offenders.

Extreme levels of Assuming the Worst can be recognized in clinical mental health populations. The psychiatric diagnosis of "delusional paranoid" is applied when individuals assume the worst regarding events and behavior irrelevant to themselves. An agitated paranoid patient of Beck's interpreted the laughing of a lively group of strangers at a street corner "as a sign that they were plotting to embarrass him" (Beck, 1999, p. 28).

Physical abuse is apparently a risk factor for the development of self-protective or Assuming the Worst biases and aggression. Dodge, Bates, and Pettit (1990) found in a longitudinal study that 4-year-olds who were physically abused subsequently evidenced hostile attributional bias and other distortions in a vignette-based assessment, followed by high rates of aggressive behavior in kindergarten. Hence, Assuming the Worst about others' intentions and other "deviant" modes of social information processing mediate the relation between physical abuse and subsequent aggressive behavior. Beck (1999) suggested that "harsh parenting shapes the child's [overgeneralized] inimical views of others and his view of himself as vulnerable to the hostile actions of others" (p. 134). Beck described the following clinical case of reactive aggression:

> Terry, an eight-year-old boy, was referred to the clinic because of a history of demandingness, disobedience, disruptive behavior at school, continuous fights with his younger siblings, and rebellion against his parents and teachers. . . . Spanking and slapping by his father in order to curb his attacks on his younger brother were largely unsuccessful. . . . By the time Terry was six, his father would slam him against the wall, wrestle with him, or drag him to his room and lock the door. . . . One of Terry's most common complaints was, "Everybody is against me." This belief shaped his interpretation of other boys' behavior. If a fellow student walked by without making a sign of noticing him, he took this as a deliberate attempt to put him down. His interpretation was, "He's trying to show that I'm a nobody, not worth noticing." . . . After his initial hurt feeling, he felt a craving to salve his injured self-esteem by yelling at the other student, precipitating a fistfight. He regarded his "counterattack" as defensive and justified. (pp. 132–133)

Like Blaming Others, Assuming the Worst distorts in part insofar as it overgeneralizes (e.g., "*every*body is against me"). Highly aggressive adolescents have been found to endorse frequently statements such as "If you back down from a fight, *every*one will think you're a coward" (Slaby & Guerra, 1988, emphasis added) and "*Every*one steals—you might as well get your share" (Gibbs, Barriga, & Potter, 2001; emphasis added). As Beck (1999) observed, "It is obviously far more painful for a person to be 'always' mistreated than mistreated on a specific occasion. The overgeneralized explanation, rather than the event itself, accounts for the degree of anger" (p. 74).

Among the secondary cognitive distortions, Assuming the Worst is distinctive in that it is not only aggressogenic but also *depressogenic*: Antisocial individuals (at least reactive offenders) often assume the worst not only about others but also about *themselves* (their capabilities, future, etc.). We (Barriga, Landau, Stinson, Liau, & Gibbs, 2000) have studied not only self-serving but also self-debasing cognitive distortions (e.g., "I can never do anything right").[4] The main picture is one of specific cognition-behavior relationships: The more closely matched the cognition to the behavior, the stronger the correlation (Dodge, 1986). In our study, self-*serving* distortion correlated more strongly with *externalizing* behavior disorders than it did with *internalizing* behavior disorders, and self-*debasing* distortion correlated more strongly with *internalizing* disorders than it did with *externalizing* disorders (Barriga et al., 2000). Essentially, exaggerated *other* blaming is *aggress*ogenic, whereas exaggerated *self*-blame is *depress*ogenic. Self-serving cognitive distortions do correlate, however, with internalizing behavior problems; this weak but significant relationship is accounted for, among the self-serving categories, mainly by Assuming the Worst (Barriga, Hawkins, & Camelia, 2008). Hence, although ego protective like the other secondary distortions, Assuming the Worst can also function as a self-*debasing* distortion (Barriga et al., 2000; cf. Quiggle, Garber, Panak, & Dodge, 1992), especially among comorbid (aggressive but also self-destructive) individuals.

Minimizing/Mislabeling   Antisocial behavior can be protected from inhibiting factors (empathy, inconsistency with self-concept) not only by blaming or attributing the worst of intentions to the victim but also by disparaging the victim or minimizing the victimization. We (Gibbs et al., 1995) define Minimizing/Mislabeling as "depicting antisocial behavior as causing no real harm or as being acceptable or even admirable, or referring to others with belittling or dehumanizing labels" (p. 113). One of our group members who had grabbed a purse dangling from a supermarket cart recalled thinking that the theft taught the purse's owner a good lesson to be more careful in the future. Similarly, group members have suggested Gary's stabbing his girlfriend was good for her, to teach that "bitch" her "place." Vandalism is sometimes minimized as "mischief" or "a prank" (Sykes & Matza, 1957), premeditated violent crimes as "mistakes" (Garbarino, 1999, p. 134). Slaby and Guerra (1988) found that highly aggressive adolescents were more likely to endorse statements such as "People who get beat up badly probably don't suffer a lot." Beck (1999) noted a common belief among rapists that a woman will "enjoy" being raped (p. 141; cf. McCrady et al., 2008).

The linguistic abuse entailed in Minimizing/Mislabeling can be quite noticeable for nonviolent as well as violent offenses. A manufacturing company executive and his engineers altered test result data so that a prospective military aircraft brake assembly, that in fact had failed all tests, would nonetheless be approved for production. Borrowing from—and abusing—the notion of poetic license, the executive explained to federal prosecutors that he and his associates were not "really lying. All we were doing was interpreting the figures the way we knew they should be. We were just exercising engineering license" (Vandivier, 2002, 163). In a television interview, an incarcerated offender who had murdered a sales clerk explained his lack of remorse: The woman had after all refused to "cooperate" and "follow the rules." In addition to blaming the victim, he was using certain words to obscure his self-centered aggrandizement: *Cooperation*, a socially decentered word that means "working together toward a common end," was abused to mean "giving me what I unfairly want," and *the rules* was similarly seized and abused to mean "my desires."

Minimizing and mislabeling such as dehumanization is a staple feature of ideological "crimes of obedience" (Kelman & Hamilton, 1989). A common practice during combat training of soldiers—or, for that matter, of gang members who are to fight another gang—is to use derogatory and dehumanizing labels for the class of human beings who are to be the enemy, so that harming or killing them will be easier. Many government torturers, to be able to continue, must frequently be reminded that their victims are "vermin" (Haritos-Fatouros, 2003; cf. Moshman, 2004, 2007).

> *A Nazi camp commandant was asked why the Nazis went to such extreme lengths to degrade their victims, whom they were going to kill anyway. The commandant chillingly explained that it was not a matter of purposeless cruelty. Rather, the victims had to be degraded to the level of subhuman objects so that those who operated the gas chambers would be less burdened by distress. (Bandura, 1999, p. 200)*

In addition to dehumanizing their victims, glorifying or ennobling their behavior may be essential if non-psychopathic individuals are to continue to engage in otherwise obviously immoral acts. Consider the troubled recollection of a communist activist who aided in the forced starvation of 14 million Ukrainian peasants and had to see and hear "the children's crying and the women's wails":

> *It was excruciating to see and hear all this. And even worse to take part in it. . . . I persuaded myself, explained to myself I mustn't give in to debilitating pity. [They were enemies of the Plan.] We were realizing historical necessity. We were performing our revolutionary duty. We were obtaining grain for the socialist fatherland. For the Five Year Plan. (Conquest, 1986, p. 233)*

This former activist's previous resistance against "debilitating pity" became guilt-wracked, belated compassion as Stalin's monstrous regime ended and reality sank in. Persistent guilt despite Minimizing/Mislabeling can be a factor in posttraumatic stress disorder among military combat veterans (Grossman, 1995).

One can also attempt to minimize and insulate oneself from the enormity of one's actions through their "routinization" (Kelman, 1973; Kelman & Hamilton, 1989) or "deconstruction" (Baumeister, 1991; Ward, Hudson, & Marshall, 1995), i.e., selective or tunnel-vision attention to concrete details or ordinary, repetitive, and mechanical details of the offending activity. Beck's (1999; cf. Hollander, 1997) term for this cognitive strategy was *procedural thinking*, which was "typical of the bureaucrats in the Nazi and Soviet apparatus":

> *This kind of "low level" thinking is characteristic of [fastidious] people whose attention is fixed totally on the details of a destructive project in which they are engaged. . . . These individuals can be so focused on what they are doing—a kind of tunnel vision—that they are able to blot out the fact that they are participating in an inhuman action. (p. 18)*

Facilitating Research on Self-Serving Cognitive Distortions: The How I Think (HIT) Questionnaire

The primary (Self-Centered) and secondary (Blaming Others, Assuming the Worst, Minimizing/Mislabeling) self-serving cognitive distortions play an important role, then, in the maintenance of antisocial behavior. Accordingly, it is important to have a means of assessing such distortions reliably and validly. Building from previous assessment advances (e.g., Bandura, Barbaranelli, Caprara, & Pastorelli, 1996; Paciello et al., 2008), we (Barriga, Gibbs, Potter, & Liau, 2001; cf. Barriga, Gibbs, Potter, Konopisos, & Barriga, 2008) developed the How I Think (HIT) questionnaire (Gibbs Barriga, & Potter, 1992, 2001). The HIT questionnaire is a group-administrable, paper-and-pencil measure that is composed of items representing mainly the four categories of self-serving cognitive distortion. To provide broad and meaningful content for the cognitive distortions, these items also refer to one or another of four main categories of antisocial behavior derived from the conduct disorder and oppositional defiant disorder syndromes listed in the fourth edition of the *Diagnostic and Statistical Manual of Mental Disorders* (*DSM-IV*; American Psychiatric Association, 1994): disrespect for rules, laws, or authorities (i.e., opposition-defiance); physical aggression; lying; and stealing. For example, the item "People force you to lie if they ask too many questions" represents a Blaming Others cognitive distortion applied to a "lying" category of behavioral referent. Also included were "Anomalous Responding" items (for screening out approval-seeking, impression management, incompetent, or otherwise suspect responding) and positive filler items (e.g., "When friends need you, you should be there for them"), used mainly for camouflaging the distortion items and encouraging full use of the response scale.

The HIT would appear to be a valid and reliable assessment contribution to study the role of self-serving cognitive distortions in the initiation and maintenance of antisocial behavior. The factor structure of the HIT questionnaire was supported by confirmatory factor analysis. Internal consistency estimates were very high, with alphas ranging from .92 to .96. The cognitive distortion subscales, behavioral referent subscales, and Anomalous Responding scale were also high, with alphas ranging from .63 to .92. The measure correlated with self-report, parental report, and institutional indices of antisocial behavior, indicating good convergent validity. It did *not* correlate with socioeconomic status (SES), intelligence, or grade point average, indicating good divergent validity. Regarding discriminant validity, the measure consistently discriminated (incarcerated and nonincarcerated) adolescent samples with antisocial behavior problems from comparison samples. Additional construct validity results are reported by Alvaro Barriga and colleagues (Barriga et al., 2001; Barriga, Morrison, et al., 2001; Barriga et al., 2008; McCrady et al., 2008).

Social Skill Deficiencies

Antisocial youths evidence not only moral developmental delays and self-serving cognitive distortions but also social skills deficiencies—the third of the "three Ds" found in the literature. *Social skills* typically refers to the consolidated and implicit mental schemas that activate and regulate balanced and constructive behavior in difficult interpersonal situations. An example is the behavior of a youth who deals constructively with deviant peer pressure by suggesting a nondeviant alternative. Another example is that of a youth who calmly and sincerely offers clarification or apologizes to an angry accuser. Such behavior is "neither aggressive nor obsequious" (Carducci, 1980, p. 161; cf. Jakubowski & Lange, 1978); that is, it achieves a fair balance between one's own perspective and that of another. Similarly, Robert Deluty (1979) conceptualized social skills as appropriately assertive responses intermediate between threats or aggression, on one hand, and submission or running away, on the other (although calmly leaving the scene can be appropriate or balanced in some circumstances). While asserting or explaining his or her own perspective, the socially skilled individual also communicates awareness of the other person's viewpoint, feelings, and legitimate expectations. The use of social skills by participants in a dialogue should reduce self-centration and promote mutual respect. Arnold Goldstein and Ellen McGinnis (1997) operationalized various types of balanced, constructive social problem solving in terms of concrete and limited sequences of "steps" or component schemas.

Social Skill Deficiencies as Unbalanced Behavior

Research on social skills has generally found deficiencies among antisocial youths relative to comparison groups, corroborating Carducci's (1980) impression that these youths typically "do not know what specific steps [in a social conflict] . . . will result in [the conflict's] being solved" (pp. 157–158). Such deficiencies are perhaps not surprising given the typical absence of models of constructive problem solving in the youths' home environments (Kazdin, 1995). Barbara Freedman and colleagues (Freedman, Rosenthal, Donahoe, Schlundt, & McFall, 1978) found evidence of extensive social skill deficits or deficiencies among male incarcerated juvenile offenders, as measured by a semistructured interview rating measure, the Adolescent Problems

Inventory (API). Lower API scores were found not only for the delinquents overall but also for a delinquent subgroup that frequently violated institutional rules. Relations between social skill deficits and antisocial behavior were replicated by Dishion, Loeber, Stouthamer-Loeber, and Patterson (1984) but not by Hunter and Kelly (1986). We (Simonian, Tarnowski, & Gibbs, 1991) corrected for a procedural flaw in the Hunter and Kelly study and used a streamlined and adapted version of the API, the Inventory of Adolescent Problems–Short Form (IAP-SF) (Gibbs, Swillinger, Leeman, Simonian, Rowland, & Jaycox, 1995). Using the IAP-SF, we found that social skills did correlate inversely with numerous indices of antisocial behavior (most serious offense committed, number of correctional facility placements, self-reported alcohol problems, and AWOL attempts and successes). We (Leeman et al., 1993) also found that social skills as measured by the IAP-SF correlated inversely with frequency of unexcused school absences, preincarceration offenses, institutional misconduct, and institutional incident reports.

Given our framework for conceptualizing social skills as balanced and constructive interpersonal behavior in difficult situations, socially unskilled behavior involves unbalanced and destructive behavior in two categories of interpersonal situations: (a) irresponsibly submissive behavior in deviant peer pressure situations (an imbalance that favors others and is tantamount to disrespect for self) and (b) irresponsibly aggressive behavior in anger provocation situations (favoring self and tantamount to disrespect for the other; more typical and another aspect of pronounced egocentric bias or self-centeredness). Using factor-analytic techniques, Susan Simonian and colleagues (Simonian et al., 1991) confirmed the validity of these categories. They labeled the peer pressure category Antisocial Peer Pressure ("peer pressure to engage in serious violation of social norms/legal mandates," p. 24). The anger provocation category was represented by "response demand" or provocative pressure situations. The Provocation Pressure items either required an immediate response in the face of a clear and present provocation or permitted "more response planning time" (p. 23; example: one is late for work and knows one will be facing an irate employer). Socially skilled responses to Antisocial Peer Pressure and Provocation Pressure situations correlated inversely with covert and overt forms of antisocial behavior, respectively.

A Case Study

Although atypical in some respects, an antisocial individual introduced in the last chapter—the infamous terrorist Timothy McVeigh—would seem to reflect as a young man in his 20s many of the limitations we have discussed under Moral Judgment Developmental Delay, Self-Serving Cognitive Distortions, and Social Skill Deficiencies.

Moral Judgment Developmental Delay

McVeigh, even as a young adult, evidenced both concrete morality and egocentric bias. As we noted in Chapter 5, eye-for-an-eye reciprocity was "a theme that became McVeigh's philosophy" (Michel & Herbeck, 2001, p. 68). His description of his philosophy—dirty for dirty, you reap what you sow, payback time—is an explicit description of the concrete logic of Kohlbergian moral judgment Stage 2. "Anyone who mistreated McVeigh—or made him think he was being mistreated—was making a formidable enemy with a long memory" (Michel & Herbeck, 2001, p. 68). Indeed, anyone who even disagreed with McVeigh was likely to induce in McVeigh a perception of mistreatment and a motive to retaliate.

McVeigh's moral developmental delay can be understood—but only to some extent—from what we know about his home history. Although McVeigh's home history did not entail significant abuse, it bordered on neglect and apparently did not provide opportunities to take the perspective of others. McVeigh had "very few memories of interactions" with his parents and "never really felt close" to them or most other relatives (Michel & Herbeck, 2001, p. 21). His father did not offer support or advice even after an incident in which McVeigh was humiliated by a bully. McVeigh did experience some nurturance through a close relationship with his grandfather; their relationship, however, "revolved around an interest the two had in common: their mutual enjoyment of guns" (p. 23).

Self-Serving Cognitive Distortions

Both primary (Self-Centered) and secondary (Blaming Others, Assuming the Worst, Minimizing/Mislabeling) cognitive distortions were amply evident in McVeigh's mental life.

Self-Centered

McVeigh's egocentric bias consolidated into a Self-Centered cognitive distortion. Aspects of his Self-Centered orientation suggested grandiosity or even psychopathy. In quitting college, he declared that he knew more than the teachers and that the classes were "just too boring" (Michel & Herbeck, 2001, p. 38). In the Army, he arrogantly expressed disdain for others—even officers—who seemed less knowledgeable regarding weapons and procedure manuals. Although the Army initially offered "thrills" (p. 103) and glory, McVeigh eventually became "suffocated by the repetition of ordinary life" and "restless, dissatisfied by daily life, increasingly eager to set his own rules" (pp. 112, 196). To impress his younger sister, he fabricated a military adventure. Alluding to the planned bombing, he bragged that "something big is going to happen" (p. 196). His plans were methodical, and he manipulated or intimidated others into helping him. He was convinced that "historians would call him a martyr, maybe even a hero" (p. 166). Incidentally, McVeigh's anticipated glory of martyrdom belied his self-presentation as a humble, selfless, sacrificial crusader. In David Moshman's (2004) terminology, McVeigh evidenced a *false moral identity*.

Yet it is not clear that McVeigh was psychopathic in the classic sense. His absence of guilt over harm to others seemed to stem not from an absence of empathy so much as the effective use of self-righteous, self-serving distortions. As described in the last chapter, he at times seemed to evidence a genuine empathy. He also at times evidenced an insecurity and vulnerability suggestive of the reactive offender. In a rambling letter to his sister, he expressed "an urgent need for someone in the family to understand me." He even made reference to his "lawless behavior and attitude" (Michel & Herbeck, 2001, p. 145), although he quickly attributed it to a (fabricated) encounter with lawless government agents.

McVeigh's volatile shifts between extremes in self-esteem were also more suggestive of the reactive than the proactive offender. After the thrills and status of the Army, back in his small home town, McVeigh felt "it was all crashing down ... the long hours in a dead-end job, the feeling that he didn't have a home, his failure to establish a relationship with a woman" (Michel & Herbeck, 2001, p. 103). After considering suicide, he "regrouped," taking "to the notion of becoming a hunter—not just any hunter, but one who could kill his quarry with a single long-range shot" (p. 104).

Especially consistent with the interpretation of McVeigh as a reactive offender is his preoccupation with his status, with whether he was receiving respect or humiliation from the world. Upon receiving an invitational magazine subscription form letter referring to "the readership of leading professionals such as yourself," McVeigh commented, "It's about time someone gave me the proper respect" (Michel & Herbeck, 2001, p. 376). McVeigh felt humiliated and wronged not only by the bullying incidents of his own childhood but also by government actions against his "people": "The government, he felt, was laughing at people in the Patriot and gun communities" (p. 167). It was "time to make them all pay" (p. 168), to silence "the laughter of the bully" (p. 167). He wrote to his sister, "My whole mindset has shifted, from intellectual to ... animal, Rip the bastards (sic) heads off and shit down their necks!" (p. 196). Indeed, to the Bureau of Alcohol, Tobacco, and Firearms, he wrote, "All you tyrannical mother fuckers will swing in the wind one day" (p. 180).

The nuances of McVeigh's Self-Centered orientation seemed to reflect, then, a mixture of proactive and reactive features. Such cases of mixture or comorbidity are not uncommon. Although there do seem to be qualitatively distinct types of aggressors, the prevalence of mixed types among aggressive individuals has prompted some researchers to advocate a continuum-of-features rather than dichotomy-of-types model of aggressive behavior (Bushman & Anderson, 2001).

Blaming Others

The secondary distortions, including Blaming Others, were also thematic. In high school, McVeigh insisted that his flagging interest in academics was "the teachers' fault" (Michel & Herbeck, 2001, p. 32). His list of blameworthy agents included "crooked politicians, overzealous governmental agents, high taxes, political correctness, gun laws" (p. 2). He even blamed "American women" for "sexually shortchanging the opposite sex" (p. 114). At his trial, he sought to present a "necessity defense" to the effect that "Waco, Ruby Ridge, and other government excesses ... *drove him*" to respond in kind (p. 277, emphasis added).

Assuming the Worst

Much the way highly aggressive boys point to the hostility they create as proof they were right all along about others' attitudes toward them (Lochman & Dodge, 1998), McVeigh welcomed execution as proving "that the American government was heartless and cruel" (Michel & Herbeck, 2001, p. 350). McVeigh explicitly Assumed the Worst regarding the ostensible threat from the government:

> "If a comet is hurtling toward the earth, and it's out past the orbit of Pluto,... it is an imminent threat." And if the U.S. government was allowed to get away with what happened at Waco and Ruby Ridge, there was an imminent threat to the lives of gun owners, McVeigh said. (Michel & Herbeck, 2001, pp. 285–286)

McVeigh saw the world as a dangerous place, necessitating constant vigilance and preparedness. He kept guns "all over" (Michel & Herbeck, 2001, p. 89) his house and in his car because of the ever-present danger, in his mind, of attack. While in the Army, he rented a storage shed where he stockpiled a hundred gallons of fresh water, food rations, guns, and other supplies in case "all hell broke loose in the world" (p. 60).

McVeigh's habitual overreaction to perceived dangers or threats may have had a heritable component. Such a possibility is suggested by his mother's subsequent commitment to a psychiatric hospital in part for paranoid delusions (an extreme level of Assuming the Worst) (Beck, 1999). McVeigh himself

> first noticed odd [even for him] behavior in his mother more than two years before the bombing. ... She constantly pulled plugs from electrical outlets. At first, he thought she was trying to save electricity; only later did he realize she was afraid of health dangers from electromagnetic fields. (Michel & Herbeck, 2001, p. 381)

Minimizing/Mislabeling

Numerous examples were provided in Chapter 5 of McVeigh's minimizing and mislabeling of his crime. Much of his Minimizing/Mislabeling and prideful ego strength entailed the abuse of a military metaphor: "War means action. Hard choices. Life and death" (Michel & Herbeck, 2001, p. 212). In this hard war, he was a courageous patriot, or perhaps a Robin Hood. At times, he would refer to himself as "we," as if he were part of a political group or military organization, obscuring the fact that in the end he was alone with his bomb in his truck. The innocent people he killed were, after all, "part of the evil empire" (p. 225), providing the "body count" (p. 300) he desired; the dead babies were "collateral damage" (p. 331). Much as did the communist activist quoted earlier—and as does the typical ideological terrorist— McVeigh saw himself as having a necessary "duty," in terms of which empathy for his victims was a sign of debilitating weakness. McVeigh had learned from example in childhood that "the men of the McVeigh family were not supposed to cry" (p. 19). To his victims and their families, he minimized that death "happens every day"

(p. 324). In a perverse expression of ego strength, he rejected suggestions that he show empathic distress or guilt for the victims' losses as a pathetic capitulation: "I'm not going to ... curl into a fetal ball, and cry just because the victims want me to do that" (p. 325).

McVeigh also minimized empathic affect in diverting his thoughts and perceptions from the crime. His extraordinary attention to detail preparing the bomb as if it were a "science project" (Michel & Herbeck, 2001, p. 288) is suggestive of the tunnel vision strategy described earlier. Also, after positioning and activating the bomb, he walked briskly away, wearing earplugs and not looking back at the devastation upon hearing the blast. Later, seeing on television the children among his victims "did cause him a moment's regret." His overall reaction, however, was disappointment that the effect of his bomb was not more spectacular. " '*Damn*,' he thought, '*the whole building didn't come down*' " (Michel & Herbeck, 2001, p. 245).

Social Skill Deficiencies

McVeigh was, to say the least, socially unskilled in difficult interpersonal situations. His biographers (Michel & Herbeck, 2001) do not report a single instance in which McVeigh maintained a balanced perspective to deal with and resolve a problem constructively. Instead, McVeigh would (a) prematurely withdraw, (b) threaten or attack, or (c) strategically withdraw in order to plan an attack. Starting work at a gun shop, McVeigh had a dispute with one of the other workers; "instead of trying to work things out, McVeigh backed off. He quit his job at the gun shop after just a few weeks" (p. 101). Finding resistance to his assertions among people met in mainstream contexts, he gravitated toward gun shows where he encountered fewer challenges requiring him to "justify his positions" (p. 125).

McVeigh would also make threats. Merely disagreeing with him was a provocation for McVeigh.[5] Again, we can speculate that McVeigh was in part a reactive offender, for whom the distorted Assuming the Worst belief, "If people disagree with me, it means they don't respect me," is readily activated by provocations (Beck, 1999). As is typical, the hurt quickly transformed to anger. In response to a prank, McVeigh called the prankster's mother and said in a frightening tone, "'Listen very carefully, ma'am, ... If your son doesn't stop this shit—and he knows what I'm talking about—I know where you live. I'm going to burn your fucking house down'" (Michel & Herbeck, 2001, p. 98).

McVeigh was perhaps most dangerous when his withdrawal was strategic. After hearing a complaint from a friend, McVeigh became extremely angry but "never said anything. He set his jaw and sat down and picked up a magazine and started reading" (Michel & Herbeck, 2001, p. 152). McVeigh might even at that point have been thinking of vengeance; he did subsequently mastermind a brutal and terrifying robbery. Although pleased by the success of the robbery, McVeigh was intensely disappointed that the man had not been murdered but only severely beaten and terrified.

Case Study Summary and Comments

Overall, then, McVeigh was a very self-centered, vindictive, and threatening individual. Among McVeigh's possessions at the time of his arrest was a copy of the U.S. Constitution, on the back of which McVeigh had written, "Obey the Constitution of the United States and we won't shoot you" (Michel & Herbeck, 2001, p. 228). Translation: "Agree with me and I won't kill you." There lies an epitome of McVeigh's self-centration as manifested in classic limitations characteristic of chronic and serious antisocial youth: the egocentric bias and payback-and-then-some morality (moral developmental delay); the arrogant judge-jury-executioner attitude supported by externalizations of blame, hostile attributions, and euphemisms (self-serving cognitive distortions); and the habits of threat rather than balanced communication and constructive conflict resolution (social skill deficiencies).

McVeigh's self-centration or failure to take others' perspectives meant that he was generally neither fair nor empathic in his interactions with others, as per the theories of Kohlberg and Hoffman. Yet McVeigh's case also presents those theories with some challenges. Consider the implicit challenge to Kohlbergian theory. Given McVeigh's developmental delay in his moral understanding of fairness, should he not have come from a home more severely deficient in social perspective-taking opportunities—say, a home of abuse and of more serious neglect? Perhaps McVeigh was temperamentally ill-suited to benefit from whatever modest social perspective-taking opportunities might have come his way in school and elsewhere.

Consider as well the challenge (at least at first blush) to Hoffman's theory. What happened to the multidetermined reliability of empathy, especially for those of one's group? Surely McVeigh was cognizant that his victims were fellow Americans; how could he not have felt empathy for them? Was McVeigh simply a cold psychopath? Probably not. His childhood empathic distress for injured animals was noted in Chapter 5. He did have to "brush aside" moments of empathic distress for his victims both before and after the bombing. Indeed, Hoffman might argue cogently that McVeigh's crime reflected not the absence so much as the *presence* of empathy. Tragically, McVeigh's empathy only made things worse: His intense empathic distress at seeing the victims at Waco was structured and channeled into vindictive, self-righteous rage by his "payback" level of moral reciprocity, cognitive distortions, and habits of threat. For a more mature, veridical, and balanced individual, the empathic distress would have helped to motivate a constructive and appropriately targeted response.

Although Kohlberg's and Hoffman's theories can address these challenges to some extent, their theories must include self-serving cognitive distortions to account for severe or chronic antisocial behavior. With a sufficient prevalence of such distortions, aggression can be initiated and perpetuated even in empathic individuals from nonabusive homes. Nor do the theories integrate into their frameworks the positive contribution of social skills to the cultivation of schemas or habits of constructive and balanced social behavior. These theories need expansion, then, in their application not only to prosocial but also to *anti*social behavior. With the key concepts of moral judgment developmental delay, cognitive distortions, and social skill deficiencies in place, we now shift from understanding to treating antisocial behavior.

Notes

[1]Self-Centered on the group level is termed *in-group* or *ethnocentric bias* (cf. empathic bias). Although in-group bias or favoritism does not necessarily lead to out-group derogation or hostility (Brewer, 2007), it often does. As Edgerton (1992) noted, "People in many [tribal] societies refer to themselves as 'the people' and regard all others as alien and repellent, if not downright subhuman. ... Many people believe that their way of life is the only one" (p. 148). Where the group's beliefs are perceived to be uniquely pure and superior (as in ideological extremist groups), group members may even consider it a "duty" to kill outsiders. After all, the very existence of these impure inferiors—especially if they seem to be flourishing—is in effect an affront to the superior group and its rightful domination (Husain, 2007).

Interestingly, Edgerton noted the dangers to a group that does not even try to rationalize or ennoble its ethnocentric aggression as a religious or ceremonial duty:

> *Unlike most of the North American Indian societies that practiced cannibalism, the Tonkawa ate people without religious justification or ceremonial purpose. The open gusto with which they consumed human flesh was offensive to neighboring tribes, and the frequent Tonkawa raids in search of more captives were so threatening that in 1862 a coalition of six disparate tribes, united only by their detestation of the Tonkawa, attacked them and killed half the people in the tribe. (p. 100)*

[2]The dynamics of harm and self-protective distortion do not always start with Self-Centered presumptions (whether proactive or reactive). David Moshman (2004, 2007; cf. Wainryb & Pasupathi, in press) described such dynamics among soldiers indoctrinated and pressured to commit atrocities. Many crimes of obedience are accomplished by "otherwise considerate people" (Bandura, 1999, p. 205; cf. Kelman & Hamilton, 1989). Bystanders who could but do not intervene may blame the victim to preserve their "just world hypothesis" (Chapter 4). To Edmund Burke's famous statement "the only thing necessary for the triumph of evil is for good men to do nothing," Bandura added: "The triumph of evil requires a lot of good people doing a bit of it in a morally disengaged way with indifference to the human suffering they collectively cause" (p. 206).

[3]Edgerton (1992) evaluated as maladaptive the cultural belief among the Ojibwa and North American Indian tribes that serious "acts committed while drunk were not intended" and hence were excusable. Such cultural extenuations, Edgerton argued, can jeopardize group survival:

> *By excusing drunken acts such as murder, rape, incest, and child abuse, the Ojibwa can only have encouraged such acts to take place. ... When a society adopts a belief that ... no one is to be blamed for anything done while drunk, it has adopted a fully-warranted prescription for self-destruction. (p. 185)*

[4]Interestingly, individuals with pronounced self-debasing cognitive distortions and internalizing disorders evidence higher levels of ego development than do individuals with pronounced self-serving cognitive distortions and externalizing disorder (reviewed by Noam, 1998).

[5]Misperceiving any disagreement as a provocation is not uncommon among extremists. Bin Laden and his loyalists were said to "keep expanding their list of enemies," defined as anyone "who doesn't precisely share their world view" (Bergen & Cruikshank, 2008, June 11, p. 21).

CHAPTER 7

Treating Antisocial Behavior

IN 1993, AT A JUVENILE CORRECTIONAL FACILITY IN COLUMBUS, OHIO, a group of eight residents and a staff group leader were having a "mutual help" meeting. The focus of the meeting was the problem reported by 15-year-old Mac, one of the group members. Mac had resisted and yelled profanities at a staff member who, in accordance with institutional policy, had begun to inspect his carrying bag. The group and Mac agreed that Mac's defiance and profanity represented, in the language of the program, an "Authority Problem," but what was the *meaning* of that problem, its underlying thinking error (cognitive distortion)? In the ensuing discussion, Mac explained that the bag contained something very special and irreplaceable—photos of his grandmother—and that he was not going to let anyone take the photos from him. Mac's peers understood his point of view but saw it as one-sided. Mac thought only of his photos, without considering for a moment the staff member's perspective: She was only carrying out institutional policy concerning inspection for possible contraband. Nor did Mac consider that she was not abusive and that he thus had no reason to assume that the photos would be confiscated. Generating the anger and overt behavior identified as Authority Problem, then, were Self-Centered and Assuming the Worst thinking errors. The group also critiqued Mac's anger at staff for his subsequent disciplinary write-up: In reality, Mac could blame no one but himself for those consequences. In program terms, Mac also had an Easily Angered problem generated by a Blaming Others thinking error. Helpful in addressing Mac's self-centered or one-sided viewpoint were certain tools, acquired elsewhere in the program. These tools included the mature reasons for an institution's rules against contraband, how Mac could have corrected his thinking errors and used other skills to manage his anger, and how he could have expressed his concern to the staff member in a balanced and constructive fashion.

As the meeting progressed (it lasted more than an hour), Mac's anger dissipated considerably, and he began to regret his verbal assault on the staff member. He started to take into account her perspective. He could see the unfairness of his behavior toward her, empathize with her, and attribute blame to himself (correcting his

Blaming Others thinking error). Over the course of subsequent sessions, Mac continued to work on correcting or remediating his cognitive limitations and taking the perspectives of others in various ways, as prescribed in both Kohlberg's and Hoffman's theories. With practice, social perspective taking became easier, more spontaneous. Constructive and responsible behavior was increasingly evident as Mac's Authority and Easily Angered problems attenuated.

Processes of treatment for antisocial behavior are more concentrated, systematic, and short term than are the processes of moral development or socialization. In essence, however, the principle of treatment does not differ from that of moral development: namely, self-centration and its remedy in social decentration through social perspective taking. As we saw in the last chapter, *multiple* limitations associated with self-centeredness (moral developmental delays, social cognitive distortions, social skill deficiencies) contribute to antisocial behavior. Accordingly, treatment programs for antisocial youth must be *multicomponential* (Kazdin, 1995) and address these limitations. As we discuss the treatment of antisocial behavior in this chapter, we will focus on a multicomponent treatment program that incorporates a wide variety of social perspective-taking opportunities, namely, our EQUIP program (DiBiase, Gibbs, & Potter, 2005; Gibbs, 1994; Gibbs, Potter, & Goldstein, 1995; Gibbs, Potter, DiBiase, & Devlin, in press; Horn, Shively, & Gibbs, 2007; Potter, Gibbs, & Goldstein, 2001; cf. Glick & Gibbs, in press).

EQUIP is multicomponential primarily in the sense that it integrates two basic approaches to treating antisocial behavior: the mutual help approach and the cognitive behavioral approach. The cognitive behavioral approach is itself multicomponential, encompassing areas that include moral judgment development, anger management (including the correction of cognitive distortion), and social skills training (e.g., see Glick, in press). Our description of the mutual help and cognitive behavioral approaches and how they are integrated in EQUIP will emphasize the ways in which they induce social perspective taking. We conclude the chapter with a consideration of more intensive perspective-taking techniques such as crime reenactment role-play, used with severe offenders.

The Mutual Help Approach

The 1993 "mutual help" meeting illustrated mainly one component of the EQUIP program, namely, our cognitive version of Positive Peer Culture (Vorrath & Brendtro, 1985) or, more generally, what we call the mutual help approach. Positive Peer Culture has sought to "make caring fashionable" (p. 21) and thereby motivate erstwhile antisocial youth to help one another change.

Although people have been motivated to help one another in groups for thousands of years, the modern support group or mutual help movement originated in 1935 with the founding of Alcoholics Anonymous. Such groups quickly proliferated. Approximately 500,000 mutual help groups have emerged in the United States alone, involving more than 12 million Americans (Hurley, 1988; Wuthnow, 1994). Like Alcoholics Anonymous, some of these groups address the struggle against an addictive behavior (e.g., Gamblers Anonymous). Other groups are composed of individuals enduring stressful or painful situations (e.g., single parenthood, widowhood, heart disease, breast cancer, rape or incest, or murder of one's child). Still other groups (e.g., Al-Anon and NAMI) aim to provide help for friends and relatives of the person with the problem.

Beginning in the 1940s, the mutual help approach began to be applied to individuals who regularly victimize others and society. At a psychiatric hospital in Great Britain, Maxwell Jones (1953) innovated techniques for cultivating a "therapeutic community" among sociopathic patients. Independently and concurrently in New Jersey, Lloyd McCorkle, Albert Elias, and Lovell Bixby (1958) applied similar techniques to delinquent boys in an intervention they termed *guided group interaction*. These techniques were subsequently refined by Vickie Agee (1979) for use with violent adolescents and for a broader population of antisocial youth by Harry Vorrath and Larry Brendtro (1985). Vorrath and Brendtro called their mutual help program Positive Peer Culture.

The Challenge of a Negative Youth Culture

Aggressive and other antisocial youths represent a formidable challenge to the mutual help approach. Unlike most mutual help groups, which are initiated voluntarily by participants, mutual help groups for antisocial youths are initiated by adults and may be mandated by the courts. Hence, forming such groups typically encounters at least initial resistance ("storming" or "limit-testing" is in fact an early phase of group development; Vorrath & Brendtro, 1985). Researchers and practitioners have noted the negative (and, we would add, distorted) group norms of antisocial youths: "Drug use is cool [Minimizing/Mislabeling], sexual exploitation proves manliness [Minimizing/ Mislabeling], and you have to watch out for number one [Self-Centered]" (Brendtro & Wasmund, 1989, p. 83). In the analysis of the "moral atmosphere" (also called moral climate) of a Bronx, New York, high school, Kohlberg and Higgins (1987) identified certain *oppositional* or "counter norms" (in our terms, culturally normative cognitive distortions) such as Assuming the Worst or Blaming Others, e.g., "Look at me the wrong way and you're in for a fight," or "It's your fault if something is stolen—you were careless and tempting me" (p. 110). In correctional settings, the negative youth culture is generally "characterized by opposition to institutional rules and goals, norms against informing authorities about rule violations, and the use of physical coercion as a basis of influence among inmates" (Osgood, Gruber, Archer, & New-comb, 1985, p. 71). Although Kohlberg and Higgins (1987) did not explicitly characterize negative or oppositional norms as distortive, they did emphasize that such norms undermine adherents' "capacity to empathize" or perspective take (p. 110). In longitudinal studies, the oppositional or "rule-breaking" content of social interchanges with anti-social peers predicted subsequent violent behavior, delinquency, and substance abuse (Dishion, McCord, & Poulin, 1999).

Mutual help programs applied to antisocial youths aim to transform this self-centered, distorted, and harmful culture. The goal is to create a caring and *positive* peer culture in which group members work with one another's perspectives and thereby help themselves and one another to change toward responsible behavior. Techniques for accomplishing this aim include selecting for the initial peer group relatively positive (or at least less limited) peers; the cognitive behavioral technique of relabeling, reframing, or cognitive restructuring (e.g., characterizing helping others as a *strong* rather than weak or sissy thing to do); confronting or reversing responsibility (see below); encouraging the honest sharing of personal histories ("life stories"); isolating and redirecting specific negative group members; and providing community service (cf. Hart, Atkins, & Donnelly, 2006) as well as faith-building opportunities[1] (see Vorrath & Brendtro, 1985).

Mutual Help Perspective Taking

The 1993 EQUIP mutual help meeting illustrated some of the features of Positive Peer Culture, especially the problem language. Antisocial youths' (such as Mac's) typical problems with authority, anger, stealing, lying, and so forth are identified in terms of a standard Problem List (see Table 7.1), of which one of the most basic is Inconsiderate of Others—implying the need for remedial work in social perspective taking.

A Positive Peer Culture technique particularly relevant to social perspective taking and inductive discipline is called confronting or reversing responsibility (cf. correcting Blaming Others), in which group members (such as Mac) are made aware of the effects of their actions on others. Essentially, the group or group leader respectfully but forthrightly challenges the antisocial group member to put himself or herself in others' positions, to consider their legitimate expectations, feelings, and circumstances.

Vickie Agee (1979) argued that effectively confronting violent offenders typically requires concrete, personal, and "blunt" techniques if they are to grasp the harm their violence has caused others. If a violent offender has a sister and cares about her, for example, that is an opening. The therapist might frame a female victim as someone's sister and appeal to moral reciprocity: " 'If it's okay for you to do that to someone else's sister, is it okay for them to do it to your sister?" ' (pp. 113–114). Another example of a concrete, blunt confrontation is provided by a question asked of the then-incarcerated Timothy McVeigh by Oklahoma City psychiatrist John R. Smith several years before McVeigh's execution:

> Smith once tried to confront McVeigh about the pain his bomb had caused others. Smith had noted how much McVeigh seemed to enjoy talking to people, and now he tried to use this quality to provoke a reaction from him. "Instead of the death penalty, Tim, they should put you in a tiny little cell," Smith said. "You wouldn't be allowed to talk to anyone, ever again."

(text continues on p. 161)

Table 7.1   Problem Names and Thinking Errors

Name _____   Date _____

Read the entire document, then reread each item and follow the instructions.

Social/behavioral problems are actions that cause harm to oneself, others, or property.

1. Has someone else's problem(s) ever hurt you? ☐ yes ☐ no
   Think of a time that someone's problem(s) have hurt you. Choose the best name for that problem from the list below and write it here.

   _____

2. Has your problem ever hurt someone else? ☐ yes ☐ no
   Think of a time your problem hurt someone else. Choose the best name for that problem from the list below and write it here.

   _____

General problems

The first three problems are general problems. These general problems may be related to any of the specific problems. When you use one of the general problem names to describe a behavior, to get a good understanding of the situation you *must* also name one of the specific problems (see the next page).

1. Low Self-Image

The person has a poor opinion of him- or herself. Often feels put down or of little worth. Quits easily. Plays "poor me" or sees him- or herself as the victim even when harming others. Feels accepted only by other people who also feel bad about themselves.

Briefly describe a situation where you or someone you know showed a low self-image problem.

_____

_____

Was a specific problem shown at the same time? ☐ yes ☐ no
What was the problem?

_____

_____

2. Inconsiderate of Self

The person does things that are damaging to him- or herself. He or she tries to run from problems and often denies them.

(Continued)

Table 7.1 (Continued)

Briefly describe a situation where you or someone you know showed an Inconsiderate of Self problem.

_____

_____

Was a specific problem shown at the same time?   ☐ yes   ☐ no
What was the problem?

_____

3. Inconsiderate of Others

The person does things that are harmful to others. Doesn't care about needs or feelings of others. Enjoys putting people down or laughing at them. Takes advantage of weaker people or those with problems.

_____

Briefly describe a situation where you or someone you know showed an Inconsiderate of Others problem.

_____

_____

Was a specific problem shown at the same time?   ☐ yes   ☐ no
What was the problem?

_____

Specific problems

4. Authority Problem

The person gets into major confrontations with teachers, parents, and others in authority, often over minor matters. Resents anyone telling him or her what to do or even giving advice. Won't listen. Even when complying, glares, sulks, or curses.

I know someone who has this problem.   ☐ yes   ☐ no
I have this problem.   ☐ yes   ☐ no

5. Easily Angered

The person quickly takes offense, is easily frustrated or irritated; throws tantrums.

I know someone who has this problem.   ☐ yes   ☐ no
I have this problem.   ☐ yes   ☐ no

6. Aggravates Others

The person threatens, bullies, hassles, teases, or uses put-downs to hurt other people. "Pays back," even when others didn't mean to put the person down.

I know someone who has this problem.   ☐ yes   ☐ no
I have this problem.   ☐ yes   ☐ no

7. Misleads Others

Manipulates others into doing the dirty work; will abandon that person if the person is caught.

I know someone who has this problem.	☐ yes	☐ no
I have this problem.	☐ yes	☐ no

8. Easily Misled

The person prefers to associate with irresponsible peers and is easily drawn into their antisocial behavior. Willing to be their flunky—hopes to gain their approval.

I know someone who has this problem.	☐ yes	☐ no
I have this problem.	☐ yes	☐ no

9. Alcohol or Drug Problem

The person misuses substances that hurt him or her, and is afraid of not having friends otherwise. Is afraid to face life without a crutch. Avoids issues and people through substance abuse. Usually is very self-centered and minimizes the use of drugs by saying they are not bad or within his or her control. When the person does something wrong, he or she blames the drugs by saying, "I was high—I couldn't help it."

I know someone who has this problem.	☐ yes	☐ no
I have this problem.	☐ yes	☐ no

10. Stealing

The person takes things that belong to others. Doesn't respect others. Is willing to hurt another person to take what he or she wants.

I know someone who has this problem.	☐ yes	☐ no
I have this problem.	☐ yes	☐ no

11. Lying

The person cannot be trusted to tell the truth or the whole story. Twists the truth to create a false impression. Denies everything when he or she thinks it is possible to get away with it. Finds it exciting to scheme and then get away with a lie—in other words, to "get over" on people. May even lie when there is nothing to be gained.

I know someone who has this problem.	☐ yes	☐ no
I have this problem.	☐ yes	☐ no

12. Fronting

The person tries to impress others, puffs him- or herself up, puts on an act. Clowns around to get attention. Is afraid to show his or her true feelings.

I know someone who has this problem.	☐ yes	☐ no
I have this problem.	☐ yes	☐ no

(Continued)

Table 7.1 (Continued)

How many problems do you have? _____

What are your most serious problems?

Number 1 problem _____

Number 2 problem _____

Number 3 problem _____

By correctly identifying your problems, you have taken a big step in helping yourself. Save this handout to use later in the program. You may find it very useful.

Thinking Errors

The following terms are used to identify thinking errors. These terms are used in the group meetings and throughout the program. When you name your behavioral problem, the thinking error that caused it is also named. *Remember: It is your thinking error that leads to your social/behavioral problem.*

The Primary thinking error

1. Self-Centered

Self-Centered thinking means that you think your opinions and feelings are more important than the opinions and feelings of other people. You may not even consider how another person might feel about things. Self-Centered thinking can also mean that you think only about what you want right now and do not think about how your behaviors will affect you or others in the future.

Self-Centered is the "primary," or basic, thinking error. The Self-Centered thinking error can severely limit one person's consideration for the viewpoint of another person.

Does someone you know seem to have a Self-Centered thinking error? How do you know? Explain without using the person's name.

_____

_____

_____

It is important to understand that a person's thoughts cannot be known by anyone other than that person. You can guess what a person is thinking, but you will not know for sure until that person shares his or her thoughts.

Has anyone ever said to you, "I know what you are thinking," but then was wrong? Explain.

_____

_____

_____

If you want to know what another person is thinking, what do you have to do?

_____

Secondary thinking errors

The Self-Centered person uses other (secondary) thinking errors to avoid feeling bad (guilt, remorse, low self-concept) about his or her bad (antisocial) behavior and to allow the selfish thoughts and behaviors to continue. The Self-Centered person almost always shows his or her basic self-centered thinking error *and* one of the following secondary thinking errors.

2. Minimizing/Mislabeling

Minimizing means that you think your problems or behaviors are not as bad or wrong as they really are.

Mislabeling means that you put a label on your wrong or harmful behavior to try to make it OK or good. Minimizing/Mislabeling can also mean that you may call other people bad names so it will seem OK to hurt them.

Examples

- "We just went for a little joyride!" What really happened: "We stole someone's car and rode around for hours, then left the car when it ran out of gas."
- "It really didn't hurt her. I only pushed her." What really happened: "The girl is in pain because I slammed her hard against the wall."
- "He was a snitch and got jumped." What really happened: "I punched and kicked him because he told his neighbor the truth, that I was the person who stole the neighbor's stereo." Or, what really happened: The young man was brutally beaten because he told the principal that someone had a gun and threatened some other kids.

Write another example and explain.

_____

_____

_____

3. Assuming the Worst

Assuming the Worst means that you think that only bad things can happen to you and that you cannot do anything about what happens. It also means that you think that you or other people will not be able to change or make improvements. Assuming the Worst can also mean that you think that others are always selfish or out to get you or someone else.

Examples

- A guy bumped into you and your friend. You think that he did it on purpose instead of thinking it was an accident. What really happened: Everyone was late and rushing to get to class on time, the bump was accidental, and the guy said, "Excuse me," but you think because the guy was bigger he was being a bully.
- You have a problem, and you say that no one will help you. What's really happening: You have not shared your problem with anyone and don't intend to because you think other people are always selfish.
- Someone left a CD player and headphones on the library table. You think that you should take them for yourself because if you don't, someone else will.

Write another example and explain.

_____

_____

_____

(Continued)

Table 7.1   (Continued)

4. Blaming Others

Blaming Others means that you do not take responsibility for your own behavior. Instead, you blame other people for your harmful behavior when it is really your fault. It can also mean that you think that your bad behaviors are OK because you were high on drugs or in a bad mood, or because you were once the victim of discrimination or abuse.

Examples

- "I got mixed up with the wrong people." What really happened: You agreed to help your friend take something that belonged to someone else.
- "I was drunk when I beat up that new guy." What really happened: You and your friends were drinking and thought it would be fun to beat up the new guy. You knew it was wrong!
- "She got me mad and got me thinking about those times I was abused. That got me even madder, and I had to lash out." What really happened: The young woman told you to leave her alone, that she didn't want to talk with you. You became angry and punched her in the face. You didn't punch the young man, who is bigger and stronger than you are, when he told you the same thing.

Write another example and explain.

_____

_____

_____

Are thinking and behaving connected? Explain.

_____

_____

_____

How many thinking errors do you have? _____

What are your most common thinking errors?

Number 1 thinking error _____

Number 2 thinking error _____

Number 3 thinking error _____

By identifying your thinking errors you have taken a big step in helping yourself to correct faulty thinking. It takes a strong person to admit to thinking errors and the behavioral problems they cause.

Source: G. B. Potter, J. C. Gibbs, & A. P. Goldstein (2001). *The EQUIP implementation guide.* Champaign, IL: Research Press. Reprinted with permission.

McVeigh looked surprised. He stood straight up from his chair. "You'd put me in a little cell like that?" he said.

"Tim, that's what you did to your victims and their families," Smith said. "They'll never be able to communicate with each other again." (Michel & Herbeck, 2001, p. 289)

Samuel Yochelson and Stanton Samenow (1977) suggested that confrontation should include teaching the "chain of injuries" (p. 223)—extended to absent and indirect victims—resulting from every crime. Similarly, Hoffman (2000) suggested that "these confrontings should also include the other's life condition beyond the immediate situation, ... which the delinquents seem to ignore on their own" (p. 292). Agee's emphasis on bluntness notwithstanding, Vorrath and Brendtro (1985) stressed that, to be effective, confronting must be conveyed in a constructive and caring fashion.

Value and Limitations of Mutual Help Programs

Outcome evaluation studies of Positive Peer Culture and related programs at schools, juvenile correctional facilities, detention centers, private residential facilities, and community group homes have yielded a mixed picture. Although these programs have generally been found to promote youths' self-concept or self-esteem, reductions in recidivism were less likely to be found in more rigorously controlled studies (see Gibbs et al., 1996). Worse, some peer group programs have actually *increased* participants' delinquency and substance use (see Dishion et al., 1999).

In our view, mutual help-only programs have had mixed success at least partly because they do not adequately address the limitations of antisocial youths (Carducci, 1980; see Chapter 6). Such programs can succeed for a while in inducing erstwhile antisocial youths to become "hooked on helping," perhaps because, as Vorrath and Brendtro (1985) suggested, the helper in the process "creates his own proof of worthiness" (p. 6) and thereby a genuine basis for self-respect. In the absence of constructive resources for helping recalcitrant peers, however, antisocial youths often eventually become frustrated in their helping attempts and fall back on what they know best: putdowns and threats. To investigate mutual help problems and needs for improvement, Brendtro and Albert Ness (1982) surveyed 10 schools and facilities using Positive Peer Culture or related programs. Cited as a problem at 9 out of 10 centers was "abuse of confrontation" (e.g., "harassment, name-calling, screaming in someone's face, hostile profanity, and physical intimidation," p. 322)—going rather beyond Agee's call for bluntness! The pervasiveness of such abuse should not be surprising: How can a youth with antisocial behavior problems be helped by fellow group members who lack skills and maturity for dealing with such problems—and who have such problems themselves? How can such "deviant peer influence" be "minimized" (Dodge, Dishion, & Lansford, 2006, p. 12)? To promote its effectiveness, the mutual help approach needs the helping resources provided by a cognitive behavioral approach.

Remedying the Limitations: The Cognitive Behavioral Approach

Mac's mutual help meeting in 1993 illustrated more than the traditional Positive Peer Culture approach. For example, Mac reported and the group discussed not only Mac's Authority and Easily Angered problems but also the underlying thinking errors generating those problems—an innovation that deepens Positive Peer Culture problem work. Even such deeper problem work, however, does not fully address a basic problem: the limitations of antisocial youths (see Chapter 6) and hence their groups. These limitations include not only distorted thinking but in general a paucity of skills and maturity needed for behavioral change (cf. Carducci, 1980). In other words, juvenile offenders and other behaviorally at risk youths must be not only adequately motivated but also adequately *equipped* if they are to succeed in helping one another and themselves.

Corresponding to the two basic approaches (mutual help, cognitive behavioral) integrated in EQUIP are two basic types of group meetings. In their mutual help meeting, Mac and the group applied the thinking errors and other helping-skill tools learned as part of a cognitive behavioral approach (see Glick, in press). The cognitive behavioral curriculum (featuring cognitive change, behavioral practice) remedies the limitations that undermine antisocial youths' effectiveness as they—both as individuals and collectively as a group—become motivated to try to help one another. Once a group is sufficiently motivated to be receptive, mutual help meetings are supplemented or interspersed with "equipment" meetings, so called because they equip the group with the skills and maturity needed for helping others and themselves to achieve cognitive and behavioral change. One facility conducted its mutual help meetings Monday through Wednesday and its equipment meetings on Thursday and Friday each week.

Whereas a peer culture of caring and mutual help is cultivated during mutual help meetings, then, the needed social perspective-taking skills and maturity are taught during the equipment meetings. It was during its equipment meetings that the 1993 prototypic EQUIP group was learning relevant insights and tools such as the need for institutions to have rules against contraband, techniques for correcting thinking errors and managing anger, and steps of constructive and balanced social behavior. These resources were crucial as Mac worked on his Authority and Easily Angered problems during the meeting and beyond. Put in general terms, groups in the EQUIP program become equipped with skills and maturity that address the youths' limitations (see Chapter 6). Hence, the curriculum components include: (1) mature moral judgment (moral education or social decision-making); (2) skills to correct thinking errors and manage anger; and (3) social skills (for constructive and balanced behavior). Hence, in addition to being multicomponential in the sense that mutual help and cognitive behavioral approaches are integrated and expanded (e.g., with attention to the self-serving cognitive distortions), EQUIP is also multicomponential in another crucial respect: *Its cognitive behavioral approach entails three interrelated curricula that correspond to the three interrelated limitations of antisocial youths.*

Synergy between Cognitive Behavioral and Mutual Help Approaches in EQUIP and Related Programs

The equipment meetings are introduced to the EQUIP groups with the explanation that what they learn in those meetings will help them to help one another more effectively. Given its emphasis on group members' helping potential rather than on their targeted limitations, this explanation itself tends to promote antisocial youths' amenability to treatment. Litwack (1976) found that both the juvenile offenders' motivation to learn constructive skills and the learning itself improved when they were told that they would subsequently be using the skills to help other adolescents. In contrast, traditional or direct psychoeducational teaching or cognitive-behavioral training programs may implicitly stigmatize the learner as dependent and inadequate, thereby eliciting defensiveness and exacerbating resistance and noncompliance problems (Riessman, 1990).

The motivational benefits deriving from introducing the curriculum with the mutual help rationale make the point that the mutual help approach can enhance the effectiveness of the cognitive behavioral approach. Indeed, cognitive behavioral or psychoeducational programs may not accomplish much if young offenders' resistance to treatment and negative group norms are not addressed, i.e., if a receptive group is not first cultivated.[2] Yet as noted, the contributions flow in the reverse direction as well. If their cultivated good intentions are to fare well, prospective helpers must gain skills, knowledge, and maturity so that they can help constructively. This bidirectionality or interdependence is worth emphasizing: The two approaches need each other. A kind of program synergy can emerge through the integration of mutual help and cognitive behavioral approaches. To adapt Einstein's famous observation about religion and science, one might say that motivation without equipping knowledge is blind, equipment without motivation is lame!

The synergistic integration of the mutual helping and cognitive behavioral approaches can be discerned in various treatment contexts besides that of EQUIP. Recovery Training and Self Help (National Institute on Drug Abuse, 1993), a program for supporting recovery from alcohol or substance addiction, features "a recovery skills training curriculum in combination with a guided peer support group" (p. 19). The skills training curriculum was added to the support group because "an aftercare group could do more than just talk about whatever came up at a given meeting and need not be limited to the ideas of whoever happened to be at that meeting" (p. 33).

Goldstein and colleagues' (Goldstein, Glick, Irwin, Pask-McCartney, & Rubama, 1989) skills training program for dysfunctional families of antisocial youths takes place in a support group context. In cooperative learning programs, teaching skills or competence is an implicit component insofar as more capable students are included in each cooperative learning group (e.g., Carducci & Carducci, 1984). Skills are typically provided in youth-to-youth service programs, wherein motivated older youths are trained in how to help at-risk younger youths.

Social Perspective Taking and the Three EQUIP Curriculum Components

In the EQUIP program, social perspective taking characterizes not only mutual help but also cognitive behavioral training or facilitating. The three-component EQUIP cognitive behavioral curriculum as taught in the equipment meetings is summarized in Table 7.2 (the sessions progressively build and hence are best conducted in the sequence indicated). Although the self-serving cognitive distortions are assimilated into one component (anger management) of the curriculum, the thinking error language is crucially important for the entire program, not only for the youth culture but for the staff "culture" as well. Hence, the language is introduced in a preliminary session using a hands-on activity specifically tailored for that purpose (the *EQUIPPED for Life* game; Horn, Shively, & Gibbs, 2007). The perspective-taking opportunities entailed in the EQUIP curriculum are described below in terms of its three components.

Component 1: Equipping with Mature Moral Judgment (Social Decision-Making)

In Kohlbergian theoretical terms, morally delayed youths need an enriched, concentrated "dosage" of social perspective-taking opportunities to stimulate them to catch up to age-appropriate levels of moral judgment. As others' perspectives are considered in their own right (not just as a means to one's own ends), more ideal and mutual moral understanding begins to displace superficial and egocentrically biased judgments. A Stage 1- or Stage 2-thinking participant—who may usually dominate peers—may lose in a challenge from a more mature peer and may accordingly experience an inner conflict or disequilibration that could stimulate a more mature moral understanding.

Delayed youths are challenged to consider the perspectives of others in the context of either a macrointervention (involving reform of the institution itself) or microintervention (small-group) program. In the macrointervention, or Just Community program, attempts are made to restructure the institution (school or correctional facility) in accord with principles of democracy and justice, such that subjects (students, residents, or inmates) participate as much as is feasible in the rule-making and enforcement processes that affect institutional life (e.g., Power & Higgins-D' Alessandro, 2008). Macrointerventions such as Multi-Systemic Therapy (MST)

Table 7.2 The Equipment Meeting Curriculum in a Nutshell

Numbers at the top of each box indicate the order in which the different types of meetings are delivered.

Anger Management/ Thinking Error Correction	Social Skills	Social Decision Making

1
Evaluating and Relabeling Anger/Aggression
 	
Reevaluating, relabeling
Anger management, not
  elimination
	2
	Expressing a Complaint Constructively
	
	Think ahead what you'll
	  say, etc.
	Say how you contributed
	  to the problem.
	Make a constructive
	  suggestion.
		3
		Martian's Adviser's Problem
		
		Planet A is seen as
		  self-centered
		Planet B labeled truly
		  strong
		Making the group
		  Planet B

4
Anatomy of Anger (AMBC)
 	
Mind as the source of anger
Early warning signs (body)
Anger-reducing self-talk
	5
	Caring for Someone Who Is Sad or Upset
	
	Notice and think ahead.
	Listen, don't interrupt.
	"Be there."
		6
		Jerry's Problem Situation
		
		Loyalty, commitment
		Value of close friendships
		  Mark's Problem Situation
		Breaking up in a considerate
		  way
		Getting even is immature

7
Monitoring and Correcting Thinking Errors
 	
Gary's Thinking Errors
  exercise
Daily logs
	8
	Dealing Constructively with Negative Peer Pressure
	
	Think, "Why?"
	Think ahead to
	  consequences.
	Suggest something else
	  (less harmful).
		9
		Jim's Problem Situation
		
		Can't trust "friend" with a
		  stealing problem
		Stealing is wrong even from
		  a stranger

10
More Anger Reducers
 	
Deep breathing, backward
  counting, peaceful
  imagery
Anger reducers to
  "buy time"
	11
	Keeping Out of Fights
	
	Stop and think.
	Think ahead to
	  consequences.
	Handle the situation
	  another way.
		12
		Alonzo's Problem Situation
		Sarah's Problem Situation
		
		Shouldn't let friends steal
		  (car, store items)
		Harm from stealing
		True friend would not
		  put you on the spot
		Closing gap between
		  judgment and behavior
		  (relabeling, using
		  social skills)

(Continued)

Table 7.2 (Continued)

Anger Management/ Thinking Error Correction	Social Skills	Social Decision Making
13 *Thinking Ahead to Consequences* Thinking ahead (if-then thinking) Types of consequences (especially for others) TOP (think of the other person)	14 *Helping Others* Think, "Is there a need?" Think ahead how to help, when, etc. Offer to help.	15 *George's Problem Situation* *Leon's Problem Situation* Should tell on drug-dealing brother, friend planning an escape Others could get killed Important to jail drug dealers
16 *Using "I" Statements for Constructive Consequences* "You" statements (put-downs, threats) Use of "I" statements instead of "you" statements	17 *Preparing for a Stressful Conversation* Imagine ahead your feelings and the other person's feelings (TOP). Think ahead what to say. Think ahead how the other person might reply.	18 *Dave's Problem Situation* Shouldn't deliver drugs for friends Sister's life may be at stake Closing gap between judgment and behavior (relabeling, correcting thinking errors, exhorting)
19 *Self-evaluation* Self-evaluation, self-reflection Talking back to thinking errors Staying constructive	20 *Dealing Constructively with Someone Angry at You* Listen openly and patiently. Think of something you can agree with, say the person is right about that. Apologize or explain, make a constructive suggestion.	21 *Juan's Problem Situation* Should tell on suicidal friend Suicide is Self-Centered thinking error Existential/spiritual concerns
22 *Reversing* Things you do that make other people angry Reversing exercise (correcting Blaming Others error)	23 *Expressing Care and Appreciation* Think if the person would like you to care. Think ahead to what you will say, when, etc. Tell the person how you feel.	24 *Sam's Problem Situation* Should tell on a friend who shoplifted Important to prosecute shoplifters Store owner is not to blame (Blaming Others)

Anger Management/ Thinking Error Correction	Social Skills	Social Decision Making
25 *More Consequences for Others/Correcting Distorted Self-views*	26 *Dealing Constructively with Someone Accusing You of Something*	27 *Reggie's Problem Situation*
Victims and Victimizers exercise	Think how you feel, tell yourself to calm down.	Should reveal violent dad's drinking
Consequences for victims One's own victimization is no excuse for victimizing others	Think if the accuser is right (TOP). If the accuser is right, apologize/ make restitution; if	Should do what's best for the family Wouldn't want someone to lie to you
Think of the pain your actions have caused others (TOP)	wrong, say it isn't true, it's a wrong impression, etc.	But mother is wrong to put Reggie on the spot
28 *Victimizer and Grand Review*	29 *Responding Constructively to Failure*	30 *Antonio's Problem Situation*
Mind of the Victimizer exercise	Ask if you did fail. Think what you could do	Shouldn't help friend cheat Can't trust "friend" with
Conclusion of consciousness raising	differently. Decide, plan to try again.	cheating problem Correcting thinking errors

31
The Final Session: Up or Down?
(33 thoughts, skills, behaviors)
Up represents mature, accurate, constructive, responsible.
Down represents immature, inaccurate, distorted, destructive, irresponsible.
  Spans all three curriculum components and provides opportunites for motivational comments.
  Tests knowledge of the content of curriculum components.
  Encourages the use of concepts or skills learned in equipment meetings to help others and self.

Source: G. B. Potter, J. C. Gibbs, & A. P. Goldstein (2001). *The EQUIP implementation guide.* Champaign, IL: Research Press. Reprinted with permission.

(Henggeler et al., 1998) have sought to provide services both directly to youths and indirectly at the family and community levels. Particularly promising are Youth Charter Programs in which those who influence the youths in a community (parents, teachers, sports coaches, police, clergy, employers) meet to orchestrate and implement coherent standards and expectations (Damon, 1997; cf. Hart, Atkins, & Donnelly, 2006).

The narrower microintervention programs focus on peer group discussion of relevant sociomoral problem situations as a stimulus for perspective-taking experiences. Participants must justify their problem-solving decisions in the face of challenges from more developmentally advanced peers (or, in the case of a highly limited group, initially from a group leader; e.g., Gibbs, Arnold, Ahlborn, & Cheesman, 1984; cf. Taylor & Walker, 1997). Although the EQUIP program emphasizes the importance of a just and caring "staff culture" as well as youth culture, along with the system-wide use of the thinking error vocabulary (Self-Centered, Blaming Others, etc.) and other "equipment," EQUIP's focus on the youth group means that it is, at its core, a microintervention.

Moral judgment interventions target basic, long-term developmental processes. Although moral judgment-based macro- and microinterventions generally stimulate more mature moral judgment, the reduction of antisocial or aggressive behavior does not necessarily follow (Gibbs, Arnold, Ahlborn, & Cheesman, 1984; Niles, 1986). One intervention that did effect behavioral change was a 4-month group program by Jack Arbuthnot and Donald Gordon (1986). Antisocial juveniles (as identified by teachers) showed gains not only in their moral judgment stage but also in their behavior (in terms of disciplinary referrals, tardiness, and grades), both on conduct assessments made 2 to 3 weeks after the intervention and on 1-year follow-up posttests, relative to a randomly assigned, passage-of-time control group. Interestingly, subsequent classroom conduct (in terms of absenteeism and teachers' ratings) did not reveal significant improvement for the experimental group relative to the controls *until* the 1-year follow-up, suggesting a possible sleeper effect. In a similar study, we (Leeman et al., 1993) also found a sleeper effect: Although we found no significant moral judgment gains overall for the EQUIP group, individual group members who gained the most in moral judgment were the least likely to have recidivated *a year later* (at 12 months but not at 6 months following release from the institution).

It is probably not coincidental that the two moral judgment programs that produced long-term behavioral gains (those of Arbuthnot & Gordon, 1986, and Leeman et al., 1993) were also the ones that were multicomponential in two senses. First, as does EQUIP, the Arbuthnot and Gordon (1986) program worked on peer culture and interaction issues before initiating the moral judgment intervention. This preliminary group work entailed exercises designed to promote group cohesiveness, openness, and rapport. Second, also like EQUIP, the Arbuthnot and Gordon program was multicomponential: Beyond moral judgment, several sessions were spent "on active listening and communication ([non-threatening] 'I' messages) skills, an unplanned diversion from the dilemma discussions *necessitated by the participants' general lack in these skills, a lack which appeared to impede effective discussions*" (p. 210, emphasis added). Arbuthnot and Gordon concluded that a comprehensive program should encompass not only moral discussion but also (a) techniques to promote group cohesion and mutual caring (cf. Positive Peer Culture) and (b) "social skills (for translation of new reasoning into action)" (p. 215).

Some of EQUIP's equipment meetings pertain, then, to moral education or "social decision-making." In these sessions, already-motivated group members strive to develop moral reasons, decisions, and values (especially, to develop *mature* moral reasons for those decisions and values) pertaining to socially relevant problem situations and probe questions. The situational contexts for the problems range from the home to the school or correctional facility to the workplace. The situations themselves are designed to stimulate ethical discussion and perspective taking and thereby promote a deeper understanding of the reasons for moral values or decisions such as telling the truth, keeping promises, not stealing or cheating, having honest peer and family relationships, resisting drugs, and preventing suicide. Helpful to Mac's contraband-related problem work in the 1993 meeting, for example, was Juan's problem situation, pertaining to whether Juan should reveal to a staff member where Juan's depressed and suicidal roommate Phil has hidden some razor blades (through discussion, the group came to understand and accept the need for an institutional policy against contraband).

The potential of problem situations to stimulate perspective taking is exploited through their associated probe questions. The final question for Juan's problem situation, for example, asks, "Who might be affected (in addition to Phil himself) if Phil were to commit suicide?" (Gibbs et al., 1995, pp. 94–95; see also Potter et al., 2001). This question prompts group members to take the perspectives of loved ones, specifically, to empathize with the distress and grief caused by suicide and hence to identify the Self-Centered thinking error in Phil's intentions. In another problem situation, Alonzo's (see Table 7.3), Question 7—"Let's say the car is *your* car"—directly stimulates the group participants to take the perspective of the prospective victim in the spirit of ideal moral reciprocity. There is a certain clever irony to how this "you're the victim" technique uses Self-Centered against itself! Other questions stimulate group members to consider possible adverse consequences for Alonzo's friend Rodney (Question 8) as well as Rodney's family. Still other questions remove impediments to perspective taking in that they "plant" secondary cognitive distortions such as Blaming Others (Question 2) and Minimizing/Mislabeling (Questions 3 and 4) for participants to identify and correct.

Other problem situations and probe questions encourage group members to take the perspective of someone not immediately present in the situation, as when the group decides that stealing an audio deck is wrong even if from a stranger's car or—considering that the life of one's drug-dependent sister may be at stake—decides against making a drug delivery to her neighborhood. Like the "you're the victim" technique that uses egocentric bias against itself, encouraging participants to imagine harm to someone close to them "is a way of turning empathy's familiarity and here-and-now biases against themselves and recruiting them in the service of prosocial motive development" (Hoffman, 2000, p. 297; Chapter 4).

Besides the stimulation from the probe questions, challenges to take the perspectives of others are also cultivated through the format of the meeting, specifically its four phases: introducing the problem situation, cultivating mature morality, remediating developmental delay, and consolidating mature morality (see DiBiase et al., 2005; Gibbs, 2004; Glick & Gibbs, in press; Potter et al., 2001). In the best group

Table 7.3 Alonzo's Problem Situation

Name_____   Date_____

Alonzo is walking along a side street with his friend Rodney. Rodney stops in front of a beautiful new sports car. Rodney looks inside and then says, excitedly, "Look! The keys are still in this thing! Let's see what it can do! Come on, let's go!"

What should Alonzo say or do?

1. Should Alonzo try to persuade Rodney not to steal this car?
   should persuade / should let steal / can't decide (circle one)
2. What if Rodney says to Alonzo that the keys were left in the car, that anyone that careless deserves to get ripped off? Then should Alonzo try to persuade Rodney not to steal the car?
   should persuade / should let steal / can't decide (circle one)
3. What if Rodney says to Alonzo that the car's owner can probably get insurance money to cover most of the loss? Then should Alonzo try to persuade Rodney not to steal the car?
   should persuade / should let steal / can't decide (circle one)
4. What if Rodney tells Alonzo that stealing a car is no big deal—that plenty of his friends do it all the time? Then what should Alonzo do?
   should persuade / should let steal / can't decide (circle one)
5. What if Alonzo knows that Rodney has a wife and child who will suffer if Rodney gets caught, loses his job, and goes to jail? Then should Alonzo try to persuade Rodney not to steal the car?
   should persuade / should let steal / can't decide (circle one)
6. Let's say the car is *your* car. Alonzo is Rodney's friend, but Alonzo is also your friend. Alonzo knows it's your car. Then should Alonzo try to persuade Rodney not to steal the car?
   should persuade / should let steal / can't decide (circle one)
7. In general, how important is it for people not to take things that belong to others?
   very important / important / not important (circle one)
8. Let's say that Alonzo does try to persuade Rodney not to take the car, but Rodney goes ahead and takes it anyway. Alonzo knows Rodney is in bad shape from being high—he could have a serious accident, and someone could get killed. Then what should Alonzo do?
   contact the police / not contact the police / can't decide (circle one)

Source: G. B. Potter, J. C. Gibbs, & A. P. Goldstein (2001). *The EQUIP implementation guide.* Champaign, IL: Research Press. Reprinted with permission.

sessions, each phase flows into the next. Once the group understands clearly what the problem situation is and how it relates to their lives (Phase 1), the group's potential for mature morality can be cultivated (Phase 2); once the group has voiced some degree of mature morality (Phase 2), the group's mature (or at least less delayed) members are in a stronger "cultural" position to effectively challenge other group members' delayed and distorted judgments (Phase 3); and, finally, reducing pockets

Persuade	Important
Help your friends not get in trouble	<u>Put yourself in the other's position</u>
<u>Rodney needs to think about his family</u>	Bible says stealing is wrong
Could be your car	You get locked up
Rodney might get caught, in trouble, shot, killed, or in a wreck	<u>Hurts trust</u>
	I've been robbed—it sucks
	You'd feel bad, scared, angry, <u>guilty</u>

Let steal, Not important

It's not important for people not to steal

You'd be a big shot

Lots of fun

Exciting

Now you can drive, get money, booze, girls, whatever you want

Figure 7.1   Alonzo's Problem Situation: Reasons for Proposed Group Decisions
Note: "Best" reasons for group's decisions underlined.
Source: Adapted from J. C. Gibbs (2004). Moral reasoning training. In A. P. Goldstein, R. Nensten, & B. Daleflod (Eds.), *New perspectives on Aggression Replacement Training.* Chicester, UK: John Wiley & Sons. Reprinted with permission.

of delay (Phase 3) means the strengthening of mature reasons and decisions that can then be consolidated as the group is helped to achieve some consensus concerning decisions and reasons (Phase 4). In the final phase, the "best" (typically, the most mature) reasons for the group's decision (typically, the responsible decision) are underlined, as illustrated for Alonzo's problem situation in Figure 7.1.

Social Decision-Making and Cultivating a Positive Youth Culture

Cultivating a mature morality through perspective taking in the social decision-making meeting not only contributes to remedying a limitation of antisocial youth but also contributes "back" to the important foundational need for a culture of caring. In fact, the first problem situation, the Martian's Adviser's Problem Situation, is designed mainly to facilitate the discovery of common values and to foster a cohesive, prosocial group spirit. It reads as follows:

> *A man from Mars has decided to move to another planet. He has narrowed his search down to two planets, Planet A and Planet B. Planet A is a violent and dangerous place to live. People just care about themselves and don't care when they hurt others. Planet B is a safer, more peaceful place. People on Planet B do care*

about others. They still have fun, but they feel bad if they hurt someone. Planet B people try to make the planet a better place.

You're the Martian's adviser. Which planet should you advise him to move to? Planet A / Planet B / can't decide (circle one)

Through this exercise, a group of antisocial youths can discover that they do after all share values of caring and prosocial behavior. Moving to the prosocial planet, Planet B, is typically the majority decision. When asked for the reasons for their decision, many group members appeal to the respective planet descriptions: There's not as much violence on Planet B, it's safer, it's more peaceful, people have fun without hurting others, and people want to help one another, work to make things better, and feel bad and apologize if they do hurt others. In a poignant moment, a younger group member once wistfully added that, on Planet B, "parents spend more time with their kids." Planet B offers a concrete representation of the mature moral climate toward which the group should be working.

Component 2: Equipping with Skills to Manage Anger and Correct Thinking Errors

Although egocentric bias is reduced as mature moral judgment is cultivated during the perspective taking of the Social Decision-Making component, egocentric bias in its consolidated cognitive distortion form, Self-Centered, is such a major, immediate problem that it requires treatment attention in its own right. Beck (1999) was right to characterize righteous self-centeredness (the key problem of the reactive offender) as "the eye ('I') of the storm" (p. 25) of anger in antisocial behavior. Fifteen-year-old Mac, with his Authority and Easily Angered problems in the illustrative 1993 mutual help meeting, was typical of this type of antisocial youth. Our description of the 10 sessions of the EQUIP anger management component will refer to relevant previous cognitive-behavioral literature (reviewed by Beck & Fernandez, 1998; see also Dahlen & Deffenbacher, 2000) and will emphasize the perspectives, techniques, and other information pertinent to the management of anger.

Session 1—Reevaluating and Relabeling Anger/Aggression   Like a number of anger control programs, EQUIP anger management begins with a metacognitive discussion of anger and aggression that induces antisocial youths to gain perspective or "distance" on their anger, reevaluate it, and see its disadvantages, and gain insights that often emerge from continued discussion of its superficial and short-term advantages. In EQUIP discussions, some group members mentioned liking the "rush" or feeling of power they get from pushing people around. With continued discussion, however, that sense of power was seen to involve a Self Centered thinking error and to lead to disadvantages: "You lose friends" because people "can't trust you;" other people fear you but "don't respect you, don't want to be around you." Similarly, proposed advantages of anger and aggression (that they enable you to "get even" and "not let others get away with putting me down or pushing me around") provoked reflection: "Then the other guy would try to get back at you." As a particularly verbal and morally nondelayed EQUIP group member put it, "The cycle of revenge never stops".[3]

Beyond the reflective discussion, anger is also reevaluated through relabeling or reframing. The group leader makes the point that a self-controlled, nonviolent individual is not necessarily a loser or wimp by drawing on illustrations from prominent athletes and other popular figures who have succeeded through self-control and self-discipline—or have failed when they have lost control. Group members "are *more powerful* when they are in control of their reactions to others despite the attempts of others to provoke them" (Goldstein, 1999, p. 83; cf. Feindler & Ecton, 1986). Similarly, to a man who hit his wife because her criticism made him feel like "less of a man," Beck (1999) made this point: "Is he more of a man by hitting a weaker person? Or is he more of a man by being cool: taking insults without flinching and maintaining control of himself and the problematic situation?" Like group members, the man could then manage his anger partly by reminding himself "that the way to feel more manly was to be cool and masterful [and self-controlled]" (p. 267). A particularly helpful visual exercise provides group members with the image of a provocateur as a clown who "wants to attach his strings to you, pull you into the clown ring with him, and make you a clown, too" (adapted from Feindler & Ecton, 1986). Developing nonviolent, self-controlled options is labeled *empowering* in that it bestows flexibility by reducing one's dependency on a single (violent) response. Although some situations require self-defense, other situations are better handled through a nonviolent response. The point is the constructive control or management, but not the elimination, of anger.

Session 2—Key Role of Mind in Anger; Monitoring Mind and Body; Reducing Anger   Gaining perspective or distance on the problem of anger continues in Session 2. This session entails teaching the sequential dynamics of anger and aggression: an activating event or provocative "hot spot," mind activity in response to that activating event, bodily responses (tense muscles, etc.) to that mind activity, and consequences (summarized in the acronym AMBC). The point of the teaching is to convey the key role of the mind—not the outer event—in generating either anger or calm (cf. Novaco, 1975). The group learns to monitor anger-generating thoughts and to displace them with responsible self-talk (e.g., "If he wants to make a fool of himself he can, but he's not gonna make a fool out of me") that reduces anger and buys time for more controlled, constructive behavior (see Social Skills). Particularly helpful is self-talk that corrects Self-Centered thinking (e.g., "I can't expect people to act the way I want them to" or "For someone to be that irritable, he must be awfully unhappy"). Group members also learn to recognize and monitor bodily "Early Warning" signs (rapid heartbeat, flushed face, clenched fists, etc.) that anger is building and must be reduced. Similarly, Beck (1999) teaches clients how to recognize that they are approaching their "red zone" (p. 263) and take corrective action.

Session 3—Monitoring and Correcting Thinking Errors   The third session focuses on mind activity, especially thinking errors. Because anger is caused by the schema-based meaning of the activating event and not the event directly, mind activity deserves special attention in anger management (although techniques such as deep breathing [Session 4] are also valuable, especially as quick and easy buy-time techniques). The group begins use of a structured daily log that helps them monitor and become more aware of their problem behaviors and associated generative thinking errors. The group leader uses the exercise Gary's Thinking Errors (introduced in Chapter 6; see Table 7.4) to bring home the connection between distorted thinking and violence and, accordingly, the importance of correcting thinking errors before it is too late. For example, to correct Self-Centered thinking, one group member at the 1993 meeting suggested that, like the hypothetical Gary, the group member Mac could say to himself, "She has a right to expect better from me."

If Gary—or group members in such a situation—are to become more fair and empathic, however, they must also learn to identify and "talk back to" or correct their secondary thinking errors. Group members have suggested that Blaming Others thoughts to the effect that violence against Cecilia is her fault could be corrected with self-talk such as, "Nobody's forcing me to grab that knife—it's my fault if I do." Assuming the Worst thoughts of hopelessness can be corrected with, "There's hope for us if I start treating her decently." Correcting an intention to "teach her a lesson" (Minimizing/Mislabeling) might be a thought such as, "You don't teach anybody anything by stabbing and maybe killing them."

Session 4—Relaxation Techniques for Reducing Anger   A key technique in anger management is engaging in activities incompatible with anger (counterconditioning). Calming self-talk is one example. Other activities, covered in the fourth session, are breathing deeply, counting backward, and invoking peaceful imagery. These activities are important because they are simpler and therefore more readily used than self-talk. For example, one can prevent anger buildup by starting to take deep breaths even before one begins to deal with thinking errors, thereby "buying time" for cognitive correction.

Session 5—Self-talk Techniques for Reducing Anger: Thinking Ahead to Consequences and TOP (Think of the Other Person)   The group leader in this session returns to anger-reducing techniques that involve self-talk. One of the two techniques taught has been called "if-then" thinking or "thinking ahead" (Feindler & Ecton, 1986); its importance is suggested by findings that highly aggressive, poorly adjusted children are poorer at anticipating and describing the possible consequences of a completed action for themselves and others (Spivack & Shure, 1989). To develop an awareness of consequences that can then be used in self-talk, the group leader teaches thinking ahead to consequences in a way that includes systematic discussion of the many ramifications of aggressive or antisocial behavior (immediate and long term, practical and emotional, for self and for others). With its emphasis on consequences for others, the discussion naturally leads into a second self-talk technique that has the acronym TOP, for "think of the other person."

Session 6—Constructive Consequences   In this session, group members learn that accurate self-talk enables them to engage in calm, noninflammatory communication (social skills) that leads to constructive consequences. For example,

Table 7.4   Gary's Thinking Errors

Name_____   Date_____

Gary is in the kitchen of his apartment. Gary's girlfriend, Cecilia, is angry at him for something he did to hurt her. She yells at him. She pushes his shoulder. Thoughts run through Gary's head. Gary does nothing to correct the errors in his thoughts. Gary becomes furious. He swears at Cecilia. A sharp kitchen knife is nearby. Gary picks up the knife and stabs Cecilia, seriously wounding her.

1. What thoughts ran through Gary's head, do you think, both during the situation and afterward? Suggest some sample thoughts.

   _____

   _____

   _____

   _____

2. What are the errors in these thoughts? Cecilia was mad at Gary because he did something to hurt her. What do you think that might have been?

   _____

   _____

   _____

   _____

3. What might Gary have told himself in this situation? In other words, how might Gary have "talked back" to his thinking errors? Suggest some things Gary could have said to himself to correct each type of thinking error.

   _____

   _____

   _____

   _____

4. If Gary had corrected his thinking errors, would he still have stabbed Cecilia?

   _____

   _____

   _____

   _____

Source: G. B. Potter, J. C. Gibbs, & A. P. Goldstein (2001). *The EQUIP implementation guide.* Champaign, IL: Research Press. Reprinted with permission.

group members learn to replace "you" statements (e.g., "You jerk—you'd better return my radio") with "I" statements (e.g., "I need the radio back now") in conflict situations. "I" statements are more likely to induce empathy (in Hoffman's terms, other-focused perspective taking; see Chapter 4), whereas "you" statements are more likely to be counterproductive insofar as they provoke defensive responses.

Session 7—Self-evaluation   Self-talk is important not only in correction but also in self-evaluation (self-reward and constructive self-criticism), the focus of this session. Group members' development of a habit of self-evaluation promotes moral self-relevance (see Chapter 5) and provides an excellent prelude to the more metacognitive or consciousness-raising material encountered in the remaining sessions.

Session 8—Reversing   Given the declines in self-righteous defensiveness that should be evident by this point in the program, the eighth session should successfully shift the perspective in anger management from oneself as the victim of provocations to oneself as a provocateur of others.[4] The focus, then, is on group members' (such as Mac's) tendencies to ignore their own provocations and to blame others totally when they are in fact partly at fault, that is, to make Self-Centered and Blaming Others thinking errors. Each group member suggests two things he or she does to aggravate or hurt others. Group members then discuss how to correct their Self-Centered and Blaming Others thinking errors and practice the "reversing" technique for helping group members who inappropriately blame others. For example, a group member may say, "I don't have any problems. You dudes are the ones with the problems, man. The only problem I have is you keep hassling me, man." A sample "reversing" response: "You know, it'll be great when you get the courage to face your problems. Then you'll thank people trying to help you instead of putting them down and blaming them" (cf. Vorrath & Brendtro, 1985). The EQUIP for Educators (DiBiase et al., 2005) version of this session includes a supplementary exercise called "A Story from Two Points of View" (upon finishing rewriting a story from the other person's point of view, the student is asked, "Is the story more complete now that both sides are included?").

Sessions 9 and 10—More Consequences for Others; Correcting Distorted Self-views; Developing Commitment to Change   The aim of the final sessions is to induce empathy-based guilt and a genuine commitment to maintain the mind of a person who manages anger and lives responsibly. Certain exercises (e.g., Victims and Victimizers, see Table 7.5) are used to make the key points pertaining to the Self-Centered mind of a victimizer: the many ways in which acts of victimization harm others, the fact that most victims are not in turn victimizers, the error of thinking that having been a victim entitles one to "get back at the world" by victimizing innocent others (that deadly combination of moral judgment Stage 2 and Blaming Others), and the acknowledgment by many group members that they have been victimizers more than victims. The group leader expands the meaning of TOP from "think of the other people" to include "think of the pain your actions have caused other people":

Table 7.5 Victims and Victimizers

Name_____ Date_____

You are attending a family wedding when you are asked to drive your grandparents home. Your grandparents have lived in that home for many years. You arrive home and help your grandparents into the house. When you open the front door, you see that the house has been broken into. Many of your grandparents' things have been thrown all around. Their crystal glasses have been smashed. The family photo album has been destroyed. Some of their things, like a wedding ring that belonged to your great grandmother, have been stolen.

1. What would be the first thing that you would do?

   _____

   _____

2. How do you think you would be feeling? Have you ever had anything stolen from you? How did you feel? Does that help you understand how your grandparents feel?

   _____

   _____

3. Would you leave your grandparents in the house alone for the night? Why or why not? Do you think your grandparents would feel afraid or worried? When have you felt afraid or worried? Does that help you understand how your grandparents would feel?

   _____

   _____

4. Do you think your grandparents will get their things back? Do you think the insurance (if they have any) can make the situation all right? Why or why not?

   _____

   _____

5. Who are the victims in this situation? Can you think of any long-term or indirect victims? List some ways that victims suffer (in body, in mind, in money, in daily living, with their friends).

   _____

   _____

6. Who are the main victimizers in this situation? If a victimizer were to think ahead to the many ways a victim would suffer, would he or she still go ahead and do the crime?

   _____

(Continued)

Table 7.5   (Continued)

7. Have you been a victim? From whom? Have you victimized others? Whom have you victimized? Do most people who have been victimized go on to victimize others?

_____

_____

8. Which have you been more of, victim or victimizer?

_____

_____

Source: G. B. Potter, J. C. Gibbs, & A. P. Goldstein (2001). *The EQUIP implementation guide.* Champaign, IL: Research Press. Reprinted with permission.

> *This is self-evaluation on a big scale—evaluating your life, how you've harmed others, where you want to go from here. In the Alcoholics Anonymous 12-step program, this step is called "taking a searching and fearless moral inventory." Now instead of thinking ahead, you're thinking back. And that's the best way to think ahead to consequences for others—to think back to how your past irresponsible behavior has harmed them. Imagine yourself as your victim—the pain, how it feels. Continue to think TOP, to think of the other person and the pain you've caused, to stop yourself before you harm yourself or someone else again. (Gibbs et al., 1995, p. 160)*

Component 3: Equipping with Social Skills

Anger-managing skills are requisite to the use of social skills: After all, as long as rage grows rather than declines in difficult situations, balanced and constructive behavior is virtually impossible. Following the learning of anger management skills, then, EQUIP group members learn 10 social skills (cf. Goldstein & McGinnis, 1997; McGinnis & Goldstein, 1997) through four phases: modeling or "showing the skill," role-playing or "trying the skill" (if a group member cannot think of a relevant situation, a list of typical situations is provided), providing feedback on the role-play or "discussing the skill," and practicing the skill (at the facility or in the community).

Social skills can in many instances be construed as step-by-step, practical training in reducing self-centration or taking the perspectives of others in specific social situations. Perspective taking is implicitly involved in many of the social skills and is an explicit step in several of them (e.g., "How might the other person feel at the start of the stressful situation? Why?" in Preparing for a Stressful Conversation, or "Think, 'What is the other person accusing me of? Is he or she right?'" in Dealing Constructively with Someone Accusing You of Something).

Illustration

We can illustrate social skills learning as practical social perspective-taking training with the social skill Expressing a Complaint Constructively. This was the social skill recommended to Mac in the 1993 meeting. The steps of this skill operationalize perspective taking in specific interpersonal situations involving the need to express a complaint.

Step 1: Identify the problem. *How are you feeling? What is the problem? Who is responsible for it? Did you contribute—or are you contributing—to the problem in any way?*

Step 2: Plan and think ahead. *To whom should you express your complaint? When? Where? What will you say? (See Step 3.)*

Step 3: State your complaint. *Greet the person in a friendly way. Calmly and straightforwardly tell the person the problem and how you feel about it. If you've contributed to the problem, mention how you may be partly at fault and what you are willing to do.*

Step 4: Make a constructive suggestion. *Tell the person what you would like done about the problem. Ask the other person if he or she thinks your suggestion is fair. If the other person makes a constructive suggestion, say that you appreciate the suggestion or that it sounds fair. (Potter et al., 2001, p. 81)*

After seeing the skill modeled, an EQUIP youth named Joe role-played a situation "between me and my father ... him always wanting to go to the bar instead of spending time talking to me." Going through the steps, he reported that he was feeling "angry." He said that his father was responsible for the problem but that he did contribute by trying to avoid it, for example, by "running off and partying" (Step 1). Joe planned to bring the matter up when his dad was "at home when he's in a good mood and just say it in a polite way" (Step 2). A very touching interchange followed: After acknowledging his own contribution to the problem (running away), Joe constructively expressed the complaint to his "dad" (a fellow group member):

Dad, I'd like to talk to you about how you like to go to the bar and not spend time with me. I feel that I'm coming home from school and you're at the bar and I'm upset about something and want to talk to you and you're not there to talk to me.

Joe and his "dad" worked out times when "Dad" agreed to be home and available (Step 3). Furthermore, "Dad" agreed that Joe's complaint and suggestion were fair, and Joe said that he appreciated "Dad's" responsiveness (Step 4). The group and group leader gave Joe feedback on his role-play (he did all the steps well). Applied practice of the skill followed group completion of the role-plays (unfortunately, we do not know whether Joe ever found an occasion to express his complaint constructively to his father, but at least he became "equipped" for that and similar situations).

Because they involve maintaining balance through an ongoing social interplay of perspectives, social skills might more accurately be called social *interaction* skills. For example, Joe considered the moment when his "dad" would be approachable, anticipated and accepted his "dad's" likely viewpoint by acknowledging at the outset his own runaway behavior, listened openly to his "dad's" ideas as an understanding was reached, solicited his "dad's" feelings about the agreement, and expressed appreciation for the "dad's" cooperation.

Adaptations and Evaluations: Issues of Implementation

Since its introduction in the early 1990s, the EQUIP Program has been implemented, adapted, and (to some extent) evaluated at various facilities or institutions in North America, Europe (especially, the Netherlands), and Australia. The institutions include juvenile correctional facilities, community-based adult correctional facilities (or halfway houses), and middle schools; the young persons served have ranged in age from preadolescence through young adulthood.

Implementations of EQUIP typically involve adaptations and include the program in an array of services. One implementation of EQUIP has been accomplished at the Minnesota Correctional Facility in Red Wing, which provides treatment, education, and transition services for chronic male juvenile offenders. The Red Wing implementation has adapted use of the Problem Names (only the generic names "Inconsiderate of Others" and "Inconsiderate of Self" are used) and Cognitive Distortions (Minimizing is separated from Mislabeling). To promote coherence and reduce program isolation, the Red Wing staff uses their adapted version of the EQUIP problem and thinking error language throughout the facility's Restorative Justice, Reflection Journaling, Substance Abuse Treatment, Sex Offender Treatment, and Relapse Prevention programs. Some implementations are only partial; for example, the Alvis House, a halfway house for adults in Columbus, Ohio, does not include Mutual Help meetings in its adaptation.

Some adaptations have modified or even eliminated the EQUIP name. Although Colorado's Youthful Offender System (YOS) does not identify EQUIP by name, much of the material, in consultation with one of us (Potter), has been assimilated into the YOS core program interventions (the Colorado consultation resulted in our *EQUIP Implementation Guide*; Potter, Gibbs, & Goldstein, 2001). Potter has also adapted EQUIP for use at Ohio's Franklin County Community-Based Correctional Facility, where it is called Responsible Adult Culture (RAC). Ann-Marie DiBiase and colleagues (DiBiase, Gibbs, & Potter, 2005) innovated a well-crafted prevention version of EQUIP for behaviorally at-risk middle school children, a version called *EQUIP for Educators*.

EQUIP should, in theory, be at least as effective as other cognitive behavioral programs given that EQUIP also addresses motivational issues. One-year recidivism at Red Wing declined from 53 percent to 21 percent following implementation of EQUIP in 1998 (a contemporaneous comparison sample was not available; Handy, personal communication, February 2, 2008). One-year recidivism following the RAC version of EQUIP was also at 21 percent, significantly lower than the 29 percent at a facility with a program that was equivalent except that it did not include cognitive restructuring techniques such as correcting thinking errors (see Devlin, 2008). Nonetheless, like that of other cognitive behavioral programs, EQUIP's effectiveness appears to vary with quality of implementation. Mark Lipsey and colleagues' (Lipsey, Chapman, & Landenberger, 2001; cf. Landenberger & Lipsey, 2005) meta-analysis of studies comparing cognitive behavioral with non-cognitive behavioral programs found an overall effectiveness for the cognitive behavioral programs, e.g., a mean recidivism rate substantially less than that of the non-cognitive behavioral programs (37 versus 53 percent, respectively). Lipsey and colleagues noted that the weakest recidivism results were found with cognitive behavioral programs "low in strength and fidelity of implementation" (p. 155), e.g., inadequate staff training, two or three rather than five weekday meetings, and high turnover among participants. Four outcome evaluation studies of EQUIP conform to Lipsey et al.'s pattern: a high-fidelity implementation of EQUIP was found to have substantial institutional conduct and recidivism effectiveness (12-month recidivism rate at 15.0 percent versus 40.5 percent for the control group; see Leeman, Gibbs, & Fuller, 1993; cf. Devlin, 2008), in contrast to weaker or negligible results for lower-fidelity implementations (Liau, Shively, Horn, Landau, Barriga, & Gibbs, 2004; Nas, Brugman, & Koops, 2005). EQUIP can be included among the referents for Lipsey et al.'s conclusion that "a great deal of improvement may be possible in the implementation of [cognitive behavioral] programs" (p. 155).

Social Perspective-Taking for Severe Offenders

The outcome evaluation research on EQUIP suggests, then, that—given adequate implementation—the program can induce responsible behavior among broad groups of initially antisocial youth. To be effective with narrower groups of more serious and chronic offenders, however, EQUIP perspective taking may require supplementation. EQUIP can be strengthened, in other words, through integration with programs emphasizing even more intensive and extensive modes of social perspective taking. Quite compatible with EQUIP, for example, are 12 Step and victim awareness programs (e.g., California Department of the Youth Authority, 1994; Hildebran & Pithers, 1989; Mendelson, Quinn, Dutton, & Seewonarain, 1988; Murphy, 1990; but cf. Hilton, 1993). These programs aim to induce perspective taking and empathy for victims through specific depicted situations (e.g., our Victims and Victimizers exercise [see Table 7.5], adapted from the California Department of the Youth Authority [1994] victim awareness program), as well as other stimulations of victim awareness through video or film presentations, newspaper or magazine articles, guest speakers (especially recovering victims or family survivors of murder victims), role-plays, personal journals, homework, and reminder posters.

A particular type of powerful or intense role-play that deserves special attention entails the reenactment of a crime perpetrated by the offender. Reenactive role-play as perpetrator and then as victim has been used in the Texas Youth

Commission Capital Offender Group program (Alvarez-Saunders & Reyes, 1994), an intensive 4-month therapy designed "to break a participant's psychological defenses to force him to see his victim's suffering, to help him discover his conscience and feel remorse" (Woodbury, 1993, p. 58). The juveniles role-play many aspects of their own histories, including family relationships and the homicidal events themselves. In a role-played reenactment of a crime, the perpetrator must remain at the scene even though in the actual event he typically had fled. He must hear the pleas and see the suffering of the victim (played by a group peer), and thereby experience empathic distress and guilt ("great care must be taken," however, to insure that the role play does not instead elicit violent or predatory desires among the group members; Marshall, Anderson, & Fernandez, 1990, p. 90). In a second reenactive role-play, the perpetrator must directly put himself in the victim's place: This time the perpetrator feels what it is like to be the victim by taking the victim's role (cf. reverse role-play activity in Beck, 1999). Outcome evaluations of the Capital and Serious Violent Offenders Treatment Program have indicated substantial reductions in rearrest and reincarceration, e.g., 15.0% recidivism (vs. 40.6% for non-enrolled controls; Texas Youth Commission, 2007; cf. Heide, 2003).

Agee and McWilliams (1984; cf. Pithers, 1999) used vivid crime reenactment role-play to achieve therapeutic breakthroughs with violent juvenile offenders in the context of a mutual help program. Particularly powerful and worth quoting at length is the apparent realization of empathic guilt in 14-year-old Larry, a serious sex offender. Larry

> asked for the agenda. He was committed to the unit for the kidnap and rape of a two-year-old girl. Several times he had attempted to have group on his crime, but was unsuccessful in doing more than a very mechanical, emotionless relation of the details. By prearrangement, he had agreed to act out the crime on a large baby doll in the hopes of bringing out more of the emotion in the situation. Larry proceeded to describe the situation in the room where he kidnapped the baby and [to] talk about what was going through his mind. He saw the sleeping child as a good opportunity to have sex and thought about where he could take her where he would be undiscovered. He left the home with the baby, with his hand over her mouth so she couldn't cry. He went to a nearby park, and with considerable difficulty, raped the baby, and then left her there injured. He stated he had no interest in whether she lived or died, but did feel a little scared at what he had done.
>
> When the role play with the baby [doll] was acted out, there was clearly shock and disgust among all the group members, both male and female, and also the Group Leader. All of the group members took some physical action wherein they were trying to distance themselves from Larry, such as scooting their chairs back. One girl (who had been sexually abused herself in childhood) screamed when another youth accidentally touched her as he moved his chair back. After some difficulty in getting started, the peers expressed their shock and disgust to Larry. He had frequently stated that he had no feeling for his victim, but in this group, he seemed to be stunned by the enormity of what he had done. He listened mutely

to the feelings of his peers and appeared noticeably stricken when the Group Leader also told him of his feelings of disgust for what he had done. The group concluded in somewhat of a shocked state, and one of the girls in the group asked the Group Leader to please take the doll off the unit.

It was not until two or three months later that the effects of this particular group on Larry were seen. At that time, he had a repeat court appearance, and when asked by the judge what he felt for his victim, gave an extremely moving and honest statement which showed much awareness of the harm he had done to his victim. This was in sharp contrast to his earlier behavior in court when he had been very cocky and unrepentant. (Agee, 1979, pp. 292–293)

The contribution of crime reenactment role-play to Larry's problem work is extraordinary. The vivid reenactment certainly did bring out "more of the emotion" of his horrific crime—first for Larry's peers and the group leader and then, as a result, for Larry. Note that once Larry completed his role-play, the reaction of every other person in the room was a shock and disgust[5] so total and profound that it at first could scarcely even be expressed. All of Larry's peers literally distanced themselves from him. The reenactment using the large doll had communicated the horror of Larry's crime so effectively that Larry now found himself utterly isolated, with no physical, emotional, social, or other connection to anyone else, not even the group leader—the group leader's feedback of disgust left Larry "noticeably stricken." The deep harm and wrong of Larry's unconscionable crime pierced through Larry's callous smugness and cognitive distortions. In a powerful and profound way, he decentered. That is, he saw his crime through clear, third-person eyes and was himself shocked and stricken by what he saw. No longer "mechanical" or emotionless and devoid of feelings for his victim, Larry now "seemed to be stunned by the enormity of what he had done." At court months later, instead of displaying an unrepentant and even cocky demeanor, Larry evidenced contrition and awareness of the grievous harm. Although Larry continued to need therapy, a breakthrough was evident.

The chapters in the final section of Aaron Beck's (1999) *Prisoners of Hate* concern "the brighter side of human nature" and the promise of cognitive therapy as it uses human resources of rationality or social decentration, ideal moral reciprocity, and empathy. Role reversal or crime reenactment role-plays constitute useful supplementary techniques for activating and helping to develop these resources and may be especially needed in working with the severe offender population. Although Larry's crime shocks and disgusts us in its depravity, Larry's redemption is inspiring: Through social perspective taking, conscience finally emerged in the mind of the perpetrator of an unconscionable crime. Larry's case appears to vindicate not only Beck's emphasis on rationality but also Kohlberg's (or Piaget's) emphasis on social decentration, Hoffman's emphasis on the reliability of the empathic predisposition, and the emphasis of all three theorists on the attainability of veridical moral perception.

The title of Beck's (1999; cf. Garbarino, 1999) final section, on change, is "From Darkness to Light." Does Larry's change represent a transition from the darkness of distortion to the light of truth in some sense that goes beyond metaphor? In other words, did Larry change in a deeper spiritual sense? In the next chapter, we will go beyond Kohlberg's and Hoffman's theories of moral development and behavior to consider their ontological implications and foundations.

Notes

[1]The provision of faith-building opportunities in Positive Peer Culture adds crucially to the cognitive behavioral approach in EQUIP, addressing James Garbarino's (1999) concern that

> cognitive behavioral programs [by themselves] are not enough to initiate and sustain the deep changes necessary for rehabilitation in the long run. Conventional programs may succeed in providing some of the needed psychological and social anchors, but they are unlikely to provide the spiritual anchors that are required for success with the most traumatized, troubled, and violent boys. (pp. 216–217).

[2]Cultivating a positive or receptive group "culture" for caring and change is important even for younger groups that are merely at risk. Fortunately, such groups may be less recalcitrant and hence may require less group-building work (see DiBiase et al., 2005).

[3]Because a cycle of lethal revenge continues indefinitely, the ultimate consequence is death to all or most of the disputants. To make this point with a gang member who was plotting revenge at the funeral of his murdered brother, a youth worker asked: "Look around, do you see any old guys here?" (many of the older youths had already been murdered in cycles of revenge; Kotlowitz, 2008, May 4, p. 54). Fortunately, in this case, the appeal to ultimate consequences was successful and cycles of retaliatory killings were thereby preempted.

[4]Where self-centered orientations in the group have *not* declined, introducing this session may be counterproductive. One still Self-Centered youth remarked with respect to a victim awareness program: "What about me, man? What about what I have gone through? I mean, I want to talk about what hurts me, and all they want to talk about is the people I hurt. I won't do it. The whole program stinks" (Garbarino, 1999, p. 139).

[5]"Disgust" in this context probably stems from a perceived wrong and sympathetic distress for the victim (see Chapter 4) more than from a perceived impurity (see Chapter 1).

CHAPTER 8

Beyond the Theories: A Deeper Reality?

Just why Homo sapiens *should carry the spark of rationality that provides the key to the universe, is a deep enigma. We, who are children of the universe—animated stardust—can nevertheless reflect on that same universe, even to the extent of glimpsing the rules on which it runs. How we have become linked into this cosmic dimension is a mystery. Yet the linkage cannot be denied. (Davies, 1992, p. 232)*

As we have seen, growing beyond superficiality characterizes the primarily affective and primarily cognitive strands of human development toward mature moral perception and behavior. Consider first Hoffman's theory of the primarily affective (empathic) strand. According to Hoffman's theory, cognitive development, language acquisition, and socialization enable the child's empathic predisposition to evolve beyond simple attention to the surface cues of another's emotions and thereby to attain a deeper, more veridical or authentic *caring* for others. In Piaget's and Kohlberg's theories of the *cognitive* strand, that evolution beyond simple attention to surface cues is a constructive process leading to a decentered *understanding* of the intangible, ideal bases in mutuality for interpersonal relationships and society. In the related context of nonsocial cognitive development, simple attention to surface cues gives way to *logical* understanding: The child is said to penetrate through superficial, sometimes misleading appearances by constructing conservation and other "necessary" knowledge of "underlying reality" (Flavell et al., 2002, p. 141).

Flavell et al.'s (2002) characterization of conservation and related necessary logic as a reality that underlies physical appearances and impressions is reminiscent of mathematician Roger Penrose's (1994) reference to "profound mathematical substructure[s]" or "underpinnings" that are "hidden in the very workings of the world" (p. 415). Indeed, conservation, transitivity, class inclusion, and so forth, insofar as their properties are logico-mathematical (see Chapter 9), are integral to these substructures. Perhaps in cognitive development, then, we not only construct and understand but in the last analysis *discover* conservation and, more systematically, using the methods of science, *discover* in logic and mathematics the very substructures or foundations of the physical world.

We are indeed "linked" to the universe, but what is the ontological significance of that linkage? When we use our "spark of rationality" to discover and thereby "glimpse the rules on which it [the universe] runs," as astrophysicist Paul Davies put it in the opening quotation, do we in effect glimpse a more fundamental reality? Penrose's neo-Platonist answer is yes. He argued that the world of tangible impressions and appearances—and in part the rational minds of those who perceive and seek to understand that tangible world—derive ultimately from those underpinnings, that substructural realm of logic and mathematics.

Testifying to this enigmatic linkage of the physical (and, in turn, mental) worlds with a deeper logico-mathematical reality is "the amazing precision and subtle applicability of sophisticated mathematics that physicists continually and increasingly find in their descriptions" (Penrose, 1994, p. 415) of the workings of the physical world. Reimannian space and imaginary numbers illustrate constructions that, despite their purely abstract origins in mathematical deduction, subsequently came to "serve as indispensable frameworks for physical phenomena" (Piaget, 1967/1971, p. 341). Similarly, Davies (1992) asked how such abstract, pure mathematics, "worked out . . . long before it was applied to the real world," nonetheless proved to be so "spectacularly successful" once technology permitted its application to nature (p. 151). Penrose answers that logical or mathematical "rules" or necessary relations, regardless of when they are discovered, partake of a primary ("profound, timeless, and universal," p. 413) reality.[1]

As we know from Chapter 2, Piaget and Kohlberg argued that morality—especially, ideal moral reciprocity—is akin to logic. If so, then might the prescriptive truths of mature morality join those of logic and mathematics in reflecting a deeper reality?[2] In an essay aptly titled "Right and Wrong as a Clue to the Meaning of the Universe," C. S. Lewis (1943) likened the reciprocation of kindnesses and unselfishness to necessary and universal truths such as those of mathematics:

> Think of a country where . . . a man felt proud of double-crossing all the people who had been kindest to him. You might just as well try to imagine a country where two and two made five. Men have differed as regards what people you ought to be unselfish to—whether it was only your own family, or your fellow countrymen, or everyone. But they have always agreed that you ought not to put yourself first. Selfishness has never been admired. (p. 5)

Although the right of reciprocity is distinct from the good of caring (or although betrayal of kindness and trust is distinct from selfishness), Lewis legitimately included both in his universalist appeal. Do not both represent cross-cultural ideals, even if they are honored in the breach?[3] And is not the ideal of justice, of mutual respect, of honoring and reciprocating others' kindnesses congruent with the ideal of unselfishness, of veridical empathy, of, we might even say, love? As Piaget (1932/1965) noted, "Between the more refined forms of justice and love properly so called, there is no longer any real conflict" (p. 324). Ideal moral reciprocity, in other words, formulates what love looks like when the perspectives of all concerned are taken into account. (Granted, how broadly we can or should apply ideal moral reciprocity [one's own family? fellow citizens? everyone?] can be an issue, one that we will have occasion to visit later in this chapter.)

Perhaps "growing beyond superficiality" in the right and the good, then, has a transcendent significance. Are love and the ethic of mutual respect clues to the meaning of the universe? Do they, like logico-mathematical knowledge, reflect a primary reality? Can that primary reality be to some extent accessed? Can one thereby gain insight and inspiration for living the moral life? These ontological (nature of reality), existential, and moral questions are addressed in this chapter. To ponder them, we venture beyond Kohlberg's and Hoffman's theories to explore the relationship of moral development and behavior to a deeper reality.

We need not start from scratch. Hoffman implicitly takes an objective ontological stand in his argument for the human potential to overcome biases and to connect *veridically* with another. Mature caring, after all, is deeply accurate or true. It is Kohlberg, however, who offers the stronger line of continuity from moral to existential and ontological concerns. On the basis of case studies and philosophical literature, as we saw in Chapter 3, Kohlberg answered the ontological question affirmatively: In the throes of existential crisis, some morally mature persons begin to see daily life from the vantage point of its cosmic "ground." They begin to sense or identify with a unitary "whole of nature" of which we are individually but parcels. From that vantage point ("Stage 7"), one transcends existential despair and experiences inspiration from a deeper reality for living in the light of love and justice—albeit in a world often dark and divisive from self-centered, angry distortion as well as genuine injustice.

Darkness and light have been used as a metaphor (by Beck, 1999; see Chapter 7) to characterize the perspective-taking progress of initially antisocial individuals from self-centeredness to the ideals of love and ideal moral reciprocity. We ask, Could this progress from "darkness to light," from self-centeredness and antisocial behavior to love and ideal reciprocity, be more than a metaphor?

Like Kohlberg, we will suggest an affirmative answer to the question of whether there is a deeper reality to the strands of moral development (or, for that matter, the remedial moral development of erstwhile antisocial individuals). If there is a deeper reality represented by love and ideal reciprocity, perhaps it is sometimes glimpsed and even accessed not only through meditation or existential crises but also, serendipitously, through life-threatening crises. In particular, we refer to an extraordinary phenomenon of human perception that has been the subject of increasing attention in the medical literature: the so-called "near-death experience" (Moody, 1975), defined by Greyson (2000b; cf. Kelly et al., 2007) as "profound psychological events with transcendental and mystical elements, typically occurring to individuals close to death or in situations of intense physical or emotional danger" (p. 316). Because of its potentially major implications for our understanding of moral development and reality, the phenomenon will be studied at some length.

Two Case Studies

We will introduce the near-death experience phenomenon through the presentation and extensive study of two independent cases involving life-threatening physical crises (radical surgery and serious accident). The first case, that of Pamela Reynolds (a pseudonym), was described by cardiologist Michael Sabom (1998); the second, that of Tom Sawyer, by biographer Sydney Farr (1993). Tom had not heard of near-death experiences prior to his near-death event; whether Pam had heard of such experiences is not known. Pam and Tom provided the interview and other data for these accounts at least 2 years after their near-death events. Recollections reported sooner after the events would probably have been highly similar, however. Cardiologist Pim van Lommel and colleagues (van Lommel, van Wees, Meyers, & Elfferich, 2001) found almost no longitudinal difference in survivors' near-death recollections at three points in time (a few days, 2 years, and 8 years later).[4] Greyson (2007) found similar results for consistency of reports across two longer time intervals (20 and 40 years later).

Pam Reynolds's Near-Death Experience

Starting in the morning of August 15, 1991, at the Barrow Neurological Institute in Phoenix, Arizona, a 35-year-old musical composer and mother of three named Pamela Reynolds underwent a daring surgical procedure and had a near-death experience. The surgery was daring in that its aim was to remove a brain aneurysm so large and deep as to be inoperable by traditional procedures. Excision of the giant aneurysm required its collapse ("like a deflated balloon," Sabom, 1998, p. 45) as the blood in the arteries of the brain was drained "like oil from a car" (p. 43).

Preliminary procedures prepared Pam for surgery. Her eyes were taped shut. Instruments were inserted or attached first to anesthetize Pam intravenously and then to monitor many vital signs: her blood pressure, pulmonary pressure, heart rate and rhythm, blood oxygen level, body temperature, and brain (cerebral cortex, brain stem) electrical activity. The brain stem monitoring device, inserted through Pam's ear canals, meant that physical hearing was impossible. The surgical scene is depicted in Figure 8.1.

Pam's near-death experience began as neurosurgeon Robert Spetzler opened her skull with a cranial saw (she was already "under deep anesthesia," Spetzler, personal communication, July 2, 2002). She recounts:

> The next thing I recall was the sound: It was a natural D [tone]. As I listened to the sound, I felt it was pulling me out of the top of my head. The further out of my body I got the more clear the tone became. . . . I remember seeing several things in the operating room when I was looking down. I was the most aware that I think that I have ever been in my entire life. . . . I was metaphorically sitting on Dr. Spetzler's shoulder. It was not like normal vision. It was brighter and more focused and clearer than normal vision. . . .

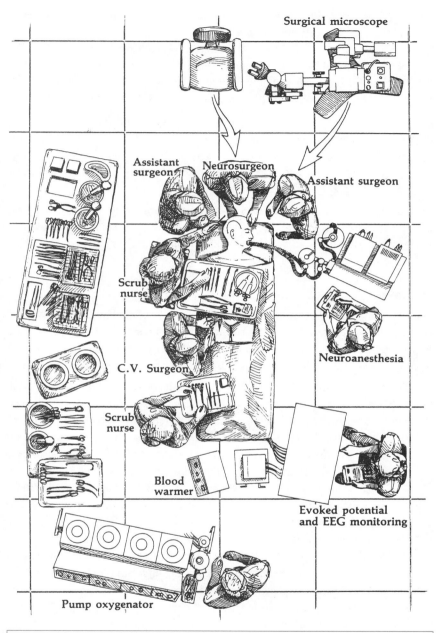

Surgical microscope

Assistant surgeon

Neurosurgeon

Assistant surgeon

Scrub nurse

Neuroanesthesia

C.V. Surgeon

Scrub nurse

Blood warmer

Evoked potential and EEG monitoring

Pump oxygenator

Figure 8.1 Diagram of the operating room at the Barrow Neurological Institute
Source: M. Sabom, M.D. (1998). *Light and death*. Grand Rapids, MI: Zondervan. Reprinted with permission.

I thought the way they had my head shaved was very peculiar. I expected them to take all of the hair, but they did not. . . .

The saw thing that I hated the sound of looked like an electric toothbrush. . . . The [electric saw] blades were in what looked like a socket wrench case. . . . I heard the saw crank up. . . . It was humming at a relatively high pitch and then all of a sudden it went Brrrrrrrrrr! like that. (Sabom, 1998, p. 41)

The neurosurgeon was cutting through Pam's skull. Through a cranial opening, a microscope was inserted into Pam's brain to inspect the aneurysm deep in her brain. The aneurysm's giant size meant that its reduction through a radical procedure, called hypothermic cardiac arrest, would indeed be necessary. A cardiovascular surgeon began preparing access to Pam's blood vessels.

Someone said something about my veins and arteries being very small. I believe it was a female voice and that it was Dr. Murray, but I'm not sure. She was the cardiologist [cardiac surgeon]. I remember thinking that I should have told her about that. (Sabom, 1998, p. 42)

The vein and artery in Pam's left groin area (those in the right groin area had been found to be too small) were connected to a cardiopulmonary bypass machine, so that her blood could circulate through the machine and be cooled by it. The machine lowered Pam's body temperature to the point that her heart stopped beating and her brain ceased electrical activity.[5] Her blood was then drained from her brain and body and temporarily stored in the cylinders of the machine. Her near-death experience continued:

There was a sensation like being pulled, but not against your will. I was going on my own accord because I wanted to go. I have different metaphors to try to explain this. It was like the Wizard of Oz—being taken up into a tornado vortex, only you're not spinning around like you've got vertigo. You're very focused and you have a place to go. The feeling was like going up in an elevator real fast. And there was a sensation, but it wasn't a bodily, physical sensation. It was like a tunnel but it wasn't a tunnel.

At some point very early in the tunnel vortex I became aware of my grandmother calling me. But I didn't hear her call me with my ears. . . . It was a clearer hearing than with my ears. I trust that sense more than I trust my own ears. The feeling was that she wanted me to come to her, so I continued with no fear down the shaft. It's a dark shaft that I went through, and at the very end there was this very little tiny pinpoint of light that kept getting bigger and bigger.

The light was incredibly bright, like sitting in the middle of a light bulb. It was so bright that I put my hands in front of my face fully expecting to see them [the hands] and I could not. But I knew they were there. Not from a sense of touch. Again, it's terribly hard to explain, but I knew they [my hands] were there. . . .

The "incredibly bright" light "was real warm and real comfortable and real loving." Pam

began to discern different figures in the light . . . they were all covered with light, they were light, and had light permeating all around them . . . they began to form shapes I could recognize and understand. I could see that one of them was my grandmother. I don't know if it was reality or projection, but I would know my grandmother, the sound of her voice, anywhere.

Everyone I saw, looking back on it, fit perfectly into my understanding of what that person looked like at their best during their lives.

I recognized a lot of people. My uncle Gene was there. So was my great-great-Aunt Maggie, who was really a cousin. On Papa's side of the family, my grandfather was there. . . . They were specifically taking care of me, looking after me.

They would not permit me to go further. . . . It was communicated to me—that's the best way I know how to say it, because they didn't speak like I'm speaking—that if I went all the way into the light something would happen to me physically. They would be unable to put this me back into the body me, like I had gone too far and they couldn't reconnect. So they wouldn't let me go anywhere or do anything.

I wanted to go into the light, but I also wanted to come back. I had children to be reared. (Sabom, 1998, pp. 44–45)

With the aneurysm sac drained of blood, the neurosurgeon was able to excise it. Then the machine began to warm Pam's blood and reintroduce it into her body; Pam's brain and heart began to resume electrical activity.

Then they [deceased relatives] were feeding me. They were not doing this through my mouth, like with food, but they were nourishing me with something. The only way I know how to put it is something sparkly. Sparkles is the image that I get. I definitely recall the sensation of being nurtured and being fed and being made strong. I know it sounds funny, because obviously it wasn't a physical thing, but inside the experience I felt physically strong, ready for whatever.

Pam "returned" to her physical body:

My grandmother didn't take me back through the tunnel or even send me back or ask me to go. She just looked up at me. I expected to go with her, but it was communicated to me that she just didn't think she would do that. My uncle said he would do it. He's the one who took me back through the end of the tunnel. Everything was fine. I did want to go.

But then I got to the end of it and saw the thing, my body. I didn't want to get into it. . . . It looked terrible, like a train wreck. It looked like what it was: dead. I believe it was covered. It scared me and I didn't want to look at it.

It was communicated to me that it was like jumping into a swimming pool. No problem, just jump right into the swimming pool. I didn't want to, but I guess I was late or something because he [the uncle] pushed me. I felt a definite repelling and at the same time a pulling from the body. The body was pulling and the tunnel was pushing. . . . It was like diving into a pool of ice water. . . . It hurt! . . . When I regained consciousness, I was still on the respirator. (Sabom, 1998, pp. 46–47)

Pam made an adequate recovery from her operation. In addition to citing her children ("I had children to be reared") as her purpose for returning, she subsequently referred as well to social harmony (expressed in terms of her background in musical composition): "Everyone has a different tone ... the beauty is in the harmony.... My reason for being is to learn to make harmony ... with all the variables that present themselves in my little world" (Benz, 2001). Although Pam has continued to have health problems, she has in fact been raising her children (Sabom, personal communication, July 1, 2008).

Thomas Sawyer's Near-Death Experience

On May 23, 1978, in Rochester, New York, Thomas Sawyer, a 33-year-old father of two boys was crushed under his truck and had a near-death experience. Tom was working under his truck with the help of his older son Todd when a support gave way; the frame of the truck depressed the center of his chest, rendering him unable to breathe. Todd screamed and phoned for an ambulance. Hearing Todd's scream, Tom's wife also arrived, as did neighbors. Tom lost consciousness and his heart stopped beating. Despite losing consciousness, Tom reportedly heard "the ... rough and hard ... conversation of the paramedics getting into the ambulance a couple of miles away ... just as though I was with them for the ride" (Farr, 1993, p. 25). He then

> had a feeling of absolutely, positively, waking up, very quickly and sufficiently.... All pain and pressure [were] gone. I felt I could see very clearly, but the problem was I saw nothing but absolute, total blackness.... I had the desire to look around inquisitively. What is this place? Where am I? ... Instantaneously [with my questions], this darkness took the shape of a tunnel. It was very vast.... If you took a tornado and stretched it out straight, it would be similar to that, without the houses and doors floating around inside.... I had the feeling of floating, or that I was moving through it—and it was okay; it was comfortable.... I went faster and faster....
>
> The next thing is that way, way off in the distance—to infinity—there appeared this little speck of light. That light was very special; it was ... extremely bright.... brighter than something that would immediately blind you.... It was utter beauty.... The light was way off in the distance and got larger as I got closer to it.... There were such feelings of warmth and love coming from the light that it made me feel good. (p. 28)

Tom communicated with the light concerning the meaning of his life as well as the nature of God and the universe. The communication "was not in words.... Instantaneously it emanated ... thought-pattern to thought-pattern.... As I thought of and formulated a desire or a question, it would already have been recognized, acknowledged, and ... answered" (Farr, 1993, p. 28). Tom interpreted the light as divine, although he found adequate description difficult:

> There are characteristics and aspects of that part of my experience that I would really wish to talk about a little deeper. I've not found the words.... Some of the things are regarding the aspect of, "What is the Light?" Well, the light is God. And what is God? God is unconditional love. God is total beauty. God is everything! (Farr, 1993, p. 38)

In order to choose "intelligently" whether to return or "become part of the light" (p. 29), Tom also experienced a "complete" or "total" (p. 29) review of the events of his life "from the first breath of life right through the accident" (p. 35). He saw and relived the events simultaneously from multiple perspectives: (a) as his adult self, observing the events "from a third-person viewpoint" (p. 37) looking down at the scene; (b) as his self at the time; and (c) as another person involved in the event. An example is an incident that occurred when he was 8. His father had told him

> to mow the lawn and cut the weeds in the yard.... [Regarding some weeds in the back, Aunt Gay had said,] "Leave them alone now, Tom ... and as soon as they blossom we'll make tiaras for all the girls, and flower necklaces for some of the guys." ... We were looking forward to that.... [But] I deliberately decided to be bad, to be malicious.... I called it "Operation Chop-Chop."... And I went ahead.... I thought, "Wow, I got away with it; I did it. And if Aunt Gay ever says anything I'll just tell her father told me to do it. Or if father asks me I'll say, well that's what you told me to do." ... My Aunt Gay never said a word to me; nothing was ever mentioned; I got away with it totally.
>
> [In my life review] I was observing this entire event.... I not only re-experienced my eight-year-old attitude.... I also experienced it exactly as though I was my Aunt Gay, several days later after the weeds had been cut ..."Oh my goodness, what has happened? Oh well, he must have forgotten. But he couldn't have forgotten, everyone was looking forward to—Oh no, knock it off. Tommy is—he's—He's never done anything like that. I love him so—Oh, come on, cut it out. Gee, it was so important. He had to know ... he couldn't have known."... I was in my Aunt Gay's body, I was in her eyes, I was in her emotions, I was in her unanswered questions. I experienced the disappointment, the humiliation. It was very devastating to me. (Farr, 1993, pp. 29–30)

Tom also relived an event that occurred in 1968, when he was 23. Upon arriving at the airport in Chicago for Olympic Trials, Tom discovered that his racing bicycle had been irreparably damaged by a baggage handler:

> I was myself [in the life review] in all of my rage and indignation and righteousness. But I was simultaneously that young kid who had worked his first day at the airport and didn't know what "Escort Service" meant. It was, to him, simply a canvas bag in the way. He had no idea there was a bicycle in there.... He made a mistake through ignorance.
>
> Did that help me to understand? Of course it did. I realized that there was, in his life, almost no interaction at all with me, Tom Sawyer. It was only a moment in his life, trying desperately to do a good job. (Farr, 1993, p. 32)

Tom also reviewed an altercation with a man who had darted in front of his truck in the street. The man had almost made contact with Tom's truck: "Now my attitude in those days was, God forbid that you should put even a smudge on my truck. A smudge made me furious." In the course of the original altercation, the man swore at and slapped Tom, which "instantly gave me license to annihilate him. ... I almost killed that man" (Farr, 1993, p. 32). Once again, in the life review reexperiencing of the event, Tom was observing not only himself at the time (at age 19) but also the other person. He experienced

> Tom Sawyer's fist come directly into my face. And I felt the indignation, the rage, the embarrassment, the frustration, the physical pain. ... I felt my teeth going through my lower lip—in other words, I was in that man's eyes. I was in that man's body. I experienced everything of that interrelationship between Tom Sawyer and that man that day. ...
>
> Okay. He hit me first. Try that in your life review! ... I wish that I could tell you how it really felt and what the life review is like, but I'll never be able to do it accurately. (Farr, 1993, pp. 32–34, emphasis added)

Like Pam, Tom wanted to go into the light. Whereas Pam also wanted to return, Tom wanted to stay. Nonetheless, just as he was "becoming homogeneous" and experiencing "total knowledge" (p. 38) with the light, Tom "reversed through the tunnel" (p. 40). Like Pam's, Tom's return to his body was jolting:

> As I reentered my body, it was with a bang. It was a very slamming experience, a shocking experience similar to grabbing on to a 220-volt line. (Farr, 1993, p. 40)

Immediately after reentering his body, Tom regained consciousness and could again breathe as the truck was lifted. As Tom was removed from underneath the truck, paramedics administered oxygen. Tom momentarily lost consciousness again and was taken to the hospital, where x-rays showed no broken bones. He recuperated at home. In retrospect, he described himself as having "abruptly" changed after the accident "from a [self-]righteous, self-motivated person to a spiritually motivated individual who now prioritizes helping others" (Farr, 1993, p. 60).

A Deeper Reality?

What are we to make of such experiences? Interestingly, Pam Reynolds explicitly raises the ontological issue in noting that she did not know whether her perception of her deceased grandmother "was reality or projection." In Susan Blackmore's (1993) terms, the near-death experience is basically either "a glimpse ... penetrating into [an] underlying reality" of human existence or a composite of "hallucinations, imaginings, and mental constructions" (such subjective mental projections, attributed to a dying brain, presumably "stop when the brain's activity stops;" pp. 3–4, 161). In Mark Fox's (2003) stark terms, near-death experiences are either "windows into transcendent realities" or "mere mirrors reflecting nothing more than a bundle of culturally derived fantasies and psychosocial expectations" (p. 100).

A full treatment of this ontological issue is not feasible within the space of this chapter (see literature reviews and related articles of mine, Gibbs, 1985, 1997, 1999, 2005; as well as those by Fox, 2003; Greyson, 2000b; Kelly et al., 2007; Parnia, 2006; Parnia, Spearpoint, & Fenwick, 2007; Potts, 2002; and Sabom, 1982, 1998). "Dying brain" explanations of the phenomenon have included references to endorphins, cerebral hypoxia, hypercarbia, hallucinogenic agents such as ketamine and phencyclidine, serotonin pathways, limbic system activation, and temporal lobe anoxic seizures (Blanke, Ortigue, Landis, & Seeck, 2002; Fox, 2003; Parnia, 2006; Parnia & Fenwick, 2002).

Using our case studies and the research literature, we will ponder five ontologically relevant questions: (1) Does the context of the near-death experience influence and even determine its content? (2) Do near-death experiencers interpret the experience as real? (3) Are verifiable aspects of the near-death experience in fact accurate or veridical? (4) Is the likelihood or depth of the experience associated with proximity to physical death? and finally, (5) Does the typical near-death experience actually take place during near-death?

Again, a literature review based on these questions could easily consume a book in its own right; even the "brief" treatment given here will be lengthy. Yet moral development and *reality* is a crucial relation to ponder, as Kohlberg recognized. Could it be that the near-death experience does afford some sort of access into a deeper reality, a glimpse that then promotes existential and moral development? Once we attain some tentative closure regarding the ontological significance of this phenomenon, we will be in a position to move to existential and moral questions.

1. Does the Context of the Near-Death Experience Influence and Even Determine the Content of the Experience?

Near-death experiences have occurred across a broad range of life contexts. A context is a relevant background, condition, or surrounding set of circumstances. The immediate context of the near-death experience is a life-threatening situation (in our case studies, radical surgery or serious accident; other near-death circumstances include serious illnesses, suicide attempts, and intense danger). More broadly, however, the context includes everything brought to the experience by the experiencers themselves: their age, gender, educational level, ethnic status, marital status, occupation, culture, religious background, mental health, knowledge of near-death experiences, historical time period, and so on, to say nothing of their particular lifestyles, schemas, and schema-related attitudes, beliefs, needs, desires, hopes, and expectations at that point in time.

Although near-death experience survivors do not differ in most contextual respects from nonexperience survivors[6] (Greyson, 2000b; Schwaninger, Eisenberg, Schechtman, & Weiss, 2002), context may nonetheless make a difference in the particular content of the experience or how the experience is interpreted. For example, experiencers may project what they need, hope, expect, or are readily able (have the schemas) to see. Pam's grandmother was one of the "shapes" (formed from figures in the light) that Pam "could recognize and understand." Furthermore, each shape "fit perfectly into [Pam's] understanding of what that person looked like at their best during their lives." During her life-threatening operation, Pam may have needed to see and so projected an image of her familiar, nurturant, optimally healthy grandmother, just as Tom, desiring to understand his dark surroundings, may have projected something he *could* understand (he reported that his surroundings—instantaneously with his desire to understand them—"took the shape of a tunnel").

Part of the context that Pam and Tom brought to their near-death experiences was their technology- and industry-oriented Western culture. Their references to elevators, light bulbs, electric tooth brushes, lawn mowers, and voltage lines are absent from many non-Western and most historical accounts. The more broadly the features of the near-death experience have been defined, of course, the more they have been evaluated as universal, that is, evident across diverse individual, situational, demographic, and cultural or historical contexts. Allan Kellehear (1996; 2008) found that descriptions such as movement through a tunnel or cylinder (such as a pipe; a truck driver experienced being "shot through a tailpipe toward a brilliant light," Cox-Chapman, 1995, p. 17) are generally provincial to Western near-death experiences. Indian, Chinese, Melanesian, and other rural or village cultures described experiences such as walking through dark fields or emerging through the calyx (throat) of a lotus flower or traveling through subterranean caves. Although Western and non-Western respondents brought different contexts to their experience, Kellehear (1996; cf. 2008) inferred that respondents in both types of culture were "attempting to describe some kind of movement through darkness" (p. 37) and into some otherworldly, usually bright realm.

Various typologies for classifying and studying broad features of the near-death experience have been proposed (see Greyson, 2000b). The most elegant of these typologies is Sabom's (1982, 1998) tripartite classification of near-death experiences as (a) autoscopic (literally, self-visualizing; more broadly, perceiving from an elevated vantage point one's physical body and its surrounding earthly situation), (b) transcendental (or moving through a dark region or void to an otherworldly realm; encountering and mentally communicating in that realm with a being or beings of light, deceased loved ones, or spiritual figures; reviewing events of one's earthly life; and reaching some border, limit, barrier, or juncture point), and (c) combined or comprehensive, such that "the transcendental portion of the experience followed the autoscopic portion in a continuous, unbroken sequence" (Sabom, 1982, p. 52).

In Sabom's (1982) Western culture study of 78 hospital patients who had had a physical near-death crisis event, more than one third (34) had had a near-death experience (this proportion was also found by Ring, 1980; in prospective studies, however, the incidence rate has been found to range from 10% to 23%; Greyson, 1998; Parnia, Waller, Yeates, & Fenwick, 2001; Schwaninger et al., 2002; van Lommel et al., 2001). Slightly more than one half (38) of the near-death experiences in Sabom's total collection of 71 such cases were transcendental, slightly less than one third (21) were autoscopic, and approximately one sixth (12) were comprehensive. In our case studies, Pam's category was comprehensive, whereas Tom's was transcendental (although his reported hearing of the distant conversation in the ambulance might be classifiable as autoscopic, rendering his experience comprehensive as well). In these basic terms, Kellehear (1996) found autoscopic, comprehensive, and especially transcendental near-death experiences to be broadly evident across diverse Western and non-Western cultural contexts.

One feature of the transcendental or comprehensive near-death experience—namely, the life review (such as Tom's)—is widespread but not universal. Kellehear (1996; 2008) found this feature among Western and Asian (Chinese, Indian, Thai, and Tibetan) accounts but not among those from the Pacific Area (such as Hawaii and Guam) and Hunter-Gatherer Societies (Native American, Aboriginal Australian, African). He speculated that the life review may have relevance in Western or Asian cultures but not in the latter cultural contexts. For example, whereas Judao-Christian and Hindu moral and religious worldviews emphasize the conscience and evaluation of the individual soul, Hunter-Gatherer and Pacific village cultures' attributes emphasize family or tribal history over individual narrative and attribute much of human personality and behavior to the forces and influences of nature (animals, vegetation, landscapes, climatic conditions, etc.); hence, a moral life review would make sense in the former more than in the latter type of cultural context.

Even within Western, Indian, and Chinese cultures, where the life review is more common, its incidence varies considerably from sample to sample. In our two cases, the life review occurred for the accident victim but not for the surgery patient; this fact is consistent with findings that life reviews are more likely to occur in the context of serious accidents. In fact, life reviews occur in more than 50% of accident-related near-death experiences, a significantly higher percentage relative to the incidence rate for near-death experiences associated with other types of near-death events (Ring, 1980; Stevenson & Cook, 1995). Ring (1980) speculated that life reviews may be especially needed in such *unexpected* near-death crises, in which one must suddenly prepare for apparently imminent death (Stevenson and Cook found only a trend in this direction, however). Even given the circumstances of a life-threatening accident, the life review is relatively rare in childhood near-death experiences, perhaps because children "don't yet have much of a life ... to review" (Morse, 1990, p. 142).

Life reviews are not uncommon among the relatively rare (or underreported), "distressing," "frightening," or "less than positive" versions of the near-death experience (Bush, 2002; Greyson & Bush, 1992; Rommer, 2000; not included are cases that convert to a positive experience). Bruce Greyson and Nancy Bush (1992) classified these distressing near-death experiences into four categories. First are experiences that have fairly typical broad features, yet are distressing. These respondents seem to have been terrified by their inability to control the anomalous events experienced (Barbara Rommer called these experiences "misinterpreted"; "most" of her experiencers in this category said that they had been "used to being in total control of all situations in their lives," p. 35). A second category is defined as a void or realm of total blackness, engendering a sense of emptiness, aloneness, and despair (we wonder whether Tom Sawyer was at risk for such affect in his "problem" of "absolute, total blackness" had his experience not converted to movement toward the light). The third category entails hellish imagery idiosyncratic to the experiencer.

Life reviews occurred in approximately one third of cases in the first (lack-of-control) and second (void/blackness) categories and in approximately one fifth of the hellish-imagery cases. Life reviews occurring in the distressing near-death experience tend to be negative or frightening. After finding a number of cases consisting chiefly of a frightening life review, Rommer (2000) proposed this experience as a fourth category of the distressing near-death experience. In this category, the primary transcendental experience is a life review in which the experiencer typically feels negatively judged and then laments his or her earthly actions (cf. near-death experience accounts in medieval folklore;[7] Zaleski, 1987).

In the life review category as well as the other categories of distressing near-death experiences, suicide attempts ("either intentionally or unintentionally, through self-destructive behavior," p. 41) constituted approximately one-third (on average) of the precipitating situational contexts. A "very frequent" impression gained by survivors of distressing near-death experiences was "that suicide is not an [acceptable] option," (p. 44) at least for the self-centered sorts of suicidal cases reviewed by Rommer.

Context does make a difference, then, in the content of the near-death experience. Although movement through a dark region or void (usually toward a lighter, increasingly bright and dominant realm or being) is universally evident across cultures, the way a person makes sense of and describes that experience will depend partly on cultural context: Characterizations of that dark region in the imagery of a tunnel, cylinder such as a pipe, and so on are more likely in the context of cultures in which those objects are familiar. And although the life review is a fairly widespread feature, its incidence may be higher in situational contexts such as accidents, as well as in cultures that attribute accountability to individual human choice or decision rather than to ecological forces or animistic influences. So contextual factors do influence the imagery and likelihood of particular features of the near-death experience.

Does context not only influence but also *determine* the experience? In other words, is the near-death experience entirely reducible to an individual's imaginal projection of some sort, such as a dream or hallucination? After all, we do know "that the imagination can be made to produce realistic images that can … be projected outward as though a part of the perceived world" (Blackmore, 1993, p. 69). Some of the "events" of the experience do seem like imaginal projections (e.g., hellish imagery). The "feeding" or "nourishing" of Pam by her loved ones could have been dreamlike imagery epiphenomenal to the fact that her brain and heart were reactivating as the increasingly warm blood circulated through her body.

In general, however, although the near-death experience is context influenced, we doubt that it is entirely attributable to contextual factors such as culture, expectation, and situation. Autoscopic, transcendental, and comprehensive near-death experiences have been evident even among persons who (like Tom and perhaps Pam) had not known of near-death experiences. With the exception of the life review, such experiences have been reported even by young children despite their limited and idiosyncratic cultural or religious expectations. It is intriguing that child survivors whose parents were present and highly salient nonetheless generally report having encountered in the light *deceased* loved ones (Greyson, 2000b).

Furthermore, unlike a typical dream or hallucination, the near-death experience does not accommodate *entirely* to the experiencer's schemas of cultural imagery and personal expectations. Prior to his experience, Tom not only had been unaware of near-death experiences but had regarded notions of spirituality as "hocus-pocus bullshit" (Farr, 1993, p. 55). Tom and Pam were surprised by specific aspects of their experience. Tom expected to stay with the light but instead found himself returning to his body. Pam knew her hands were there and "fully expected" to see them, yet she could not. And although Pam expected her grandmother to escort her on her return, her grandmother "just didn't think she would do that" (her uncle instead escorted her and facilitated her return). Departures from specific personal or religious expectations are not uncommon in near-death experiences (Abramovitch, 1988; Morse, 1990; Ring, 1984). Although they do not constitute strong evidence (Blackmore, 1993), unexpected or surprising events—especially those that continue to baffle—do suggest an ontological status beyond subjective imagination. An experiencer named Elinor remembered that her

> father loved having friends and family around. The fact that it still seems odd to Elinor that her father would have turned down her company ["All he said to me was, 'Sweetheart, don't come'"] gives credence to the possibility that her vision is not simply a construct of her imagination. (Cox-Chapman, 1995, p. 134)

Also suggestive of something beyond ordinary imagination is the difficulty encountered by experiencers as they seek to communicate their experiences. Pam and Tom found it difficult adequately to convey numerous extraordinary and anomalous aspects of their experiences. An example is their movement through a dark region, channel, or void. Although both Pam and Tom invoked the tunnel imagery, neither was entirely content with that characterization. Declaring that "it was like a tunnel but it wasn't a tunnel," Pam also invoked the "metaphors" of tornado vortex and elevator but found nothing quite adequate. Similarly, the dark region only *partially* took on the character of a tunnel for Tom, who had to add the image of a straightened tornado. Their interchanges with the figures or the light took place through a nonauditory "communication" ("that's the best way I [Pam] know how to say it") or instant "emanations" (Tom) of thoughts. Pam "found it terribly hard to explain" how she could sense yet not see her "hands" in the experience. Tom's particular frustration was in attempting to convey aspects of the light, inadequately communicated with phrases such as "unconditional love" and "total beauty." Typical in the literature was Tom's and Pam's reference to the light as extremely bright, loving, warm, and "comfortable" such that one "feels good."

In this connection, we note that a classic criterion of a genuinely transcendent or mystical experience is "ineffability," that is, that "no adequate report of its contents can be given in words" (W. James, 1903/1958, pp. 292–293). By this criterion,

Pam's and Tom's experiences were genuinely transcendental. It is perhaps not coincidental that ineffability (as implied in expressions of communicative frustration, surprise, or bafflement) was totally absent from a near-death experience account that was subsequently acknowledged to have been a fabrication (reported by Ring & Lawrence, 1993; see Gibbs, 1997).

2. Do Near-Death Experiencers Interpret the Experience as Real?

Although Pam expressed uncertainty as to whether her encounter with her deceased grandmother was a matter of projection or reality, she also reported her impression that the sound, as it were, of her grandmother's calling her was extraordinarily clear ("a clearer hearing than with my own ears") and authentic ("I trust that sense more than I trust my own ears ... I would know my grandmother, the sound of her voice, anywhere"). Similarly, the pitch of the cranial saw became "clearer" with her sense of emergence from her physical body. Her visual perception as well was "brighter and more focused and clearer than normal vision." Tom also referred to "waking up" and seeing "very clearly" (even though all he saw at first was "absolute, total blackness"). Finally, Pam felt that during the experience she "was the most aware that I think I have ever been in my entire life." Such impressions of heightened conscious awareness and clarity of perception are commonly evident in these experiences (see Kelly et al., 2007).

Experiencers usually report not only enhanced awareness and perceptual clarity but as well a sense that their experience was real. In contrast to Pam's initial uncertainty as to whether her perception of her Grandmother was projected or real, Tom was emphatic that his experience was real. Experiencers who remember their dreams or have had hallucinations typically distinguish their near-death experience as neither dream nor hallucination (Ring, 1980; Sabom, 1982). One respondent said, "It was too real. Dreams are always fictitious. *This* was *me,* happening at *that* time and there was no doubt that it was reality" (Ring, 1980, p. 82). Regarding the distinguishability of hallucinations as only pseudo-real in comparison, Bruce Greyson (2001) recounted an astonishing incident in which a psychiatric patient began a suicide attempt (by overdosing on a medication), changed his mind and dialed the phone for help, started hallucinating (seeing little people in his kitchen and crawling around his legs), and then had an autoscopic near-death experience:

> He drew back out of his body and from a position of about 10 feet behind his body he looked at himself holding the phone. He saw his body looking around. . . . He couldn't see any little people; he was mentally clear. But he remembered being inside the body and he knew that his body was hallucinating. He told me: "I wasn't hallucinating but my body was!"

Some near-death experiencers even suggest that their experience was more real than is the physical world. According to Tom, "The reality in which we are currently existing is in fact a lesser reality than the reality of the Light" (Farr, 1993, p. 51).

Similarly, one of Sabom's (1982) patients described the experience as "realer than here" (p. 16). Nonetheless, this "lesser" or less-real reality of earthly existence is evidently of some ontological status and importance in its own right: An additional common impression of near-death experiencers is that their return has some reason or purpose, typically involving spiritual growth, learning or education, and helping or caring for others,[8] including in some cases broad humanitarian concerns. Although interpreting an experience as real does not make it so (Blackmore, 1993), the "reality" claim does invite investigation as to whether it is to any degree supportable. To that question we now turn.

3. Are Verifiable Aspects of the Near-Death Experience in Fact Accurate or Veridical?

A crucial empirical strategy for assessing whether near-death experiences are purely subjective imaginal projections or something more than that is to investigate the empirical accuracy or veridicality of their confirmable features. Most amenable to such investigations are, of course, perceptions reported in the autoscopic near-death experience (or the autoscopic portion of the comprehensive near-death experience).

Vague reports, of course, could derive from purely imaginal projections. In his one possibly autoscopic feature, Tom reportedly heard a distant ambulance conversation that was "rough and hard," but that report is difficult to evaluate given the lack of specifics or of corroboration. Tom's claims to paranormal abilities *following* his experience are more specific but uncorroborated. Such claims are common in the near-death experience literature but their validity status remains controversial (e.g., Bem, Palmer, & Broughton, 2001; Bierman, 2001; LaBerge & Gackenbach, 2000; Radin, 2006; Targ, Schlitz, & Irwin, 2000).

Pam, however, provides us with more specific and hence more verifiable earthly recollections. Recall that throughout the surgery Pam's eyes were taped shut, ear canals occluded, and body deeply anesthetized. Nonetheless, she reported numerous idiosyncratic visual and auditory details (e.g., the pitch and shape of the cranial saw, her partially shaven head, and surgeons' comments)—all of which were corroborated by the medical staff. Sabom (1998) was particularly "shocked with the accuracy of Pam's description of the saw as an 'electric toothbrush' with 'interchangeable blades' ... and with a 'socket wrench' in which this equipment is kept" (p. 187), although he did also note a minor inaccuracy (Pam mislabeled an overhanging edge along the cranial saw as a "groove" near the "top" of the saw). Sabom tentatively attributed this misimpression to Pam's viewing the instrument "from a distance" (p. 189).

Pam's accuracy corroborates an earlier finding by Sabom (1982) of veridicality in autoscopic near-death experiences. Before his first study, Sabom had been convinced that "the near-death experience, if properly studied, could be reduced to a simple scientific explanation" (Sabom, 1998, p. 175). At the onset of his first near-death experience study of hospital patients, Sabom (1982)

*was anxiously awaiting the moment when a patient would claim that he had
"seen" what had transpired in his room during his own resuscitation. Upon such
an encounter, I intended to probe meticulously for details that would not
ordinarily be known to nonmedical personnel. In essence, I would pit my
experience as a trained cardiologist against the professed visual recollections of
lay individuals. ... [In so doing,] I was convinced [that] obvious inconsistencies
would appear which would reduce these purported "visual" observations to no
more than "educated guesses." (p. 83)*

Sabom (1982) interviewed 32 such patients. All of their accounts of hospital CPR
procedure were accurate, including six particularly detailed recollections. The recollected details in each case were "fairly specific for the actual resuscitation being
described and ... not interchangeable with the clinical circumstances of other near-
death crisis events" (p. 114). One participant did make apparent errors in his
describing the operation of a defibrillating meter—until Sabom, to his astonishment, discovered that that description matched an older model that was "still in
common use in 1973, at the time of [the patient's] cardiac arrest" (p. 104).

To establish a baseline rate of accuracy attributable to educated guesses,
Sabom (1982) also interviewed a control group of 25 patients with comparable
cardiac-related background and hospital experience but who had *not* reported a
near-death experience. These patients were asked what they would expect to see if
they were to watch a hospital CPR procedure. The baseline rate of accuracy was
extremely low: only 2 of these 23 participants *avoided* making a "major error" (p. 85)
in their imaginative descriptions. The accuracy rate of the group reporting specific
autoscopic recollections, then, was overwhelming and not attributable to projections
from common knowledge.

Other cases of verified perceptual recollections, from experiences apparently
taking place during clinical death or coma, have been reported in the literature. In
one case, a 7-year-old girl, deeply comatose from having nearly drowned, nonetheless subsequently recalled idiosyncratic details of her emergency care such as her
unusual intubation (nasal instead of oral; Morse, 1990). In another case, a man who
remained deeply comatose and under artifical respiration for days, nonetheless
upon recovering recognized a nurse who had removed his dentures for intubation.
He asked for the return of his dentures, correctly identifying their whereabouts
(behind "a sliding drawer underneath" a top drawer). He also accurately described
details of the operating room, the procedure, and the appearance of other staff
members (van Lommel et al., 2001, p. 2041; cf. Smit, 2008a). In yet another case, a
surgery patient under anesthesia subsequently described leaving his body and
watching the cardiac surgeon "flapping his arms as if trying to fly." The surgeon
verified this description of his movements, explaining that he moved his arms in
this way after scrubbing in an effort to prevent contamination (Cook et al., 1998, pp.
399–400).[9] That these idiosyncratic recollections, like Pam's, were corroborated by
medical professionals on the scene supports the claim that the recollections were
to some extent "real" or accurate.

Although verifiability refers mainly to the earthly perceptions of the autoscopic near-death experience, it can also apply in an indirect way to transcendental near-death perceptions of deceased loved ones. In the transcendental portion of Pam's near-death experience, she "recognized a lot of people" (all deceased) among the "figures in the light" that "began to form shapes." In some cases, experiencers describe encounters with unfamiliar figures whose identities are only subsequently recognized. For example,

> Child near-death experients purportedly describe meeting persons, whom they did not know, in sufficient detail to allow their parents to recognize those persons as deceased relatives, or the child may later identify the person from the NDE [near-death experience] in a family portrait [or photograph] he or she had never seen before. (Greyson, 2000b, p. 341)

An adult whose near-death experience occurred in childhood reported that while in the light, he became aware that

> there were some presences there. There were some ladies. . . . I didn't know them at the time. . . . They were so loving and so wonderful and I just didn't want to come back. . . . I didn't see any pictures of them until I was an adult, but then I said, "Oh, yeah.". . . They were my great-grandmothers who had died years before I was born. (Wilson, 1995)

Such corroboration of encounters that could scarcely be projections of the familiar also sometimes occurs in connection with the related phenomenon of deathbed visions or "nearing-death awarenesses" (Callanan & Kelley, 1992), in which the experiencer sees—often with some surprise—recently deceased loved ones whose deaths were unknown to them (Greyson, 2000b). Maggie Callanan and Patricia Kelley (1992) recounted the case of a dying 93-year-old woman, Su, whose visions began to include not only her late husband but also her sister:

> "Why is my sister with my husband?," she asked. "They are both calling me to come."
> "Is your sister dead,?" I [Callanan] asked.
> "No, she still lives in China," she said. "I have not seen her for many years."
> When I related this conversation to the daughter [Lily], she was astonished and tearful.
> "My aunt died two days ago in China," Lily said. "We decided not to tell Mother—her sister had the same kind of cancer. It was a very painful death; she lived in a remote village where good medical care wasn't available. We didn't want to upset or frighten Mother, since she is so sick herself.". . .
> When Lily tearfully told her mother about her sister's illness and death, Su said, with a knowing smile, "Now I understand." Her puzzle solved, she died three weeks later, at peace and with a sense of anticipation. (pp. 98–99)

In sum, although some projective participation does seem to be involved, the findings on balance seem to suggest that there is some noteworthy degree of accuracy or veridicality to verifiable aspects of the perceptions reported in autoscopic and even transcendental near-death experiences. We next consider the questions of whether the accurate recollections are in fact associated with a proximity to physical death, and whether they are attributable to perceptions occurring during the near-death experience.

4. Is the Likelihood or Depth of the Experience Associated with Proximity to Physical Death?

Despite her documented condition of brain death, Pam not only felt she experienced extraordinary perceptual awareness and clarity but as well reported a comprehensive-type and "deep" near-death experience. Although measures of near-death experience "depth" raise questions of validity (see Greyson, 2000b, pp. 342–345), it is worth noting that Pam's depth score on Greyson's (1983) Near-Death Experience Scale was 27 of a possible maximum score of 32. (She responded, for example, not merely that time "seemed to go faster than usual [1 point]," but that "everything seemed to be happening all at once [2 points];" she felt not only peace or happiness or had unusually vivid senses [1 point each], but "incredibly" so [2 points each]; she not only "lost awareness" of her body [1 point], but "clearly left the body and existed outside it" [2 points]; she was not only in an "unfamiliar, strange place" [1 point] but a "clearly mystical or unearthly realm" [2 points]; she not only "sensed the presence of deceased persons [1 point] but "saw them" [2 points]; etc; data supplied by M. Sabom, personal communication, November 3, 2001.) Overall, Pam's total score of 27 far exceeded the mean of 13.3 in Sabom's (1998) sample of 47 experiencers and in fact was the highest score of anyone in the sample.

The concurrence of a clinically extreme near-death condition with a deep near-death experience is consistent with research findings of an association between proximity to physical death and likelihood of having an NDE. Although many aspects of the so-called near-death experience can occur in deep meditation or "situations of intense physical or emotional danger," typically it occurs "to individuals [actually] close to death" (Greyson, 2000b, pp. 315–316). Ring (1980) and Sabom (1982) both found that NDE likelihood or depth correlated with closeness to physical death in their samples. Van Lommel and colleagues (van Lommel et al., 2001) partially replicated this relationship in their prospective study. On the one hand, survivors in the van Lommel et al. study who remained unconscious for longer periods during their cardiac arrest, or whose resuscitation required intubation, were not more likely to have had an NDE. On the other hand, those survivors who died within 30 days following their initial interview were more likely to have reported an NDE, and this greater likelihood was *highly* significant for those who had reported a "deep" NDE.

5. Does the Typical Near-Death Experience Actually Take Place During Near Death?

If near-death perceptions are to some remarkable degree veridical or accurate, experienced as real, and even highly conscious and clear, then how could they be taking place at a time of severe mental and bodily compromise, of proximity to death? One answer attributes the experience to special effects of a dying or severely compromised brain. Blackmore (1993; cf. Blanke et al., 2002) argued that the disinhibited and seizure activity of a dying brain could generate seemingly "real" hallucinations. Sam Parnia and Peter Fenwick (2002) countered that the "disorganized and compromised cerebral function" evident during near-death states is unlikely to produce the "lucid, well structured thought processes" characteristic of the near-death experience (p. 8; cf. Owens, Cook, & Stevenson, 1990). In any event, seizures can be ruled out as an explanation at least in Pam Reynolds's case, where the absence of such activity is documented by the EEG record (Sabom, personal communication, September 20, 2002).

"Compromised" is an understatement as a description of Pam's brain function. By the time Pam was experiencing the transcendental aspects of her experience, the EEG record was showing that her brain was not only functionally compromised but "dead" by all three of the standard clinical criteria: (a) a "flat" EEG, indicating nonfunction of the cerebral cortex; (b) absence of auditory evoked potentials, indicating nonfunction of the brain stem; and (c) cessation of blood flow to and through the brain (Sabom, 1998, p. 49). Yet Pam's near-death experience continued during clinical brain death, contradicting the dying-brain hypothesis that the experience should "stop when the brain's activity stops" (Blackmore, 1993, p. 4).[10]

Another answer challenges the premise of the question. Perhaps the recollections do not in fact derive from the time of the near-death conditions. Perhaps these purportedly highly conscious "perceptions" can be accurate because the perceivers *were* conscious in the ordinary sense. Their perceptions might actually have been projections constructed from the informational stimuli of a time period mainly *prior* to or *following* the time of near-death, while the person's mental functioning was unimpaired (indeed, perhaps even from the early moments of near-death, given that the auditory sense often persists even as conscious mental functioning fades). The person's ostensibly recollected "experience" might then be fabricated from these sources and misattributed to the near-death time period (Blackmore, 1993; French, 2001; Hyman, 2001). For example, Pam's reference to having heard a "female" voice could have been fabricated from her prior familiarity with a female member (Dr. Murray) of the surgery team.

As Sabom (1998) pointed out, the fabrication hypothesis has difficulty in cases where the reported details were not initially in view. Most of the details reported in Pam Reynolds's case were of this sort (the pitch or shape of the cranial saw, the partial shaving of Pam's head hair, etc.). Pam's surgeon, Dr. Robert Spetzler, commented: "The drill and so on, those things were. ... in their packages. You really don't begin to open until the patient is completely asleep so that you maintain a sterile environment" (Broome, 2002).

Sabom (1998) was particularly interested in Pam's recollection of the cardiovascular surgeon's comment that certain blood vessels were too small. Given her occluded ear canals ("altogether eliminat[ing] the possibility of physical hearing," p. 184) as well as the obscuring auditory stimuli of the brain stem monitoring devices, Pam could not have *physically* heard this comment during the operation. As Spetzler (quoted in Smit, 2008b) commented, "I find it inconceivable that ... there was any way for her to hear ... through the normal auditory pathways" (p. 309). Yet somehow she did hear a specific comment that was corroborated as accurate. Moreover, the comment was reported at the appropriate point in her near-death experience:

> Pam stated that she did not hear or perceive anything prior to her out-of-body experience, and that this experience began with hearing the bone saw. At this point in the operation, she had been under anesthesia for about 90 minutes. ... The [use of] the bone saw was simultaneous with the conversation about Pam's small blood vessels—and, as it turns out, with her out-of-body experience. This correspondence of Pam's recollections from an out-of-body experience with the correct bit of intraoperative conversation during a six-hour operative procedure is certainly intriguing evidence. (p. 185)

Pam's sequence of recollected perceptions corresponded, then, with the actual sequence of steps in the surgical procedure.

The post hoc version of the fabrication hypothesis posits that the "experience" was retrospectively projected from details mentioned afterward. For example, Pam Reynolds might have heard about the details of her operation from medical staff or records (Hyman, 2001).[11] Such a possibility is unlikely, given the idiosyncratic character of many of the recounted details in Sabom's and other studies. Such idiosyncratic details are "not what would likely be explained to a patient recovering from a cardiac arrest" (Sabom, 1982, p. 114). Cardiac patients might be told

> that their "heart stopped beating" and that an "electrical shock" was used on the chest to stabilize cardiac rhythm, but there is no conceivable reason to supply the details reported in the typical autoscopic NDE—the insertion of a plastic airway, the checking for a carotid pulse or pupillary response in the eye, the drawing of arterial blood from the hand or the groin, the movement of the needles on the face of the defibrillator, etc. (p. 75; cf. Cook, Greyson, & Stevenson, 1998; Ring, 1980)

In general, it would appear that the evident accuracy and perceived consciousness of some near-death recollections cannot be interpreted in terms of remembered auditory or visual pre-post stimuli, not only for the reasons given but also because loss of consciousness typically induces anterograde and retrograde amnesia (Parnia & Fenwick, 2002). It is also difficult for before- or after-the-fact fabrication explanations to account for correlations between closeness to death and likelihood or depth of the near-death experience.

A Deeper Reality? Summary and Conclusion

We can reach some tentative closure, then, as to whether the near-death experience is an imaginal projection or a glimpse of a deeper reality: It is evidently some subtle mixture (cf. Morse, 1992, pp. 119–120, 127). Perceptions in the experience do seem to entail imaginal projections (or assimilations) based on contextual factors such as the experiencer's mental schemas of familiarity, needs, and expectation. In other words, the experiencer does seem to influence that which is perceived.[12] Nonetheless, the experience does not reduce entirely to subjective projection, interpretation, and particular context. The experience is in good measure ineffable and typically elicits surprise or bafflement. The autoscopic, comprehensive, and especially transcendental types of near-death experience are fairly universally evident across personal, situational, cultural, and historical contexts. Experiencers recollect heightened awareness and perceptual clarity and interpret their experience as real; those who can compare their near-death experience to dreams or hallucinations typically insist that the near-death experience is neither dream nor hallucination but reality. There is a remarkable degree of accuracy to autoscopic perceptions, and there are reports of indirect empirical confirmation even for some transcendental perceptions. The experience is more likely to occur, as well as more extensive or profound, for those experiencers who are closer to physical death. The accuracy and conscious, clear qualities of the experience are unlikely to be attributable to fabrications from information gained when mental function was unimpaired (prior or subsequent to the near-death event) or from auditory information during the event—impossible in Pam Reynolds's case. Astonishingly, Pam's deep near-death experience occurred despite the documented cessation of brain wave activity.

A definitive conclusion regarding the significance of this phenomenon would be premature. At the least, the near-death experience overall would seem to be a challenging anomaly (e.g., Parnia, 2006; Vaitl et al., 2005). Parnia and Fenwick (2002) concluded from a research review of cases of cardiac arrest that the near-death experience may point to the need for a new science of consciousness. Similarly, we conclude, given our own review above, that the phenomenon may point to a deeper reality of human existence. As did Parnia and Fenwick, we call for large-scale studies.

Although tentative, these conclusions suggest that hypothetical (or not so hypothetical) reflection on the phenomenon's possible implications may be worthwhile. If the near-death experiencer does glimpse even partially a deeper reality of human existence, what would be the phenomenon's existential and moral implications? Accordingly, we move now from ontological to existential and moral questions.

Moral Insight, Inspiration, and Transformation

Kohlberg's cases of existential crisis and "Stage 7" epiphany seem to access a deeper reality relevant to the moral life. In these cases, morally mature but existentially and ontologically anguished thinkers attain (through deep thought, soul-searching, meditation) a cosmic perspective deriving from "the whole of nature" and thereby lose their *angst*. They begin to see human life from that primary vantage point, sense an answer to the existential "Why be moral?" question, and are endowed with inspiration to embrace life. But is such insight and inspiration from a deeper reality the exclusive province of the morally mature? Is the soul-searching of existential crises the only way to penetrate this deeper reality with its evident potential to inspire faith in the moral and meaningful life?

Near-death experiencers differ in some ways from Kohlberg's cases. The very name "*near-death* experience" reminds us that the crisis is generally physical rather than existential. Also, in contrast to Kohlberg's cases, near-death experiencers prior to the event—as in the cases of Pam Reynolds and Tom Sawyer—were not necessarily deep thinkers, soul-searchers, or idealists. Despite these differences, the life-changing reality accessed, we suspect, is one and the same. Consider the claims of "Stage 7" individuals that they experienced a cosmic perspective with an associated sense of "union, love, joy, and grace" (p. 347) and that "love is somehow the key which unlocks the door which leads to ultimate reality" (Martin Luther King, Jr., quoted in Kohlberg & Power, 1981). Such claims seem indistinguishable from what many near-death experiencers say and seem to evidence in their subsequent lives. Reminiscent of "Stage 7" experiencers' identification with "the whole of nature," Pam responded (on Greyson's [1983] near-death experience scale) that her experience included "a sense of harmony or unity with the universe."

The life-changing effects of a near-death experience give new meaning to "growing beyond superficiality" in moral or existential human development. A high school student said his near-death experience stimulated him to realize that "there's more to life than Friday night movies and the football game" (Moody, 1975, p. 89). One of Sabom's (1998) patients, after his near-death experience, "no longer had time for . . . little country club things" (p. 88). Furthermore, such an experience "appears to herald a wide range of pervasive and durable personality transformations, including a decreased interest in materialism and competition and an increased interest in altruism and spirituality" (Greyson, 1992–1993, pp. 81–82). Relative to a comparison (non-near-death experience) sample of survivors of major cardiac surgery, survivors who had had a near-death experience reported greater postsurgery gains in terms of intrinsic faith (e.g., "inner sense of God's presence"), meaning in life, family life involvement, and "capacity for love" (understanding of others or insight into their problems; ability to express love and listen to others; compassion, tolerance, and acceptance of others; and desire to help them) (Sabom, 2000). Similarly, in a recent prospective and controlled study, "people who had NDEs had a significant increase in belief in an afterlife and decrease in fear of death compared with people who had not had this experience" in their near-death events. Furthermore, "depth of NDE was linked to . . . showing love and accepting others" (van Lommel et al., 2001, p. 2042). In his earlier study, Sabom (1982) observed among his near-death experience patients behavioral changes such as "becoming a hospital volunteer" and a new commitment to "humanitarian concerns," changes that they "would invariably attribute" to the near-death experience (p. 157). Pam Reynolds came back to care for her children and contribute to "harmony" among people; Tom Sawyer's new priority was on helping others and on certain global dangers (Tom's moral transformation is explored below). Helping others, understanding their needs, focusing on humanitarian concerns—life changes in this direction are of particular relevance to the "caring" strand of moral development and behavior.

The Light

When present among the features of the near-death experience, the light plays an "overwhelmingly positive—and hence beneficial—role" (Fox, 2003, p. 302). Indeed, Melvin Morse (1992) argued that the key feature in the near-death experience accounting for moral and personality transformations is the encounter with the light. In his study, experiencers who met the light—even if not physically near death—had significant decreases in death anxiety and increases in zest for life not only relative to nonexperience survivors but even relative to experiencers whose out-of-body experiences did not include the light.

Two cases from his study illustrate this role of the light in evoking a deeper insight, inspiration, and subsequent life changes, including a new earnestness about life and other people. One case was that of James, an 18-year-old African American teenager living in the housing projects of St. Louis, Missouri. James nearly drowned and had a comprehensive near-death experience when he was 9 years old. Interviewed at age 18 (Morse, 1992), James was actively resisting peer pressure to sell drugs or engage in gang violence and was instead applying himself academically (at least as of Morse's writing). He attributed his responsible lifestyle to the impact of his near-death experience during the near drowning:

> [After I stopped struggling to breathe] I just floated out of my body into a safe place. It was all bright; I felt peaceful.... Suddenly, I realized that we are all the same. There ain't no black and there ain't no white. I saw that bright light and I knew it was all the colors there were, everything was in that light....
>
> I feel better about myself. I know that I am different. I don't think about putting people down for fun like I used to.... I see life the way it really is. It is not meant to be played with. (Morse, 1992, pp. 17–18)

Whereas James had "put other people down" and was at risk for developing an anti-social lifestyle, Ann, another of Morse's cases, was depressed and self-destructive ("internalizing" rather than "externalizing" her hurt and anger; see Chapter 6). At a party, upon hearing that her boyfriend was leaving her for another girl, she decided to commit suicide

> just the way my mother had. I took a handful of barbiturates and swallowed them with vodka, lots of it.... It took me a while to realize that I was out of my body and floating up by the ceiling.... I remember feeling love and peace and also feeling as though I had escaped from all the tension and frustration in my life. I felt kind of enveloped by light. It was a wonderful feeling.... I was shown the beauty of my body and of every body. I was told that my body was a gift and I was supposed to take care of it, not kill it. After hearing this, I felt very, very

ashamed of what I had done and hoped that I would live. I began to beg the light for life. The feeling that came back was the strongest feeling of love I have ever experienced. (Morse, 1992, pp. 152–153)

Annie's near-death experience abruptly transformed her lifestyle. She stopped thinking about her mother's suicide and about committing suicide herself, stopped abusing drugs and alcohol, eschewed the old friends and parties, developed more responsible friendships, married, and started a family (Morse, 1992).

Again, these cases illustrate Morse's point: Encountering the light seems to play the key role in the induction of subsequent major life changes, changes less likely to be seen following nonlight experiences. Exceptions should be noted, however. Peter and Elizabeth Fenwick (1995) noted cases in which the survivors' near-death experiences entailed a sense of transcendent comfort or joy, timeless peace, and familiarity or "coming home"—but no light—and who nonetheless attributed to their experience their subsequent dramatic declines in fear of death. Also, apparently absent from Morse's nonlight near-death experience cases were "distressing" yet life-changing near-death experiences. In these cases, *not* experiencing the light induces "loneliness, fear, desolation, alienation, and separation" (Lorimer, 1990, p. 86)—the inverse of the feelings experienced by union with the light. Rommer (2000) pointed out, based on her sample of such cases, that feelings such as fear in the absence of the light can elicit some degree of change as well. Indeed, she concluded that such experiences can be "blessings in disguise" (the title of her book), insofar as they can provide a much-needed wake-up call. A drug abuser named Del who had a distressing life review described the experience and its effect:

The review of my life happened so quick. . . . It was going so fast, I really couldn't grasp everything I was seeing, but I knew it was me. It was like my life was just goin' away, real quick. . . . What was scary was: This is it! This is the end! . . . So when I didn't die, I thought: "Well, I'd better do something different." (Rommer, 2000, p. 61)

After this "scary" experience of his life as too fleeting and wasted even to grasp or assess, Del stopped abusing drugs and started maintaining stable employment (Rommer, 2000). Del's moral and existential insight had been simply to see the waste and fleeting insignificance of his life of severe drug abuse. That simple insight was sufficiently frightening to inspire reform.

More positive moral insight and inspiration were engendered in Tom's near-death experience, which encompassed a beginning hint of a distress experience, the light, and a life review. Prior to his accident and experience, Tom's lifestyle had been not only superficial but self-centered and arrogant to an extent approaching that of the proactive offender (see Chapter 6). Tom's wife Elaine recalled that, before the accident, Tom was physically and verbally abusive to her ("stupid" was one name he had called her), threw shoes and other nearby objects at her, and was very controlling, precipitating a separation at one point. Tom corroborated Elaine's recollection: "I was the head of my family and I would tell them [including their two sons] what they could do!" He was "blind to her needs" (Farr, 1993, p. 95) and, to some extent, the needs of the family. His Self-Centered cognitive distortion and control extended to his having "a fit" upon learning that Elaine had listened to classical music (which Tom at that time did not listen to) on his radio when he wasn't home: "On *my* radio, she was only to listen to *my* music" (p. 94).

Following his near-death experience, Tom was transformed. His self-centered attitudes, abusive behavior, and rages were replaced by an attitude of love and a priority on helping others. "All of a sudden, he was a different person. *He loved everybody!*" (Farr, 1993, p. 99), exclaimed Elaine. Tom's love and altruism included humanitarian concerns: In 1980, several years after his experience, he began to speak against the planetary dangers of chemical pollution and global warming.

The Life Review

Although Tom attributed a "good" feeling to the "warmth and love coming from the light," he seemed to derive particular moral insights and inspiration from his life review. Speaking to Farr (and to a prospective audience), Sawyer said,

> I wish I could tell you how it really felt and what the life review is like, but I'll never be able to do it accurately. I'm hoping to give you just a slight inkling. . . . Will you be totally devastated by the crap you've brought into other people's lives? Or will you be . . . enlightened and uplifted by the love and joy that you have shared in other people's lives? . . . You will be responsible for yourself, judging and reliving what you have done to everything and everybody in very far-reaching ways. (Farr, 1993, pp. 34–35)

As noted, the life review is not universally reported in near-death experiences and may even be absent in some cultures. Nonetheless, given its major role in Tom's moral inspiration and subsequent life changes, the life review merits further study. David Lorimer (1990) suggested that Russell Noyes and Roy Kletti's (1977) term *panoramic memory* applies to brief visions of one's life (e.g., the mountain climber who somehow survives a fall during which time seems to slow down as he sees his "whole life pass before" him); Lorimer applied the term *life review* only to those retrospective experiences that evoke "emotional involvement and moral assessment" (p. 10). Apropos of this distinction, Melvin Morse (1992) related the case of a heart patient in the Netherlands who experienced first a panoramic memory and then a life review (in Lorimer's sense) as his car rammed into the back of a truck:

> When he realized that collision was imminent, the patient said that time seemed to slow down as he hit his brakes and went into an uncontrolled slide. Then he seemed to pop out of his body. While in this state, he had a life review [or panoramic memory episode] which consisted of brief pictures—flashes—of his life. . . . His car struck the truck and the truck bed crashed through the window, causing multiple injuries to his head and chest. Medical reports show that he was in a coma and nearly died. Yet he had a vivid sensation of leaving his

physical body and entering into darkness. ... He had the feeling of moving up through a dark tunnel toward a point of light. Suddenly a being "filled with love and light" appeared to him. Now he had a second *life review [or life review proper], one guided by the being of light. He felt bathed in love and compassion as he reviewed the moral choices he had made in his lifetime. He suddenly understood that he was an important part of the universe and that his life had a purpose. (pp. 197–198)*

Among such moral life reviews, a particularly evocative type is what Lorimer (1990) termed "empathetic" (p. 20), "in which people relive events through the consciousness of the person with whom they were interacting at the time" (pp. 1–2). Lorimer described several cases of initially rather self-centered individuals who nearly died, encountered a loving light and experienced an empathetic life review (one individual exclaimed, "I was the very people I hurt, and I was the very people I helped to feel good," p. 21), and dramatically transformed into persons who loved and attempted to help everyone. So Tom's experience and transformation were not unique.

Such a life review experience of another's consciousness—indeed, of adopting another's *identity*—takes "empathy," "perspective taking" and "social decentration" beyond the normal ken of Hoffman and Kohlberg! (Adam Smith [1759/1965] was writing in a subjective, phenomenological vein when he defined *empathy* as experiencing another's emotion through "*enter[ing]*, as it were, into [his] body" and becoming "in some measure *the same person* with him," p. 261, emphases added.) In Tom's empathetic life review, he not only "had empathy for" or "took the perspective of" his Aunt Gay seeing the would-be flowers chopped down, or of the baggage handler ignorantly handling his bicycle, or of the man in the street slapping him; instead, he *was* Aunt Gay, *was* the baggage handler, *was* the man in the street! Yet at the same time, he was also still his own self at the time, as well as his older self viewing the scene from a decentered or third-person perspective.

This extraordinary social perspective taking would seem to imply that in some ultimate sense, ideal justice or moral reciprocity is not successfully violated, that the "world" in the deepest sense of the word is just after all. Furthermore, the extraordinary perspective taking seemed to lead to moral insight and transformation. In comprehensively reliving the flower-killing incident, for example, Tom in effect received the "perfect justice" (Lorimer, 1990, p. 13) of having to be Aunt Gay in her distress; in the final analysis, he did not "get away with" his mischief:

I was in my Aunt Gay's body. I was in her eyes, I was in her emotions, I was in her unanswered questions. I experienced the disappointment, the humiliation. It was very devastating to me. I changed my attitude quite a bit as I experienced it. (Farr, 1993, p. 30)

Needless to say, Tom could not retain his "arrogance, ... snide little thoughts [such as Operation Chop-Chop], [and] excitement [Wow, I got away with it]" (Farr, 1993, pp. 30–31)—what we would call his Self-Centered and other self-serving cognitive distortions—in that light.

Tom's depiction of the baggage-handling incident suggests that he may have originally Assumed the Worst regarding the handler's intentions and egocentrically personalized them ("Damn the jerk at the airport that broke my bike," p. 31). In Tom's empathetic life review, he saw that the handler actually "had no idea there was a bicycle in there" and "made a mistake through ignorance" but was not maliciously intending to sabotage Tom's plans ("There was, in his life, almost no interaction with me, Tom Sawyer"). Accordingly, Tom could understand and forgive.

In the street altercation, Tom had Minimized/Mislabeled his near-killing of the man as "self-defense" and engaged in Blaming Others ("he started it") because the man had slapped him; that action, he had felt, "instantly gave me license to annihilate this man" (Farr, 1993, p. 32). In his self-righteous rage, Tom was merciless: The man "went straight back [from Tom's blows] and hit the back of his head on the pavement. And of course I followed him right down; I broke his nose and really made a mess of his face" (p. 34). In the empathetic life review, however, Tom realized the truth, that is, the inadequacy of self-serving rationalizations and immature, egoistically motivated, eye-for-an-eye-and-then-some reciprocity justifications ("Okay. He hit me first. Try *that* in your life review!"). As Lorimer (1990) put it, "There is a kind of spiritual nakedness as dimensions of life and truth are unfurled. Question-begging rationalizations and petty excuses are swept aside" (p. 21).

Prior to the light of this revelation, Tom had been benighted by his self-serving cognitive distortions. Although Tom was not a chronic offender or criminal, his moral and cognitive condition was in principle no different in this respect. Lorimer (1990) observed that, in the absence of an experience with the light, the "hardened criminal is willfully ignorant ... [of] what he is creating" ("willfully" may be apt; McVeigh had to dismiss a moment of moral insight into the enormity of what he was about to do). Lorimer asked, "Would the terrorist or criminal really go through with an act of violence if they knew for certain that they would eventually experience the event through the consciousness of the victim?" (p. 286). (Personally, I must admit that Lorimer's question prompts me to wish near-fatalities upon budding young criminals or terrorists! Upon realizing the spiritual near-contradiction in this wish, I return to advocacy of the more mundane techniques for inducing perspective taking outlined in Chapter 7.) For severe offenders, the experience of vividly reenacting their crime from the perspective of their victim may have a profound significance. Was a glimmer of the transcendent, from darkness to light, evident in the sudden insight and sustained contrition of Larry, the adolescent child molester?

The Dilemma of Multiple Claimants

Astonishingly, when asked what had been the "hardest thing" for her to "deal with" in her marriage with Tom, Elaine mentioned not the old Tom but the new one! Her response seems counterintuitive. Whereas Tom had previously abused, demeaned, and controlled her, after his near-death experience, he "was suddenly seeing her in a different light" (Farr, 1993, p. 98), loving her as a precious human being, a person in her own right. Recall, however, that now Tom had a humanitarian scale of agape love: In Elaine's words, "He loved *everybody!*" *Everybody* was precious; to some extent, Elaine was no longer particularly special. To illustrate the problem, Elaine mentioned that when she was ill once and needed Tom to help her, he was not in a position to because he was "on the phone helping someone else" (p. 94).

Elaine's complaint pertains to the dilemma of "multiple claimants" to one's love or caring (Hoffman, Chapter 4), an issue of positive or distributive justice (Damon, 1977; Eisenberg, 1982). It is the issue touched upon by C. S. Lewis (1943) in the opening quotation: What is the optimal balance of care among the legitimate claimants of family, nation, world? There is no easy answer. In fact, the moral exemplars studied by Colby and Damon (1992; see Chapter 5) "commonly expressed regret" (p. 68) that they had neglected their families. For Tom, it became a critical issue. Piaget or Kohlberg might have said that Tom was extending social decentration to a fault, Hoffman might say Tom was at risk for empathic overarousal from a loss of empathic bias (Chapter 4), or we might just say that Tom in his universal love and humanitarian compassion was spreading himself too thin and neglecting the needs of his own family.

Greyson (2000b) noted that experiencers often evidence life changes of "unconditional [or agape] love" incompatible with "the conditions and limitations of human relationships.... The value incongruities between near-death experients and their families" can "lead to a relatively high divorce rate" (p. 329; Christian & Holden, in press). Fortunately, the Sawyer marriage weathered the "pretty hard" times with the new Tom (Farr, 1993; T. Sawyer, personal communication, March 13, 2003) because, despite everything, they still "really care about each other a lot" (p. 97) and "compromise" (p. 94).

Conclusion

We have in this chapter attempted to explore the relation of moral development and behavior to a deeper reality—in Penrose's (1994) term, an *underpinning* or foundation. Our exploration is not without precedent; Kohlberg claimed that moral inspiration is gained as one sees life from the cosmic perspective of the whole of nature. Furthermore, one sees the ethic of love and ideal reciprocity as (in C. S. Lewis's terms) clues to the meaning of the universe and its evolution. Our investigation of the near-death experience in effect corroborated such a cosmic insight: Near-death experience survivors seem to access a deeper reality wherein the "whole of nature" is "an interconnected web of creation" of which we are "interdependent strands" (Lorimer, 1990, p. 20). Although speculative (Blackmore, 1993), such a view seems indicated by Pam Reynolds's NDE-inspired suggestion that, although "everyone has a different tone," the "beauty is in the harmony;" the St. Louis youth's experience of seeing "everything"—including the full diversity or "colors" of humanity—encompassed within the light; the instantaneous communication in the deeper realm; the social and moral emphasis in the life review, especially in "empathetic" life reviews such as Tom's bizarre participation in the consciousnesses and feelings of those whom he had hurt or helped; the dramatic pre-post shifts from self-centeredness and superficiality to earnest lives of humanitarian dedication; and Tom's conclusion that the choices we make and actions we take have a far-reaching impact.

Accordingly, we tentatively conclude with Lorimer (1990) that "human beings are connected at a deep level which is occasionally experienced by those who transcend the boundaries and limitations of ordinary perception" (p. 104). This profound interconnection means, in moral terms, that one reaps what one sows: "The feedback of loving thoughts and actions is love and joy, while hatred and bitterness breed isolation and sorrow" (p. 267). If life is profoundly interrelated, if we are somehow part of each other, then to put oneself in another's place is to experience not only the other but also part of oneself, and to help or hurt others is ultimately to help or hurt oneself. Put more ideally, acts of love may contribute to the deep flow of life, enriching one and all.

Notes

[1]Also suggestive of an atemporal reality or realm of necessary logico-mathematical truths are (a) the cumulative, non-contradictory character of the history of mathematical ideas (Piaget, 1967/1971); (b) independent, contemporaneous publications of the same mathematical advance; (c) sudden mathematical inspiration or revelation; and (d) the astonishing, effortless abilities of mathematical savants (see Davies, 1992). Just as knowledge is not only "necessary" but also contingent or empirical (see Chapter 9), however, primary reality is not only invariant but also dynamic and evolving. Paul Davies (1992) noted "the paradoxical conjunction of the temporal and atemporal, of being and becoming" in the nature of ultimate reality (p. 38).

[2]The question of objective or deeply true morality is controversial (see Chapter 1). Haidt and Bjorklund (2008b) explicitly discounted any notion of objective morality: "Moral facts are facts only with respect to a community of human beings that have created them. ... [There are no] objective [moral] facts which would be true for any rational creature anywhere in the universe" (p. 214). Pinker (2008, January 13), while disavowing a strong form of Platonism, suggested that moral ideals such as the interchangeability of perspectives may be "in the nature of things" or a "feature of reality" (p. 56). Piaget (1932/1965) suggested that ideal moral necessities of reciprocity and equality are akin to their counterparts in logic or mathematics. Penrose (1994) accorded ontologically real (Platonic) foundational status to mathematical (and possibly moral) truths "discovered" by the human mind.

[3]Whether some cultures lack these ideals altogether is debated. Even blood vengeance cultures, insofar as positive social exchanges are normatively prescribed in some circumstances, can be said to partake of moral ideals to some extent. Genuine exceptions are not known. In the famous case of the Ik tribe of East Africa, selfishness and cruelty were not only common but, according to Turnbull (1972), normative. The Ik "culture" was viewed as having degenerated as a result of severe food shortages, however (deWaal, 1996; Edgerton, 1992). Other degenerative cases are discussed by Robert Edgerton (1992). No such degenerative conditions

were attributed to the Sawi, a tribe of headhunting cannibals in New Guinea known for their idealization and practice of treachery and deceit (specifically, "fattening with friendship" a prospective victim before slaughtering him). Yet even the Sawi prescribed genuine inter-group friendship, trust, and peace under certain conditions (following an exchange of babies for rearing in one another's villages and a joint celebration featuring an interweaving non-cannibalistic "you-in-me-I-in-you" dance) (Richardson, 1974, p. 205).

[4]Of 37 patients not reporting a near-death experience 1 to 3 days after the near-death event, 4 reported at Time 2 (2 years later) that they *did* have a near-death experience; such cases raise the question of susceptibility to false memories (French, 2001).

[5]Administration of certain drugs also contributed to the cessation of brain wave activity (Robert Spetzler, personal communication, June 2, 2002).

[6]Two possible exceptions have been reported. Greyson (2000a) found elevated but subclinical levels of dissociation among near-death experiencers. Because the study was correlational, however, the direction (or directions) of causation between near-death experiences and dis-sociative tendencies (daydreaming, etc.) could not be determined. Fenwick and Fenwick (1995) pointed out that the affectless and dreamlike qualities of dissociated states contrast with the intense emotions and vivid perceived reality of the near-death experience. A second possible exception: Near-death experiences may be more likely if the near-death condition occurred at younger ages (studies reviewed by van Lommel, 2001).

[7]Intriguingly, although judgment and penitence are much more prominent in medieval narratives,

> In accounts of the light, contemporary testimony bears a striking resemblance to medieval narratives. Both medieval and modern descriptions of otherworld light blend visual qualities such as splendor, clarity, and transparency with sensory/emotional effects such as warmth and energy. . . . This mixture of imagery suggests a convergence of knowledge and love. . . . The visionary may behold a light that is at once all-knowing and all-loving. (Zaleski, 1987, p. 125)

[8]A particularly dramatic instance of returning from an NDE to care for others was reported by Sabom (2008). During a devastating fire aboard an airplane (the accident occurred on December 17, 1973), a flight attendant, struggling for breath, "crawled onto" the two remaining seats not yet on fire. She recounted:

> That's when I had my experience. It was just all light. It was just incredible happiness and joy! It was indescribable. I saw myself. I was lying there in my uniform. I could see myself clearly through the smoke and I thought, "Why aren't I moving?" There was fire everywhere. . . . But I really didn't care because I was so happy where I was. . . .
> And I am looking at myself and I'm lying there with my eyes closed because I couldn't breathe. All of a sudden a passenger screamed "Open the window. Somebody open the win-dow. Help me!" I thought "I have to help that lady." The next thing I knew, I was back in my body. (p. 106)

[9]Noteworthy are the comments of the operating cardiovascular surgeon at Hartford Hospi-tal, Hiroyoshi Takata, and his colleagues. Dr. Takata commented: "I cannot explain how he [Al Sullivan, the patient] saw these things under the complete sleep of anesthesia." Dr. Takata's colleague, Dr. Anthony F. Lasala, commented: "Al Sullivan would not know of this peculiar behavior of Dr. Takadata. I did not tell him [Al] that. . . . Even if he was conscious, it would be impossible for Al to see Dr. Takata's stance or arm movement because Al [was] behind the drape that blocks the vision of the patient and his eyes [were] taped shut." Another colleague,

Dr. Kathy E. Maliato, Director of the Brain Injury Research Center at UCLA, exclaimed, almost in exasperation: "So explain that to me. Explain that, through chemicals or some other scientific explanation. Please explain to me why that man knows that" (Ling, 2008).

[10]Since Pam was not yet clinically dead and may have still had some residual (if undetected) brain activity during the autoscopic portion of her experience, perhaps brain activity somehow generated these aspects. Yet the "how" is problematic: She had "no sight (eyes taped shut), no hearing (ear canals plugged), no touch (arms secured under drapes), no taste (endotracheal tube in mouth . . .), no seizure activity, and was under anesthesia deep enough to allow for the painless removal of the top of her skull" (Sabom, personal communication, September 20, 2002). Parnia (2006) pointed out that thought processes are normally mediated by interacting neural regions in the brain, and that any such "minute" residual activity "would be unlikely to lead to adequate electricity being generated for the brain cells to communicate with each other" (p. 94).

[11]Ray Hyman (2001) suggested that Pam Reynolds had "the complete report of the proceedings" of her operation, from which she could have reconstructed her "experience." In fact, however, Pam had only a five-page summary of the operation, which made no mention of the idiosyncratic details that she accurately reported (concerning the appearance of the cranial saw and instrument case, surgery team conversation, etc.; Sabom, personal communication, September 20, 2002).

[12]One is reminded of the influence of the observer on that which is observed at the subatomic level. The influence is not totally determinative, however. The restriction of observational or measurement influence to certain ranges of probability (Lindley, 1996), reflecting the "precise . . . mathematical laws that govern the quantum world," suggests that subatomic reality is not *totally* a function of the subjective observer (Penrose, 1994, p. 313).

CHAPTER

Conclusion

IF, AS NEAR-DEATH EXPERIENCE SURVIVORS (ALONG WITH AN IMPRESSIVE assortment of mystics, poets, religious leaders, moral exemplars, and "Stage 7" thinkers) insist, each individual is in some ultimate sense integral with the whole of humanity, then we are deeply connected with two fellow human beings named Emroz and Bakhtiar:

> Emroz Khan destroys for a living. He dismantles car engines, slicing them open with a sledgehammer and a crooked chisel, prying apart the cylinders, tearing out pistons, dislodging screws and bolts and throwing the metal entrails into a pile that will be sold for scrap. He is 21 and has been doing this sort of work for 10 years, 12 hours a day, six days a week, earning $1.25 a day.
>
> His hands and arms are ... stained a rich black like fresh asphalt and ribboned with scars. ... A bulge on his forearm [contains] a stretch of pipe he drove into his body by mistake. He cannot afford to pay a doctor to take it out.
>
> "I've had it for three years," he says.
>
> He opens his left palm and places two fingers alongside what looks like a crease, then pulls apart the crease to reveal a two-inch gash that runs an inch deep. ... The raw flesh was covered with grease, like the rest of his palm and arm. The wound is two years old.
>
> [Not far from the scrap metal shop where Emroz works is] Bakhtiar Khan, [who] began working in the pits [making bricks] when he was 10. He is now 25 or 26. He isn't sure, because nobody keeps close track; time passes, that is all. He works from 5 in the morning until 5 in the afternoon, making 1,000 bricks a day, six days a week, earning a few dollars a week. He is thin, he wears no shirt or shoes. ...
>
> The situation is worse than it appears. [Emroz and Bakhtiar] carry an invisible burden. They don't earn enough to live on, so they must borrow. ... They have no hope of paying back the loans. (Maass, 2001, pp. 48 ff.)

Emroz's and Bakhtiar's plight exceeds that of Edward, the man whose unfair torment at a summer camp introduced us, by way of negative example, to the non-relative right and good of morality. Emroz and Bakhtiar are "young men for whom life is abuse" (Maass, 2001, p. 50). They live not in the relatively affluent West but in desperate poverty in Peshawar, Pakistan, and they represent all too many among the world's population. Now in their 20s, in the early 21st century, they lack adequate food, clothing, and medical care. They have no way to emerge from debt. Although worse than Edward's, their plight, too, is one of wrong and harm.

Justice and care have been the themes of this book. We have argued, in fact, that the right and the good, moral reciprocity and empathy, the primarily cognitive and the primarily affective, constitute the chief strands of moral development. We have explored moral development, perception, and behavior in these terms through the theories of Lawrence Kohlberg and Martin Hoffman. Especially, we have explored Kohlberg's and Hoffman's thesis that children grow beyond the superficial in moral knowing and feeling at least partly by taking into account the perspectives and situations of others. We introduced existential development as part of a new view of Kohlberg's theoretical approach and championed "primary" cognitive motivation in our critique of Hoffman's theory. Furthermore, we found that both theories needed certain elaborations in their application to social behavior. In particular, we elaborated on moral self-relevance (or moral identity) in exemplary prosocial behavior and on self-serving cognitive distortion and social skill deficiencies in chronic antisocial behavior. We identified an affect-regulating ability that serves either prosocial or antisocial behavior, namely, ego strength. Finally, we explored the question of a deeper reality to the moral life, an exploration that brought new meaning to "taking the perspectives of others" and "growing beyond the superficial."

Superficial levels of perception do contribute to morality. Think of the wrong and harm endured by Emroz and Bakhtiar. Most observers young and old would sense a wrong and respond empathically to their highly salient signs of distress: the metal-induced bulge in Emroz's forearm, his scars, his open gash of raw flesh; and Bakhtiar's gaunt appearance, his lack of shirt or shoes. Such sights would surely activate at least the automatic, involuntary modes of empathic arousal described by Hoffman. Were Emroz and Bakhtiar still children, young observers' empathic distress for them would be all the more intense, according to the similarity bias also described by Hoffman.

Young children would be less likely, however, to imagine themselves in the life conditions of Emroz and Bakhtiar or to understand the deeper and broader context of their injustice. As Peter Maass (2001) noted, Emroz and Bakhtiar's situation is even worse than it appears. These men's plight includes an intangible or "invisible"— and deeply unfair—burden of labor abuse, of hopelessly indebted servitude. Their crushing debt is not unlike that of the nations where they and others with similar plights were born.

With cognitive and language development, expanding social interaction, reflection, and moral socialization, children—while still responding to direct or pictured signs of the distress of similar others—tend to grow beyond the superficial. They grow especially through social perspective taking, leading at least potentially to a deeper understanding of and feeling for others' plights. And out of that understanding and feeling, one hopes, they act.

The Canadian activist youth Craig Kielburger is, in Colby and Damon's (1992; see Chapter 5) terms, a moral exemplar. Kielburger (1998) reflected on what drove him, one morning when he was 12 years old, to found his youth-run, now-international anti–child labor organization Free the Children. "Staring back at" Kielburger that morning before school was a front-page newspaper headline ("BATTLED CHILD LABOR, BOY, 12, MURDERED") and photo of a boy his age who had been murdered in Muridke, Pakistan, after crusading against child labor abuses. "It was a jolt." Kielburger started reading the accompanying article, "hardly believing the words." The murdered crusader had known the problem of child labor abuse well: His own parents had sold him into slavery when he was 4 years old. Until he was freed and his crusade began at age 10, he had been shackled many hours each day to a carpet-weaving loom, "tying tiny knots hour after hour." Kielburger was shocked. "What kind of parents would sell their child into slavery at four years of age? And who would ever chain a child to a carpet loom?" he asked himself.

After school that day, Kielburger researched the problem of child labor abuse at a library. Once home, he found that

> images of child labour had imbedded themselves in my mind: children younger than me forced to make carpets for endless hours in dimly lit rooms; others toiling in underground pits, struggling to get coal to the surface; others maimed or killed by explosions raging through fireworks factories.... I was angry at the world for letting these things happen to children. Why was nothing being done to stop such cruelty?
>
> That evening I had great difficulty concentrating on my homework.... For some reason these descriptions of child labour had moved me like no other story of injustice.... Perhaps it was because the stories were of people my own age, and many even younger. Perhaps it was because these few words had shattered my ideas of what childhood was all about—school, friends, time to play. I had work to do around my house—carrying out the garbage, cleaning up the backyard—but it all seemed so trivial compared to what these children had to do.... I thought how I would react if I found myself in their place....
>
> As I walked through my middle-class neighborhood, my thoughts were on the other side of the world. And my own world seemed a shade darker.... Do all children, even the poorest of the poor, have the right to go to school? Are all children created equal? If child labour is not acceptable for white, middle-class North American kids, then why is it acceptable for a girl in Thailand or a boy in Brazil? (Kielburger, 1998, pp. 7–8, 12, 297)

"We never quite know," Robert Coles (1986) once observed, "how an event will connect with ourselves" (p. 29). Kielburger's imaginal perspective taking, empathic anger, and sense of global injustice upon his discovery of child labor abuse connected with his self-perception and motivation to act. Specifically, the event connected with what he could and could *not* see himself doing. He reflected, "You begin to believe so deeply in a [moral] cause that you can't *see yourself* just standing on the sidelines, waiting for other people to act" (Kielburger, 1998, p. 12, emphasis added;

cf. Kielburger & Kielburger, 2006). Craig's moral perception and goals became so relevant to his self-schema that his identity became, in crucial respects, a *moral* identity, adding its own power to his moral motivation from the right and the good. Kielburger's and similar activist organizations have done much to fight against child labor or slavery, promote education, and encourage debt relief for impoverished nations.[1]

In this final chapter, we conclude our use of Kohlberg's and Hoffman's theories to explore the development of moral perception and behavior; we will close with some final thoughts on moral development and reality. To conclude our case for coprimacy in moral motivation, we relate these theories to the differing motivational properties of fundamentally distinct categories of knowledge. In that light, we see that Kohlberg's and Hoffman's theories of the right and the good, respectively, are complementary if not integrable. Finally, beyond the theories, we conclude our use of the near-death experience to explore a love and deep connection that may underlie moral insight and transformation.

Revisiting the Issue of Moral Motivation and Knowledge

Imagine for a moment that the theoretical vehicles of our exploration are tour buses. We are at this moment student tourists, with Kohlberg and Hoffman as our prospective guides. Each man is offering an educational tour of the land of moral motivation, in particular, the landscape (or mindscape?) of Craig Kielburger's moral event that morning in Toronto. Whether we take Kohlberg's or Hoffman's tour first does not really matter, so long as we eventually take both tours. Which tour we take first *does* affect, however, which sight we see first. Hoffman might take us first to Craig's involuntary and sudden "jolt" of empathic distress at seeing the picture of a boy his age who had been murdered. After all, for Hoffman, the empathic predisposition (especially its basic arousal modes) is primary in moral motivation. Kohlberg might take us first to Craig's shock at the headline and article, at the scarcely believable *unfairness* of a parent or businessman so severely exploiting a child. After all, for Kohlberg, the violation or affirmation of ideals of justice is primary in moral motivation.

Were we but casual students, either tour would suffice. After all, we would learn much either way, and each guide would also take us to the (in their view) nonprimary site. Nor would our wait be long; the two sites are so nearby and so functionally interrelated that they are nearly one and the same place. But we are in fact not so casual; we seek a fully adequate understanding, and for that we shall require the complementary wisdom of our two guides, their collective expertise. So we take both tours. We learn from Hoffman much of empathic motivation and how exploitation or nonreciprocity (or other cognitions) transform and mediate empathic distress. It is mainly from Kohlberg (or his senior partner Jean Piaget), however, that we learn how knowledge of a reciprocity violation can, in its *own* right, motivate action. With only Hoffman's tour, we would miss what is special, what is irreducible, what is dynamic and motivating in their own right about structures of logic, consistency, and justice or moral reciprocity. Yet if we take only Kohlberg's tour, although we would learn much of such motivating structures, we would miss learning about the empathic predisposition and the moral internalization of norms of caring. Finally, to learn more about how the event led to Craig's subsequent moral identity—or, more broadly, about moral self-relevance and consistency with self (see Chapter 5), another can't-be-missed site in moral motivation[2]—we might seek an extended tour from Anne Colby and William Damon.

The Good, the Right, and Categories of Knowledge

Review our chapters and consider the following statements of knowledge concerning morality, conservation, and mathematics:

- Craig Kielburger encountered news of a child crusader's murder in the *Toronto Star.* He was jolted, in part, by reading the headline and seeing from the photo that the victim was a boy his own age.
- A White student rescued an African American student from imminent attack by fellow White segregationists in Atlanta, Georgia. The White student knew that he had joined in tormenting the student. That knowledge combined with empathic distress for the victim to create a feeling of guilt. As the rescuer broke up the imminent attack, he blurted out an apology.
- The norm of reciprocity, that you should return a kindness, is taught and internalized in many societies.
- In a discipline encounter, parents may use other-oriented inductions (proscribing harm to others and prescribing prosocial behavior). Such messages, particularly when the victim's suffering is salient, can elicit in the child empathic distress and guilt. Infused with such empathic distress, the inductive information thereby becomes "hot" enough to prevail against egoistic motives and motivate prosocial behavior or inhibit antisocial behavior. The child may internalize or appropriate the induction, attributing to himself or herself its origin.
- Through social interaction, children actively construct schemas, which encompass affectively charged scripts of knowledge such as, "My actions can harm others."
- Water is often the liquid used to fill the containers in the conservation of quantity task. The amounts of water are the same in the first comparison of the task but appear to be different in the second comparison.
- Different notations can be used in the addition and subtraction of numbers.

Much could be said of the above statements, but for present purposes, one question is paramount: What do they have in common? Can they all fit under a common rubric, a basic category of knowledge? Especially, are they all distinguishable in some fundamental way from the following statements of knowledge concerning morality, conservation, and mathematics?

- It is wrong for one person to exploit another. Seeing or experiencing exploitation tends to motivate an effort to right the wrong.
- Bad things should not happen to good people. Those who see themselves as good and whose social perspective taking is generally veridical may feel distress if they do an obviously bad thing to a good person. Also, the appreciation of a good person who remains above the level of trading insults can promote depth or maturity of moral perception (the White student in Atlanta began to see not a "nigger" but a fellow human being).
- Through social interaction, children actively construct schemas, including stages of moral judgment (especially moral reciprocity). At the core of the mature stages is ideal moral reciprocity, namely, that you should take into account others' perspectives in how you treat them.
- A quantity that undergoes neither addition nor subtraction is conserved (or better, "$x + 0 - 0 = x$"). Apparent logical violations, contradictions, or inconsistencies can be distressing and can motivate efforts to explain or correct.
- The combination of two actual quantities is greater than either of the original quantities (in one notation, "$1 + 1 = 2$").

What do these *latter* instances of knowledge have in common? Can *they* all fit under a common rubric, a basic category of knowledge? Are they all distinguishable in some fundamental way from the first set of statements listed? Obviously, they are more generally formulated than was the first set of statements, but is that all that can be said? Piaget (e.g., Piaget, 1967/1971) and Kohlberg would have claimed that the two sets of statements represent two fundamental and crucially distinct categories of knowledge, namely, "empirical" and "logico-mathematical," respectively. Under the latter rubric fit not only logic and mathematics but also the kindred themes of justice, reciprocity, or equality; balance or proportion; and consistency, harmony, or noncontradiction. "Everyone is aware of the kinship between logical and ethical [ideals]," wrote Piaget (1932/1965). "Logic is the morality of thought just as morality is the logic of [social] action" (p. 398). And this logic-related category of morality is, in turn, intimately related to the empirical or caring category in a way that we term "coprimacy" or "dual process" (see Chapters 1 and 5).

Although intimately interrelated, the two categories are distinguishable. We cannot adequately address the issue of moral motivation (or, for that matter, the issue of whether Kohlberg's and Hoffman's theories are integrable) unless we grasp this crucial distinction between empirical and logico-mathematical knowledge. So let us revisit the issue of moral motivation through this epistemological exploration. The two categories of knowledge differ in at least three major ways: (a) chance versus necessity, (b) internalization versus construction in the Piagetian sense, and (c) "external" versus "internal" motivation.

1. Chance Versus Necessity

Perhaps the most readily evident distinction between the categories pertains to chance versus necessity. Whereas empirical knowledge happens by chance to be true, logico-mathematical knowledge *must* be true; it could not be otherwise. It happened to be true that Kielburger was reading the *Toronto Star* or that the rescue took place in Atlanta. For that matter, it is true that the liquid in a conservation task was water and that addition can be accomplished in the base 10 system. Those truths could have been otherwise, however. Although less likely, Kielburger might have been reading the *Columbus Dispatch,* or the rescue might have taken place in Birmingham. The liquid in the conservation task might have been lemonade, and addition can be done in base 2.

Consider, in contrast, the truths of the second category. Is it ever right (without adding premises) for one person to exploit another or for bad things to happen to good people? Or, for that matter, is it even possible for x plus zero minus zero ever to equal something other than x (cf. conservation), or for one plus one to equal something other than two? These latter truths are *necessary*; although they can be violated in certain respects, they remain true. They are *necessarily* true (Laupa, 2000; Miller et al., 2000). Unlike the younger child's continued perceptual judgments in the conservation tasks, the older child's logical judgment "appears to have a necessity to it that removes it from the sphere of matters requiring empirical verification" (Brown, 1965, p. 201).

2. Internalization Versus Construction in the Piagetian Sense

The happenstance facts of empirical knowledge constitute information abstracted from "objects as such...that is, the experience of external objects or of whatever appertains to them" (Piaget, 1967/1971, p. 266). It is knowledge of the empirical world, the world of liquids, containers, and appearances, of photos, newspapers, and events— even of cities, cultural norms, and conventions of notation. In a broad sense, the acquisition of empirical knowledge can be depicted as a process of "construction." After all, "to construct" means simply "to build." The child can be said to build schemas through interaction with the environment (cf. Neisser, 1976). This interaction might even be described à la Piaget as an assimilation-accommodation interplay, involving the activation of schemas that are then refined or built up by accommodation of new information from the environment. For example, over the course of moral socialization, the child's causal schemas build, in a moral dimension, to become something like, "My actions can harm others" (Hoffman, 2000). That such schemas can be called "scripts" of generic events, however, connotes their empirical character. Such knowledge has been inductively abstracted from the given empirical world of social interaction, perhaps from among the norms in a particular culture. Although construction, even in the broad sense, is helpful to remind us of the active child (whose acquisitions do not purely copy environmental events or elements), one would not lose much in stating rather that the child *acquires* or *internalizes* scripts (or, for that matter, inductive teachings) from patterns in the prior givens of the empirical world. Hoffman (1983) wrote that the problem of moral socialization is that of how an "initially external" prescriptive norm becomes internalized or self-attributed (p. 236). Moral reciprocity is interesting in that it is *both* a norm that is, in many societies, taught and internalized and as well as an ideal that is constructed (in the Piagetian sense) through social interaction.

Let us elaborate on the Piagetian sense of "construction." As we discussed in Chapter 2, "construction," as in the construction of an *ideal*, can have a special meaning. In a classic series of experiments with dyads of preconservational children, for example, two conflicting "wrongs" (a quantity is now greater vs. a quantity is now less) in effect made a "right" (a quantity is conserved). Although the epistemology of conservation knowledge is a major topic in its own right, one thing is certain in these experiments: The children did not acquire the right answer from one another (they both started with wrong answers), from the experimenter (who refrained from modeling an answer), or from some other source of information in the environment. Rather, they *constructed* the knowledge through a dialectic of thesis and antithesis, a mental coordination or equilibration of opposing centrations on partial features. Analogously, although justice (in the form of ideal reciprocity) can and should be socialized as a cultural norm, it also tends naturally to be constructed as an "ideal [and necessary] equilibrium ... born of the actions and reactions of individuals upon each other," that is, "naturally" emergent from "a long *reciprocal education of the children by each other*" (Piaget, 1932/1965, p. 318, emphasis added; see Chapter 2). Piaget (1951/1971) argued that such knowledge is neither invented nor internalized nor discovered but rather *constructed* (following the "bursting" of instinctual programming) from the "general coordinations of action" of the living system (p. 366). Construction in this special sense is not reducible to internalization.

3. External Versus Internal Motivation

Whether empirical or logical or whether pertaining to the good or the right, knowledge can imply obligation. We may experience an obligation (or, more loosely, a moral motivation) to help others, just as we may experience such a motivation to right a wrong. And of course, moral motivation in either case may or may not prevail against egoistic motives given a particular individual in a particular situation.

Yet there is a crucial epistemological difference in moral motivation between the good and the right. In the former case, knowledge concerning beneficence per se is inert; it entails no inherent property of motivation. Such information (an inductive message, causal attribution, script, etc.) motivates only insofar as it is infused, charged, or rendered hot by an affect such as empathic distress (cf. classical conditioning). Accordingly, Hoffman's theory champions the empathic predisposition as the basic "infuser" of knowledge with moral motivation (affective primacy). In contrast, in the case of the right, the motivation is in some sense inherent or internal to the necessary properties of the knowledge. Decades ago,

Leon Festinger (1957) argued that "the existence of nonfitting relations among cognitions [or cognitive dissonance] is a motivating factor in its own right" (Festinger, 1957, p. 143). Cognitive primacy in motivation means that "the *recognition* of inconsistency *comes first*, and the feeling that this [inconsistency] should be avoided *follows from* it" (Singer, 1981, p. 142, emphasis added). In other words, the feeling to avoid or correct partly "*derives from* our capacity...to recognize inconsistency" (p. 142, emphasis added). As we saw in Chapter 2, violations of necessity—moral non-reciprocity, logical contradiction—tend to generate in their own right an affect of distress and a motivation to explain or correct.

Piaget (1967/1971) suggested that ideals of logical consistency or non-contradiction require a sophisticated understanding of evolutionary processes of adaptation:

> *A precise application of logic presupposes, among other things, the constant obligation not to contradict. ... Lack of intellectual honesty may be of a certain practical use (it is usually more convenient to be able to contradict oneself). ... When scruples about truth finally triumph, it is certainly not because there has been competition or selection in terms of utility alone but rather because of certain choices dictated by the internal organization of thought. ... The victory of one idea over another depends, in the final analysis, on the truth contained in it. ... Factors of utility and survival would have led only to intellectual instruments of a crudely approximate kind, loosely sufficient for the life of the species and its individual members, and never [directly] to that precision and, above all, that intrinsic necessity which demand a much more penetrating explanation of adaptation.[3] (Piaget, 1967/1971, pp. 274).*

There need be no delay in action from "intellectual honesty," "scruples about truth" and "choices dictated by the internal organization of thought." That the motivation to right a wrong or correct a logical violation can activate *quickly* is suggested by the Atlanta youth's sudden intervention or the promptness with which a conservation-judging child typically justifies a conservation evaluation (Brown, 1965). Thus, the claims of some theorists (e.g., Krebs & Denton, 2005) notwithstanding, established rational judgments of logic or justice do participate in the "quick" or "hot" response system (see Chapter 5; Gibbs, 2006).

We have labeled these positions, respectively, affective primacy and cognitive primacy in moral motivation. In philosophical terms, the issue is in general terms that of deontology versus utilitarianism and, in particular, that of whether motivation is *external* or *internal* to obligatory knowledge (Frankena, 1958; Straughan, 1983; see Wren, 1991). The external associationism of affective primacy means that knowledge is secondary in the sense that it is motivationally dependent on some prior force. In contrast, the internal pull of cognitive primacy means the *affect* is secondary in the sense that it owes its very existence to the knowledge that a "necessary" truth or ideal has been violated. Hoffman (2000) pointed out that the latter motivation can be deconfounded from the former when a *good* thing happens to a *bad* person: Empathy is generally not generated in such a case,[4] yet we still feel some moral motivation (to correct the violation). Nonetheless, Hoffman referred to cognitive moral reciprocity as only a possible preference, one that had not been established as an alternative primary motive.

"External" or extrinsic (primarily affective) and "internal" or intrinsic (primarily cognitive) sources of moral motivation typically cohere and jointly motivate. Indeed, in the usual ecology of the moral life, they are difficult to disentangle. Some confluence of empathic and violation-of-fairness distresses seemed to motivate Kielburger as well as the Atlanta youth (see Chapter 5), for example. Moreover, the guilt that prompted the Atlanta youth to blurt out an apology was attributed in our view not only to the affective charge of his self-attribution (he had joined in the tormenting), but also to consistency violation (his prior behavior contradicted his putative self-schema as one who does not unjustifiably harm others). Our epistemological analysis has led to support, then, for coprimacy in moral motivation.

So Are Kohlberg's and Hoffman's Theories Integrable?

The logical and the empirical are intimately interrelated. It is ironic, for example, that the logic of *imaginary* numbers is "at the very foundational structure of the *actual* physical world in which we live" (Penrose, 1994, p. 256; emphasis added). And in the other direction, empirical statements refer to the logical sooner or later. (I found it difficult to craft the first set of statements above without making even implicit reference to fairness, logic, or consistency.) Yet as noted, for all their intimacy, the two categories of knowledge remain fundamentally distinct. The categories are not integrable (at least not in the sense that happenstance could acquire an intrinsic necessity or that necessity could ever reduce to happenstance).

This point corresponds to the mutual irreducibility of the right and the good (as discussed in Chapter 1) and bears a major implication for the corresponding theories of moral development. Are Kohlberg's and Hoffman's theories integrable? Well, no. They are as mutually irreducible as are the right and the good, the logical and the empirical. Do the theories complement one another? We hope that the answer to that question is at this point clear: Yes, they intimately interrelate and complement one another quite nicely. Like the right and the good for morality, Kohlberg's and Hoffman's theories need to be taken together for a comprehensive understanding of basic moral development.

We end this study of morality and epistemology with a comment regarding its implications for moral *ontology*, that is, moral development and *reality*. Roger Brown (1965) suggested that to infer conservation is to "transcend immediate perception" to "*discover* a deeper reality" (p. 222, emphasis added). Piaget's emphasis on construction notwithstanding, discovery may indeed also be involved in the inference of necessary, internally motivating knowledge. Did the sudden *moral* perception and action of Craig Kielburger or the Atlanta youth also represent, in effect, the discovery of a deeper reality?

Moral Perception and Reality

Our phenomenally local world is in actuality supported by an invisible reality [of non-local connection] which is unmediated, unmitigated, and faster than light. (Herbert, 1985, p. 227)

Reality involves a paradox. Although the objects of this world interrelate, their connections are "local" (i.e., mediated, mitigated, and temporal). Gravity, electromagnetism, and other forces that connect the parts of this world are mediated (through particles or field waves). They mitigate (i.e., weaken with distance from one another) and take time (albeit often infinitesimal). Yet one implication of mathematical and experimental work deriving in part from certain predictions of quantum mechanics (Aspect & Grangier, 1986; Bell, 1966; Bouwmeester et al., 1997) is that our world of "local" events and connections that mitigate across time and space—the train whistle's sound waves take time to reach our ears, the "connection" from whistle to ear weakening as the waves travel in space—is somehow supported by a totally different, *non*-local reality. The supportive reality is one of immediate connections or relations, a realm that mathematical physicist Roger Penrose (1994) called "profound, timeless, and universal" (p. 413). Is it not paradoxical that this profound reality of *non*local connection both supports and contradicts our phenomenally *local* world of mediated connections? And the "togetherness"[5] of nonlocal connection is immediate indeed: "The mechanism for this instant connectedness is not some invisible [classical] field that stretches from one part to the next, but the fact that a bit of each part's 'being' is lodged in the other" (Herbert, 1985, p. 223).

Physical reality's ontological paradox—mediated connections between separate parts of the world supported by instant connectedness—can perhaps be discerned as well in terms of *human social and moral* reality. Are we humans—despite our individuality—deeply connected? It would certainly seem nonsensical to say that a bit of each human being is somehow lodged in others, that an affluent Westerner is somehow deeply connected with an Emroz or a Bakhtiar, living in crushing poverty in Pakistan halfway around the world. Even in largely collectivist cultures such as Pakistan's, each individual is *separate:* Although we socially decenter and feel emotionally close to others or integral with the group (socialization), we do also differentiate ourselves as separate and independent individuals:

It seems obvious and fundamental that the human brain and its associated cognitive structures guarantee at the very least that all humans are aware of the continuous kinesthetic sensations from their own bodies. This continuing kinesthetic awareness not only provides infants with an early sense of separation of self from other ... but also continues past infancy to ensure a certain minimum of separation of self from others through a person's life. .... It should therefore be impossible for an adult with a normal brain to feel that his or her self is merged with others. (Hoffman, 2000, p. 276, emphases added)

Moreover, throughout life we remain egocentrically biased at least to some extent (Chapter 2) and engage to varying degrees in self-centered and self-serving cognitive distortions (Chapter 6). Hence the importance of self-corrective and social skills (Chapter 7), as well as cultural support for social perspective-taking and mature moral judgment (Chapter 2).

And is not our world of separate individuals also one of local interindividual interactions, processes, and effects? Whether the emphasis is on justice or empathy, the point remains: Moral development, perception, and behavior normally take place over *time* through *mediating* processes (neural, maturational, social perspective taking). Even sudden moral acts take place in time and are often "primed" by earlier real-time attributions, inferences, and other empirical and logical schemas. And empathic distress generally *mitigates* or weakens where the distressed other is different, a stranger, or distant in location or history (empathic bias).

It would appear that the locality of this world does impose some practical moral constraints. Although Hoffman (Chapter 4) stresses the need to reduce egoistic motives and empathic bias through socialization and education, he also notes a "virtue" of empathic bias: It does afford a kind of protection. Were we to empathize equally with everyone, with no gradient of caring, we might affectively overload (empathic overarousal) and would chronically experience the paralysis and agony of not knowing whom to help first (the so-called multiple-claimants dilemma).

Nonetheless, let us consider the possibility that our ostensible human state of individual separation and local effects belies a deeper interconnectedness. Especially, perhaps human moral existence does entail the ontological paradox of local phenomena contradicted yet supported by their nonlocal underpinnings. Perhaps, just as justice presupposes caring (Frankena, 1973), individuality presupposes relatedness. Is morality ultimately love and connection? Although Kohlberg's and Hoffman's generally are local theories, Kohlberg did go beyond his own six-stage theory to claim that some reach a holistic perspective (his metaphorical "Stage 7"). In that ultimate "stage" of moral development, as we have seen, the existentially anguished soul-searcher morally revives after seeing human life from the perspective of the cosmos or "whole of nature."

Relevant to the perspective of a holistic reality that supports yet contradicts ordinary life is the so-called near-death experience (Chapter 8). Cherie Sutherland (1992) suggested that "the experiencer has undergone an ontological shift" (p. 193), a participation to some extent in an anomalous deeper reality. Certainly, the experience is rife with (for the local realm) bizarre anomalies: seeing despite closed eyelids, observing one's own three-dimensional body, moving through a tunnel that's not actually a tunnel, seeing a blinding light that does not blind, encountering love beyond earthly description, meeting dead yet alive loved ones, speaking without audibly speaking, hearing without audibly hearing, communicating instantaneously, and so forth. Near-death experiencers' continuing surprise, puzzlement, and difficulties in conveying their experience stem in part from such violations in their ordinary anticipations of, or schemas for, reality (Gibbs, 1997).

Like anyone, these persons can only process and describe their experience through the personal and cultural schemas they bring to the encounter. Yet to adapt, they must not experience only what they can anticipate, make ready sense of, or control (highly controlling individuals tend to have frightening near-death experiences). Beyond assimilating, they must somehow accommodate to the bizarre anomalies—even if the resulting disequilibration is severe. Finally, they must resist the temptation either to *over*assimilate (i.e., to misperceive or minimize as ordinary the ontological challenges of their experience) or to *over*accommodate (i.e., to change so radically as to lose any sense of continuity with their erstwhile identity and life contexts).

One can scarcely assimilate and accommodate to these anomalies adaptively without some disequilibration and reequilibration, some transformation of life and worldview. Somehow, "meaning has to be re-created, renegotiated within the context of this changed worldview" (Sutherland, 1992, p. 193). Sutherland discussed the social and personal aspects of typical renegotiations of meaning in this disequilibration-reequilibration process.

Timelessness and other anomalies of the near-death experience would seem to suggest that we individual humans can to some extent glimpse a realm of nonlocal (instantaneous, unmediated, unmitigated) connection. Pam Reynolds reported that in her comprehensive near-death experience, she felt "a sense of harmony or unity with the universe" (cf. Kohlberg's Stage 7 "cosmic perspective") and that "everything seemed to be happening all at once" (unpublished data, Sabom, November 3, 2001). In Tom Sawyer's transcendent near-death experience, the light

> *instantly began communicating with me ... emanating to me, thought-pattern to thought-pattern. ... It was pure communicating that was complete in every respect. ... As I thought of and formulated a desire or a question, it would already have been recognized, acknowledged, and therefore answered. ... The dialogue ... took place in no time. (Farr, 1993, p. 28)*

By "pure" communicating, Tom seems to refer to an interaction that is neither mediated nor sequential in time (at the point of asking or even intending to ask, questions have already been answered); yet, by definition, communicating entails causal signals propagated in time. That Tom must in effect reduce nonlocal phenomena to local language (e.g., "communicating") perhaps accounts for his expressive frustrations. In any event, Tom not only engaged in this "pure" interaction but even "became" other interactants in his empathetic life review. Tom saw self-serving excuses for acts such as assault to be benighted and utterly futile: "OK. He hit me first. Try *that* in your life review!" (see Chapter 8).

So perhaps in some ultimate sense, some aspect of each of us *is* lodged in others. Perhaps, on some foundational level, we are not so separate and independent after all. Extending from Nick Herbert in this section's opening quotation, could our phenomenally local world of individual persons even be *supported* by a reality of connection and commonality? Might we thereby grow beyond the superficial in existential and spiritual understanding? In Tom's empathetic life review, there seemed to be some connection of his "being" with the beings he became: with the drunk man he assaulted and nearly killed, with his shocked and bewildered Aunt Gay, with the well-meaning airport baggage handler he had hated but had never actually met, and so forth. Connection and commonality were also evident in the life-transforming experience of James, the St. Louis youth who saw racial distinctions of color as superficial and contained within the loving light he encountered. Connection and commonality certainly characterized the experience of Pam Reynolds, for whom figures of loved ones formed in the light, and who saw in the different "tones" of human individuality the potential for social harmony.

Deep connection is implied not only by the near-death experience but, more broadly, by the subatomic foundation of a physical world that includes our own bodies. On both counts, this deep human connection has ethical implications. Physicist Henry P. Stapp (2006) suggested that "non-local connectedness... opens the way to the construction of science-based ethical theories" that emphasize each person's "deep connectedness to the community of human beings, and to nature itself" (p. 619–620). David Lorimer (1990) suggested that the near-death experience and commonalities of mystical experience should be used as the "empirical soil" (p. 1) for a new ethic of interconnectedness—specifically, of profound love and universalized ideal reciprocity. Similarly, David Fontana (2004) urged the replacement of our materialist "philosophy of separation" with a "recognition of the interconnectedness of all things"(p. 158). Extending from a non-materialist conceptualization of mind, consciousness, and the self, Mario Beauregard and Denyse O'Leary (2007) proposed "a new scientific frame of reference" that could "significantly contribute to the emergence of a planetary type of consciousness," an awareness that "is absolutely essential if humanity is to successfully solve the global crises that confront us" (pp. 294–295).

That the deeply connected self can evidently function apart from the mediating processes of biology is perhaps the greatest anomaly of the near-death experience. Did not Hoffman (2000; see Chapter 4) and others identify certain *prerequisites* in the structures and pathways of the brain for moral functioning? How could Thomas Sawyer "wake up" as he lost consciousness? Even more astonishing, how could Pam Reynolds—with no detectable brain waves, little blood in the brain, not even any brain stem response—have been "the most aware" of her "entire life"? How could she have seen and heard details of her operation despite the unavailability of sensory organs (eyes blindfolded, ear canals totally occluded)? Moreover, how could individuals blind since birth nonetheless accurately see during their near-death experience (Ring & Cooper, 1997, 1999; Fox, 2003)? That the mind and identity can somehow function apart from the mediation of brain activity is suggested in a psychiatric patient having been "mentally clear" while out of his body even as he knew that his brain was still generating hallucinatory images (Chapter 8)! Perhaps Penrose (1989) is correct that "there must always be something missing" from the notion of the mind as merely an epiphenomenon of "extraordinarily complicated" computational activity of the brain (p. 447; cf. Neisser, 1992; Penrose, 1994). Mind-brain and other issues stimulated by the near-death experience may even go to "the very heart" of our "understanding of what it is to be human, and what it is for human beings to die" (Fox, 2003, p. 5).

At the very least, the anomaly—however disequilibrating it may be—must be faced. Pam Reynolds's chief neurosurgeon, Robert Spetzler, declared,

> It struck me that this [Pam's near-death experience] was incredibly perplexing and not understandable with what we know about the brain. Without any brain wave activity, it is inconceivable to me that the brain can receive, internalize, and maintain a memory. But at the same time, I think it is the height of egocentrism to say something can't happen just because we can't explain it. (Benz, 2001)

Ultimately incompatible with local morality is the agape sense of love often seen in the aftermath of the near-death experience. The urgently needed "planetary consciousness" notwithstanding, we are back to the multiple-claimants dilemma. Shouldn't a balance be struck between a global morality and caring for one's local loved ones? Bruce Greyson and Barbara Harris (1987) suggested that it is not always easy for the experiencer to find "a way to actualize in daily life the love he or she received in the NDE [near-death experience]" (p. 51; cf. Christian & Holden, in press). As described in Chapter 8, Thomas Sawyer's empathy for years after his return was nonlocal. His caring for others lost all similarity-familiarity bias, that is, was unmitigated with distance: Tom wanted to help *any* needy person he encountered, whether friend or stranger, and did—even when that meant at one point his unavailability to his wife who was ill and also needed his care. Reestablishing *some* gradient of care, *some* empathic bias as Hoffman calls it, was part of Tom's reequilibration process back into our local world of separate selves (Sawyer, personal communication, March 13, 2003).

Let us finally suggest, however, a less than total divorce in this paradoxical state of affairs between our local world and its nonlocal underpinnings. Although Tom was "back" and had to adjust to some extent, his inspiration and deeper understanding of life endured. Indeed, perhaps "a unity with the workings of Nature is potentially present within each of us," our insights and sensitivities resonant with those workings (Penrose, 1994, p. 420). The inference through misleading superficial appearances to discover an underlying necessity of conservation-related logic is a humble example in nonsocial cognitive development. Plato declared and Penrose suspects that ultimate reality encompasses the moral (and aesthetic) along with the mathematical. We have had occasion to cite numerous epiphanies of profound moral insight in our exploration of the right and the good strands of moral development and behavior. Some veridical insights and feelings have been heartbreakingly sabotaged by self-serving cognitive distortion, as in the case of the 17-year-old burglar who recollected, "If I started to feel bad [for one or another of my victims], I'd say tough rocks for him, he should have had his house locked better and the alarm on" (Samenow, 1984, p. 115). Presumably, Timothy McVeigh summoned some such dark externalization of blame to sabotage what we might call his moment of light, of insight into the enormity of what he was about to do.

Other moments of profound moral perception were more successful, sometimes resulting in total, life-changing moral transformations. Short of a near-death or even a meditative "Stage 7" experience, perhaps ordinary local processes can inspire insights that resonate with the nonlocal underpinnings of the moral life. The moment may be powerful and even "strange" (to use the Atlanta rescuer's word), as one finds oneself changed. Larry, the severe sex offender studied in Chapter 7, seemed to experience a shift abruptly out of darkness and into a transforming epiphany through group processes we can understand: He vividly role-played his crime in his adult-led peer group and, through connecting with human revulsion, decentered from self and felt with intense remorse the deep harm of his crime. Other cases of deep and transformative perception through local processes have included those of Mark Mathabane (the South African whose appreciation of a past kindness enabled him to see humanity within the individuals of an oppressive out-group), the Yanomamo villager (who discovered and excitedly begged for legal institutions so his people could grow beyond blood vengeances), 15-year-old Mac (who began to regret his verbal assault as he saw its roots in self-serving distortions), a reminiscing former ideologue (who, stripped of his old distortions, reexperienced empathic distress and felt guilt over having starved to death countless innocent women and children), and a girl who gained moral self-relevance as she reflected on how her stealing had disappointed her parents' expectations. Featured in this chapter has been the transformation of Craig Kielburger, whose life as a moral exemplar started with a jolt and shock at the news of brutal exploitation and murder in Pakistan, the land of our fellow human beings Emroz and Bakhtiar. Perhaps every deep moral perception offers at least a glimmer of insight into the deeper reality of human connection.

Notes

[1]As noted (Chapter 1), however, moral reform can be trickier than moral evaluation. Kielburger (1998) found that, to be taken seriously as a social activist, he had to deal with issues such as whether eliminating child labor would "send local currencies plummeting, causing unemployment and economic chaos" in those countries, and whether children freed from child labor might end up in even worse circumstances (p. 22). Issues of moral reform do not invalidate principles of moral evaluation. Indeed, like moral evaluation in the first place, issues of reform pertain to what is right and good.

[2]Although drawing on cognitive and affective primacies, moral self-relevance may be best seen as constituting in its own right as a source—a third or "meta" primacy, if you will—of moral motivation. As noted in Chapter 5, high levels of moral self-relevance have been termed *moral identity* (Blasi, 1995; Moshman, 2004, 2005).

[3]"Intellectual honesty" and "scruples about truth" tend to receive short shrift from evolutionary moral psychologists (e.g., Greene, 2008a, b; Haidt & Bjorklund, 2008a, b; Krebs, 2008), whose evolutionary reconstructions of human morality generally make precisely the pragmatic and utilitarian claims that Piaget rejected. But how do we account for intellectual honesty and scruples about truth? How might we have evolved in our mental functioning from the practical to the logic-related moral, mathematical, and scientific? As physicist Paul Davies (1992) put the question: "Our brains have evolved in response to environmental pressures, such as the ability to hunt, avoid predators, dodge falling objects, etc. What has this got to do with discovering the laws of electromagnetism or the structure of the atom?" (p. 149).

Singer speculated on a possible evolutionary pathway from the practical to the logical and mathematical:

> It is said that if four hunters go into a thicket and only three come out, baboons will keep away . . . baboons who can count a little may sometimes survive when less gifted baboons perish. The ability to count may have conferred a similar advantage on our own ancestors. . . . Long before writing developed, people made permanent records of their counting by cutting notches on a stick or stringing shells on twine. They had no idea that they had stepped on an escalator of reasoning that leads by strictly logical steps to square roots, prime numbers, and the differential calculus. (Singer, 1981, p. 89; see pp. 89–90.)

This "escalator of reasoning" leading by "inherent logic" to a "level of thought removed from the needs of ordinary people" (Singer, 1981, pp. 89–90) was characterized by Piaget (1967/1971) as the construction of formal operational cognitive structures. Penrose (1994) argued that this level of thought permitted the "uncovering" of "a profound mathematical substructure . . . hidden in the very [astrophysical, subatomic] workings of the world" (p. 415). Singer's, Piaget's, and Penrose's arguments transcend but do not contradict Donald T. Campbell's (e.g., Cook & Campbell, 1979) evolutionary critical-realist epistemology.

[4]Empathic distress may be activated even in this case if one thinks of others who may be left out and hurt because of the undeserving individual's benefits (Hoffman, 2000).

[5]At the subatomic level represented by "quantum systems," one finds

> an unexpected degree of togetherness [of elementary particles]. Mere spatial separation does not divide them from each other. It is a particularly surprising conclusion for so reductionist a subject as physics. After all, elementary particle physics is always trying to split things up into smaller and smaller constituents with a view to treating them independently of each other. (Polkinghorne, 1984, p. 76)

Surprising though this conclusion may be, the evidence for nonlocal interconnectedness (at least of electrons or photons whose waveforms have been entangled) is compelling. Hence, "until a measurement has actually been performed, it is wrong to think of the two [elementary particles] as having a completely independent existence" (Lindley, 1996, p. 146). As Dean Radin (2006) put the point: "One of the most surprising discoveries of modern physics is that objects aren't as separate as they seem. When you drill down into the core of even the most solid-looking material, separateness dissolves" (p. 1). David Lindley (1996) was skeptical of claims (e.g., by Laszlo, 2003) that the entire universe is fundamentally interconnected in this nonlocal sense, however.

References

Abelson, R. P., Aronson, E., McGuire, W. J., Newcomb, T. M., Rosenberg, M. J., & Tannenbaum, P. H. (Eds.). (1968). *Theories of cognitive consistency: A sourcebook.* Chicago: Rand McNally.

Abramovitch, H. (1988). An Israeli account of a near-death experience: A case study of cultural dissonance. *Journal of Near-Death Studies, 6,* 175–184.

Ackerman, P., & Duvall, J. (2000). *A force more powerful: A century of nonviolent conflict.* New York: St. Martin's.

Ackerman, P. L., Beier, M. E., & Boyle, M. O. (2005). Working memory and intelligence: The same or different constructs? *Psychological Bulletin, 131,* 30–60.

Adelson, J., Green, B., & O'Neil, R. P. (1969). Growth of the idea of law in adolescence. *Developmental Psychology, 1,* 327–332.

Agee, V. L. (1979). *Treatment of the violent incorrigible adolescent.* Lexington, MA: Lexington Books.

Agee, V. L., & McWilliams, B. (1984). The role of group therapy and the therapeutic community in treating the violent juvenile offender. In R. Mathias (Ed.), *Violent juvenile offenders* (pp. 283–296). San Francisco: National Council on Crime and Delinquency.

Al-Krenawi, A., Slonim-Nevo, V., Maymon, Y., & Al-Krenawi, S. (2001). Psychological responses to blood vengeance among Arab adolescents. *Child Abuse & Neglect, 25,* 457–472.

Alexander, R. D. (1987). *The biology of moral systems.* New York: Aldine de Gruyter.

Ali, A. H. (2008). *Infidel.* New York: Free Press.

Aloniz, V. (1997, April 27). Fort Worth man charged in wife's slaying. *The Dallas Morning News,* p. 5A.

Alvarez-Saunders, C., & Reyes, L. S. (1994). *Capital offender group program.* Giddings: Giddings State Home and School of the Texas Youth Commission.

American Psychiatric Association (1994). *Diagnostic and statistical manual of mental disorders* (4th ed.). Washington, DC: Author.

Ames, G., & Murray, F. B. (1982). When two wrongs make a right: Promoting cognitive changes by social conflict. *Developmental Psychology, 18,* 894–898.

Anderson, R., & Morgan, C. (Producers). (2007). *Exposing the truth: Anderson Cooper interviews Joe Darby.* New York: CBS "60 Minutes."

Anderson, S. (1999, December 26). The curse of blood and vengeance. *New York Times Magazine,* pp. 29–34, 44, 54–57, 149.

Andrews, E. L. (2006, December 3). Blowing the whistle on big oil. *New York Times Sunday Edition Business Section,* pp. 1, 8–9.

Aquino, K., & Reed, A., II. (2002). The self-importance of moral identity. *Journal of Personality and Social Psychology, 83,* 1423–1440.

Aquino, K., Reed, A., Thau, S., & Freeman, D. (2007). A grotesque and dark beauty: How moral identity and mechanisms of moral disengagement influence cognitive and emotional reactions to war. *Journal of Experimental Social Psychology, 43,* 385–392.

Arbuthnot, J., & Gordon, D. (1986). Behavioral and cognitive effects of a moral reasoning development intervention for high-risk behavior-disordered adolescents. *Journal of Consulting and Clinical Psychology, 85,* 1275–1301.

Arsenio, W. F., Gold, J., & Adams, E. (2006). Children's conceptions and displays of moral emotions. In M. Killen & J. G. Smetana (Eds.), *Handbook of moral development* (pp. 581–610). Mahwah, NJ: Erlbaum.

Aspect, A., & Grangier, P. (1986). Experiments on Einstein-Podolsky-Rosen-type correlations with pairs of visible photons. In R. Penrose & C. J. Isham (Eds.), *Quantum concepts in space and time* (pp. 1–15). Oxford, UK: Oxford University Press.

Ayer, A. J. (1952). *Language, truth, and logic.* New York: Dover Publications.

Azar, B. (1997, November 11). Defining the trait that makes us human. *American Psychological Association Monitor, 28,* 1 ff.

Baier, K. (1965). *The moral point of view: A rational basis of ethics.* New York: Random House.

Baldwin, M. W. (1992). Relational schemas and the processing of social information. *Psychological Review, 112,* 462–484.

Bandura, A. (1977). Self-efficacy theory: Toward a unifying theory of behavioral change. *Psychological Review, 84,* 191–215.

Bandura, A. (1999). Moral disengagement in the perpetration of inhumanities. *Personality and Social Psychology Review, 3,* 193–209.

Bandura, A., Barbaranelli, C., Caprara, G. V., & Pastorelli, C. (1996). Mechanisms of moral disengagement in the exercise of moral agency. *Journal of Personality and Social Psychology, 71,* 364–371.

Bargh, J. A. (1996). Automaticity in social psychology. In E. T. Higgins & A. W. Kruglanski (Eds.), *Social psychology: Handbook of basic principles* (pp. 169–183). New York: Guilford.

Barriga, A. Q., & Gibbs, J. C. (1996). Measuring cognitive distortion in antisocial youth: Development and preliminary evaluation of the *How I Think* questionnaire. *Aggressive Behavior, 22,* 333–343.

Barriga, A. Q., Gibbs, J. C., & Potter, G. B., Konopisos, M., & Barriga, K. T. (2007). *How I Think about Drugs and Alcohol (HIT D & A) Questionnaire.* Champagne, IL: Research Press.

Barriga, A. Q., Gibbs, J. C., Potter, G. B., & Liau, A. K. (2001). *How I Think (HIT) questionnaire manual.* Champaign, IL: Research Press.

Barriga, A. Q., Hawkins, M. A., & Camelia, C. R. T. (2008). Specificity of cognitive distortions to antisocial behaviors. *Criminal Behaviour and Mental Health, 18,* 104–116.

Barriga, A. Q., Landau, J. R., Stinson, B. L., Liau, A. K., & Gibbs, J. C. (2000). Cognitive distortion and problem behaviors in adolescents. *Criminal Justice and Behavior, 27,* 333–343.

Barriga, A. Q., Morrison, E. M., Liau, A. K., & Gibbs, J. C. (2001). Moral cognition: Explaining the gender difference in antisocial behavior. *Merrill-Palmer Quarterly, 47,* 532–562.

Barry, B. (1995). *Justice as impartiality.* Oxford, UK: Clarendon.

Basinger, K. S., & Gibbs, J. C. (1987). Validation of the Sociomoral Reflection Objective Measure–Short Form. *Psychological Reports, 61,* 139–146.

Basinger, K. S., Gibbs, J. C., & Fuller, D. (1995). Context and the measurement of moral judgment. *International Journal of Behavioral Development, 18,* 537–556.

Batson, C. D., Batson, J. G., Todd, R. M., Brummeth, B. H., Shaw, L. L., & Aldeguer, C. M. (1995). Empathy and the collective good: Caring for one of the others in a social dilemma. *Journal of Personality and Social Psychology, 68,* 619–631.

Baumeister, R. F. (1989). The optimal margin of illusion. *Journal of Social and Clinical Psychology, 8,* 176–189.

Baumeister, R. F. (1991). *Escaping the self: Alcoholism, spirituality, masochism, and other flights from the burden of selfhood.* New York: Basic Books.

Baumeister, R. F. (1997). *Evil: Inside human violence and cruelty.* New York: W. H. Freeman.

Baumrind, D. (1971). Current patterns of parental authority. *Developmental Psychology Monograph, 4*(1, Pt. 2).

Baumrind, D. (1989). Rearing competent children. In W. Damon (Ed.), *Child development today and tomorrow* (pp. 349–379). San Francisco: Jossey-Bass.

Bavelas, J. B., Black, A., Chovil, N., Lemery, C. R., & Mullett, J. (1988). Form and function in motor mimicry: Topographical evidence that the primary function is communication. *Human Communication Research, 14*, 275–299.

Beah, I. (2007). *A long way gone: Memoirs of a boy soldier.* New York: Farrar, Straus and Giroux.

Beauchamp, T. L., & Childress, J. F. (2001). *Principles of biomedical ethics* (5th ed.). New York: Oxford University Press.

Beauregard, M., & O'Leary, D. (2007). *The spiritual brain: A neuroscientist's case for the existence of the soul.* New York: HarperOne.

Beck, A. T. (1999). *Prisoners of hate: The cognitive basis of anger, hostility, and violence.* New York: HarperCollins.

Beck, R., & Fernandez, E. (1998). Cognitive-behavioral therapy in the treatment of anger: A meta-analysis. *Cognitive Therapy and Research, 22*, 63–74.

Beilin, H. (1992). Piaget's enduring contribution to developmental psychology. *Developmental Psychology, 28*, 191–204.

Bell, J. S. (1966). On the problem of hidden variables in quantum theory. *Research in Modern Physics, 38*, 447–452.

Bem, D. J., Palmer, J., & Broughton, R. S. (2001). Updating the Ganzfeld database: A victim of its own success? *Journal of Parapsychology, 65*, 207–218.

Benz, G. R. (Producer). (2001, May 28). *Beyond human limits* [Television broadcast]. New York: Discovery Channel.

Bergen, P., & Cruickshank, P. (2008, June 11). The unraveling: Al Qaeda's revolt against bin Laden. *The New Republic*, pp. 16–21.

Bergman, R. (2004). Identity as motivation: Toward a theory of the moral self. In D. K. Lapsley & D. Narvaez (Eds.), *Morality, self, and identity* (pp. 21–46). Mahwah, NJ: Lawrence Erlbaum.

Bergman, R. (2006). Gibbs on Kohlberg on Dewey: An essay review of John C. Gibbs' Moral Development and Reality. *European Journal of Developmental Psychology, 3*, 300–311.

Berk, L. (2009). *Child development* (8th ed.). Boston: Allyn & Bacon.

Berkowitz, M. W., & Gibbs, J. C. (1983). Measuring the developmental features of moral discussion. *Merrill-Palmer Quarterly, 29*, 399–410.

Berkowitz, M. W., & Gibbs, J. C. (1985). The process of moral conflict resolution and moral development. In M. W. Berkowitz (Ed.), *Peer conflict and psychological growth: New directions for child development* (No. 29, pp. 71–82). San Francisco: Jossey-Bass.

Bierman, D. J. (2001). On the nature of anomalous phenomena: Another reality between the world of subjective consciousness and the objective world of physics? In P. Van Loocke (Ed.), *The physical nature of consciousness* (pp. 269–292). Amsterdam: John Benjamins.

Bjorklund, D. F., & Pellegrini, A. D. (2002). *The origins of human nature: Evolutionary developmental psychology.* Washington, DC: American Psychological Association.

Blackmore, S. (1993). *Dying to live: Near-death experiences.* New York: Prometheus.

Blair, R. J. R. (2006). *The psychopath: Emotion and the brain.* Oxford, UK: Blackwell Publishing.

Blanke, O., Ortigue, S., Landis, T., & Seeck, M. (2002). Stimulating illusory own-body perceptions. *Nature, 419*, 269.

Blasi, A. (1980). Bridging moral cognition and moral action: A critical review of literature. *Psychological Bulletin, 88*, 1–45.

Blasi, A. (1995). Moral understanding and the moral personality: The process of moral integration. In W. Kurtines & J. L. Gewirtz (Eds.), *Moral development: An introduction* (pp. 229–253). Boston: Allyn & Bacon.

Bloom, P. (2004). *Descartes' baby: How the science of child development explains what makes us human.* New York: Basic Books.

Bodansky, Y. (1999). *Bin Laden: The man who declared war on America.* New York: Random House.

Bouwmeester, D., Pan, J. W., Mattle, K., Eibl, M., Weinfurther, H., & Zeilinger, A. (1997). Experimental quantum teleportation. *Nature, 390,* 575–579.

Bowlby, J. (1980). *Attachment and loss: Vol. 1. Attachment.* New York: Basic Books.

Boyes, M. C., & Chandler, M. (1992). Cognitive development, epistemic doubt, and identity formation in adolescence. *Journal of Youth and Adolescence, 21,* 277–304.

Boysen, S. T. (1993). Counting in chimpanzees: Nonhuman principles and emergent properties of number. In S. T. Boysen & E. J. Capaldi (Eds.), *The development of numerical competence* (pp. 39–59). Hillsdale, NJ: Lawrence Erlbaum.

Boysen, S. T., Berntson, G., Shreyer, T. A., & Quigley, K. S. (1993). Processing of ordinality and transitivity by chimpanzees *(Pan troglodytes). Journal of Comparative Psychology, 107,* 208–215.

Brabeck, M. (1984). Ethical characteristics of whistle blowers. *Journal of Research in Personality, 18,* 41–53.

Brandt, R. B. (1959). *Ethical theory: The problems of normative and critical ethics.* Englewood Cliffs, NJ: Prentice Hall.

Brendtro, L. K., & Ness, A. E. (1982). Perspectives on peer group treatment: The use and abuse of Guided Group Interaction/Positive Peer Culture. *Children and Youth Services Review, 4,* 307–324.

Brendtro, L. K., & Wasmund, W. C. (1989). The Positive Peer Culture model. In R. Lyman, S. Prentice-Dunn, & S. Gabel (Eds.), *Residential treatment of emotionally disturbed children* (pp. 81–93). New York: Plenum.

Brewer, M. B. (2007). The importance of being *we:* Human nature and intergroup relations. *American Psychologist, 62,* 728–738.

Bronfenbrenner, U., & Morris, P. A. (2006). The bioecological model of human development. In W. Damon & R. M. Lerner (Series Eds.) & R. M. Lerner (Vol. Ed.), *Handbook of child psychology: Vol. 1. Theoretical models of human development* (6th ed., pp. 793–828). New York: John Wiley.

Broome, K. (Producer) (2001). *The day I died* [Television broadcast]. UK: British Broadcasting Corporation (BBC).

Brothers, L. (1989). A biological perspective on empathy. *American Journal of Psychiatry, 146,* 10–19.

Brown, R. (1965). *Social psychology.* New York: Free Press.

Brown, R., & Herrnstein, R. J. (1975). *Psychology.* Boston: Little, Brown.

Brugman, D., & Aleva, A. E. (2004). Developmental delay or regression in moral reasoning by juvenile delinquents? *Journal of Moral Education, 33,* 321–338.

Bruni, P. (2004, February 1). Doctor in Italy tries to ease pain of an African tradition. *The New York Times,* p. 3.

Bugental, D. B., & Grusec, J. E. (2006). Socialization processes. In W. Damon & R. M. Lerner (Series Ed.) & N. Eisenberg (Vol. Ed.), *Handbook of child psychology: Vol. 3. Social, emotional, and personality development* (6th ed., pp. 366–428). New York: John Wiley.

Burgess, R. L., & Huston, T. L. (1979). *Social exchange in developing relationships*. New York: Academic Press.

Bush, N. (2002). Afterward: Making meaning after a frightening near-death experience. *Journal of Near-Death Studies, 21,* 99–133.

Bushman, B. J., & Anderson, C. A. (2001). Is it time to pull the plug on the hostile versus instrumental aggression dichotomy? *Psychological Review, 108,* 273–279.

Bussey, K. (1992). Lying and truthfulness: Children's definitions, standards, and evaluative reactions. *Child Development, 63,* 1236–1250.

California Department of the Youth Authority. (1994). *Victim awareness/community safety: Student and teacher's manuals* (Rev. version). Sacramento, CA: Department of the Youth Authority.

Callanan, M., & Kelley, P. (1992). *Final gifts: Understanding the special awarenesses, needs, and communications of the dying.* New York: Bantam Books.

Campbell, D. T. (1972). On the genetics of altruism and the counter-hedonic components in human culture. *Journal of Social Issues, 28,* 21–37.

Campbell, R. L., & Christopher, J. C. (1996). Moral development theory: A critique of its Kantian presuppositions. *Developmental Review, 16,* 1–47.

Carducci, D. J. (1980). Positive Peer Culture and assertiveness training: Complementary modalities for dealing with disturbed and disturbing adolescents in the classroom. *Behavioral Disorders, 5,* 156–162.

Carducci, D. J., & Carducci, J. B. (1984). *The caring classroom: A guide for teachers troubled by the difficult student and classroom disruption.* New York: Bull.

Carlson, R. (1982). Studies in script theory: II. Altruistic nuclear scripts. *Perceptual and Motor Skills, 55,* 595–610.

Carr, M. B., & Lutjemeier, J. A. (2005). The relation of facial affect recognition and empathy to delinquency in youth. *Adolescence, 40,* pp. 601–620.

Case, R. (1998). The development of conceptual structures. In W. Damon (Series Ed.) & D. Kuhn & R. S. Siegler (Vol. Eds.), *Handbook of child psychology: Vol. 2. Cognition, perception, and language* (5th ed., pp. 745–800). New York: John Wiley.

Cason, D. R., Resick, P. A., & Weaver, T. L. (2002). Schematic integration of traumatic events. *Clinical Psychology Review, 22,* 131–153.

Chagnon, N. A. (1988). Life histories, blood revenge, and warfare in a tribal population. *Science, 239,* 985–992.

Chandler, M., & Carpendale, J. I. M. (1998). Inching toward a mature theory of mind. In M. Ferrari & R. Sternberg (Eds.), *Self-awareness: Its nature and development* (pp. 148–190). New York: Guilford Press.

Chapman, M., & Lindenburger, U. (1989). Concrete operations and attentional capacity. *Journal of Experimental Child Psychology, 47,* 236–258.

Chase, K. A., O'Leary, D., & Heyman, R. E. (2001). Categorizing partner-violent men within the reactive-proactive typology model. *Journal of Consulting and Clinical Psychology, 69,* 567–572.

Christian, S. R., & Holden, J. (in press). Till death do us part: Marital satisfaction and stability after the near-death experience of one of the spouses. *Journal of Near-Death Studies.*

Colby, A. (1978). Evolution of a moral developmental theory. In W. Damon (Ed.), *New directions for child development* (No. 2). San Francisco: Jossey-Bass.

Colby, A. (2000). The place of moral interpretation and habit in moral development. *Human Development, 43,* 161–164.

Colby, A. (2002). Moral understanding, motivation, and identity [Commentary]. *Human Development, 45*, 130–135.

Colby, A. (2008). Fostering the moral and civic development of college students. In L. P. Nucci & D. Narvaez (Eds.), *Handbook of moral and character education* (pp. 391–413). New York: Routledge.

Colby, A., & Damon, W. (1992). *Some do care: Contemporary lives of moral commitment.* New York: Free Press.

Colby, A., & Kohlberg, L. (1987). *The measurement of moral judgment: Vol. 1. Theoretical foundations and research validation.* Cambridge, UK: Cambridge University Press.

Colby, A., Kohlberg, L., Gibbs, J. C., & Lieberman, M. (1983). A longitudinal study of moral judgment. *Monographs of the Society for Research in Child Development, 48*(1–2, Serial No. 200).

Colby, A., Kohlberg, L., Speicher, B., Hewer, A., Candee, D., Gibbs, J., & Power, C. (1987). *The measurement of moral judgment* (Vol. 2). Cambridge, UK: Cambridge University Press.

Coles, R. (1986). *The moral life of children.* Boston: Houghton Mifflin.

Coll, S. (2008). *The bin Ladens: An Arabian family in the American Century.* New York: Penguin Books.

Collins, W. A., Maccoby, E. E., Steinberg, L., Hetherington, E. M., & Bornstein, M. H. (2000). Contemporary research on parenting: The case of nature and nurture. *American Psychologist, 55*, 218–232.

Comunian, A. L., & Gielen, U. P. (1995). A study of moral reasoning and prosocial action in Italian culture. *Journal of Social Psychology, 135*, 699–706.

Comunian, A. L., & Gielen, U. P. (2000). Sociomoral reflection and prosocial and antisocial behavior: Two Italian studies. *Psychological Reports, 87*, 161–175.

Comunian, A. L., & Gielen, U. P. (2006). Promotion of moral judgement maturity through stimulation of social role-taking and social reflection: An Italian intervention study. *Journal of Moral Education, 35*, 51–69.

Conquest, R. (1986). *The harvest of sorrow: Soviet collectivization and the terror-famine.* New York: Oxford University Press.

Cook, E. W., Greyson, B., & Stevenson, I. (1998). Do any near-death experiences provide evidence for the survival of human personality after death? Relevant features and illustrative case reports. *Journal of Scientific Exploration, 12*, 377–406.

Cook, T. D., & Campbell, D. T. (1979). *Quasi-experimentation: Design & analysis issues for field settings.* Chicago: Rand McNally.

Cowan, P. A. (1978). *Piaget with feeling: Cognitive, social, and emotional dimensions.* New York: Holt, Rinehart, & Winston.

Cowan, P. A., Powell, D., & Cowan, C. P. (1998). Parenting interventions: A family systems perspective. In W. Damon (Series Ed.) & I. E. Sigel & K. A. Renninger (Vol. Eds.), *Handbook of child psychology: Vol. 4. Child psychology in practice* (5th ed., pp. 3–72). New York: John Wiley.

Cox-Chapman, M. (1995). *The case for heaven.* New York: Berkley.

Crick, N. R., & Dodge, K. A. (1994). A review and reformulation of social information processing mechanisms in children's social adjustment. *Psychological Bulletin, 115*, 74–101.

Dahlen, E. R., & Deffenbacher, J. L. (2000). A partial component analysis of Beck's cognitive therapy for the treatment of general anger. *Journal of Cognitive Therapy, 14*, 77–95.

Damasio, A. (1994). *Descartes' error: Emotion, reason, and the human brain.* New York: Grosset/ Putnam.

Damasio, A. (1999). *The feeling of what happens: Body and emotion in the making of consciousness.* New York: Harcourt Brace.

Damon, W. (1977). *The social world of the child.* San Francisco: Jossey-Bass.

Damon, W. (1980). Patterns of change in children's social reasoning: A two-year longitudinal study. *Child Development, 51,* 1010–1017.

Damon, W. (1981). Exploring children's social cognition on two fronts. In J. H. Flavell & L. Ross (Eds.), *Social cognitive development: Frontiers and possible futures* (pp. 154–175). Cambridge, UK: Cambridge University Press.

Damon, W. (1984). Peer education: The untapped potential. *Journal of Applied Developmental Psychology, 5,* 331–343.

Damon, W. (1988). *The moral child: Nurturing children's natural moral growth.* New York: Free Press.

Damon, W. (1995). *Greater expectations: Overcoming the culture of indulgence in America's homes and schools.* New York: Free Press.

Damon, W. (1996). The lifelong transformation of moral goals through social influence. In P. B. Baltes & U. M. Staudinger (Eds.), *Interactive minds: Lifespan perspectives on the social foundation of cognition* (pp. 198–220). Cambridge, UK: Cambridge University Press.

Damon, W. (1997). *The youth charter: How communities can work together to raise standards for all our children.* New York: Free Press.

Damon, W. (2006). Preface to Handbook of Child Psychology, Sixth Edition. In W. Damon & R. M. Lerner (Series Ed.) & W. R. M. Lerner (Vol. Ed.), *Handbook of child psychology: Vol. 1. Theoretical models of human development* (6th ed., pp. ix–xvi). New York: John Wiley.

Damon, W., & Hart, D. (1988). *Self-understanding in childhood and adolescence.* New York: Cambridge University Press.

Damon, W., & Killen, M. (1982). Peer interaction and the process of change in children's moral reasoning. *Merrill-Palmer Quarterly, 28,* 347–367.

Darling, N., & Steinberg, L. (1993). Parent style as context: An integrative model. *Psychological Bulletin, 113,* 487–496.

Davies, P. (1992). *The mind of God: The scientific basis for a rational world.* New York: Simon & Schuster.

Day, J. M., & Tappan, M. B. (1996). The narrative approach to moral development: From the epistemic subject to dialogical selves. *Human Development, 39,* 67–82.

Decety, J., & Chaminade, T. (2003). Neural correlates of feeling sympathy. *Neuropsychologia, 41,* 127–138.

DeLoache, J., Miller, K. F., & Pierroutsakos, S. L. (1998). Reasoning and problem solving. In W. Damon (Series Ed.) & D. Kuhn & R. S. Siegler (Vol. Eds.), *Handbook of child psychology: Vol. 2. Cognition, perception, and language* (5th ed., pp. 801–850). New York: John Wiley.

Deluty, R. H. (1979). Children's Action Tendency Scale: A self-report measure of aggressive-ness, assertiveness, and submissiveness in children. *Journal of Consulting and Clinical Psychology, 47,* 1061–1071.

Devlin, R. (2008). *Responsible Adult Culture (RAC): Cognitive and behavioral changes at a com-munity-based correctional facility.* Unpublished doctoral dissertation, The Ohio State University, Columbus.

de Waal, F. B. M. (1996). *Good natured: The origins of right and wrong in humans and other animals.* London: Harvard University Press.

de Waal, F. B. M. (2008). Putting the altruism back into altruism: The evolution of empathy. *Annual Review of Psychology, 59,* 279–300.

Dewey, J., & Tufts, J. H. (1908). *Ethics*. New York: Holt.

Diamond, J. (2008, April 21). Annals of Anthropology: Vengeance is ours. What can tribal societies tell us about our need to get even? *The New Yorker*, 74, 76–78, 80–82, 84–87.

DiBiase, A.-M., Gibbs, J. C., & Potter, G. B. (2005). *EQUIP for educators: Teaching youth (grades 5–8) to think and act responsibly*. Champaigne, IL: Research Press.

Dishion, T. J., Loeber, R., Stouthamer-Loeber, M., & Patterson, G. R. (1984). Skill deficits and male adolescent delinquency. *Journal of Abnormal Child Psychology*, 12, 37–54.

Dishion, T. J., McCord, J., & Poulin, F. (1999). When interventions harm: Peer groups and problem behavior. *American Psychologist*, 54, 755–764.

Dodge, K. A. (1986). A social informational processing model of social competence in children. In M. Perlmutter (Ed.), *Minnesota symposia on child psychology: Vol. 18. Cognitive perspectives on children's social and behavioral development* (pp. 77–125). Hillsdale, NJ: Lawrence Erlbaum.

Dodge, K. A. (1993). Social-cognitive mechanisms in the development of conduct disorder and depression. *Annual Review of Psychology*, 44, 559–584.

Dodge, K. A., Bates, J. E., & Pettit, G. S. (1990). Mechanisms in the cycle of violence. *Science*, 250, 1678–1685.

Dodge, K. A., & Coie, J. D. (1987). Social information-processing factors in reactive and proactive aggression in children's playgroups. *Journal of Personality and Social Psychology*, 53, 1146–1158.

Dodge, K. A., Coie, J. D., & Lynam, D. (2006.) In W. Damon & R. M. Lerner (Series Eds.) & N. Eisenberg (Vol. Ed.), *Handbook of child psychology: Vol. 3. Social, emotional, and personality development* (6th ed., pp. 719–788). New York: John Wiley.

Dodge, K. A., Dishion, T. J., & Lansford (Eds.) (2006). *Deviant peer influences in programs for youth: Problems and Solutions*. New York: Guilford Press.

Dodge, K. A., McLoyd, V. C., & Lansford, J. E. (2005). The cultural context of disciplining children. In V. C. McLoyd, N. E. Hill, & K. A. Dodge (Eds.), *African American family life: Ecological and cultural diversity* (pp. 245–263). New York: Guilford Press.

Dodge, K. A., Price, J. M., Bachorowski, J. A., & Newman, J. P. (1990). Hostile attributional biases in severely aggressive adolescents. *Journal of Abnormal Psychology*, 99, 385–392.

Dodge, K. A., & Schwartz, D. (1998). Social information processing mechanisms in aggressive behavior. In D. M. Stoff, J. Breiling, & J. D. Maser (Eds.), *Handbook of antisocial behavior* (pp. 171–180). New York: John Wiley.

Doise, W., & Mugny, G. (1984). *The social development of the intellect* (A. St. James-Emler & N. Emler, Trans.). Oxford, UK: Pergamon. (Original work published 1979)

Dondi, M., Simion, F., & Caltran, G. (1999). Can newborns discriminate between their own cry and the cry of another newborn infant? *Developmental Psychology*, 35, 418–426.

Edgerton, R. B. (1992). *Sick societies: Challenging the myth of primitive harmony*. New York: Free Press.

Edwards, C. P. (1975). Social complexity and moral development: A Kenyan study. *Ethos*, 3, 505–527.

Edwards, C. P. (1978). Social experience and moral judgment in East African young adults. *Journal of Genetic Psychology*, 133, 19–29.

Edwards, C. P. (1982). Moral development in comparative cultural perspective. In D. A. Wagner & H. Stevenson (Eds.), *Cultural perspectives on child development* (pp. 248–279). San Francisco: W. H. Freeman.

Edwards, C. P. (1985). Rationality, culture, and the construction of "ethical discourse": A comparative perspective. *Ethos: The Journal of Psychological Anthropology, 13,* 318–339.

Edwards, C. P. (1986). Cross-cultural research on Kohlberg's stages: The basis for consensus. In S. Modgil & C. Modgil (Eds.), *Lawrence Kohlberg: Consensus and controversy* (pp. 419–430). Sussex, England: Falmer Press Ltd.

Eisenberg, N. (1982). The development of reasoning regarding prosocial behavior. In N. Eisenberg (Ed.), *The development of prosocial behavior* (pp. 219–249). New York: Academic Press.

Eisenberg, N. (1996). In search of the good heart. In M. R. Merrens & G. G. Brannigan (Eds.), *The developmental psychologists: Research adventures across the life span* (pp. 89–104). New York: McGraw-Hill.

Eisenberg, N., Fabes, R. A, & Spinrad, T. L. (2006). Prosocial development. In W. Damon & R. M. Lerner (Series Eds.) & N. Eisenberg (Vol. Ed.), *Handbook of child psychology: Vol. 3. Social, emotional, and personality development* (6th ed., pp. 646–718). New York: John Wiley.

Ellis, A. (1977). Rational-emotive therapy: Research data that support the clinical and personality hypotheses of RET and other modes of cognitive-behavioral therapy. *Counseling Psychologist, 7,* 2–42.

Epstein, S. (1991). Cognitive-experiential self theory: Implications for developmental psychology. In M. R. Gunnar & L. A. Sroufe (Eds.), *Self processes and development: The Minnesota symposia on child development* (Vol. 23, pp. 79–124). Hillsdale, NJ: Lawrence Erlbaum.

Epstein, S., & Morling, B. (1995). Is the self motivated to do more than enhance and/or verify itself? In M. H. Kernis (Ed.), *Efficacy, agency, and self-esteem* (pp. 9–29). New York: Plenum.

Fabes, R. A., Eisenberg, N., Nyman, M., & Michealieu, Q. (1991). Young children's appraisals of others' spontaneous emotional reactions. *Developmental Psychology, 27,* 858–866.

Farr, S. S. (1993). *What Tom Sawyer learned from dying.* Norfolk, VA: Hampton Roads.

Feffer, M. (1970). Developmental analysis of interpersonal behavior. *Psychological Review, 77,* 197–214.

Feindler, E. L., & Ecton, R. R. (1986). *Adolescent anger control: Cognitive-behavioral techniques.* New York: Pergamon.

Fenwick, P., & Fenwick, E. (1995). *The truth in the light.* New York: Berkley.

Ferrari, M., & Sternberg, R. J. (1998). The development of mental abilities and styles. In W. Damon (Series Ed.) & D. Kuhn & R. S. Siegler (Vol. Eds.), *Handbook of child psychology: Vol. 2. Cognition, perception, and language* (5th ed., pp. 899–946). New York: John Wiley.

Festinger, L. (1957). *A theory of cognitive dissonance.* Stanford: Stanford University Press.

Fischer, K. W., & Bidell, T. R. (2006). Dynamic development of action and thought. In W. Damon & R. M. Lerner (Series Ed.) & R. M. Lerner (Vol. Ed.), *Handbook of child psychology: Vol. 1. Theoretical models of human development* (6th ed., pp. 313–399). New York: John Wiley.

Flavell, J. H. (1996). Piaget's legacy. *Psychological Science, 7,* 200–203.

Flavell, J. H., & Miller, P. H. (1998). Social cognition. In W. Damon (Series Ed.) & D. Kuhn & R. S. Siegler (Vol. Eds.), *Handbook of child psychology: Vol. 2. Cognition, perception, and language* (5th ed., pp. 851–898). New York: John Wiley.

Flavell, J. H., Miller, P. H., & Miller, S. A. (2002). *Cognitive development* (4th ed.). Upper Saddle River, NJ: Prentice Hall.

Fontana, D. (2004). Science, religion, and psychology: The case for the transpersonal. In D. Lorimer (Ed.), *Science, consciousness, and ultimate reality.* Exeter, UK: Imprint Academic.

Fowers, B. J., & Richardson, F. C. (1996). Why is multiculturalism good? *American Psychologist*, *51*, 609–621.

Fowler, R. C. (2007). *Reestablishing the limits: A response to Turiel and Smetana's commentary.* Unpublished manuscript, Salem State College, MA.

Fox, M. (2003). *Religion, spirituality, and the near-death experience.* New York: Routledge.

Frankena, W. K. (1958). Obligation and motivation in recent moral philosophy. In A. I. Melden (Ed.), *Essays in moral philosophy* (pp. 40–81). Seattle: University of Washington Press.

Frankena, W. K. (1973). *Ethics* (2nd ed.). Englewood Cliffs, NJ: Prentice Hall.

Frankena, W. K. (1980). *Thinking about morality.* Ann Arbor: University of Michigan Press.

Freedman, B. J., Rosenthal, L., Donahoe, C. P., Schlundt, D. G., & McFall, R. M. (1978). A social behavioral analysis of skills deficits in delinquent and nondelinquent adolescent boys. *Journal of Consulting and Clinical Psychology*, *46*, 1148–1462.

French, C. C. (2001). Commentary. *The Lancet*, *358*, 2010–2011.

Fromm, E. (1955). *The sane society.* New York: Holt, Rinehart, & Winston.

Funk & Wagnalls new international dictionary of the English language. (2000). Chicago: World Publishers.

Gannon, T. A., Polaschek, D. L. L., & Ward, T. (2005). Social cognition and sex offenders. In M. McMurran & J. McGuire (Eds.), *Social problem solving and offending: Evidence, evaluation, and evolution* (pp. 223–247). New York: John Wiley & Sons.

Garbarino, J. (1999). *Lost boys: Why our sons turn violent and how we can save them.* New York: The Free Press.

Garmon, L. C., Basinger, K. S., Gregg, V. R., & Gibbs, J. C. (1996). Gender differences in stage and expression of moral judgment. *Merrill-Palmer Quarterly*, *42*, 418–437.

Gergen, K. J. (2001). Psychological science in a postmodern context. *American Psychologist*, *56*, 803–813.

Gibbs, J. C. (1972). *Opinion change after mild and strong prohibitions.* Unpublished doctoral dissertation, Harvard University.

Gibbs, J. C. (1977). Kohlberg's stages of moral judgment: A constructive critique. *Harvard Educational Review*, *47*, 43–61.

Gibbs, J. C. (1979). Kohlberg's moral stage theory: A Piagetian revision. *Human Development*, *22*, 89–112.

Gibbs, J. C. (1985). Moody's versus Siegel's interpretation of the near-death experience: An evaluation based on recent research. *Anabiosis*, *5*, 67–81.

Gibbs, J. C. (1991a). Sociomoral developmental delay and cognitive distortion: Implications for the treatment of antisocial youth. In W. M. Kurtines & J. L. Gewirtz (Eds.), *Handbook of moral behavior and development* (Vol. 3, pp. 95–110). Hillsdale, NJ: Lawrence Erlbaum.

Gibbs, J. C. (1991b). Toward an integration of Kohlberg's and Hoffman's moral development theories. *Human Development*, *34*, 88–104.

Gibbs, J. C. (1994). Fairness and empathy as the foundation for universal moral education. *Comenius*, *14*, 12–23.

Gibbs, J. C. (1997). Surprise—and discovery?—in the near-death experience. *Journal of Near-Death Studies*, *15*, 259–278.

Gibbs, J. C. (1999). God, tragedy, and the near-death experience: Evaluating Kushner's perspectives on theodicy. *Journal of Near-Death Studies*, *17*, 223–259.

Gibbs, J. C. (2003). *Moral development and reality: Beyond the theories of Kohlberg and Hoffman* (1st. ed.). Thousand Oaks, CA: Sage.

Gibbs, J. C. (2004). Moral reasoning training: The values component. In A. P. Goldstein, R. Nensen, M. Kalt, & B. Daleflod (Eds.), *New perspectives on aggression replacement training* (pp. 51–72). Chicester, UK: Wiley.

Gibbs, J. C. (2005). Reply to Michael Sabom's commentary. *Journal of Near-Death Studies, 24,* 105–107.

Gibbs, J. C. (2006a). Reply [to R. Bergman's "Gibbs on Kohlberg on Dewey: An essay review of John C. Gibbs' *Moral Development & Reality*"]. *European Journal of Developmental Psychology, 3,* 312–315.

Gibbs, J. C. (2006b). Should Kohlberg's cognitive developmental approach be replaced with a pragmatic approach? Comment on Krebs and Denton. *Psychological Review, 113,* 666–671.

Gibbs, J. C., Arnold, K. D., Ahlborn, H. H., & Cheesman, F. L. (1984). Facilitation of sociomoral reasoning in delinquents. *Journal of Consulting and Clinical Psychology, 52,* 37–45.

Gibbs, J. C., Arnold, K. D., & Burkhart, J. E. (1984). Sex differences in the expression of moral judgment. *Child Development, 55,* 1040–1043.

Gibbs, J. C., Arnold, K. D., Morgan, R. L., Schwartz, E. S., Gavaghan, M. P., & Tappan, M. B. (1984). Construction and validation of a multiple-choice measure of moral reasoning. *Child Development, 55,* 527–536.

Gibbs, J. C., Barriga, A. Q., & Potter, G. (1992). *The How I Think questionnaire.* Unpublished manuscript, The Ohio State University.

Gibbs, J. C., Barriga, A. Q., & Potter, G. B. (2001). *How I Think (HIT) questionnaire.* Champaign, IL: Research Press.

Gibbs, J. C., Basinger, K. S., & Fuller, D. (1992). *Moral maturity: Measuring the development of sociomoral reflection.* Hillsdale, NJ: Lawrence Erlbaum.

Gibbs, J. C., Basinger, K. S., & Grime, R. L. (2003). Moral judgment maturity: From clinical to standard measures. In S. J. Lopez & C. R. Snyder (Eds.), *Handbook of positive psychological assessment* (pp. 361–373). Washington, DC: American Psychological Association Books.

Gibbs, J. C., Basinger, K. S., Grime, R. L., & Snarey, J. R. (2007). Moral judgment development across cultures: Revisiting Kohlberg's universality claims. *Developmental Review, 27,* 443–500.

Gibbs, J. C., Clark, P. M., Joseph, J. A., Green, J. L., Goodrick, T. S., & Makowski, D. G. (1986). Relations between moral judgment, moral courage, and field independence. *Child Development, 57,* 185–191.

Gibbs, J. C., Kohlberg, L., Colby, A., & Speicher-Dubin, B. (1976). The domain and development of moral judgment: A theory and a method of assessment. In J. R. Meyer (Ed.), *Reflections on values education* (pp. 19–46). Waterloo, Ontario: Wilfrid Laurier University Press.

Gibbs, J. C., Potter, G. B., Barriga, A. Q., & Liau, A. K. (1996). Developing the helping skills and prosocial motivation of aggressive adolescents in peer group programs. *Aggression and Violent Behavior, 1,* 285–305.

Gibbs, J. C., Potter, G. B., DiBiase, A.-M., & Devlin, R. (in press). The EQUIP program: Social perspective-taking for responsible thought and behavior. In B. Glick (Ed.), *Cognitive behavioral interventions for at-risk youth* (2nd ed.). Kingston, NJ: Civic Research Institute.

Gibbs, J. G., Potter, G., & Goldstein, A. P. (1995). *The EQUIP program: Teaching youth to think and act responsibly through a peer-helping approach.* Champaign, IL: Research Press.

Gibbs, J. C., & Schnell, S. V. (1984). Moral development "versus" socialization: A critique. *American Psychologist, 40,* 1071–1080.

Gibbs, J. C., & Schnell, S. V. (1986). *The Opportunities for Role-Taking (ORT) questionnaire.* (Available from John C. Gibbs, Psychology Department, The Ohio State University, 1835 Neil Avenue, Columbus, OH 43210)

Gibbs, J. C., Swillinger, A., Leeman, L. W., Simonian, S. S., Rowland, S., & Jaycox, C. (1995). Inventory of Adolescent Problems—Short Form (IAP-SF). Appendix B in J. C. Gibbs, F. B. Potter, & A. P. Goldstein, *The EQUIP program: Teaching youth to think and act responsibly through a peer-helping approach.* Champaign, IL: Research Press.

Gibbs, J. C., & Whiteford (Mason), M. G. (1989). *The Post-Childhood Opportunities for Role-Taking Measure.* (Available from John C. Gibbs, Psychology Department, The Ohio State University, 1835 Neil Avenue, Columbus, OH 43210)

Gibbs, J. C., Widaman, K. F., & Colby, A. (1982). Construction and validation of a simplified, group-administrable equivalent to the Moral Judgment Interview. *Child Development, 53,* 895–910.

Gielen, U. P., Comunian, A. L., & Antoni, G. (1994). An Italian cross-sectional study of Gibbs's Sociomoral Reflection Measure–Short Form. In A. L. Comunian & U. P. Gielen (Eds.), *Advancing psychology and its applications: International perspectives.* Milan, Italy: Franco-Arneli.

Giesbrecht, N., & Walker, L. (2000). Ego development and the construction of a moral self. *Journal of College Student Development, 41,* 157–171.

Gilligan, C. (1982). *In a different voice: Psychological theory and women's development.* Cambridge, UK: Cambridge University Press.

Glachan, P., & Light, M. (1982). Peer interaction and learning: Can two wrongs make a right? In G. Butterworth & P. Light (Eds.), *Social cognition: Studies of the development of understanding* (pp. 238–262). Sussex, UK: Harvester.

Glassman, M., & Zan, B. (1995). Moral activity and domain theory: An alternative interpretation of research with young children. *Developmental Review, 15,* 434–457.

Glazer, M. P. (2002). Ten whistleblowers: What they did and how they fared. In M. D. Erman and R. J. Lundman (Eds.), *Corporate and governmental deviance: Problems of organizational behavior in contemporary society* (6th ed.; pp. 229–249). New York: Oxford University Press.

Glick, B. (in press). *Cognitive behavioral interventions for at-risk youth* (Vol. 2). Kingston, NJ: Civic Research Institute.

Glick, B., & Gibbs, J. C. (in press). Aggression Replacement Training: A comprehensive intervention for aggressive youth (3rd ed.). Champaign, IL: Research Press.

Gnepp, J. (1983). Children's social sensitivity: Inferring emotions from conflicting cues. *Developmental Psychology, 19,* 805–814.

Golding, W. (1962). *Lord of the flies.* New York: Coward-McCann. (Original work published 1954)

Goldstein, A. P. (1999). *The Prepare curriculum: Teaching prosocial competencies* (Rev. ed.). Champaign, IL: Research Press.

Goldstein, A. P., Glick, B., & Gibbs, J. C. (1998). *Aggression Replacement Training: A comprehensive intervention for aggressive youth* (2nd ed.). Champaign, IL: Research Press.

Goldstein, A. P., Glick, B., Irwin, M. J., Pask-McCartney, C., & Rubama, I. (1989). *Reducing delinquency: Intervention in the community.* New York: Pergamon.

Goldstein, A. P., & McGinnis, E. (1997). *Skillstreaming the adolescent: New strategies and perspectives for teaching prosocial skills* (Rev. ed.). Champaign, IL: Research Press.

Goleman, D. (1995). *Emotional intelligence.* New York: Bantam Books.

Goodall, J. (1990). *Through a window: My thirty years with the chimpanzees of Gombe.* Boston: Houghton Mifflin.

Gopnik, A. (1996). The post-Piaget era. *Psychological Science, 7,* 221–225.

Gopnik, A., & Wellman, H. M. (1994). The 'theory' theory. In L. A. Hirschfeld & S. A. Gelman (Eds.), *Mapping the mind: Domain specificity in cognition and culture* (pp. 257–293). Cambridge, UK: Cambridge University Press.

Gottman, J. M., Jacobson, N. S., Rushe, R. H., Shortt, J. W., Babcock, J., La Taillade, J. J., & Waltz, J. (1995). The relationship between heart rate reactivity, emotionally aggressive behavior, and general violence in batterers. *Journal of Family Psychology, 9,* 227–248.

Gouldner, A. (1960). The norm of reciprocity: A preliminary statement. *American Sociological Review, 25,* 161–179.

Greene, J. D. (2008a). The secret joke of Kant's soul. In W. Sinnott-Armstrong (Ed.), *Moral psychology, vol. 3. The neuroscience of morality: Emotion, brain disorders, and development* (pp. 35–79). Cambridge, MA: The MIT Press.

Greene, J. D. (2008b). Reply to Mikhail and Timmons. In W. Sinnott-Armstrong (Ed.), *Moral psychology, vol. 3. The neuroscience of morality: Emotion, brain disorders, and development* (pp. 105–117). Cambridge, MA: The MIT Press.

Greene, J. D., Morelli, S. A., Lowenberg, K., Nystrom, L. E., & Cohen, J. D. (2008). Cognitive load selectively interferes with utilitarian moral judgment. *Cognition, 107,* 1144–1154.

Greene, J. D., Sommerville, R. B., Nystrom, L. E., Darley, J. M., & Cohen, J. D. (2001). An fMRI investigation of emotional engagement in moral judgment. *Science, 293,* 2105–2108.

Gregg, V. R., Gibbs, J. C., & Basinger, K. S. (1994). Patterns of developmental delay in moral judgment by male and female delinquents. *Merrill-Palmer Quarterly, 40,* 538–553.

Greyson, B. (1983). The Near-Death Experience Scale: Construction, reliability, and validity. *Journal of Nervous and Mental Disease, 171,* 369–375.

Greyson, B. (1992–1993). Near-death experiences and antisuicidal attitudes. *Omega, 26,* 81–89.

Greyson, B. (1998). The incidence of near-death experiences. *Medicine & Psychiatry, 1,* 92–99.

Greyson, B. (2000a). Dissociation in people who have near-death experiences: Out of their bodies or out of their minds? *The Lancet, 355,* 460–463.

Greyson, B. (2000b). Near-death experiences. In E. Cardena, S. J. Lynn, & S. Krippner (Eds.), *Varieties of anomalous experience: Examining the scientific evidence* (pp. 315–352). Washington, DC: American Psychological Association.

Greyson, B. (2001, August). *Are NDErs out of their bodies or out of their minds?* Paper presented at the meeting of the International Association of Near-Death Studies, West Hartford, CT.

Greyson, B. (2007). Consistency of near-death experience accounts over two decades: Are reports embellished over time? *Resuscitation, 73,* 407–411.

Greyson, B., & Bush, N. E. (1992). Distressing near-death experiences. *Psychiatry, 55,* 95–110.

Greyson, B., & Harris, B. (1987). Clinical approaches to the near-death experiencer. *Journal of Near-Death Studies, 6,* 41–52.

Grim, P., White, S., & Kohlberg, L. (1968). Some relationships between conscience and attentional processes. *Journal of Personality and Social Psychology, 8,* 239–253.

Gross, P., & Leavitt, N. (1994) *Higher superstition: The academic left and its quarrels with science.* Baltimore: Johns Hopkins University Press.

Grossman, D. L. (1995). *On killing: The psychological cost of learning to kill in war and society.* Boston: Little, Brown.

Groth, A. N., & Birnsbaum, J. J. (1979). *Men who rape.* New York: Plenum.

Guisinger, S., & Blatt, S. J. (1994). Individuality and relatedness: Evolution of a fundamental dialectic. *American Psychologist, 49,* 104–111.

Haaga, D. A., & Beck, A. T. (1994). Perspectives on depressive realism: Implications for cognitive theory of depression. *Behaviour Research and Therapy, 33*, 41–48.

Hafer, C. L., & Begue, L. (2005). Experimental research on Just-World theory: Problems, developments, and future challenges. *Psychological Review, 131*, 128–167.

Haggbloom, S. J., Warnick, R., Warnick, J. E., Jones, V. K., Yarbrough, G. L., Russell, T. M., et al. (2000). The 100 most eminent psychologists of the twentieth century. *Review of General Psychology, 6*, 139–152.

Haidt, J. (2003). The moral emotions. In R. J. Davidson, K. R. Scherer, & H. H. Goldsmith (Eds.), *Handbook of affective sciences* (pp. 852–870). Oxford, UK: Oxford University Press.

Haidt, J., & Bjorklund, F. (2008a). Social intuitionists answer six questions about moral psychology. In W. Sinnott-Armstrong, *Moral psychology, Vol. 2. The cognitive science of morality: Intuition and diversity* (pp. 181–218). Cambridge, MA: The MIT Press.

Haidt, J., & Bjorklund, F. (2008b). Social intuitionists reason, in conversation. In W. Sinnott-Armstrong, *Moral psychology, Vol. 2. The cognitive science of morality: Intuition and diversity* (pp. 241–254). Cambridge, MA: The MIT Press.

Halford, G. S., & Andrews, G. (2006). Reasoning and problem-solving. In W. Damon & R. M. Lerner (Series Ed.) & D. Kuhn & R. S. Siegler (Vol. Ed.), *Handbook of child psychology, Volume 2: Cognition, perception, and language* (6th ed.) (pp. 557–608). New York: John Wiley & Sons.

Hamilton, W. D. (1971). Selection of selfish and altruistic behavior in some extreme models. In J. F. Eisenberg & W. S. Dillon (Eds.), *Man and beast: Comparative social behavior* (pp. 57–91). Washington, DC: Smithsonian Institute Press.

Hammock, G. S., Rosen, S., Richardson, D. R., & Bernstein, S. (1989). Aggression as equity restoration. *Journal of Research in Personality, 23*, 398–409.

Haritos-Fatouros, M. (2003). *The psychological origins of institutionalized torture.* New York: Routledge.

Harkness, S., Edwards, C. P., & Super, C. (1981). Social roles and moral reasoning: A case study in a rural African community. *Developmental Psychology, 17*, 595–603.

Hart, D., Atkins, R., & Donnelly, T. M. (2006). Community service and moral development. In M. Killen & J. G. Smetana (Eds.), *Handbook of moral development* (pp. 633–656). Mahwah, NJ: Erlbaum.

Harter, S. (1999). *The construction of self: A developmental perspective.* New York: Guilford Press.

Harter, S. (2006). The self. In W. Damon & R. M. Lerner (Series Eds.) & N. Eisenberg (Vol. Ed.), *Handbook of child psychology: Vol. 3. Social, emotional, and personality development* (6th ed., pp. 505–570). New York: John Wiley.

Hauser, M. D. (2006). *Moral minds: How nature designed our universal sense of right and wrong.* New York: HarperCollins.

Havighurst, H. J., & Taba, H. (1949). *Adolescent character and personality.* New York: John Wiley.

Heide, K. M. (2003). Youth homicide: A review of the literature and a blueprint for action. *International Journal of Offender Therapy and Comparative Criminology, 47*, 6–36.

Heider, F. (1958). *The psychology of interpersonal relations.* New York: John Wiley.

Helwig, C. C., & Prencipe, A. (1999). Children's judgments of flags and flag-burning. *Child Development, 70*, 132–143.

Helwig, C. C., Turiel, E., & Nucci, L. P. (1996). The virtues and vices of developmental theorists. *Developmental Review, 16*, 69–107.

Henggeler, S. W., Schoenwald, S. K., Borduin, C. M., Rowland, M. D., & Cunningham, P. B. (1998). *Multisystemic treatment of antisocial behavior in children and adolescents.* New York: Guilford.

Herbert, N. (1985). *Quantum reality: Beyond the new physics.* New York: Anchor.

Heyert, M. (1976). The new kid. In R. C. Pooley, E. Daniel, E. J. Farrell, A. H. Grommon, & O. S. Niles (Eds.), *Projection in literature* (pp. 216–226). New York: Scott Foresman.

Hickling, A. K., & Wellman, H. M. (2001). Emergence of children's causal explanations and theories: Evidence from everyday conversation. *Developmental Psychology, 37,* 668–683.

Hildebran, D., & Pilthers, W. D. (1989). Enhancing offender empathy for sexual-abuse victims. In D. R. Laws (Ed.), *Relapse prevention with sex offenders* (pp. 236–243). New York: Guilford.

Hill, T. E., Jr. (1996). Moral dilemmas, gaps, and residues: A Kantian perspective. In H. E. Mason (Ed.), *Moral dilemmas and moral theory* (pp. 167–188). New York: Oxford University Press.

Hilton, N. Z. (1993). Childhood sexual victimization and lack of empathy in child molesters: Explanation or excuse? *International Journal of Offender Therapy and Comparative Criminology, 27,* 287–296.

Hoffman, M. L. (1960). Power assertion by the parent and its impact on the child. *Child Development, 31,* 129–143.

Hoffman, M. L. (1963). Parent discipline and the child's consideration for others. *Child Development, 13,* 90–126.

Hoffman, M. L. (1970). Moral development. In P. H. Mussen (Ed.), Carmichael's manual of child psychology (Vol. 2, 3rd ed., pp. 261–359). New York: John Wiley.

Hoffman, M. L. (1981a). Is altruism part of human nature? *Journal of Personality and Social Psychology, 40,* 121–137.

Hoffman, M. L. (1981b). Perspectives on the difference between understanding people and understanding things: The role of affect. In J. H. Flavell & L. Ross (Eds.), *Social cognitive development: Frontiers and possible futures* (pp. 67–81). Cambridge, UK: Cambridge University Press.

Hoffman, M. L. (1983). Affective and cognitive processes in moral internalization: An information processing approach. In E. T. Higgins, D. Ruble, & W. Hartup (Eds.), *Social cognition and social development: A socio-cultural perspective* (pp. 236–274). New York: John Wiley.

Hoffman, M. L. (1986). Affect, cognition, and motivation. In R. M. Sorrentino & E. T. Higgins (Eds.), *Handbook of motivation and personality: Foundations of social behavior* (pp. 244–280). New York: Guilford.

Hoffman, M. L. (1988). Moral development. In M. H. Bornstein & M. E. Lamb (Eds.), *Developmental psychology: An advanced textbook* (2nd ed., pp. 497–548). Hillsdale, NJ: Lawrence Erlbaum.

Hoffman, M. L. (1991). Toward an integration: Commentary. *Human Development, 34,* 105–110.

Hoffman, M. L. (2000). *Empathy and moral development: Implications for caring and justice.* Cambridge, UK: Cambridge University Press.

Hoffman, M. L. (2008). Empathy and prosocial behavior. In M. Lewis, J. Haviland-Jones, & Lisa F. Barrett (Eds.), *Handbook of emotions* (3rd ed.; pp. 440–455). New York: Guildford Press.

Hoffman, M. L., & Saltzstein, H. D. (1967). Parent discipline and the child's moral development. *Journal of Personality and Social Psychology, 5,* 45–57.

Hoffner, C., & Badzinski, D. M. (1989). Children's integration of facial and situational cues to emotion. *Child Development, 60,* 411–422.

Hoffner, C., Cantor, J., & Thorson, E. (1989). Children's responses to conflicting auditory and visual features of a televised narrative. *Human Communication Research, 16,* 256–278.

Horn, M., Shively, R., & Gibbs, J. C. (2007). *EQUIPPED for Life* (3rd ed.; therapeutic board game). Champaign, IL: Research Press.

Hudson, J. A., & Nelson, K. (1983). Effects of script structure on children's story recall. *Developmental Psychology, 19,* 625–635.

Hunter, N., & Kelly, C. K. (1986). Examination of the validity of the Adolescent Problems Inventory among incarcerated juvenile delinquents. *Journal of Consulting Clinical Psychology, 54,* 301–302.

Hurley, D. (1988, January). Getting help from helping. *Psychology Today,* pp. 63 ff.

Husain, E. (2007). *The Islamist: Why I joined radical Islam in Britain, what I saw inside, and why I left.* New York: Penguin Books.

Hyman, R. (2001). Anomalous experience in a mundane world [Review of the book *Varieties of anomalous experience: Examining the scientific evidence*]. *Contemporary Psychology APA Review of Books, 46,* 453–456.

Jacobson, D. (2008). Does intuitionism flatter morality or challenge it? In W. Sinnott-Armstrong (Ed.), Moral Psychology, Vol. 2. *The cognitive science of morality: Intuition and diversity* (pp. 219–232). Cambridge, MA: The MIT Press.

Jaffee, S., & Hyde, J. S. (2000). Gender differences in moral orientation: A meta-analysis. *Psychological Bulletin, 126,* 703–726.

Jakubowski, P., & Lange, A. J. (1978). *The assertive option: Your rights and responsibilities.* Champaign, IL: Research Press.

James, S. A. (1994). Reconciling international human rights and cultural relativism: The case of female circumcision. *Bioethics, 8,* 1–26.

James, W. (1958). *The varieties of religious experiences: A study in human nature.* New York: Mentor Books. (Original work published 1903)

Janssens, J. M. A. M., & Gerris, J. R. M. (1992). Childrearing, empathy, and prosocial development. In J. M. A. M. Janssens & J. R. M. Gerris (Eds.), *Child rearing: Influence on prosocial and moral development* (pp. 57–75). Amsterdam: Swets & Qeitlinger.

Jensen, L. A. (2008). Through two lenses: A cultural-developmental approach to moral psychology. *Developmental Review, 28,* 289–315.

Jones, M. (1953). *The therapeutic community.* New York: Basic Books.

Kahn, T., & Chambers, H. J. (1991). Assessing recidivism risk with juvenile sex offenders. *Child Welfare, 70,* 333–345.

Kane, M. J., Hambrick, D. Z., & Conway, A. R. A. (2005). Working memory capacity and fluid intelligence are strongly related constructs: Comment on Ackerman, Beier, and Boyle (2005). *Psychological Bulletin, 131,* 66–71.

Kane, R. (1994). *Through the moral maze: Searching for absolute values in a pluralistic world.* New York: Paragon House.

Kant, I. (1993). *Grounding for the metaphysics of ethics* (J. E. Ellington, Trans.). Indianapolis, IN: Hackett. (Original work published 1785)

Kazdin, A. (1995). *Conduct disorders in childhood and adolescence* (2nd ed.). Thousand Oaks, CA: Sage.

Keasy, C. B. (1971). Social participation as a factor in the moral development of preadolescents. *Developmental Psychology, 5,* 216–230.

Keenan, T., & Ward, T. (2003). Developmental antecedents of sexual offending. In T. Ward, D. R. Laws, & S. M. Hudson (Eds.), *Sexual deviance: Issues and controversies.* Thousand Oaks, CA: Sage.

Kegan, R. (1982). *The evolving self: Problem and process in human development.* Cambridge, MA: Harvard University Press.

Kellehear, A. (1996). *Experiences near death: Beyond medicine and religion.* New York: Oxford University Press.

Kellehear, A. (2008). Census of non-western near-death experiences to 2005: Overview of the current data. *Journal of Near-Death Studies, 26,* 249–265.

Kelly, E. W., Greyson, B., & Kelly, E. F. (2007). Unusual experiences near death and related phenomena. In E. F. Kelly, E. W. Kelly, A. C. Crabtree, A. Gauld, M. Grosso, & B. Greyson (Eds.). *Irreducible mind: Toward a psychology for the 21st century* (pp. 367–421). Lanham, MD: Rowman & Littlefield.

Kelly, G. (1963). *A theory of personality: The psychology of personal constructs.* Oxford, UK: W. W. Norton.

Kelman, H. C. (1958). Compliance, identification, and internalization: Three processes of attitude change. *Journal of Conflict Resolution, 2,* 51–60.

Kelman, H. C. (1973). Violence without restraint: Reflections on the dehumanization of victims and victimizers. *Journal of Social Issues, 29,* 25–61.

Kelman, H. C., & Hamilton, V. L. (1989). *Crimes of obedience: Toward a social psychology of authority and responsibility.* New Haven, CT: Yale University Press.

Kielburger, C. (1998). *Free the children: A young man fights against child labor and proves that children can change the world.* New York: HarperCollins.

Kielburger, C., & Kielburger, M. (2006). *Me to we: Finding meaning in a material world.* New York: Simon & Schuster.

Klahr, D. (1982). Nonmonotone assessment of monotone development: An information processing analysis. In S. Strauss (Ed.), *U-shaped behavioral growth* (pp. 63–86). New York: Academic Press.

Kochanska, G. (1995). Children's temperament, mother's discipline, and security of attachment: Multiple pathways to emerging internalization. *Child Development, 66,* 597–615.

Kohlberg, L. (1958). *The development of modes of moral thinking and choice in the years ten to sixteen.* Unpublished doctoral dissertation, University of Chicago.

Kohlberg, L. (1963). The development of children's orientation toward a moral order: 1. Sequence in the development of moral thought. *Vita Humana, 6,* 11–33.

Kohlberg, L. (1964). The development of moral character and ideology. In M. L. Hoffman (Ed.), *Review of child development research* (Vol. 1, pp. 383–431). New York: Russell Sage Foundation.

Kohlberg, L. (1971). From *is* to *ought:* How to commit the naturalistic fallacy and get away with it in the study of moral development. In T. Mischel (Ed.), *Cognitive development and epistemology* (pp. 151–235). New York: Academic Press.

Kohlberg, L. (1973a). The claim to moral adequacy of a highest stage of moral judgment. *Journal of Philosophy, 70,* 630–646.

Kohlberg, L. (1973b). Continuities in childhood and adult moral development revisited. In P. B. Baltes & K. W. Schaie (Eds.), *Lifespan developmental psychology: Personality and socialization* (pp. 179–204). New York: Academic Press.

Kohlberg, L. (1976). Moral stages and moralization: The cognitive-developmental approach. In T. Lickona (Ed.), *Moral development and behavior* (pp. 31–53). New York: Holt, Rinehart, & Winston.

Kohlberg, L. (1984). *Essays on moral development: Vol. 2. The psychology of moral development.* San Francisco: Harper & Row.

Kohlberg, L. (1991). My personal search for universal morality. In L. Kuhmerker (Ed.), *The Kohlberg legacy for the helping professions* (pp. 11–17). Birmingham, AL: R. E. P. Books.

Kohlberg, L., Boyd, D. R., & Levine, C. (1990). The return of Stage 6: Its principle and moral point of view. In T. Wren (Ed.), *The moral domain: Essays in the ongoing discussion between philosophy and the social sciences* (pp. 151–181). Cambridge: MIT Press.

Kohlberg, L., & Candee, D. (1984). The relationship of moral judgment to moral action. In L. Kohlberg (Ed.), *Essays on moral development: Vol. 2. The psychology of moral development* (pp. 498–581). New York: Harper & Row.

Kohlberg, L., Colby, A., Gibbs, J. C., & Lieberman, M. (1983). A longitudinal study of moral judgment. *Monographs of the Society for Research in Child Development*, 48(1–2, Serial No. 200).

Kohlberg, L., & Higgins, A. (1987). School democracy and social interaction. In W. M. Kurtines & J. L. Gewirtz (Eds.), *Moral development through social interaction* (pp. 102–108). New York: Wiley-Interscience.

Kohlberg, L., & Kramer, R. (1969). Continuities and discontinuities in childhood and adult moral development. *Human Development*, 12, 93–120.

Kohlberg, L., & Power, C. (1981). Moral development, religious development, and the question of a seventh stage. *Zygon*, 16, 203–259.

Kohlberg, L., & Ryncarz, R. A. (1990). Beyond justice reasoning: Moral development and consideration of a seventh stage. In C. N. Alexander & E. J. Langer (Eds.), *Higher stages of human development: Perspectives on adult growth* (pp. 191–207). New York: Oxford University Press.

Kopelman, L. M. (2001). Female circumcision/genital mutilation and ethical relativism. In P. K. Moser & T. L. Carson (Eds.), *Moral relativism: A reader* (pp. 307–326). New York: Oxford University Press.

Kotlowitz, A. (2008, May 4). If gang shootings and revenge killing were an infectious disease, how would you stop it? A Chicago epidemiologist thinks he has the answer. *The New York Times Sunday Magazine*, pp. 52–59, 100–102.

Krebs, D. L. (2008). Morality: An evolutionary account. *Perspectives on Psychological Science*, 3, 149–172.

Krebs, D. L., & Denton, K. (2005). Toward a more pragmatic approach to morality: A critical evaluation of Kohlberg's model. *Psychological Review*, 112, 629–649.

Krebs, D. L., & Denton, K. (2006). Explanatory limitations of cognitive developmental approaches to morality. *Psychological Review*, 113, 672–675.

Krebs, D., Vermuelen, S. C. A., Carpendale, J. I., & Denton, K. (1991). Structural and situational influences on moral judgment: An interaction between stage and dilemma. In W. M. Kurtines & J. L. Gewirtz (Eds.), *Handbook of moral behavior and development: Vol. 2. Research* (pp. 139–170). Hillsdale, NJ: Lawrence Erlbaum.

Krettenauer, T., & Edelstein, W. (1999). From substages to moral types and beyond: An analysis of core criteria for morally autonomous judgments. *International Journal of Behavioral Development*, 23, 899–920.

Krevans, J. A., & Gibbs, J. C. (1991, April). *Relations between inductive discipline, empathy, and prosocial behavior.* Paper presented at the meeting of the Society for Research in Child Development, Seattle, WA.

Krevans, J., & Gibbs, J. C. (1996). Children's use of inductive discipline: Relations to children's empathy and prosocial behavior. *Child Development*, 67, 3264–3277.

Kruger, A. (1992). The effects of peer and adult-child transactive discussions on moral reasoning. *Merrill-Palmer Quarterly*, 38, 191–211.

Kruger, A. C., & Tomasello, M. (1986). Transactive discussions with peers and adults. *Developmental Psychology*, 22, 681–685.

Kuhn, D. (1972). Mechanisms of change in the development of cognitive structures. *Child Development, 43,* 833–844.

Kuhn, D. (1997). The view from giants' shoulders. In L. Smith, J. Dockrell, & P. Tomlinson (Eds.), *Piaget, Vygotsky, and beyond: Future issues for developmental psychology and education* (pp. 246–259). New York: Routledge.

Kuhn, D., & Franklin, S. (2006). The second decade: What develops (and how). In W. Damon & R. M. Lerner (Series Ed.) & D. Kuhn & R. S. Siegler (Vol. Eds.), *Handbook of child psychology, Volume 2: Cognition, perception, and language* (6th ed.) (pp. 953–993). New York: John Wiley & Sons.

Kushner, H. (1986). *When all you've ever wanted isn't enough: The search for a life that matters.* New York: Simon & Schuster.

LaBerge, S., & Gackenbach, J. (2000). Lucid dreaming. In E. Cardena, S. J. Lynn, & S. Krippner (Eds.), *Varieties of anomalous experience: Examining the scientific evidence* (pp. 151–182). Washington, DC: American Psychological Association.

Lacayo, R. (1998, April 6). Toward the root of evil. *Time,* pp. 34–35.

Lacayo, R., & Ripley, A. (2002, December 30). Persons of the year. *Time,* pp. 32–33.

Lacey, M. (2002, January 6). Kenya's ban on female ritual divides a family. *The New York Times,* p. 4.

Landenberger, N., & Lipsey, M. (2005). The positive effects of cognitive-behavioral programs for offenders: A meta-analysis of factors associated with effective treatment. *Journal of Experimental Criminology, 1,* 451–476.

Lapsley, D. R., & Narvaez, D. (2006), Character education. In W. Damon & R. M. Lerner (Series Eds.) and K. A. Renninger & I. E. Sigel (Vol. Eds.), *Handbook of child psychology: Vol. 4. Child psychology in practice* (6th ed., pp. 248–296).

Larden, M., Melin, L., Holst, U., & Langstrom, N. (2006). Moral judgment, cognitive distortions, and empathy in incarcerated delinquent and community control adolescents. *Psychology, Crime, and Law, 12,* 453–462.

Laszlo, E. (2003). *The connectivity hypothesis: Foundations of an integral science of quantum, cosmos, life, and consciousness.* Albany: State University of New York Press.

Latane, B., & Darley, J. J. (1970). *The unresponsive bystander: Why doesn't he help?* New York: Appleton.

Laupa, M. (2000). Similarities and differences in children's reasoning about morality and mathematics. In M. Laupa (Ed.), *Rights and wrongs: How children and young adults evaluate the world* (pp. 19–32). San Francisco: Jossey-Bass/Pfeiffer.

Lawrence, J. A., & Valsiner, J. (1993). Conceptual roots of internalization: From transmission to transformation. *Human Development, 36,* 150–167.

Lazar, A., & Torney-Purta, J. (1991). The development of the subconcepts of death in young children: A short-term longitudinal study. *Child Development, 62,* 1321–1333.

Leeman, L. W., Gibbs, J. C., & Fuller, D. (1993). Evaluation of a multi-component group treatment program for juvenile delinquents. *Aggressive Behavior, 19,* 281–292.

Lerner, M. J. (1980). *Belief in a just world: A fundamental delusion.* New York: Plenum.

Levitt, M. J., Weber, R. A., Clark, M. C., & McDonnell, P. (1985). Reciprocity of exchange in toddler sharing behavior. *Developmental Psychology, 21,* 122–123.

Lewis, C. S. (1943). *Mere Christianity.* New York: Macmillan.

Lewis, C. S. (1962). *The problem of pain.* New York: Macmillan.

Lewis, M., & Brooks-Gunn, J. (1979). *Social cognition and the acquisition of self.* New York: Plenum.

Liau, A. K., Barriga, A., & Gibbs, J. C. (1998). Relations between self-serving cognitive distortions and overt vs. covert antisocial behavior in adolescents. *Aggressive Behavior, 24*, 335–346.

Liau, A. K., Shively, R., Horn, M., Landau, J., Barriga, A. Q., & Gibbs, J. C. (2004). Effects of psychoeducation for offenders in a community correctional facility. *Journal of Community Psychology, 32*, 543–553.

Lickona, T. (1983). *Raising good children.* New York: Bantam.

Lillard, A. S., & Flavell, J. H. (1990). Young children's preference for mental state versus behavioral descriptions of human action. *Child Development, 61*, 731–741.

Lindley, D. (1996). *Where does the weirdness go? Why quantum physics is strange, but not as strange as you think.* New York: Basic Books.

Ling, L. (Host). (2008). The moment of death [Television series episode]. In K. Gahagan (Coordinating Producer), *Explorer.* Washington, D.C.: National Geographic Television & Film News Corporation.

Lipsey, M. W., Chapman, G. L., & Landenberger, N. A. (2001). Cognitive-behavioral programs for offenders. *Annals of the American Academy of Political & Social Sciences, 578*, 144–157.

Litwack, S. E. (1976). *The use of the helper therapy principle to increase therapeutic effectiveness and reduce therapeutic resistance: Structured learning therapy with resistant adolescents.* Unpublished doctoral dissertation, Syracuse University, NY.

Livesley, W. J., & Bromley, D. B. (1973). *Person perception in childhood and adolescence.* London: Wiley.

Lochman, J. E., & Dodge, K. A. (1998). Distorted perceptions in dyadic interactions of aggressive and nonaggressive boys: Effects of prior expectations, context, and peer age. *Development and Psychopathology, 10*, 495–512.

Lorimer, D. (1990). *Whole in one: The near-death experience and the ethic of interconnectedness.* London: Penguin.

Lourenco, O. (2000). The aretaic domain and its relation to the deontic domain in moral reasoning. In M. Laupa (Ed.), *Rights and wrongs: How children and young adults evaluate the world* (pp. 47–62). San Francisco: Jossey-Bass/Pfeiffer.

Lourenco, O., & Machado, A. (1996). In defense of Piaget's theory: A reply to 10 common criticisms. *Psychological Review, 103*, 143–154.

Lykken, D. T. (1995). *The antisocial personalities.* Hillsdale, NJ: Lawrence Erlbaum.

Maass, P. (2001, October 21). Emroz Khan is having a bad day. *New York Times Magazine,* pp. 48–51.

Maccoby, E. E. (1980). *Social development: Psychological growth and the parent-child relationship.* New York: Harcourt Brace.

Maccoby, E. E. (1983). Let's not overattribute to the attribution process: Comments on social cognition and behavior. In E. T. Higgins, D. N. Ruble, & W. W. Hartup (Eds.), *Social cognition and social development: A sociocultural perspective* (pp. 356–370). New York: Cambridge University Press.

MacIntyre, A. (1981). *After virtue.* Notre Dame, IN: University of Notre Dame Press.

MacIntyre, A. (1988). *Whose justice, which rationality?* Notre Dame, IN: University of Notre Dame Press.

Maclean, P. B. (1985). Brain evolution relating to family, play, and the separation call. *Archives of General Psychiatry, 42*, 405–417.

Markus, H., & Wurf, E. (1987). The dynamic self-concept: A social psychological perspective. *Annual Review of Psychology, 38*, 299–337.

Marshall, W. L., Anderson, D., & Fernandez, Y. (Eds.). (1999). Cognitive behavioral treatment of sexual offenders. Chichester, UK: Wiley.

Martin, C. L. (2000). Cognitive theories of gender development. In T. Eckes & H. M. Trautner (Eds.), *The developmental social psychology of gender* (pp. 91–122). Mahwah, NJ: Lawrence Erlbaum.

Martin, G. B., & Clark, R. D. (1982). Distress crying in infants: Species and peer specificity. *Developmental Psychology, 18*, 3–9.

Mason, M. G., & Gibbs, J. C. (1993a). Role-taking opportunities and the transition to advanced moral judgment. *Moral Education Forum, 18*, 1–12.

Mason, M. G., & Gibbs, J. C. (1993b). Social perspective-taking and moral judgment among college students. *Journal of Adolescent Research, 8*, 109–123.

Mathabane, M. (2002, July 5). The cycle of revenge can be broken. *New York Times*, p. A21.

McCorkle, L. W., Elias, A., & Bixby, F. L. (1958). *The Highfields story: An experimental treatment project for youthful offenders.* New York: Holt.

McCrady, F., Kaufman, K., Vasey, M. W., Barriga, A. Q., Devlin, R. S., & Gibbs, J. C. (2008). It's all about me: A brief report of incarcerated adolescent sex offenders' generic and sex-specific cognitive distortions. *Sexual Abuse: A Journal of Research and Treatment, 20*, 261–271.

McGinnis, E., & Goldstein, A. P. (1997). *Skillstreaming the elementary school child: New strategies and perspectives for teaching prosocial skills* (Rev. ed.). Champaign, IL: Research Press.

Meichenbaum, D. H. (1990). Paying homage: Providing challenges. *Psychological Inquiry, 1*, 96–99.

Mendelson, E. F., Quinn, M., Dutton, S., & Seewonarain, K. (1988). A community treatment service for sex offenders: An account at two years. *Bulletin of the Royal College of Psychiatrists, 12*, 416–421.

Menon, M. [Madhavi], Tobin, D. D., Corby, B. C., Menon, M., Hodges, E. V. E., & Perry, D. G. (2007). The developmental costs of high self-esteem for antisocial children. *Child Development, 78*, 1627–1639.

Metcalfe, J., & Mischel, W. (1999). A hot/cool-system analysis of delay of gratification: Dynamics of willpower. *Psychological Review, 106*, 3–19.

Michel, L., & Herbeck, D. (2001). *American terrorist: Timothy McVeigh & the Oklahoma City bombing.* New York: HarperCollins.

Miller, J. G. (1986). Early cross-cultural commonalities in social explanation. *Developmental Psychology, 22*, 514–520.

Miller, M. (1987). Argumentation and cognition. In M. Hickman (Ed.), *Social and functional approaches to language and thought* (pp. 225–250). London: Academic Press.

Miller, P. H., & Aloise, P. A. (1989). Young children's understanding of the psychological causes of behavior: A review. *Children Development, 60*, 257–285.

Miller, S. A. (2007). *Developmental research methods* (3rd ed.). Thousand Oaks, CA: Sage.

Miller, S. A., Custer, W. L., & Nassau, G. (2000). Children's understanding of the necessity of logically necessary truths. *Cognitive Development, 15*, 383–403.

Mischel, H. N., & Mischel, W. (1983). The development of children's knowledge of self-control strategies. *Child Development, 54*, 603–619.

Moody, R. A. (1975). *Life after life.* New York: Bantam.

Morris, B. J., & Sloutsky, V. (2001). Children's solutions of logical versus empirical problems: What's missing and what develops? *Cognitive Development, 16*, 907–928.

Morse, M. (1990). *Closer to the light: Learning from children's near-death experiences.* New York: Villard.

Morse, M. (1992). *Transformed by the light: The powerful effect of near-death experiences on people's lives*. New York: Villard.

Moshman, D. (1998). Cognitive development beyond childhood. In W. Damon (Series Ed.) & D. Kuhn & R. S. Siegler (Vol. Eds.), *Handbook of child psychology: Vol. 2. Cognition, perception, and language* (5th ed., pp. 947–978). New York: John Wiley.

Moshman, D. (2004). False moral identity: Self-serving denial in the maintenance of moral self-conceptions. In D. Lapsley & M. Narvaez (Eds.), *Morality, self, and identity* (pp. 83–110). Mahwah, NJ: Lawrence Erlbaum.

Moshman, D. (2005). *Adolescent psychological development: Rationality, morality, and identity* (2nd ed.). Mahwah, NJ: Lawrence Erlbaum.

Moshman, D. (2007). Us and them: Identity and genocide. *Identity: An International Journal of Theory and Research, 7*, 115–135.

Moshman, D. (2008). Social equations [essay review of C. Wainryb, J. G. Smetana, & E. Turiel (Eds.), Social development, social inequality, and social justice]. *Journal of Applied Developmental Psychology, 51*, 279–281.

Moskowitz, G. B., Gollwitzer, P. M., Wasel, W., & Schaal, B. (1999). Preconscious control of stereotype activation through chronic egalitarian goals. *Journal of Personality and Social Psychology, 77*, 167–184.

Mueller, E., & Brenner, J. (1977). The origins and social skill and interaction among play-group toddlers. *Child Development, 48*, 854–861.

Murphy, W. D. (1990). Assessment and modification of cognitive distortions in sex offenders. In W. L. Marshall, D. R. Laws, & H. E. Barbaree (Eds.), *Handbook of sexual assault: Issues, theories, and treatment of the offender* (pp. 331–342). New York: Plenum.

Murray, F. B. (1982). Teaching through social conflict. *Contemporary Educational Psychology, 7*, 257–271.

Mustakova-Possardt, E. (2000). Critical consciousness and its ontogeny in the life span. In M. E. Miller & A. N. Weiss (Eds.), *Spirituality, ethics, and relationship—Adult clinical and theoretical explorations* (pp. 85–109). Madison, CT: Psychosocial Press.

Narvaez, D. (2008). Triune ethics: The neurobiological roots of our multiple moralities. *New Ideas in Psychology, 26*, 95–119.

Narvaez, D., & Rest, J. (1995). The four components of acting morally. In W. M. Kurtines & J. L. Gewirtz (Eds.), *Moral development: An introduction* (pp. 385–400). Needham Heights, MA: Allyn & Bacon.

Nas, C., Brugman, D., & Koops, W. (2005). Effects of a multicomponent peer intervention program for juvenile delinquents on moral judgment, cognitive distortions, social skills, and recidivism. *Psychology, Crime, & Law, 11*, 1–14.

National Institute on Drug Abuse. (1993). *Recovery training and self-help: Relapse prevention and aftercare for drug addicts* (NIDA Publication No. 93–3521). Rockville, MD: National Institute on Drug Abuse.

Neisser, U. (1976). *Cognition and reality: Principles and implications of cognitive psychology*. San Francisco: W. H. Freeman.

Neisser, U. (1992). Computers can't think. In B. Slife & J. Rubinstein (Eds.), *Taking sides: Clashing views on controversial psychological issues* (7th. ed., pp. 135–142). Guilford, CT: Dushkin.

Nelson, J. R., Smith, D. J., & Dodd, J. (1990). The moral reasoning of juvenile delinquents: A meta analysis. *Journal of Abnormal Child Psychology, 18*, 231–239.

Nelson, K. (1981). Social cognition in a script framework. In J. H. Flavell & L. Ross (Eds.), *Social cognitive development: Frontiers and possible futures* (pp. 97–118). Cambridge, UK: Cambridge University Press.

Niles, W. J. (1986). Effects of a moral development discussion group on delinquent and predelinquent boys. *Journal of Counseling Psychology, 33*, 45–51.

Noam, G. G. (1998). Clinical-developmental psychology: Toward developmentally differentiated interventions. In W. Damon (Series Ed.) & I. E. Sigel & K. A. Renninger (Vol. Eds.), *Handbook of child psychology: Vol. 4. Child psychology in practice* (5th ed., pp. 585–634). New York: John Wiley.

Noddings, N. (1984). *Caring: A feminine approach to ethics & moral education.* Berkeley: University of California Press.

Novaco, R. W. (1975). *Anger control: The development and evaluation of an experimental treatment.* Lexington, MA: Lexington Books.

Noyes, R., & Kletti, R. (1977). Panoramic memory: A response to the threat of death. *Omega, 8*, 181–194.

Nussbaum, M. C. (1999). Judging other cultures: The case of genital mutilation. In M. C. Nussbaum (Ed.), *Sex & social justice* (pp. 118–129). New York: Oxford University Press.

Oliner, S., & Oliner, P. (1988). *The altruistic personality.* New York: Free Press.

Orobio de Castro, B., Veerman, J. W., Koops, W., Bosch, J. D., & Monshouwer, J. J. (2002). Hostile attribution of intent and aggressive behavior: A meta-analysis. *Child Development, 73*, 916–934.

Osgood, D. W., Gruber, E., Archer, M. A., & Newcomb, T. M. (1985). Autonomy for inmates: Counterculture or cooptation? *Criminal Justice and Behavior, 12*, 71–89.

Owens, J. E., Cook, E. W., & Stevenson, I. (1990). Features of "near-death experience" in relation to whether or not patients were near death. *Lancet, 336*, 1175–1177.

Paciello, M., Fida, R., Tramontano, Lupinetti, C., & Caprara, G. V. (2008). Stability and change of moral disengagement and its impact on aggression and violence in late adolescence. *Child Development, 79*, 1288–1309.

Palmer, E. J. (2003). *Offending behavior: Moral reasoning, criminal content, and the rehabilitation of offenders.* Devon, UK: Willan Publishing.

Palmer, E. J., & Hollin, C. R. (1998). A comparison of patterns of moral development in young offenders and non-offenders. *Legal and Criminological Psychology, 3*, 225–235.

Paris, S., & Upton, L. (1976). Children's memory for inferential relationships in prose. *Child Development, 47*, 660–668.

Parke, R. D., & Buriel, R. (2006). Socialization in the family: Ethnic and ecological perspectives. In W. Damon & R. M. Lerner (Series Eds.) & N. Eisenberg (Vol. Ed.), *Handbook of child psychology: Vol. 3. Cognition, perception, and language* (6th ed., pp. 429–504). New York: John Wiley.

Parnia, S. (2006). *What happens when we die: A groundbreaking study into the nature of life and death.* Carlsbad, CA: Hay House.

Parnia, S., & Fenwick, P. (2002). Near death experiences in cardiac arrest: Visions of a dying brain or visions of a new science of consciousness? *Resuscitation, 52*, 5–11.

Parnia, S., Spearpoint, K., & Fenwick, P. B. (2007). Near death experiences, cognitive function, and psychological outcomes of surviving cardiac arrest. *Resuscitation, 74*, 215–221.

Parnia, S., Waller, D. G., Yeates, R., & Fenwick, P. (2001). A qualitative and quantitative study of the incidence, features and aetiology of near death experiences in cardiac arrest survivors. *Resuscitation, 48*, 149–156.

Patrick, R. B. (2008). [Inductive discipline and moral self-relevance in children]. Unpublished dissertation data. Columbus: The Ohio State University.

Patrick, R. B., & Gibbs, J. C. (2007). Parental expression of disappointment: Should it be a factor in Hoffman's model of parental discipline? *Journal of Genetic Psychology, 168*, 131–145.

Penrose, R. (1989). *The emperor's new mind: Concerning computers, minds, and the laws of physics.* New York: Oxford University Press.

Penrose, R. (1994). *Shadows of the mind: A search for the missing science of consciousness.* New York: Oxford University Press.

Peterson, C. C., Peterson, J. L., & Seeto, D. (1983). Developmental changes in ideas about lying. *Child Development, 54,* 1529–1535.

Piaget, J. (1962). *Comments on Vygotsky's critical remarks concerning* The language and thought of the child *and* Judgment and reasoning in the child (A. Parons, E. Hanfman, & G. Vakar, Trans.). Cambridge: MIT Press.

Piaget, J. (1965). *Moral judgment of the child* (M. Gabain, Trans.). New York: Free Press. (Original work published 1932)

Piaget, J. (1969). *Judgment and reasoning in the child* (M. Warden, Trans.). Totowa, NJ: Littlefield, Adams. (Original work published 1928)

Piaget, J. (1970). Piaget's theory (G. Gellerier & J. Langer, Trans.). In P. H. Mussen (Ed.), *Carmichael's manual of child psychology* (3rd ed., pp. 703–732). New York: John Wiley.

Piaget, J. (1971). *Biology and knowledge: An essay on the relations between organic regulations and cognitive processes* (B. Walsh, Trans.). Chicago: University of Chicago Press. (Original work published 1967)

Piaget, J. (1972). Intellectual evolution from adolescence to adulthood. *Human Development, 15,* 1–12.

Piaget, J. (1973; A. Rosen, Trans.). *The child and reality: Problems of genetic psychology.* New York: Grossman. (Originally published 1972)

Pinker, S. (2008, January 13). The moral instinct: Evolution has endowed us with ethical impulses. Do we know what to do with them? *The New York Times Magazine,* pp. 32, 34–37, 52, 55–56.

Pithers, W. D. (1999). Empathy: Definition, measurement, enhancement, and relevance to the treatment of sexual abusers. *Journal of Interpersonal Violence, 14,* 257–284.

Pizzaro, D. A., & Bloom, P. (2003). The intelligence of the moral intuitions: Comment on Haidt (2001). *Psychological Review, 110,* 193–196.

Polkinghorne, J. C. (1984). *The quantum world.* Princeton, NJ: Princeton University Press.

Potter, G. B., Gibbs, J. C., & Goldstein, A. P. (2001). *The EQUIP implementation guide.* Champaign, IL: Research Press.

Potts, M. (2002). The evidential value of near-death experiences for belief in life after death. *Journal of Near-Death Studies, 20,* 233–264.

Powell, N. (Producer). (2008). *SuperNanny.* New York: WABC.

Power, F. C., & Higgins-D'Alessandro, A. (2008). The Just Community approach to moral education and the moral atmosphere of the school. In L. P. Nucci & D. Narvaez (Eds.), *Handbook of moral and character education* (pp. 230–247). New York: Routledge.

Premack, D., & Premack, A. J. (1983). *The mind of an ape.* New York: Norton.

Quiggle, N., Garber, J., Panak, W., & Dodge, K. A. (1992). Social information processing in aggressive and depressed children. *Child Development, 63,* 1305–1320.

Radin, D. (2006). *Entangled minds: Extrasensory experiences in a quantum reality.* New York: Paraview Pocket Book.

Rathunde, K., & Czikszentmihalyi (2006). The developing person: An experiential perspective. In W. Damon & R. M. Lerner (Series Eds.) & R. M. Lerner (Vol. Ed.), *Handbook of child psychology: Vol. 1. Theoretical models of human development* (6th ed., pp. 465–515). New York: John Wiley.

Rawls, J. (1971). *A theory of justice.* Cambridge, MA: Harvard University Press.

Redl, F., & Wineman, D. (1957). *The aggressive child.* New York: Free Press.

Reed, R. R. C. (1997). *Following Kohlberg: Liberalism and the practice of democratic community.* Notre Dame, IN: University of Notre Dame Press.

Rest, J. R. (1979). *Development in judging moral issues.* Minneapolis: University of Minnesota Press.

Rest, J. R. (1983). Morality. In P. H. Mussen (Series Ed.) & J. H. Flavell & E. M. Markman (Vol. Eds.), *Handbook of child psychology: Vol. 3. Cognitive development* (pp. 556–629). New York: John Wiley.

Rest, J. R., Narvaez, D., Bebeau, M. J., & Thoma, S. J. (1999). *Postconventional moral thinking: A neo-Kohlbergian approach.* Hillsdale, NJ: Lawrence Erlbaum.

Richardson, D. (1974). *Peace child.* Ventura, CA: Regal.

Riessman, F. (1990). Restructuring help: A human services paradigm for the 1990s. *American Journal of Community Psychology, 18,* 221–230.

Ring, K. (1980). *Life at death: A scientific investigation of the near-death experience.* New York: Morrow.

Ring, K. (1984). *Heading toward Omega: In search of the meaning of the near-death experience.* New York: Morrow.

Ring, K., & Cooper, S. (1997). Near-death and out-of-body experiences in the blind: A study of apparent eyeless vision. *Journal of Near-Death Studies, 16,* 101–147.

Ring, K., & Cooper, S. (1999). *Mindsight: Near-death and out-of-body experiences in the blind.* Palo Alto, CA: William James Center/Institute of Transpersonal Psychology.

Ring, K., & Lawrence, M. (1993). Further evidence for veridical perception during near-death experiences. *Journal of Near-Death Studies, 11,* 223–229.

Robinson, R., Roberts, W. L., Strayer, J., & Koopman, R. (2007). Empathy and emotional responsiveness in delinquent and non-delinquent adolescents. *Social Development, 16,* 555–579.

Rogoff, B. (1998). Cognition as a collaborative process. In W. Damon (Series Ed.) & D. Kuhn & R. S. Siegler (Vol. Eds.), *Handbook of child psychology: Vol. 2. Cognition, perception, and language* (5th ed., pp. 679–744). New York: John Wiley.

Rommer, B. R. (2000). *Blessing in disguise.* St. Paul, MN: Llewellyn.

Rosen, H. (1980). *The development of sociomoral knowledge: A cognitive-structural approach.* New York: Columbia University Press.

Rotenberg, K. J., & Eisenberg, N. (1997). Developmental differences in the understanding of and reaction to others' inhibition of emotional expression. *Developmental Psychology, 33,* 526–537.

Rubin, K. H., Bukowski, W., & Parker, J. G. (2006). Peer interactions, relationships, and groups. In W. Damon & R. M. Lerner (Series Eds.) & N. Eisenberg (Vol. Ed.), *Handbook of child psychology: Vol. 3. Social, emotional, and personality development* (6th ed., pp. 571–645). New York: John Wiley.

Rutter, M. L. (1997). Nature-nurture integration: The example of antisocial behavior. *American Psychologist, 52,* 390–398.

Saarni, C., Campos, J. J., Camras, L. A., & Witherington, D. (2006). Emotional development: Action, communication, and understanding. In W. Damon & R. M. Lerner (Series Eds.) & N. Eisenberg (Vol. Ed.), *Handbook of child psychology: Vol. 3. Social, emotional, and personality development* (6th ed., pp. 226–299). New York: John Wiley.

Sabom, M. B. (1982). *Recollections of death: A medical investigation.* New York: Harper & Row.

Sabom, M. B. (1998). *Light and death: One doctor's fascinating account of near-death experiences.* Grand Rapids, MI: Zondervan.

Sabom, M. B. (2008). The acute dying experience. *Journal of Near-Death Studies, 26,* 181–218.

Sagi, A., & Hoffman, M. L. (1976). Empathic distress in the newborn. *Developmental Psychology, 12,* 175–176.

Samenow, S. E. (1984). *Inside the criminal mind.* New York: Random House.

Sarter, M., Berntson, G. G., & Caccioppo, J. T. (1996). Brain imaging and cognitive neuroscience: Toward strong inference in attributing function to structure. *American Psychologist, 51,* 13–21.

Schneider, S. L. (2001). In search of realistic optimism: Meaning, knowledge, and warm fuzziness. *American Psychologist, 56,* 250–263.

Schnell, S. V. (1986). *Delinquents with mature moral reasoning: A comparison with delayed delinquents and mature nondelinquents.* Unpublished doctoral dissertation, The Ohio State University, Columbus.

Schonert-Reichl, K. A. (1999). Relations of peer acceptance, friendship adjustment, and social behavior to moral reasoning during early adolescence. *Journal of Early Adolescence, 19,* 249–279.

Schwaninger, J., Eisenberg, P. R., Schechtman, K. B., & Weiss, A. N. (2002). A prospective analysis of near-death experiences in cardiac arrest patients. *Journal of Near-Death Studies, 20,* 215–232.

Sedikides, A. (1989). *Relations between role-taking opportunities and moral judgment development.* Unpublished doctoral dissertation, The Ohio State University, Columbus.

Selman, R. L. (1976). Social-cognitive understanding: A guide to educational and clinical practice. In T. Lickona (Ed.), *Moral development and behavior: Theory, research, and social issues* (pp. 299–316). New York: Holt, Rinehart, & Winston.

Selman, R. L. (1980). *The growth of interpersonal understanding.* New York: Academic Press.

Selman, R. L. (2003). *The promotion of social awareness: Powerful lessons from the partnership of developmental theory and classroom practice.* New York: Russell Sage Foundation.

Selman, R. L., & Shultz, L. H. (1990). *Making a friend in youth: Developmental theory and pair therapy.* Chicago: University of Chicago Press.

Shaver, P. R., Collins, N., & Clark, C. L. (1996). Attachment styles and internal working models of self and relationship partners. In J. O. G. Fletcher & J. Fitness (Eds.), *Knowledge structures in close relationships: A social psychological approach* (pp. 25–61). Mahwah, NJ: Lawrence Erlbaum.

Sherif, M., Harvey, O. J., White, B. J., Hood, W. R., & Sherif, C. W. (1961). *Intergroup conflict and cooperation: The Robbers Cave experiment.* Norman: University of Oklahoma.

Shultz, T. R., Dover, A., & Amsel, E. (1979). The logical and empirical bases of conservation judgments. *Cognition, 7,* 99–123.

Shweder, R. A. (1990). Ethical relativism: Is there a defensible version? *Ethos, 18,* 205–218.

Shweder, R. A. (2000). The astonishment of anthropology. In C. W. Gowans (Ed.), *Moral disagreements: Classical and contemporary readings* (pp. 102–112). London: Routledge Kegan Paul.

Shweder, R. A., Goodnow, J. J., Hatano, G., LeVine, R. A., Markus, H. R., & Miller, P. J. (2006). The cultural psychology of development: One mind, many mentalities. In W. Damon & R. M. Lerner (Series Eds.) & R. M. Lerner (Vol. Ed.), *Handbook of child psychology: Vol. 1. Theoretical models of human development* (6th ed., pp. 716–792). New York: John Wiley.

Siegler, R. S. (1996a). *Emerging minds: The process of change in children's thinking.* New York: Oxford University Press.

Siegler, R. S. (1996b). Unidimensional thinking, multidimensional thinking, and characteristic tendencies of thought. In A. J. Sameroff & M. M. Haith (Eds.), *The five to seven shift: The age of reason and responsibility* (pp. 63–84). Chicago: University of Chicago Press.

Siegler, R., & Ellis, S. (1996). Piaget on childhood. *Psychological Science, 7*, 211–215.

Sigelman, C. K., & Waitzman, K. A. (1991). The development of distributive justice orientations: Contextual influences on children's resource allocations. *Child Development, 62*, 1367–1378.

Signorella, M. L., Bigler, R. S., & Liben, L. S. (1993). Developmental differences in children's gender schemata about others: A meta-analytic review. *Developmental Review, 13*, 147–183.

Silberman, M. A., & Snarey, J. (1993). Gender differences in moral development during early adolescence: The contribution of sex-related variation in maturation. *Current Psychology: Developmental, Learning, Personality & Social, 12*, 163–171.

Simmel, G. (1902). The number of members as determining the sociological form of the group. *American Journal of Sociology, 8*, 1–46.

Simner, M. L. (1971). Newborn's response to the cry of another infant. *Developmental Psychology, 5*, 136–150.

Simonian, S. J., Tarnowski, K. J., & Gibbs, J. C. (1991). Social skills and antisocial conduct of delinquents. *Child Psychiatry and Human Development, 22*, 17–22.

Sinclair, S. (2008, January 20). A cutting tradition: Inside a female circumcision ceremony for young Muslim girls. *New York Times Magazine*, 46–50.

Singer, P. (1981). *The expanding circle: Ethics and sociobiology.* New York: Farrar, Straus, & Giroux.

Slaby, R. G., & Guerra, N. G. (1988). Cognitive mediators of aggression in adolescent offenders: 1. Assessment. *Developmental Psychology, 24*, 580–588.

Smedslund, J. (1961). The acquisition of conservation of substance and weight in children: III. Extinction of conservation of weight acquired "normally" and by means of empirical controls on a balance scale. *Scandinavian Journal of Psychology, 2*, 85–87.

Smetana, J. G. (2006). Social-cognitive domain theory: Consistencies and variations in children's moral and social judgments. In M. Killen & J. G. Smetana (Eds.), *Handbook of moral development* (pp. 119–153). Mahwah, NJ: Lawrence Erlbaum Associates.

Smit, R. H. (2008a). Corroboration of the dentures anecdote involving veridical perception in a near-death experience. *Journal of Near-Death Studies, 27*, 47–62.

Smit, R. H. (2008b). Further commentary on Pam Reynolds's NDE. *Journal of Near-Death Studies, 24*, pp. 308–310.

Smith, A. (1965). *The theory of moral sentiments.* Oxford, UK: Clarendon. (Original work published 1759)

Snarey, J. (1985). The cross-cultural universality of social-moral development: A critical review of Kohlbergian research. *Psychological Bulletin, 97*, 202–232.

Sokol, A., & Bricmont, J. (1999). *Fashionable nonsense: Postmodern intellectuals' abuse of science.* New York: MacMillan.

Spivack, G., & Shure, M. B. (1989). Interpersonal Cognitive Problem-Solving (ICPS): A competence-building primary prevention program. *Prevention in Human Services, 6*, 151–178.

Stams, G. J., Brugman, D., Dekovic, M., van Rosmalen, L., van der Laan, P., & Gibbs, J. C. (2006). The moral judgment of juvenile delinquents: A meta-analysis. *Journal of Abnormal Child Psychology, 34*, 697–713.

Stapp, H. T. (2006). Science's conception of human beings as a basis for moral theory. *Zygon, 41*, 617–621.

Staub, E. (1974). Helping a distressed person: Social, personality, and stimulus determinants. In L. Berkowitz (Ed.), *Advances in experimental social psychology* (Vol. 7). New York: Academic Press.

Stevenson, I., & Cook, E. W. (1995). Involuntary memories during severe physical illness or injury. *Journal of Nervous and Mental Disease, 183*, 452.

Straughan, R. (1983). From moral judgment to moral action. In H. Weinreich-Haste & D. Locke (Eds.), *Morality in the making: Thought, action, and the social context* (pp. 125–140). Chichester, UK: Wiley.

Sutherland, C. (1992). *Reborn in the light: Life after near-death experiences.* New York: Bantam.

Swann, W. B. Jr., Griffin, J. J. Jr., Fredmore, S. C., & Gaines, B. (1999). The cognitive-affective cross-fire: When self-consistency confronts self-enhancement. In R. F. Baumeister (Ed.), *The self in social psychology* (pp. 191–401). Philadelphia: Psychology Press.

Sykes, G. M., & Matza, D. (1957). Techniques of neutralization: A theory of delinquency. *American Sociological Review, 22,* 664–670.

Tappan, M. B. (2006). Mediated moralities: Sociocultural approaches to moral development. In M. Killen & J. Smetana (Eds.), *Handbook of moral development* (pp. 351–374). Mahwah, NJ: Lawrence Erlbaum Associates.

Targ, E., Schlitz, M., & Irwin, H. J. (2000). Psi-related experiences. In E. Cardena, S. J. Lynn, & S. Krippner (Eds.), *Varieties of anomalous experience: Examining the scientific evidence* (pp. 219–252). Washington, DC: American Psychological Association.

Taylor, H., & Walker, L. (1997). Moral climate and the development of moral reasoning: The effects of dyadic discussions between young offenders. *Journal of Moral Education, 26,* 21–43.

Taylor, S. E., & Brown, J. D. (1994). Positive illusions and well-being revisited: Separating fact from fiction. *Psychological Bulletin, 116,* 21–27.

Texas Youth Commission (2007). *Capital and serious violent offender treatment program.* Austin, TX: Texas Youth Commission FY 2007 review of agency treatment effectiveness.

Tomasello, M. (2008, May 25). Are humans unique? *New York Times Sunday Magazine,* p. 15.

Tomasello, M., Kruger, A. C., & Ratner, H. H. (1996). Cultural learning. *Behavioral and Brain Sciences, 16,* 495–552.

Tooby, J., & Cosmides, L. (1996). Friendship and the banker's paradox: Other pathways to the evolution of adaptations for altruism. In J. M. Smith, W. G. Runciman, & R. I. M. Dunbar (Eds.), *Evolution of social behavior patterns in primates and man* (Vol. 88, pp. 119–143). London: British Academy.

Trivers, R. L. (1971). The evolution of reciprocal altruism. *Quarterly Review of Biology, 46,* 35–57.

Trzebinski, J. (1985). Action-oriented representations of implicit personality theories. *Journal of Personality and Social Psychology, 48,* 1266–1278.

Turiel, E. (1974). Conflict and transition in adolescent moral development. *Child Development, 45,* 14–29.

Turiel, E. (1977). Conflict and transition in adolescent moral development: II. The resolution of disequilibrium through structural reorganization. *Child Development, 48,* 634–637.

Turiel, E. (2006a). The development of morality. In W. Damon & R. M. Lerner (Series Eds.) & N. Eisenberg (Vol. Ed.), *Handbook of child psychology: Vol. 3. Social, emotional, and personality development* (6th ed., pp. 789–857). New York: John Wiley.

Turiel, E. (2006b). Thoughts, emotions, and social interactional processes in moral development. In M. Killen & J. G. Smetana (Eds.), *Handbook of moral development* (pp. 7–36). Mahwah, NJ: Lawrence Erlbaum Associates.

Turiel, E. (2008). The trouble with the ways morality is used and how they impede social equality and social justice. In C. Wainryb, J. G. Smetana, & E. Turiel (Eds.), *Social development, social inequalities, and social justice* (pp. 1–26). New York : Lawrence Erlbaum Associates.

Turnbull, C. M. (1972). *The mountain people.* New York: Touchstone.

Tversky, A., & Kahneman, D. (1973). Availability: A heuristic for judging frequency and probability. *Cognitive Psychology, 5,* 207–232.

Vaitl, D., Birbaumer, N., Gruselier, J., Jamieson, G. A., Kotchoubey, B., Kubler, A., et al. (2005). Psychobiology of altered states of consciousness. *Psychological Bulletin, 131,* 98–127.

Valdesolo, P., & DeSteno, D. (2008). The duality of virtue: Deconstructing the moral hypocrite. *Journal of Experimental Social Psychology, 44,* 1334–1338.

Vandivier, K. (2002). Why should my conscience bother me? In M. D. Erman and R. J. Lundman (Eds.), *Corporate and governmental deviance: Problems of organizational behavior in contemporary society* (6th ed.; pp. 146–166). New York: Oxford University Press.

van Lommel, P., van Wees, R., Meyers, V., & Elfferich, I. (2001). Near-death experience in survivors of cardiac arrest: A prospective study in the Netherlands. *Lancet, 358,* 2039–2045.

Varshney, A. (2002). *Ethnic conflict & civic life: Hindus and Muslims in India.* New Haven, CT: Yale University Press.

Vasudev, J., & Hummel, R. C. (1987). Moral stage sequence and principled reasoning in an Indian sample. *Human Development, 30,* 105–118.

Viswanathan, V. (2008, February/March). [Comment.] *Scientific American Mind,* p. 35.

Vorrath, H. H., & Brendtro, L. K. (1985). *Positive Peer Culture* (2nd ed.). New York: Aldine.

Vygotsky, L. S. (1978). *Mind in society: The development of higher mental processes.* Cambridge, MA: Harvard University Press. (Original works published 1930, 1933, and 1935)

Vygotsky, L. S. (1986). *Thought and language* (A. Kozulin, Trans.). Cambridge: MIT Press. (Original work published 1934)

Wainryb, C. (2000). Values and truths: The making and judging of moral decisions. In M. Laupa (Ed.), *Rights and wrongs: How children and adults evaluate the world* (pp. 33–47). San Francisco: Jossey-Bass.

Wainryb, C., Brehl, B. A., & Matwin, S. (2005). Being hurt and hurting others: Children's narrative accounts and moral judgments of their own interpersonal conflicts. *Monographs of the Society for Research in Child Development, 70* (3, Serial No. 281).

Wainryb, C., Komolova, M., & Florsheim, P. (in press). How violent youth offenders and typically developing adolescents construct moral agency in narratives about doing harm. In K. McLean and P. Pasupathi (Eds.), *Narrative development in adolescence: Creating the storied self.* New York: Springer.

Wainryb, C., & Pasupathi, M. (in press). Developing moral agency in the midst of violence: Children, political conflict, and values. In W. McCormack (Ed.), *Values and violence: Intangible aspects of terrorism.* New York: Springer.

Walker, L. J. (1983). Sources of cognitive conflict for stage transition in moral development. *Developmental Psychology, 19,* 103–110.

Walker, L. J. (1988). A longitudinal study of moral reasoning. *Child Development, 60,* 157–166.

Walker, L. J. (1995). Sexism in Kohlberg's moral psychology? In W. M. Kurtines & J. L. Gewirtz (Eds.), *Moral development: An introduction* (pp. 83–108). Needham Heights, MA: Allyn & Bacon.

Walker, L. J., Gustafson, P., & Hennig, K. H. (2001). The consolidation/transition model in moral reasoning development. *Developmental Psychology, 37,* 187–197.

Walker, L. J., & Hennig, K. H. (2004). Differing conceptions of moral exemplarity: Just, brave, and caring. *Journal of Personality and Social Psychology, 86,* 629–647.

Walker, L. J., Hennig, K. H., & Krettenauer, T. (2000). Parent and peer contexts for children's moral reasoning. *Child Development, 71,* 1033–1048.

Walsh, M. W. (2007, November 18). Blowing the whistle, many times. *New York Times Sunday Business Section,* pp. 1, 10.

Walton, G. E., & Bower, T. G. R. (1993). Newborns form "prototypes" in less than 1 minute. *Psychological Science, 4*, 203–205.

Ward, T., Hudson, S. M., & Marshall, W. L. (1995). Cognitive distortion in sex offenders: An integrative review. *Clinical Psychology Review, 17*, 470–507.

Wegner, D. M., & Bargh, J. A. (1998). Control and automaticity in social life. In D. Gilbert, S. Fiske, & G. Lindzey (Eds.), *The handbook of social psychology* (pp. 446–496). New York: McGraw-Hill.

Weiner, B. (1985). "Spontaneous" causal thinking. *Psychological Bulletin, 8*, 226–232.

Whitbourne, S. K., & Connolly, L. A. (1999). The developing self at midlife. In S. L. Willis (Eds.), *Life in the middle: Psychological and social development in middle age* (pp. 25–45). San Diego: Academic Press.

Wilson, D. (1995, August). [Personal testimony.] Panel of Near-Death Experiencers. Presented at the meeting of the International Association of Near-Death Studies, West Hartford, CT.

Wilson, J. Q. (1993). *The moral sense.* New York: The Free Press.

Wilson, J. Q., & Herrnstein, R. J. (1985). *Crime and human nature.* New York: Simon & Schuster.

Wilson, S. J., Lipsey, M. W., & Derzon, J. H. (2003). The effects of school-based intervention programs on aggressive behavior: A meta-analysis. *Journal of Consulting and Clinical Psychology, 71*, 136–141.

Wilson, T. O. (2002). *Strangers to ourselves: Discovering the adaptive unconscious.* Cambridge, MA: Harvard University Press.

Winer, G., Craig, R. K., & Weinbaum, E. (1992). Adults' failure on misleading weight-conservation tests: A developmental analysis. *Developmental Psychology, 28*, 109–120.

Winer, G. R., & McGlone, D. (1993). On the uncertainty of conservation: Responses to misleading questions. *Developmental Psychology, 29*, 760–769.

Witkin, H. A., & Goodenough, D. R. (1977). Field independence and interpersonal behavior. *Psychological Bulletin, 84*, 661–689.

Woodbury, R. (1993, October 11). Taming the killers. *Time*, pp. 58–59.

Wren, T. E. (1991). *Caring about morality.* London: Routledge Kegan Paul.

Wright, L. (2008, June 2). The rebellion within: An Al Qaeda mastermind questions terrorism. *The New Yorker*, 36–53.

Wright, R. (1994). *The moral animal: Why we are the way we are.* New York: Pantheon.

Wuthnow, R. (1994). *Sharing the journey: Support groups and America's new quest for community.* New York: Free Press.

Yochelson, S., & Samenow, S. E. (1976). *The criminal personality: Vol. 1. A profile for change.* New York: Jason Aronson.

Yochelson, S., & Samenow, S. E. (1977). *The criminal personality: Vol. 2. The change process.* New York: Jason Aronson.

Yochelson, S., & Samenow, S. E. (1986). *The criminal personality: Vol. 3. The drug user.* Northvale, NJ: Jason Aronson.

Youniss, J., & Damon, W. (1992). Social construction in Piaget's theory. In H. Beilin & P. B. Pufall (Eds.), *Piaget's theory: Prospects and possibilities* (pp. 267–286). Hillsdale, NJ: Lawrence Erlbaum.

Zahn-Waxler, C. (2000). [Quotation on dust jack cover for *Empathy and moral development.*]

Zahn-Waxler, C., & Robinson, J. L. (1995). Empathy and guilt: Early origins of feelings of responsibility. In K. Fischer & J. Tangney (Eds.), *Self-conscious emotions: Shame, guilt, embarrassment, and pride* (pp. 143–173). New York: Guilford.

Zahn-Waxler, C., Robinson, J. L., Emde, R. N., & Plomin, R. (1992). The development of empathy in twins. *Developmental Psychology, 28,* 1038–1047.

Zajonc, R. B. (1968). Attitudinal effects of mere exposure. *Journal of Personality and Social Psychology Supplement, 9*(2, Pt. 2), 1–27.

Zajonc, R. B. (1984). On the primacy of affect. *American Psychologist, 39,* 117–123.

Zaleski, C. (1987). *Otherworld journeys: Accounts of near-death experience in medieval and modern times.* New York: Oxford University Press.

Zhou, Q., Eisenberg, N., Losoya, S. H., Fabes, R. A., Reiser, M., Guthrie, I. K., Murphy, B. C., Cumberland, A. J., & Shepard, S. A. (2002). The relations of parental warmth and positive expressiveness to children's empathy-related responding and social functioning: A longitudinal study. *Child Development, 73,* 893–915.

Appendix

Short-Answer Questions for the Chapters

Briefly discuss the following:

Chapter 1: Introduction

1. The author's conceptualization of the basis of moral evaluation or decision-making. In what sense can morality be objective, according to this conception? How does this conception differ from other conceptions or views of morality?
2. The author's conceptualization of the moral domain. How might one resolve a conflict between equally fundamental considerations?
3. "Growing beyond the superficial" in morality. What are its two major strands?
4. Antisocial behavior, even among those who may not be delayed in moral judgment development. What are three possible explanations in terms of the camp incident?

Chapter 2: "The Right" and Moral Development: Fundamental Themes of Kohlberg's Cognitive Developmental Approach

1. The thesis that early-childhood moral (and other) judgment tends to be "superficial." How does Piaget's and Kohlberg's cognitive developmental approach account for this superficiality?
2. The sense in which the social cognition of young children tends to be egocentrically biased. How may pronounced egocentric bias be integral to early childhood superficiality?
3. Superficial judgment in nonsocial cognition. What accounts for the "curious caprice of the young child" that can be seen in conservation (as well as social cognitive) tasks?
4. "Growth beyond the superficial" or "decentration" in nonsocial cognition. Describe how experiments using the conservation task have helped to distinguish construction from internalization.
5. Conservation knowledge. How does it "crucially" differ from non-conservation responses?
6. Reciprocity as (a) an internalized moral norm and (b) a socially constructed ideal. What conditions promote the likelihood that peer interaction will lead to the construction of moral reciprocity?

7. Logical necessity and cognitive primacy in the context of *social* cognitive development and behavior.
8. Moral reciprocity. Is it a uniquely human phenomenon? What stage-related distinction is important in this connection? What role might "reflective abstraction" play?
9. The difference made by ideal moral reciprocity in moral motivation. Does Hoffman specifically identify ideal reciprocity? How does ideal reciprocity help us to evaluate norms of blood vengeance?
10. Moral judgment development beyond Stage 3 in the Gibbs et al. view. Can Stage 3 represent sufficient moral judgment maturity? What social perspective-taking opportunities seem to be important for advanced development?
11. Immature and mature moral judgment stages. How are they assessed by the Sociomoral Reflection Measure-Short Form (SRM-SF)? How must "stage sequence" be understood in moral development?
12. Adaptive learning and development in terms of Piagetian theory.

Chapter 3: Kohlberg's Theory: A Critique and New View

1. The sense in which Kohlberg's claims regarding age trends in moral judgment were "bolder" than Piaget's.
2. Kohlberg's overhaul of Piaget's moral judgment phases or stages. How did the Deweyan influence "distort" moral judgment development in Kohlberg's overhaul? What was "lost" as a result? What "irony" was evident?
3. Violations of invariant-sequence expectations discovered and dealt with in the course of Kohlberg's longitudinal research. In Kohlberg's stage revisions to restore invariant sequence, what two new problems for Kohlberg's stage typology were created? These problems both reflect what generic problem, according to Gibbs?
4. Adult moral development in Kohlberg's theory. What is Gibbs's critique?
5. The author's two-phase view of life span moral judgment development. What is the role of formal operational thought?

Chapter 4: "The Good" and Moral Development: Hoffman's Theory

1. The empathic predisposition and its functional importance for human society. What factor promotes the reliability of empathic responding, according to Hoffman?
2. The question of whether empathy is unique to the human species. Make sure to include the modes of empathic arousal and the complexity of the "full-fledged" empathic predisposition in your discussion.

3. Hoffman's conception of "fully mature" perspective taking.
4. The meaning of "growing beyond the superficial" in Hoffman's (especially vis-à-vis Kohlberg's) theory.
5. Hoffman's immature stages of empathic development (refer to the pertinent empathic arousal modes).
6. Hoffman's mature stages of empathic development (refer to the pertinent empathic arousal modes).
7. The cognitive processes that mediate or "complicate" the relationship between the empathic predisposition and social behavior. Illustrate these cognitive processes. Can they not only complicate but *undermine* the empathy-prosocial behavior relationship?
8. The limitations of empathy as the "bedrock" of prosocial morality. How can these limitations be remedied?
9. The cognitive regulation of empathy in Hoffman's theory. In what sense is affect such as empathy "primary" in Hoffman's theory?
10. The role of moral socialization (and especially the discipline encounter) in the eventuation of the empathic predisposition into prosocial behavior. How does the parent give effective inductions?
11. Two empirical studies of Hoffman's moral socialization theory. How were the results supportive? What might the parents' expression of disappointment "foster" in the child?
12. The role of nurturance in moral socialization.
13. Gibbs's critique of Hoffman's theory, with particular attention to the issue of moral motivation.

Chapter 5: Moral Development, Moral Self-Relevance, and Prosocial Behavior

1. The issue of the motivation of prosocial behavior, especially in terms of the presented case study of a rescue. How do Hoffman's and the author's positions on moral motivation differ?
2. The factors that help to account for individual differences in the likelihood of prosocial behavior. What factors are involved in clear or accurate moral perception?
3. The integration of self and morality in human development.
4. The strengths and weaknesses of information-processing models of social behavior. Can such models account for quick behavioral responses?
5. "Ego strength," with particular attention to its processes and relations to honesty and to prosocial behavior.
6. Three points regarding prosocial behavior that are highlighted by considering certain counter-examples.

Chapter 6: Understanding Antisocial Behavior

1. The limitation of moral judgment developmental delay among antisocial youths.
2. The limitation of self-serving cognitive distortions among antisocial youths. What are the four categories of distortion? What is the relation of the primary distortion to proactive versus reactive aggression? What is the function of the other three categories of distortion?
3. The limitation of social skill deficiencies among antisocial youths.
4. Timothy McVeigh as a case study of the limitations of antisocial youths. What challenges to Kohlberg's and Hoffman's theories are represented by this case, and how might those challenges be addressed?

Chapter 7: Treating Antisocial Behavior

1. The mutual help (in particular, Positive Peer Culture) approach to treating antisocial behavior. What is its aim? How does it provide social perspective-taking opportunities? Why has it had only mixed success, according to the author?
2. The cognitive behavioral approach to treating antisocial behavior. How does EQUIP integrate the mutual help with the cognitive behavioral approaches? What does each approach contribute to the other?
3. The curriculum in the EQUIP program. What opportunities are "entailed" in the curriculum? How do its three components remedy, responsively, the three main limitations of antisocial youth?
4. Adaptations and evaluations of the EQUIP program.
5. Social perspective taking for the severe offender.

Chapter 8: Beyond the Theories: A Deeper Reality?

1. Kohlberg's exploration of ontological and existential questions pertaining to moral development. How does the author propose to go beyond Kohlberg's and Hoffman's theories?
2. The near-death experience, its three types, and whether it is of a deeper reality. What does the author conclude, in terms of what five ontologically relevant questions?
3. Moral insight, inspiration, and transformation from the near-death experience. What feature or features of the experience might be especially important for moral transformation? What moral issue is often raised by one of the experience's typical aftereffects?

Chapter 9: Conclusion

1. The main sources of moral motivation. How do Hoffman's and Kohlberg's theories differ? Describe the respective categories of knowledge to which the theories refer. How does this epistemological difference relate to the issue of moral motivation?

2. The integrability of Kohlberg's and Hoffman's theories. What is Gibbs's view?

3. Moral perception and the question of a deeper reality. What paradox seems to be involved?

Author Index

A

Abelson, R. P., 32, 116
Abramovitch, H., 199
Ackerman, P., 106, 110
Adams, E., 23–24, 34
Adelson, J., 45, 72
Agee, V., 153–154, 161, 182–183
Ahlborn, H. H., 168
Aldeguer, 88
Alexander, R. D., 41
Ali, A. H., 4, 14
Aleva, A. E., 130
Al-Krenawi, A., 43
Al-Krenawi, S., 43
Aloise, P. A., 21
Aloniz, V., 136
Alvarez-Saunders, C., 182
Ames, G., 29, 53
Amsel, E., 31
Anderson, C. A., 120, 146
Anderson, D., 182
Anderson, R., 114
Anderson, S., 43
Andrews, G., 30, 114
Antoni, G., 103
Aquino, K., 115–116, 135
Arbuthnot, J., 168
Archer, M. A., 153
Arnold, K. D., 47, 103, 168
Aronson, E., 32, 116
Arsenio, W., 23–24, 34
Aspect, A., 228
Atkins, R., 115, 154, 168
Ayer, A. J., 108
Azar, B., 9, 76

B

Bachorowski, J. A., 139
Badzinski, D. M., 23
Baier, K., 2–3, 6, 73
Baldwin, M. W., 53, 116

Bandura, A., 89, 118, 136, 141–142, 150
Barbaranelli, C., 142
Bargh, J. A., 119–120
Baron, R. M., 135
Barriga, A. Q., 116, 129, 132–133, 135–136, 138, 140, 142–143, 161, 181
Barriga, K. T., 142
Barry, B., 6, 38
Basinger, K. S., xv, 47–48, 50–51, 54, 56, 72, 103, 130–131
Bates, J. E., 139
Batson, C. D., 88
Batson, J. G., 88
Baumeister, R. F., 117, 127, 134, 142
Baumrind, D., 97–98
Bavelas, J. B., 80
Beah, I., 56
Beauchamp, T. L., 3, 6–7, 16, 89
Beaureagard, M., 231
Bebeau, M. J., 4, 44, 47, 52, 60, 120
Beck, A. T., 122, 125, 127, 131, 133–135, 137–140, 142, 147–148, 172–173, 182–183, 187
Begue, L., 86
Beilin, H., 19
Bell, J. S., 228
Bem, D. J., 201
Benz, G. R., 192, 232
Bergen, P., 127, 150
Bergman, R., 75, 117
Berk, L., 23, 35, 99
Berkowitz, M., 34
Bernstein, S., 35
Berntson, G., 37, 103
Bidell, T. R., 52–53, 61
Bierman, D. J., 201
Bigler, R. S., 21
Birbaumer, N., 207
Birnsbaum, J. J., 138
Bixby, L., 153
Bjorklund, D. F., 3–5, 14, 37, 40, 54–55, 93, 104, 108, 110, 126, 215, 234
Black, A., 80

Blackmore, S., 194, 198–199, 201, 205, 214
Blair, R. J. R., 78
Blanke, O., 195, 205
Blasi, A., 4, 115–117, 129, 135, 233
Blatt, S. J., 43–44
Bloom, P., 5–6, 15, 22–24, 43, 90, 108, 111, 119, 120
Bodansky, Y., 122–124
Bornstein, M. H., 43, 99, 128
Bosch, J. D., 139
Bouwmeester, D., 228
Bower, T. G. R., 83
Bowlby, J., 53
Boyd, D. R., 75
Boyes, M. C., 64
Boysen, S. T., 37
Brabeck, M., 118
Bradley, E., 123
Brandt, R. B., 74
Brehl, B. A., 21, 34
Brendtro, L. K., 136, 152–154, 161, 176
Brenner, J., 37
Brewer, M. B., 5, 150
Bricmont, J., 14
Bromley, D. B., 20, 23
Bronfenbrenner, U., 114, 128
Brooks-Gunn, J., 84
Broome, K., 205
Brothers, L., 78
Broughton, R. S., 201
Brown, R., 26, 30–31, 55, 57, 88, 127, 224, 226–227
Brugman, D., 129–130, 181
Brummeth, B. H., 88
Bruni, P., 14
Bugental, D. B., 97
Bukowski, W., 34–35
Burgess, R. L., 41
Buriel, R., 95
Burkhart, J. E., 103
Bush, N., 197
Bushman, B. J., 120, 146
Bussey, K., 20

C

Caccioppo, J. T., 103
Callanan, M., 203
Caltran, G., 83

Camelia, C. R. T., 140, 143
Campbell, D. T., 77, 234
Campbell, R. L., 3
Campos, J. J., 93
Candee, D., 45, 54, 63, 65, 103, 115, 117–118, 120
Cantor, J., 23
Caprara, G. V., 133, 135–136, 142
Carducci, D., 129–130, 136, 143, 161–162, 164
Carducci, J. B., 164
Carlson, R., 111
Carpendale, J. I., 23, 51
Carr, M. B., 133
Case, R., 22, 29
Cason, D. R., 52
Chagnon, N. A., 43
Chambers, H., 138
Chaminade, T., 78
Chandler, M., 23, 64
Chapman, G. L., 181
Chapman, M., 29
Chase, K. A., 134
Cheesman, F. L., 168
Childress, J. F., 3, 6–7, 16, 89
Chovil, N., 80
Christian, S. R., 214, 232
Christopher, J. C., 3
Clark, C. L., 53
Clark, M. C., 37
Clark, P. M., 10, 112, 117
Clark, R. D., 83
Cohen, J. D., 15, 78
Coie, J. D., 98, 119, 134, 139
Colby, A., xv, 11, 45, 51–54, 61–63, 65–67, 73, 75, 103, 106, 111–112, 114–122, 124, 214, 220, 222
Coles, R., 107–108, 112, 115, 117, 121, 220
Coll, S., 122, 124
Collins, N., 53
Collins, W. A., 43, 99, 128
Comunian, A., 46, 103, 113, 118
Connolly, L. A., 56
Conquest, R., 141
Conway, A. R. A., 29
Cook, E. W., 197, 202, 205–206
Cook, T. D., 234
Cooper, S., 231
Corby, B. C., 135
Cosmides, L., 37

Cowan, C. P., 56
Cowan, P. A., 16, 56
Cox-Chapman, M., 196, 199
Craig, R. K., 55
Crick, N., 119
Cruickshank, P., 127, 150
Csikszentmihalyi, M., 56
Cumberland, A. J., 101
Custer, W. L., 31, 55, 224

D

Dahlen, E. R., 172
Daleflod, B., 171
Damasio, A., 92, 103
Damon, W., 2, 5, 11–12, 16, 19–20, 22, 24, 29, 31,
    33–38, 44, 52, 55, 95, 97, 99, 104, 106, 111–112,
    114–122, 124, 127, 132, 168, 214, 220, 222
Darley, J. J., 77, 118
Darley, J. M., 15, 78
Darling, N., 101
Davies, P., 185–186, 215, 234
Day, J. M., 3
Decety, J., 78
Deffenbacher, J. L., 172
Dekovic, M., 129
DeLoache, J., 27
Deluty, R., 143
Denton, K., 3, 41, 51, 226
DeSteno, D., 15, 25, 125, 135, 137
Devlin, R., 13, 133, 135, 140, 143, 152, 181
de Waal, F., 37, 42, 76–78, 83, 93, 215
Dewey, J., x, 57–58, 60–62, 67, 74–75
Diamond, J., 43, 56
DiBiase, A.-M., 13, 152, 169, 176, 180, 184
Dishion, T. J., 144, 153, 161–162
Dodd, J., 129
Dodge, K. A., 97–98, 105, 118–120, 122, 134,
    139, 140, 147
Doise, W., 29
Donahoe, C. P., 143
Dondi, M., 83
Donnelly, T. M., 115, 154, 168
Dover, A., 31
Durkheim, E., 62
Dutton, S., 181
Duvall, J., 106, 110

E

Ecton, R. R., 173–174
Edelstein, W., 118
Edgerton, R. B., 4, 43, 126, 150, 215
Edwards, C. P., 44
Eibl, M., 228
Eisenberg, N., 23, 54, 58, 72, 76, 85, 92, 101, 103,
    118, 135, 214
Eisenberg, P. R., 195–196
Elfferich, I., 188, 196, 202, 204, 208
Elias, A., 153
Ellis, A., 132
Ellis, S., 19
Emde, R. N., 78
Epstein, S., 52, 135

F

Fabes, R. A., 23, 58, 92, 101, 103, 118, 135
Farr, S., 188, 192–194, 199–200,
    211–214, 230
Feffer, M., 22, 52
Feindler, E. L., 173–174
Fenwick, E., 210, 216
Fenwick, P. B., 194–196, 205–207, 210, 216
Fernandez, E., 172
Fernandez, Y., 182
Ferrari, M., 114
Festinger, L., 226
Fida, R., 133, 135–136, 142
Fischer, K. W., 52–53, 59
Flavell, J. H., 19–21, 23–28, 30, 51–52, 55, 67, 71,
    104, 185
Florsheim, P., 133
Fontana, D., 231
Fowers, B. J., 4
Fowler, R. C., 14
Fox, M., 194–195, 209, 231–232
Frankena, W. K., 6–7, 226, 229
Franklin, S., 70
Fredmore, S. C., 135
Freeman, D., 116, 135
Freedman, B. J., 143
French, C. C., 205, 216
Fromm, E., 44, 67, 71
Fuller, D., 47–48, 51, 54, 56, 72, 129, 144,
    168, 181

G

Gackenbach, J., 201
Gaines, B., 135
Gannon, T. A., 138
Garbarino, J., 140, 183–184
Garber, J., 140
Garmon, L. C., 103
Gavaghan, M. P., 47
Gergen, K. J., 3
Gerris, J., 98, 100, 104
Gibbs, J. C., ix-x, xv-xvi, 3, 10, 13, 34, 41, 44–48,
    50–52, 54, 56, 63, 65–66, 72–73, 75, 98–100,
    103–104, 112, 116–118, 129–133, 135–136, 138,
    140, 142-144, 152, 160–161, 164, 167–171,
    175–176, 178–181, 184, 194, 200, 226, 229
Gielen, U., 46, 103, 113, 118
Giesbrecht, N., 116
Gilligan, C., 76, 103
Glachan, P., 29
Glassman, M., 14
Glick, B., 152, 162–163, 169
Gnepp, J., 23
Goldstein, A. P., 13, 133, 136, 140, 143, 152, 160,
    163, 167, 169–171, 173, 175, 178–180
Gold, J., 23–24, 34
Golding, W., 35
Goleman, D., 134
Gollwitzer, P. M., 119
Goodall, J., 77
Goodenough, D. R., 114
Goodnow, J., 3
Goodrick, T. S., 10, 112, 117
Gopnik, A., 19, 53
Gordon, D., 168
Gottman, J. M., 134
Gouldner, A., 32, 37
Grangier, P., 228
Green, B., 45, 71
Green, J. L., 10, 112, 117
Greene, J. D., xvi, 3, 15–16, 78, 108, 234
Gregg, V. R., 103, 130
Greyson, B., 13, 187–188, 194–197, 199–200,
    202–204, 206, 208, 214, 216, 232
Griffin, J. J., Jr., 135

Grim, P., 121
Grime, R. L., xv, 47–48, 50, 54, 56, 72, 103, 130–131
Gross, P., 14
Grossman, D. L., 141
Groth, A. N., 138
Gruber, E., 153
Grusec, J. E., 97
Gruselier, J., 207
Guerra, N. G., 140
Guisinger, S., 43–44
Gustafson, P., 54
Guthrie, I. K., 101

H

Hafer, C. L., 86
Haggbloom, S. J., 57
Haidt, J., xvi, 3–5, 11, 14, 16, 40, 54–55, 93, 104,
    108, 110, 119, 126, 215, 234
Halford, G. S., 30
Hambrick, D. Z., 29
Hamilton, V. L., 136, 141–142, 150
Hamilton, W. D., 77
Hammock, G. S., 35
Haritos-Fatouros, M., 141
Harkness, S., 44
Harris, B., 232
Hart, D., 20, 115, 116, 154, 168
Harter, S., 20, 23–24, 34, 53
Harvey, O. J., 44
Hatano, G., 3
Hauser, M. D., 3, 5, 41, 77, 103, 108, 126
Havighurst, R., 112
Hawkins, M. A., 140, 143
Heide, K. M., 182
Heider, F., 32
Helwig, C. C., 3, 20
Henggeler, S. W., 167
Hennig, K., 34, 54, 96, 125
Herbeck, D., 123–126, 144–149, 161
Herbert, N., 228, 230
Herrnstein, R. J., 57, 138
Hetherington, E. M., 43, 99, 128
Hewer, A., xv, 45, 54, 63, 65, 103
Heyert, M., 41
Heyman, R. E., 134
Hickling, A. K., 86
Higgins, A., 153

Higgins-D'Alessandro, A., 167
Hildebran, D., 181
Hill, T. E., Jr., 7
Hilton, N. Z., 181
Hodges, E. V. E., 135
Hoffman, M. L., ix, xv-xvii, 1–2, 7–14, 19,
    34–35, 41–42, 53, 62, 70, 73, 76–104, 106,
    108–110, 117, 123, 125–126, 128, 135, 137–138,
    149, 152, 161, 169, 176, 183–185, 187, 212, 214,
    219, 221–229, 231, 234
Hoffner, C., 23
Holden, J., 214, 232
Hollander, P., 142
Hollin, C. R., 130
Holst, U., 129, 135
Hood, W. R., 44
Horn, M., 152, 164, 181
Hudson, J. A., 94
Hudson, S. M., 142
Hummel, R. C., 67
Hunter, N., 144
Hurley, D., 153
Husain, E., 150
Huston, T. L., 41
Hyde, J. S., 103
Hyman, R., 205–206, 217

I

Irwin, H. J., 201
Irwin, M. J., 163

J

Jacobson, D., 5, 14
Jaffee, S., 103
Jakubowski, P., 143
James, J., 14
James, W., 199
Jamieson, G. A., 207
Janssens, J., 98, 100, 104
Jaycox, C., 144
Jensen, L. A., 41
Jones, M., 153
Jones, V. K., 57
Joseph, J. A., 10, 112, 117

K

Kahn, T., 138
Kahneman, D., 24

Kane, M. J., 29
Kane, R., 2–3, 12
Kant, I., 3, 12, 59, 68, 70, 73–74
Kaufman, K., 133, 135, 140, 143
Kazdin, A., 128–129, 132, 143, 152
Keasy, C., 45
Keenan, T., 52
Kegan, R., 41, 69
Kellehear, A., 196–197
Kelley, P., 203
Kelly, C. K., 144
Kelly, E. F., 187, 194, 200
Kelly, E. W., 187, 194, 200
Kelly, G., 116
Kelman, H. C., 114, 135–136, 141–142, 150
Kielburger, C., 220–222, 224, 227, 233
Kielburger, M., 221
Killen, M., 35
Klahr, D., 56
Kletti, R., 211
Kochanska, G., 97
Kohlberg, L., ix-x, xv-xvii, 1–2, 8–14, 17–20, 34–36,
    38–39, 42–46, 48, 50–76, 82, 91, 102–103, 106,
    110, 113, 115, 117–118, 120–121, 125, 128, 131,
    145, 149, 152–153, 164, 183–187, 195, 207–208,
    212, 214, 219, 221–223, 227, 229–230
Komolova, M., 133
Konopisos, M., 142
Koopman, R., 130
Koops, W., 139, 181
Kopelman, L. M., 4, 14–15
Kotchoubey, B., 207
Kotlowitz, A., 184
Kramer, R., 63–64
Krebs, D., xvi, 3, 41, 51, 108, 226, 234
Krettenauer, T., 34, 96, 118
Krevans, J., xvi, 10, 98–100, 104–105, 118
Kruger, A. C., 29, 33–34, 37, 45, 67
Kubler, A., 207
Kuhn, D., 40, 55, 70
Kushner, H., 71

L

LaBerge, S., 201
Lacayo, R., 114, 138
Lacey, M., 4, 14
Landau, J. R., 133, 140, 181
Landenberger, N. A., 181

Landis, T., 195, 205
Lansford, J. E., 97, 105, 162
Lange, A. J., 143
Langstrom, N., 129, 135
Lapsley, D. K., vii, xi, 4, 115
Larden, M., 129, 135
Laszlo, E., 234
Latane, B., 77, 118
Laupa, M., 56, 126, 224
Lawrence, J. A., 96
Lawrence, M., 200
Lazar, A., 21
Leeman, L. W., 129, 144, 168, 181
Lemery, C. R., 80
Lerner, M. J., 86
Levine, C., 75
LeVine, R. A., 3
Levitt, M. J., 14, 37
Lewis, C. S., 36, 56, 186, 214
Lewis, M., 84
Liau, A. K., 116, 129, 132–133, 135–136, 138, 140,
    142–142, 161, 181
Liben, L., 21
Lickona., T., 38, 101, 113, 131
Lieberman, M., xv, 51–52, 63, 66
Light, M., 29
Lillard, A. S., 21
Lindenburger, U., 29
Lindley, D., 217, 234
Ling, L., 217
Lipsey, M. W., 181
Litwack, S. E., 163
Livesley, W. J., 20, 23
Lochman, J. E., 147
Loeber, R., 144
Lorimer, D., 71, 73, 210–215, 231
Losoya, S., 101
Lourenco, O., 6, 19
Lowenberg, K., 15
Lupinetti, C., 133, 135–136, 142
Lutjemeier, J. A., 133
Lykken, D. T., 116, 135
Lynam, D., 98, 119, 139

M

Maass, P., 218–219
Macado, A., 19

Maccoby, E. E., 43, 90, 99, 101–102, 104, 128
MacIntyre, A., 3
Maclean, P. B., 78
Makowski, D. G., 10, 112, 117
Markus, H., 3, 116
Marshall, W. L., 142, 182
Martin, C. L., 116
Martin, G. B., 83
Mason, M. G., 44, 46
Mathabane, M., 90–91, 122, 233
Mattle, K., 228
Matwin, S., 21, 34
Matza, D., 140
Maymon, Y., 43
McCord, J., 153, 161
McCorkle, L., 153
McCrady, F., 133, 135, 140, 143
McDonnell, P., 37
McFall, R. M., 143
McGinnis, E., 143, 178
McGlone, D., 55
McGuire, W. J., 32, 116
McLoyd, V. C., 97, 105
McWilliams, B., 182
Meichenbaum, D. H., 52
Melin, L., 129, 135
Mendelson, E. F., 181
Menon, M. [Madhavi], 135
Menon, M. [Meenakshi], 135
Metcalfe, J., 16, 121, 126
Meyers, V., 188, 196, 202, 204, 208
Michealieu, Q., 23
Michel, L., 123–126, 144–149, 161
Miller, J. G., 20
Miller, K., 27
Miller, M., 29
Miller, P. H., 19–21, 23–28, 30, 51–52, 55, 67, 71,
    104, 185
Miller, P. J., 3
Miller, S. A., 19–20, 23–28, 30–31, 51–52, 55, 67,
    71, 104, 185, 224
Mischel, H. N., 121
Mischel, W., 16, 121, 126
Monshouwer, J. J., 139
Moody, R. A., 187, 208

Morelli, S. A., 15

Morgan, C., 114

Morgan, R. L., 47

Morling, B., 52, 135

Morris, B. J., 55

Morris, P. A., 114, 128

Morrison, E. M., 116, 129, 136, 143

Morse, M., 197, 199, 202, 206, 209–211

Moshman, D., 3–4, 12, 33–34, 39–40, 115, 122, 141, 145, 150, 233

Moskowitz, G. B., 119

Mueller, E., 37

Mugny, G., 29

Mullett, J., 80

Murphy, B. C., 101

Murphy, W. D., 181

Murray, F., 29, 53, 55

Mustakova-Possardt, E., 67

N

Narvaez, D., 4, 44, 47, 52, 60, 115, 118, 120

Nas, C., 181

Nassau, G., 31, 55, 224

Neisser, U., 52, 224, 232

Nelson, J. R., 129

Nelson, K., 53, 94

Nensten, R., 171

Ness, A., 161

Newcomb, T. M., 32, 116, 153

Newman, J. P., 139

Niles, W. J., 168

Noam, G. G., 150

Noddings, N., 76

Novaco, R. W., 173

Noyes, R., 211

Nucci, L., 3

Nussbaum, M. C., 14

Nyman, M., 23

Nystrom, L. E., 15, 78

O

O'Leary, D., 134, 231

Oliner, P., 114, 118

Oliner, S., 114, 118

O'Neil, R. P., 45, 71

Orobio de Castro, B., 139

Ortigue, S., 195, 205

Osgood, D. W., 153

Owens, J. E., 205

P

Paciello, M., 133, 135–136, 142

Palmer, E. J., 129–130

Palmer, J., 201

Pan, J. W., 228

Panak, W., 140

Paris, S., 21

Parke, R. D., 95

Parker, J. G., 34–35

Parnia, S., 194–196, 205–207, 217

Pask-McCartney, C., 163

Pastorelli, C., 142

Pasupathi, M., 150

Patrick, R. B., xvi, 10, 100–101, 105

Patterson, G. R., 144

Pellegrini, A. D., 37

Penrose, R., 185–186, 214–215, 217, 227–228, 231–232, 234

Perry, D. G., 135

Peterson, C. C., 19–20, 24, 34

Peterson, J. L., 19–20, 24, 34

Pettit, G. S., 139

Piaget, J., ix-x, 6–9, 16–21, 24–29, 31, 33–40, 42, 45, 51–56, 58–62, 69, 71–72, 74–75, 82, 96, 102, 108, 122, 125–126, 183, 185–186, 214–215, 221, 223–227, 234

Pierroutsakos, S., 27

Pinker, S., 2–3, 5, 215

Pithers, W. D., 181–182

Pizarro, D. A., 108, 119–120

Plomin, R., 78

Polaschek, D. L. L., 138

Polkinghorne, J. C., 234

Potter, G. B., 13, 129, 132–133, 135–136, 138, 140, 142–143, 152, 160–161, 167, 169–170, 175–176, 178–180, 184

Potts, M., 194

Poulin, F., 153, 161

Powell, D., 56, 104

Power, C., xv, 45, 54, 65, 68, 70, 103, 208

Power, F. C., 164

Premack, A. J., 37

Premack, D., 37

Prencipe, A., 20
Price, J. M., 139

Q

Quiggle, N., 140
Quigley, K. S., 37
Quinn, M., 181

R

Radin, D., 201, 234
Rathunde, K., 56
Ratner, H. H., 29, 37, 69
Rawls, J., 68, 72
Redl, F., 131–132, 135–136, 138
Reed, A. H., 115–116, 135
Reed, R. R. C., 75
Reiser, M., 101
Resick, P. A., 52
Rest, J. R., 4, 16, 44, 47, 52, 59–60, 118, 120
Reyes, L. S., 182
Richardson, D., 35, 216
Richardson, F. C., 4
Riessman, F., 163
Ring, K., 196–197, 199–200, 204, 206, 231
Ripley, A., 114
Roberts, W. L., 130
Robinson, J. L., 78, 94
Robinson, R., 130
Rogoff, B., 29, 35
Rommer, B. R., 197–198, 210
Rosen, H., 19
Rosen, S., 35
Rosenberg, M. J., 32, 116
Rosenthal, L., 143
Rotenberg, K. J., 85
Rowland, S., 144
Rubama, I., 163
Rubin, K. H., 34–35
Russell, T. M., 57
Rutter, M. L., 128
Ryncarz, R. A., 68–69

S

Saarni, C., 93
Sabom, M., 188–192, 194, 196, 200–202,
    204–206, 208, 216–217, 230

Sagi, A., 83
Saltzstein, H. D., 99–100
Samenow, S. E., 132, 135, 137, 161, 233
Sarter, M., 103
Schaal, B., 119
Schechtman, K. B., 195–196
Schlitz, M., 201
Schlundt, D. G., 143
Schneider, S., 124
Schnell, S. V., xv–xvi, 45–46
Schonert-Reichl, K. A., 45
Schwaninger, J., 195–196
Schwartz, D., 119–120
Schwartz, E. S., 47
Sedikides, A., 45
Seeck, M., 195, 205
Seeto, D., 19–20, 24, 34
Seewonarain, K., 181
Selman, R., 21–22, 24, 37–39
Shaver, P. R., 53
Shaw, L. L., 88
Shepard, S. A., 101
Sherif, C. W., 44
Sherif, M., 44
Shively, R., 152, 164, 181
Shreyer, T. A., 37
Shultz, L. H., 24
Shultz, T. R., 31
Shure, M. B., 174
Shweder, R. A., 3
Siegler, R. S., 19, 22, 52, 53–54, 59
Sigelman, C. K., 20, 38
Signorella, M. L., 21
Silberman, M. A., 103
Simion, F., 83
Simmel, G., 78
Simner, M. L., 83
Simonian, S. J., 144
Sinclair, S., 4
Singer, P., 3, 11, 14–15, 40, 44, 89–90, 226, 234
Slaby, R. G., 140
Slonim-Nevo, V., 43
Sloutsky, V., 55

Smedslund, J., 31, 35, 110

Smetana, J., 3, 14

Smit, R. H., 202, 206

Smith, A., 77

Smith, D. J., 129

Snarey, J., xv, 47–48, 50, 54, 56, 66, 72, 103, 130–131

Sokol, A., 14

Sommerville, R. B., 15, 78

Spearpoint, K., 194

Speicher (Speicher-Dubin), B., xv, 45, 54, 63, 65, 103

Spetzler, R., 188, 216, 232

Spinrad, T. L., 58, 92, 103, 118, 135

Spivack, G., 174

Stams, G. J., 129

Stapp, H. T., 231

Staub, E., 77

Steinberg, L., 43, 99, 101, 128

Sternberg, R., 114

Stevenson, I., 197, 202, 205–206

Stinson, A. K., 133, 140

Stouthamer-Loeber, M., 144

Straughan, R., 226

Strayer, J., 130

Super, C., 44

Sutherland, C., 229–230

Swann, W. B., Jr., 135

Swillinger, A., 144

Sykes, G. M., 140

T

Taba, H., 112

Tannenbaum, P. H., 32, 116

Tappan, M. B., 3, 47

Targ, E., 201

Tarnowski, K. J., 144

Taylor, H., 34–35, 168

Taylor, S. E., 127

Thau, S., 116, 135

Thoma, S. J., 4, 44, 47, 52, 60, 120

Thorson, E., 23

Tobin, D. D., 135

Todd, R. M., 88

Tomasello, M., 12, 29, 33, 37, 67

Tooby, J., 37

Torney-Purta, J., 21

Tramontano, 133, 135–136, 142

Trivers, R. L., 41, 77

Trzebinski, J., 52

Tufts, J. H., 60

Turiel, E., 1, 3, 14, 19–20, 65, 115, 119

Turnbull, C. M., 215

Tversky, A., 24

U

Upton, L., 21

V

Vaitl, D., 207

Valdesolo, P., 15, 25, 125, 135, 137

Valsiner, J., 96

van der Laan, P., 129

Vandivier, K., 141

van Lommel, P., 188, 196, 202, 204, 208, 216

van Rosmalen, L., 129

van Wees, R., 188, 196, 202, 204, 208

Varshney, A., 44

Vasey, M. W., 133, 135, 140, 143

Vasudev, J., 67

Veerman, J. W., 139

Vermuelen, S. C. A., 51

Viswanathan, V., 15

Vorrath, H., 136, 152–154, 161, 176

Vygotsky, L. S., 40, 55, 62, 96

W

Wainryb, C., 14, 21, 34, 133, 150

Waitzman, K. A., 20, 38

Walker, L. J., 33–35, 51, 54, 55, 96, 103, 116, 125, 168

Waller, D. G., 196

Walsh, M. W., 114

Walton, G. E., 83

Ward, T., 52, 138, 142

Warnick, J. E., 57

Warnick, R., 57

Wasel, W., 119

Wasmund, W. C., 153

Weaver, T. L., 52

Weber, R. A., 37

Wegner, D. M., 120

Weinbaum, E., 55
Weiner, B., 86
Weinfurther, H., 228
Weiss, A. N., 195–196
Wellman, H. M., 53, 86
Whitbourne, S. K., 56
White, B. J., 44
White, S., 121
Whiteford, M. G., 46
Widaman, K. F., xv
Wilson, D., 203
Wilson, J. Q., 3, 138
Wilson, T. O., 108
Wineman, D., 131–132, 135–136, 138
Winer, G. R., 55
Witherington, D., 93
Witkin, H. A., 114
Woodbury, R., 182

Wren, T. E., 226
Wright, R., 41
Wurf, E., 116
Wuthnow, R., 153

Y

Yarbrough, G. L., 57
Yeates, R., 196
Yochelson, S., 132, 161
Youniss, J., 33

Z

Zahn-Waxler, C., 9, 76, 78, 94
Zajonc, R. B., 16, 88, 93
Zaleski, C., 198, 216
Zan, B., 14
Zeilinger, A., 228
Zhou, Q., 101

Subject Index

A

Abuse, assuming the worst and physical, 139
   See also cognitive distortions, self-serving,
      under Antisocial behavior
Adolescents, moral judgment or reflection
      of. *See* Antisocial Behavior; EQUIP
      and related programs for treating
      antisocial behavior; Kohlberg's
      moral theory; Moral judgment or
      evaluation
Adolescent Problems Inventory-Short Form
      (API-SF), 143-144
Adult moral development in Kohlberg's
      moral theory, 67–69
Affective primacy. *See* Moral motivation
Aggression, proactive or reactive. *See* Anti-
      social behavior; EQUIP and related
      programs for treating antisocial
      behavior
Aggressogenic cognitive distortion. *See* cog-
      nitive distortions, self-serving, *under*
      Antisocial behavior
Altruism. *See* Prosocial behavior
Anger, empathic. *See* Antisocial behavior; cog-
      nitive complications or transforma-
      tions *under* Empathy or empathic
      predisposition
Antisocial behavior
   aggression, proactive or reactive,
      12, 134, 137–138, 150
   case studies
      bin Laden, Osama, 121–127, 150
      McVeigh, Timothy, 121–126, 144–150, 233
      summary and comments, 149–150
   cognitive distortions, self-serving, 10,
      12–13, 86, 104, 123–127, 132–143,
      145–150, 164, 175, 183, 212, 229, 233
      assuming the worst, 138–140, 147, 151,
         159, 174, 213
      blaming others, 12–13, 86, 104, 124,
         136–138, 146, 150, 152, 160, 176

dehumanization and, 141, 150
ego or self-esteem protected by, 135, 137
empathy neutralized by, 12–13, 123–124,
   135–136, 141, 232–233
minimizing/mislabeling, 124–125, 127,
   140–142, 147–148, 159, 174, 213
physical abuse as a risk factor, 139
secondary, 135–142, 146–148, 158
self-centered or primary, 132–134,
   144–146, 151, 158–159, 169, 172, 174,
   176, 187, 210–212, 229
limitations or problematic tendencies,
   128–152
moral judgment delay, 11, 123, 129–132,
   144–145, 164
negative peer culture or peer pressure, 128,
   143–144, 151–153
psychopathy, 103, 135, 145, 149
social skill deficiencies, 10, 143–144,
   148–149, 229
wife batterers, 134
See also Bias; EQUIP and related programs
   for treating antisocial behavior; How
   I Think (HIT) questionnaire; Moral
   judgment or evaluation
Authoritative parenting. *See* Discipline,
   parental, or socialization and moral
   internalization
Autoscopic near-death experience. *See* definition and types *under* Near-death
   experience

B

Balancing and moral type B, 113
   See also Kohlberg's moral theory
Behavior, social. *See* Antisocial behavior;
   EQUIP and related programs
   for treating antisocial behavior;
   Prosocial behavior
Benevolence, is morality relative to the
   virtue of, 3–4

Benevolence, is morality relative to the
virtue of (*cont.*)
See also Moral relativism or post-
modernism
Bias
egocentric, 8, 23–27, 34, 83–84, 104, 125,
144–145, 169, 172, 213, 229.
See also Cognitive-developmental
approach to morality; Social
perspective-taking or coordination
of perspectives
empathic. *See* Empathy or empathic
predisposition, limitations of bin
Laden, Osama. *See* Antisocial
behavior, case studies
Blaming others. *See* cognitive distortions,
self-serving *under* Antisocial behavior
Bystander guilt. *See* Empathy or empathic
predisposition, cognitive complications or transformations; Hoffman's
moral theory

C

Centrations and early childhood superficiality.
See centrations or superficiality; construction, decentration, or mental
coordination; *both under* Cognitive
developmental approach to morality
Chance vs. necessity and distinction
between empirical and logico-
mathematical knowledge, 224
See also Moral motivation
Child labor and moral development, 219–220
Children, young. *See* centrations and superficiality *under* Cognitive developmental approach to morality
Classical conditioning as basic mode of
empathic arousal, 79–80
See also Empathy or empathic
predisposition
Cognitive behavioral approach. *See* EQUIP
and related programs for treating
antisocial behavior
Cognitive developmental approach to morality
centrations or superficiality, 8, 18–21,
26–28, 80

construction, decentration, or mental
coordination, 8, 18, 21–23, 26, 27–37,
40, 55, 61, 70, 183, 212, 214, 233
critiques of, 102
formal operations or hypothetical reflection and, 34, 37–39, 54, 59, 64, 69, 72, 234
fundamental themes of, 17–18, 28, 32
invariant sequence, 51, 59, 63–64
logic and morality, 35–36
reciprocity and justice, 6, 32–33, 40–41
reciprocity norm, 32
reflection, role of, 39–40
social perspective-taking, 33–35
stages as qualitative changes, 18, 36–54
working memory or executive attention,
8, 18, 22, 27, 29, 73
See also Bias, egocentric; Conservation
task/knowledge; Kohlberg's
moral theory; Moral judgment or
evaluation; Moral motivation;
Piaget's theory; Reciprocity
Cognitive distortions or thinking errors
self-debasing, 140, 150
self-serving. *See* Antisocial Behavior;
EQUIP and related programs for
treating antisocial behavior
Cognitive primacy. *See* Moral motivation
Columbus Dispatch, 224
Condition of reversibility. *See* Moral judgment
or evaluation
Conscience and Moral Type B, 113
See also Kohlberg's moral theory
Conservation knowledge/task, 25–26, 28–32,
115, 119, 185, 222–223, 225–227
See also Cognitive-developmental
approach to morality; Prosocial
Behavior; Reality
Construction
internalization and, 9, 18, 28–30, 33–35, 55,
61–62, 96, 102, 224–225
social construction, 18, 28–30, 33–35, 40,
55, 116–117
See also construction, decentration, or
mental coordination *under* Cognitive developmental approach to
morality
Conventional level. *See* Kohlberg's moral theory

Coprimacy. *See* Moral motivation

Cosmic perspective or Kohlberg's "Stage 7." *See* Kohlberg's moral theory; Near-death experience

Cultural psychology, 3–4.
See also Moral relativism or post-modernism

Culture and, 42–44.
See also Reciprocity; Moral judgment or evaluation

D

Death concept and early childhood superficiality, 20–21
See also Cognitive developmental approach to morality

Decentration or mental coordination. *See* Cognitive developmental approach to morality; Empathy or empathic predisposition

Delusional paranoia and assuming the worst, 139, 147
See also cognitive distortions, self-serving, *under* Antisocial behavior

Depression, self-debasing cognitive distortion, and assuming the worst 140

Dewey, John, 58–61, 67

Diagnostic and Statistical Manual of Mental Disorders (DSM-IV), 142

Disappointed expectations, parental expression of. *See* Discipline, parental or socialization and moral internalization

Discipline, parental, or socialization and moral internalization
authoritative parenting and, 97–98
disappointed expectations, parental expression of, 99–101, 105
empathy or empathy-based guilt and, 98–99
evidence for Hoffman's theory of moral socialization, 98–99
inductions, 10, 95–101, 105, 154
love withdrawal, 97, 99
moral internalization and, 97, 219
moral self-relevance and, 100–101
nurturance, role of, 101–102

optimal pressure and, 96–97
permissive parenting and, 102
power-assertion, 96, 101, 104–105
socialization, role of parental discipline in, 95–101

Dual-process models. *See* Moral motivation

E

Egocentric bias. *See* Bias; centrations or superficiality *under* Cognitive developmental approach to morality

Egocentric empathic distress, 79, 83–84, 104
See also modes of empathic arousal *under* Empathy or empathic predisposition

Egoistic drift, 81, 87–88
See also Empathy or empathic predisposition; Hoffman's moral theory

Egoistic motives and antisocial behavior, 12, 97, 213
See also Antisocial behavior

Ego strength or self-control. *See* Prosocial behavior

Emotions, understanding mixed, 34
See also Empathy or empathic predisposition

Empathic bias. *See* Empathy, limitations of

Empathic over-arousal. *See* Empathy, limitations of

Empathy or empathic predisposition
biological substratum, 78, 103
cognitive complications or transformations, 85–92
bystander guilt, 86
causal attribution, 86–87
empathy-based guilt, 86, 95, 99
empathic anger, 86
injustice inference, 86
cognitive development and, 9, 219
cognitive regulation of, 91–93, 95
compassion fatigue and, 87
complexity of, 78–79, 81–82, 85
conditioning and, 80, 83
decentration or mental coordination and, 80, 84–85, 104
definition, 6
discipline encounters and, 95

Empathy or empathic predisposition (*cont.*)
  diffusion of responsibility, 77, 94
  empathetic life review, 212, 215, 230–231
  hot or empathically charged cognition,
      92, 96, 98, 102
  human societal requirements and, 77–78
  justice or the right and, 6, 87
  key factors, 76–77
  language development and, 9, 81, 185, 219
  limitations of
      empathic bias (here-and-now, familiar-
          ity-similarity), 88–90, 150, 219, 229, 232
      empathic overarousal, 87–88, 214
  modes of empathic arousal
      basic or superficial, 78–80, 126, 219
      mature, 78–81, 126, 219
  moral circle and, 90
  moral principles and, 89–92, 109
  multiple claimants dilemma and, 89, 187,
      213–214, 229, 232
  reframing or relabeling and, 90–91, 154
  reliability but fragility of, 78, 94, 149
  remedying limitations of, 89–92
  self-other distinction or self-recognition,
      84, 104
  stages of, mature and immature, 79,
      82–85, 219
  sympathy, 86
  See also Cognitive distortions, self-serving
      under Antisocial behavior; Bias;
      Discipline, parental, or socialization
      and moral internalization; EQUIP
      and related programs for treating
      antisocial behavior; Moral
      Motivation; Prosocial behavior
Empirical knowledge. *See* Moral motivation
Epistemology. *See* Moral motivation
Equality. *See* Cognitive-developmental
      approach to morality; Reciprocity
Equilibration/disequilibration. *See* Piaget's
      theory
EQUIP and related programs for treating
      antisocial behavior
  cognitive behavioral approach, 152,
      162–181, 184
      anger management and correcting
          thinking errors, 162–163, 172–178

  curriculum, overview of, 164–167
  equipment meetings, 162, 165–167
  EQUIPPED for Life game, 164
  moral judgment and Social
      Decision-Making meetings,
      162, 164, 167–172
  mutual help approach, synergy with,
      163–164
  relaxation techniques, 174,
  social skills, equipping with, 13, 163,
      168, 173, 178–179, 229
  evaluation of, 180–181
  multi-component, 152, 163
  mutual help approach, 152–162
      confronting, 154, 161
      evaluation of, 161–162
      faith-building opportunities, importance
          of, 184
      mutual help meetings, 151–152, 154, 162
      Positive Peer Culture, Guided
          Group Interaction, or challenge
          of a negative youth culture, 153,
          161–162, 171
      reframing or relabeling, 154, 173
  problem names and thinking errors,
      151–152, 162–164, 169–172
  social perspective-taking in, 13, 151–152,
      154, 161–164, 168–172, 181–183
      mutual help, 154, 161, 164, 168
      theme, 13, 151–152, 162–164, 169–172
      severe offenders, 13, 181–183
      Think of the Other Person (TOP)
          technique, 174, 176, 179
  See also Antisocial behavior; Bias;
      Cognitive distortions, self-serving,
      under Antisocial behavior; Social
      perspective-taking or coordination of
      social perspectives
Ethical philosophy. *See* Kohlberg's moral
      theory
Ethnocentric bias, 150.
  See also Bias, egocentric
Evolutionary moral or pragmatic psychology
      or sociobiology, 3, 41, 77, 234
Existential development. *See* Gibbs's moral
      theory and critique of Kohlberg's
      theory

F

False moral identity. *See* Moral identity. *See also* Prosocial behavior

Familiarity-similarity empathic bias, 88. *See* Empathy or empathic predisposition

Female genital mutilation and moral relativism, 4, 14

Field dependence/independence
  Moral types A/B and, 113–115
  veridical moral perception and, 114–115
  See also Prosocial behavior

Formal operations. *See* Cognitive developmental approach to morality

Fundamental or universal valuing and moral type B, 113. *See also* Moral judgment or evaluation

G

Gender differences. *See* Moral judgment or evaluation.

Gibbs's moral theory and critique of Kohlberg's theory
  confusion of construction with internalization, 60–62, 74
  conventional level and internal contradiction, 65–66
  ethical philosophy and basic stages, 70
  existential development, 9, 59, 69–70, 71–74, 208, 219, 230–231
  rarification of post-conventional level, 66–67
  standard development, 72–74

Golden Rule, 38–39, 42
  See also condition of reversibility, moral point of view, or third-person perspective *under* Moral judgment or evaluation

Greene's argument, 15–16

Guilt. *See* Empathy or empathic predisposition; Discipline, parental, or socialization and moral internalization; Empathy

H

Here-and-now empathic bias. *See* Bias; Empathy or empathic predisposition

Heteronomy, 20

See also Centrations or superficiality *under* Cognitive developmental approach to morality

Hobbesian philosophy, 70
  See also Gibbs's moral theory and critique of Kohlberg's theory

Hoffman, Martin L., 9, 76
  See also Hoffman's moral theory

Hoffman's moral theory
  Hoffman's theory, critique of, 102–103
  Kohlberg's and Hoffman's theories, comparison or question of integration, 82, 102–103, 227
  reality, question of a deeper, 187
  Timothy McVeigh, 149
  universalist moral theories, 1
  See also Bias; Discipline, parental, or socialization and moral internalization; Empathy or empathic predisposition; Moral motivation; Prosocial behavior

Hostility and conditions for co-construction of moral reciprocity, 34–35
  See also Construction; Moral judgment or evaluation; Reciprocity; Social perspective-taking or coordination of perspectives

How I Think (HIT) questionnaire, 142–143. *See also* Cognitive distortions, self-serving, *under* Antisocial behavior; EQUIP and related programs for treating antisocial behavior.

I

Ideal moral reciprocity. *See* Kohlberg's moral theory; Moral judgment or evaluation, stages of; Reciprocity

Inductive discipline. *See* Discipline, parental, and socialization or moral internalization

Information-processing models. *See* Prosocial behavior

Injustice and poverty, 219
  See also Moral motivation; Prosocial behavior

Interconnectedness, human, 14, 214–215, 221, 228–233

Interconnectedness, human (*cont.*)
    See also Near-death experience; Reality
Internalization. *See* Discipline, parental,
    or socialization and moral
    internalization

J

Just World Hypothesis. *See* Reciprocity
Just Community programs, 164, 168 *See also*
    EQUIP and related programs for
    treating antisocial behavior
Justice. *See* Cognitive developmental approach
    to morality; Moral motivation

K

Kant or Kantian ethics, 3, 12, 68–69, 70, 74
    See also Morality or moral domain
Kaszynski, Theodore, 125
Kielburger, Craig, 220–222, 233
King, Martin, L., Jr., 208
Knowledge, categories of. *See* Moral motivation
Kohlberg, Lawrence, 1, 9, 17, 57, 74
    See also Kohlberg's moral theory
Kohlberg's moral theory
    adult moral development in, 67–69
    background, 58–67
    contribution to field of moral
        development, 9, 57
    conventional level, 60–62, 65
    Dewey's influence and trichotomy of
        levels, 58–60, 67, 74
    Heinz dilemma, 60, 63
    Hoffman's and Kohlberg's theories, com-
        parison or question of integration,
        82, 102–103, 227
    invariant sequence, 58–59, 63, 68
    life-span moral judgment development,
        72–74
    longitudinal research, discoveries of, 62–67
    moral types A/B, 65, 113–115, 118
    Piaget's work and, 58–61
    preconventional level, 60–61
    postconventional or principled level
        or post-skeptical rationalism,
        62, 63–65, 70
    "Stage 7" or cosmic perspective, 1, 9, 13,
        67–68, 187, 207–208, 214, 229–230, 233

stages as schemas, 52–53
summarizing comments, 54
Timothy McVeigh, 122–123, 144–145, 149
transition 4 $\frac{1}{2}$, 64–65, 69
universality claims or universalist moral
    theories, 1, 48, 58–59, 62
See also Cognitive developmental
    approach to morality; Cosmic
    perspective or Kohlberg's "Stage" 7;
    Gibbs's moral theory and critique of
    Kohlberg's theory; Moral motivation;

L

Language-mediated association as mature
    mode of empathic arousal, 79, 81, 126
    See also Empathy or empathic predispositon
Lewis, C. S., 186, 214
Life review. *See* Near-death experience
Logic or logico-mathematical knowledge.
    See Morality or moral domain;
    Moral judgment or evaluation;
    Moral motivation; Reality
Locality/non-locality,
    See also Moral perception; Reality
Locus of control or self-efficacy theory
    prosocial behavior and internal, 118
    See also Field dependence/independence;
    Prosocial behavior
Lord of the Flies (Golding), 35
Love
    ideal moral reciprocity and, 6, 186–187
    the near-death experience, 192, 199,
        208–209, 211–216, 232
Love-withdrawal discipline. *See* Discipline,
    parental or socialization and moral
    internalization, discipline
Loyalty, is morality relative to virtue of, 3–4
    See also Moral relativism or post-
    modernism

M

Mathabane, Mark, 90–91, 233
Mathematical substructures hidden in the
    workings of the world. *See* Reality
Maturity. *See* Empathy; EQUIP and related
    programs for treating antisocial
    behavior; Moral Judgment

McVeigh, Timothy, 122–126, 144–149
  See also Antisocial behavior
Member-of-society perspective. *See* conventional level *under* Cognitive developmental approach to morality
Metacognition. *See* Empathy or empathic predisposition; Moral judgment or evaluation
Might-makes-right philosophies, 72
  See also Gibbs's moral theory and critique of Kohlberg's theory
Mimicry as basic mode of empathic arousal, 79–80
  See also Empathy or empathic predisposition
Moral circle, 11, 44, 46, 89–90, 187
  See also empathic bias *under* Empathy, limitations of; multiple claimants dilemma *under* Empathy or empathic predisposition; Social perspective-taking or coordination of social perspectives
Moral courage. *See* Prosocial behavior
Moral development. *See* Cognitive developmental approach to morality; Empathy; Moral judgment or evaluation; Social perspective-taking
Moral exemplars. *See* Prosocial behavior
Moral identity
  commitment to helping profession or caring principle and, 87–88
  false, 122
  See also moral self-relevance or moral identity *under* Prosocial Behavior
Moral internalization. *See* Discipline, parental, or socialization and moral internalization
Moral Judgment Interview (MJI). *See* Moral judgment or evaluation
Moral Judgment of the Child (Piaget), 58
Morality or moral domain,
  ambiguity or conflict in, 7
  beneficence as a principle, 6, 16
  brain and, 103
  definition, 5–7, 54–55
  deontology, 15, 226

Greene's argument, 15–16
  logic and, 35, 55–56, 186–187, 215, 226, 234
  meta-ethical reflection, 73
  objectivity of, 1–3, 215
  social domain theory and, 14
  utilitarianism, 6, 15
  See also Cognitive developmental approach to morality; Empathy or empathic predisposition; Kant or Kantian ethics; Moral judgment or evaluation; Moral motivation; Reality; Reciprocity
Moral judgment or evaluation
  assessment of stages, 46–48
  condition of reversibility, moral point of view, or third-person perspective, 2–3, 6, 14–16, 26, 38–40, 70
  cross-cultural age trends, 48–51
  definition, 46–47
  delinquency and developmental delay in, 11, 123, 129–132, 144–145, 164
  gender differences in, 103
  mature or profound, 219
  Moral Judgment Interview, 54, 60, 103
  moral reform and, 14, 233
  moral values, 47–48
  retributive justice or vengeance, 36, 40, 43–44, 56, 172, 184, 213
  social institutions and the development of, 44
  Sociomoral Reflection Measure-Short Form, 47–51, 54, 56, 131
  stages of, 18, 28, 36–56, 58–75
  See also Antisocial behavior; Cognitive developmental approach to morality; EQUIP and related programs for treating antisocial behavior; Kohlberg's moral theory; Reciprocity; Social perspective-taking or coordination of perspectives;
Moral Life of Children, the (Coles), 107
Moral motivation
  affective primacy, intuitionist or emotivist theory, or caring, 3, 16, 42, 108–112, 221, 225, 233
  cognitive primacy, necessity, or justice, 9, 16, 18, 30–32, 35–36, 42, 55–56, 111, 221–222, 224, 226, 233

Moral motivation (*cont.*)
    coprimacy or dual-process models,
      10, 15–16, 110–112, 223, 227
    empirical knowledge and, 30, 222–226
    Kohlberg and Hoffman as guides to,
      221–222
    logico-mathematical knowledge or
      necessity and, 30–32, 185, 223–226
    moral self-relevance or moral identity as a
      source of, 11, 117, 219, 233
    unconscious cognitive processes in, 108,
      118–120
    violations of logic or justice, or reciprocity
      imbalance, 32, 35–36, 55–56, 87, 109,
      111–112, 226–227
    See also Cognitive developmental approach
      to morality; Moral judgment or evalu-
      ation; Reciprocity
Moral perception
    information-processing models of, 118–120
    reality and, 228–232
    See also Prosocial behavior; Reality
Moral point of view or third-person
      perspective. *See* condition of
      reversibility, moral point of view,
      or third-person perspective *under*
      Moral judgment or evaluation
Moral principles. *See* Cognitive developmental
    approach to Morality; Empathy or
    empathic predisposition
Moral reciprocity. *See* Recipocity
Moral relativism or post-modernism,
    2–3, 14–15, 63–65, 69, 73, 75
    See also Morality, objectivity of
Moral self-relevance or moral identity. *See*
    Prosocial behavior
Moral types A/B. *See* Kohlberg's moral
    theory
Moral values. *See* Moral judgment
    or evaluation
Motivation. *See* Moral motivation
Multiple claimants dilemma. *See* Empathy
    or empathic predisposition
Multisystemic Therapy (MST), 167
Mutual help approach, *see under* EQUIP
    and related programs for treating
    antisocial behavior

N

Narrative psychology, 3
    See also moral relativism or post-
      modernism
Near-death experience
    accurate, verifiable aspects as, 201–204,
      216–217
    anomalies of, 229, 231
    Asian accounts of, 197
    case studies
      Reynolds, Pam, 188–192, 230–231
      Sawyer, Thomas, 192–194, 230–231
    changes after experience, 191–192, 194,
      209–211, 214, 232–233,
    connection or interconnectedness and,
      209, 214–215, 218, 221, 228–233
    context, influence on content, 195–200
    death, does near-death experience hap-
      pen during near-, 204–206
    definition and types, 187, 196–198, 207
    dissociation and, 216
    distressing versions, 197
    dying brain explanations of, 194, 205, 217
    existential crisis or development
      and, 73, 187
    fabrication hypothesis, 205–206
    Hunter-gatherer society accounts of, 197
    incident rate, 196–197
    life review, 193–194, 196–198, 230
    light, 190, 192, 209–211, 214, 216
    Pacific area accounts of, 197
    proximity to death and, 204
    real, do near-death experiencers interpret
      the experience as, 200–201
    reality, nature of and
    See also Reality, local/non-local; "Stage 7"
      or cosmic perspective *under*
      Kohlberg' moral theory
Necessity vs. chance and distinction of
    logico-mathematical vs. empirical
    knowledge. *See* Moral motivation
Negative youth culture. *See* EQUIP and
    related programs for treating anti-
    social behavior
Neo-nativist views, 3
    See also Moral relativism or post-
      modernism

Newborn reactive cry as immature stage of empathic distress, 83
  See also Empathy, stages of
Nonsocial cognition. *See* Cognitive developmental approach to morality; Conservation knowledge/task
Nurturance. *See* Discipline, parental, or socialization and moral internalization

P

Paranoid behavior and assuming the worst, 139, 147
  See also Cognitive distortion or thinking errors, self-serving
Parental discipline. *See* Discipline, parental, or socialization and moral internalization
Peer interaction. *See* Piaget's theory; Social perspective-taking or coordination of perspectives
Perspective-taking. *See* Social perspective-taking
Piaget, Jean. *See* Piaget's theory
Piaget's theory
  adaptation, 53–54, 56, 226
  construction, 18, 28–30, 32, 33–35, 40, 55
  critiques of, 19, 126
  decentration or mental coordination, 8, 21–23, 26, 28–30, 36–37
  equilibration/disequilibration, assimilation, or accommodation, 53–54, 56, 64, 225, 230–232
  heteronomy, 20, 61
  influence on Kohlberg, 58–60,
  logic inherent in social relations, 17
  moral judgment phases, 20, 51–52, 59–61, 74
  peer interaction, 33–35, 44–46, 58, 73
  reflective abstraction, 40
  See also Bias, egocentric; Cognitive developmental approach to morality; Construction; Kohlberg's moral theory; Schemas
Positive Peer Culture. *See* EQUIP and related programs for treating antisocial behavior
Postconventional level. *See* Kohlberg's moral theory

Power-assertive discipline. *See* Discipline, parental, or socialization and moral internalization
Pragmatic moral reciprocity. *See* Moral judgment or evaluation, stages of
Preconventional level. *See* Kohlberg's moral theory
Primacy in moral motivation. *See* Moral motivation
Proactive aggression. *See* Aggression, proactive or reactive, *under* Antisocial behavior
Prosocial behavior
  case study, 107–112, 114–115
  definition of, 107
  ego strength or self-control and, 13, 103, 120–122, 125–126, 219
  empathy and, 77, 92, 117–118, 125
  false or spurious "moral" exemplars, 121–126
  field independence or self-efficacy, Moral Type B, or veridical moral perception and, 114–115, 117–118
  moral exemplars, moral courage, or whistle-blowers, 111–112, 114, 118, 127, 220–221, 233
  moral judgment stage and, 117–118, 122–125
  moral self-relevance or moral identity, 88, 106, 115–116, 126–127, 176, 219–221, 233
  social perspective-taking and, 93
  veridical moral perception
  See also Empathy or empathic predisposition; moral Types A/B *under* Kohlberg's moral theory; Moral motivation
Psychopathy. *See* Antisocial behavior
Purity, is morality relative to virtue of, 5

Q

Quasi-egocentric distress. *See* stages of, mature and immature, *under* Empathy or empathic predisposition

R

Rationalism
  critiques of Piaget's theory as conscious, 126
  postskeptical, 64–65

Rawls's theory of justice, 72
  See also Gibbs's moral theory and critique
    of Kohlberg's theory
Reactive aggression. See Aggression, proactive
    or reactive, under Antisocial behavior
Reality
  conservation knowledge and perception
    of a deeper, 30, 115, 227
  cognitive developmental approach to
    morality and a deeper, 1, 30, 219
  empathy or human relations and deep
    interconnectedness, 94, 214–215, 221,
    228–233
  ideal moral reciprocity and a deeper,
    186–187
  Kohlberg's and Hoffman's theories,
    venturing beyond, 187
  local and non-local, subatomic, or quantum,
    215, 217, 228–229, 232–234
  mathematical substructures or underpin-
    nings, 186- 187, 213, 215, 234
  moral perception or inspiration and a
    deeper, 232–233
  See also Kohlberg's "Stage" 7 or cosmic
    perspective under Kohlberg's moral
    theory; Near-death experience;
Reciprocity
  activation of, 119
  empathy and principle of, 92
  equality and, 30–31, 33, 111
  Just World Hypothesis, 86, 150
  ideal moral reciprocity or reciprocity as
    constructed ideal, 18, 32, 38–40, 43,
    93, 103, 123, 138, 163, 169, 183, 186, 212,
    214–216, 219, 225
  moral reciprocity as internalized norm,
    32, 37, 225
  nonsocial cognition and, 17–17, 25–32
  primate societies and, 37–38
  See also Cognitive-developmental
    approach to morality; Morality or
    moral domain; Moral motivation
Reflection, reflective abstraction, or
    metacognition
  ego strength or self-control and, 121
  moral maturity and, 28, 31, 44, 46, 54, 67,
    71, 74

social construction and, 40
  See also Cognitive developmental
    approach to morality; Kohlberg's
    moral theory; Piaget's theory
Reframing and moral development, 90–91, 154
  See also EQUIP and related programs for
    treating antisocial behavior
Relativism, moral or cultural. See Moral rel-
    ativism or post-modernism
Relaxation techniques. See cognitive
    behavioral approach under EQUIP
    and related programs for treating
    antisocial behavior
Reversibility, condition of. See Moral
    judgment or evaluation
Reynolds, Pam. See Near-death experience,
    case studies.
"Right and Wrong as a Clue to the Meaning
    of the Universe" (Lewis, C. S.), 186

S
Sawyer, Thomas. See Near-death experience
Schemas, 9, 52–54, 94, 96, 98, 115, 119, 221, 230
  See also Moral judgment, stages of;
    Piaget's theory
Self-efficacy. See locus of control or self-
    efficacy theory
Social construction. See Cognitive develop-
    mental approach to morality;
    Construction
Social contract or libertarian theories and
    moral judgment stage 2, 70–71
Social domain theory, 3, 14
Social intuitionist theory, 3, 5
  See also Evolutionary moral or pragmatic
    psychology or sociobiology; Moral
    relativism or post-modernism
Social perspective-taking or coordination of
    perspectives
  empathy or caring and, 12, 79, 93, 121,
    125, 212
  moral judgment development or expan-
    sion of moral circle and, 1–2, 18, 28,
    37, 44, 46, 73, 90, 183
  opportunities for, 11, 39, 42–46, 152, 154,
    164, 168–169, 219
  research evaluation, 45–46

role-taking, 104

severe offenders, 181–184, 233

spirituality or near-death experience and, 13, 187, 212, 219

time-out technique and, 104

See also cognitive distortions, self-serving, *under* Antisocial behavior; Bias, egocentric; Construction; Empathy or empathic predisposition; EQUIP and related programs for treating antisocial behavior; Moral judgment or evaluation; Theory of mind

Socialization. *See* Discipline, parental, or socialization and moral internalization

Social skills. *See* Antisocial behavior; EQUIP and related programs for treating antisocial behavior

Sociobiology. *See* Evolutionary moral or pragmatic psychology or sociobiology

Sociomoral development. *See* Moral Judgement, stages of

Sociomoral Reflection Measure—Short Form (SRM-SF). *See* Moral judgment or evaluation

Spetzler, Robert, 188, 216, 232

Stages. *See* Empathy or empathic predisposition; Kohlberg's moral theory; Moral judgment or evaluation

Superficiality. *See* Cognitive developmental approach to morality; Empathy

T

Texas Youth Commission Capital Offender Group program, 181–182.

See also EQUIP and related programs for treating antisocial behavior

Theory of mind, 23

See also Social perspective-taking or coordination of perspectives

Thinking errors and antisocial behavior. *See* Antisocial behavior; Cognitive distortions, self-serving; EQUIP and related programs for treating antisocial behavior

Time-out technique, 104

See also Social perspective-taking or coordination of perspectives

Toronto Star, 222, 224

Transcendental near-death experience. *See* Near-death experience, definition and types

Transgression guilt. *See* Discipline, parental, or socialization and moral internalization

Transition 4 $^1/_2$. *See* Kohlberg's moral theory

Turiel, Elliot, 1, 63, 125

See also Social domain theory

12-Step programs, 183

See also and related programs for treating antisocial behavior

U

Universal morality, Kohlberg's search for, 59

See also Kohlberg's moral theory; Morality or moral domain; Moral judgment or evaluation

V

Veridical empathic distress. *See* stages of *under* Empathy

Victim Awareness programs, 181

See also EQUIP and related programs for treating antisocial behavior

Violations of logic or justice. *See* Cognitive-developmental approach to morality; Moral motivation

Village or rural cultures and the near-death experience, 196

See also Near-death experience

Virtue or character ethics, 3, 125

See also Moral relativism or postmodernism

W

Western culture and near-death experience, 196

See also Near-death experience

Wife batterers and proactive and reactive aggression. *See* Antisocial behavior

Working memory or executive attention. *See* Cognitive developmental approach to morality

Youth culture or Positive Peer Culture. *See* EQUIP and related programs for treating antisocial behavior

Y

Yanomamo Indians, 43–44
Youth Charter Programs, 167

Z

Zone of proximal development, 53, 55, 62